ANIMATION:MASTER
A COMPLETE GUIDE

Animation:Master
A Complete Guide

David Rogers

CHARLES RIVER MEDIA

Boston, Massachusetts

Cover Design: Tyler Creative

CHARLES RIVER MEDIA
25 Thomson Place
Boston, Massachusetts 02210
617-757-7900
617-757-7969 (FAX)
crm.info@thomson.com
www.charlesriver.com

This book is printed on acid-free paper.

David Rogers. Animation:Master: A Complete Guide.
ISBN: 1-58450-475-7

All brand names and product names mentioned in this book are trademarks or service marks of their respective companies. Any omission or misuse (of any kind) of service marks or trademarks should not be regarded as intent to infringe on the property of others. The publisher recognizes and respects all marks used by companies, manufacturers, and developers as a means to distinguish their products.

Library of Congress Cataloging-in-Publication Data
Rogers, David.
  Animation:master : a complete guide / David Rogers.
      p. cm.
  Includes bibliographical references and index.
  ISBN 1-58450-475-7 (pbk. with cd : alk. paper)
  1. Computer animation. 2. Animation:Master. I. Title.
  TR897.7.R643 2006
  006.6'96—dc22
                              2006011039

06 7 6 5 4 3 2 First Edition

CHARLES RIVER MEDIA titles are available for site license or bulk purchase by institutions, user groups, corporations, etc. For additional information, please contact the Special Sales Department at 800-347-7707.

Requests for replacement of a defective CD-ROM must be accompanied by the original disc, your mailing address, telephone number, date of purchase and purchase price. Please state the nature of the problem, and send the information to CHARLES RIVER MEDIA, 25 Thomson Place, Boston, Massachusetts 02210. CRM's sole obligation to the purchaser is to replace the disc, based on defective materials or faulty workmanship, but not on the operation or functionality of the product.

This book is dedicated to my parents:
Bennie and Paulette Rogers, and to DeeDee and Frank Shoup

CONTENTS

ACKNOWLEDGMENTS

To Hash Inc. for never once getting tired of my pestering. Martin, Bob, Yves, Will, Noel, Steve, and Ken, thanks for the awesome software. It gets better every year.

To Joe Cosman (a.k.a. Joel Cosmano) for the great Facial Bump Map tutorial.

To the people who shared their knowledge with me over the years: Brian "Sweater Boy" Prince, William Eggington, Jeff Cantin, Jeffery Dates, Glen Crowell, Mike Brennan, Shaun Freeman, Sam Buntrock, Matt Peters, Stephen Millengen, and every one else I can't remember right now. Whether you know it or not I owe a debt of thanks to you all.

To all the awesome people in the A:M community: see you in #hash3d.

To Chuck Jones, Tex Avery, Bill Tytla, Preston Blair, Richard Williams, Pixar, PDI, John Coltrane, Miles Davis, Mike Watt, and Tom Waits for all the inspiration.

To R.O. Roberts for convincing me that I should do this.

To coffee, and the person who first decided to pour some hot water over that odd-looking bean. This book would not have been possible without it.

And to Denise, without whom I would still be Grammatically Challenged.

INTRODUCTION

ANIMATION:MASTER, A BRIEF HISTORY

When computer animation first emerged, it was dominated by huge main-frame computers that cost tens of thousands of dollars, running complex and equally expensive software. It was obtuse and obfuscated by layers and layers of complex equations, well outside the reach of artists, and most certainly outside the reach of any average home user. Then along came the Amiga, a low-cost, powerful (for the day) home computer with fantastic graphics capabilities. It was the Amiga and the programmers that loved it that played Prometheus and carried the fire of 3D animation down from Olympus to us mere mortals. Leading the charge was a little program called Animation:Apprentice. First released in 1985 for the Amiga, Apprentice was a fundamental shift in what was possible for an average individual. The ground broken by Apprentice was soon seeded with other programs, Lightwave and TruSpace notable among them. As the power of home computers increased, so did what was possible in 3D software. Apprentice became Journeyman, then Will Vinton's Playmation, then Martin Hash's 3D Pro, and finally Animation:Master (A:M). Along the way, it grew up from a loosely associated group of applications into an integrated 3D modeling/animating/rendering solution capable of re-creating reality in exacting detail or creating worlds of the imagination.

A:M has consistently walked a different path than the programs that it grew up alongside. Instead of building complicated tools that require studios of people to develop pipelines to use, A:M instead focused on the idea of "One Man with One Computer" telling a story. Each version of A:M brings us closer to that goal.

A RAPID-FIRE INTRODUCTION TO 3D

The concepts in this book are intended to be basic; however, there are aspects that can be difficult to understand if you do not have a basic grasp of some of the fundamental aspects of 3D.

3D, as its name indicates, represents objects on a screen (either your monitor as you work, or in the final output either still or animated) by shading pixels based on geometry, textures, and lights in a simulated 3D environment. The geometry in the environments must be wholly created from scratch by someone (either by you as you create models, or someone else if you use a purchased or premade model) to represent every aspect that can be seen in a rendered product. There are mathematical rules that govern how each object you create will look. These rules define what is known about the surface of an object, but the objects themselves have no mass or thickness to them.

Each object you model is placed in an environment, either alone or together with other objects. The position, rotation, and size of an object can be set or changed over time to create animation. These three "transformations" are the basis of all animation. The environment itself is an infinite void by default containing no light or objects. It has an arbitrary center point from which the position, rotation, and size of an object is measured. This point is called the World Space Origin: All points are referenced from this origin by their distance in three cardinal axes called *x*, *y*, and *z*. Each object has its own Local Origin often referred to as its pivot. If an object has other objects inside of itself those objects, refer to the Local Origin. Think of it like a galaxy: The galaxy itself has a center point, and all the stars and star systems in the galaxy can be thought of as being located a certain distance in 3D space from that center. While you could also look at the planets in each star system as being referenced by the galaxy, it is easier to look at the star around which they orbit to get a location.

Once an object is placed in a scene you can define how the object will be shaded by adding lights to the same scene. A light is a way to indicate from where in a scene illumination will originate. Scenes can have any number of lights, and multiple lights are often required to achieve realistic shading on a surface. Because the 3D world is completely empty, the complex interactions of light that mark reality do not exist (by default), and multiple light sources are needed to provide even illumination.

Objects are created smooth and white. In order to make them appear to be made out of a particular material (wood, plastic, metal, skin, and so on) they must be "textured" indicating what colors and other attributes an object should have. Textures can provide bump and deformation on a surface to provide small detail or indicate simple colors and patterns.

This is the basic process of all 3D work: You build, postion (and animate), texture, and light each scene in the computer. As you work, you are presented with a view that shows you an approximation of your scene. When you are finished and want to see the final product of your labors, you then ask the computer to "render" the scene. This is the mathematically intensive process that produces final quality images. During rendering, the computer looks into the scene through a camera that you place and position, finds the surfaces of the models you have created, and determines how to shade each pixel of the final image based on the shape, position, and texture of those models in relation to the lights you placed in the scene. This process can take anywhere from a couple minutes to several days depending on the complexity of the calculations involved.

ABOUT YOUR VERSION OF ANIMATION:MASTER

Hash updates and releases major new versions of its program every year (sometimes twice a year). This is partly based on the development cycle of the software and partly based on a subscription-driven revenue system. When you buy a CD-ROM from Hash, you get access to all versions released in the calendar year of that disc. So if you have the 2005 disc and want to run the 2006 release, you will need to upgrade to a new disc. It just so happens that new features added to the software tend to make the upgrade worthwhile.

Unfortunately, this makes writing a book on a calendar year a moving target at best. I can tell you what the features are now and how they work, and I can offer some idea on the best way to arrive at a given point, but there is no guarantee that some new feature won't arrive to make everything said here obsolete. The first edition of this book focused on the fundamentals, and I thought that was a fairly safe way to do things. And then sure enough, the fundamentals changed. For example, since the book was released the new Stitch tool has completely changed the way we model, porcelain has been improved, and a new rendering technology has been added. The new tools mean that what used to be the "best" way to go about something is not always the "best" way anymore.

I realize that as soon as I finish this update and have published the last chapter of it that Hash will release a new version of the software to make things easier/ different. The onus is on you, the reader, to take this information as a foundation and extrapolate it into new versions of the software. The goal of this book is not to be a complete description of every possibility in the software; rather, it is intended to serve as a complete guide to the concepts behind the software and, yes, to describe the state of features as they exist now: to give you a leg up on the basic blocks of knowledge that you need in order to use A:M effectively.

For a point of reference, this book was written with version 12 and early Alpha versions of v13 (2006 subscription) as its base. If you are looking at version 13.5 and wondering if this book is still applicable, I will tell you that yes it is. It gives you a foundation on the 3D technology that is at the heart of A:M. It may not show you what a new button does when v14 is released, but with a firm knowledge of how things tend to work, you should be able to extrapolate that on your own.

With that in mind, go ahead and get started. See you inside!

GETTING AROUND

INTERFACE

In This Chapter

- Toolbars/Global Interface
- Workflow and Project Structure

In this chapter, the goal is to familiarize you with the Animation:Master (A:M) interface. By necessity, we will also cover some of the base concepts of 3D in general and A:M in particular. You will need no outside resources for this chapter; the exercises are simple and designed to demonstrate single tools, not complex uses for them.

It is assumed that A:M is already installed on your computer. Check the Hash, Inc. Web site (*http://www.hash.com*) for any updates that may be available. The program has a rapid development cycle, and the version that you received at purchase is not likely the most recent update.

By the end of this chapter you should have a familiarity with the interface and general usage of the tools in A:M, as well as a rough understanding of the concepts behind the A:M workflow.

TOOLBARS/GLOBAL INTERFACE

Go ahead and launch A:M, and get right into things. The first time you launch A:M, it starts with the Library palette, and a default Choreography Viewport opens. Once you start working on projects, it will load in the last project you had open at startup. Like most defaults in A:M, this can be changed. The first thing you need to do, however, is to review the tools and move toward an understanding of the program. we will start with the broadest terms and then focus on individual tools and functions.

Like most modern graphical user interface (GUI)-based applications, A:M follows a basic palette/workspace philosophy where tools are presented as buttons and data is shown in windows and palettes. Most of the basic interface concepts will be very familiar to you unless, for some reason, you have never used a word processor.

Most of the interface can be docked along the edge of the screen or broken into multiple floating windows. Toolbars and information palettes can be undocked by dragging them away from the edge of the screen. When a dockable panel is dragged close to any edge of the screen, it will attempt to dock. To prevent this, hold down the Ctrl key while dragging the window. You can prevent any window from docking by right-clicking (control-clicking on the Mac) and deselecting Allow Docking from the contextual menu. This allows you to position the interface elements where you want them. This is very useful if you work with more than one monitor. As you grow comfortable with A:M, you will find a layout that agrees with you.

Contextual menus are very important to the workflow in A:M, and rather than tell you to right-click or control-click for the remainder of the book I will simply ask you to bring up a contextual menu.

A:M has a number of different types of workspace windows, each of them relating to a specific type of operation. Some display images or other information, but the focus will tend to be on the three-dimensional workspace. What you can do in a particular workspace space depends on what type of object you are looking at and how you choose to look at it, both of which we will explore as we progress.

Each 3D window is an independent view into a space with its own local coordinate system. The coordinates are mapped to standard cardinal axes labeled x, y, and z. The y-axis in A:M is up, the x-axis runs left to right, and the z-axis from front to back. The center of each workspace is the origin, or 0,0,0 in Cartesian coordinates; as you work, this will be the main point of reference for all your objects. Each workspace window can show one of a number of views in 3D space at a time, and multiple views can be opened to show any number of angles into a workspace simultaneously. If more than one window is open showing the same space (two windows of the same 3D model, for example), then they will share the same 3D space.

The three axes of the workspace windows are how the software will map points or movement in three dimensions. We will learn how to navigate through a 3D space as we progress, but understanding what the windows represent is the first real step to learning 3D.

The panels that make up the majority of the A:M interface show data regarding any aspect of a particular project or outside data, but they all represent a set of data in some form. We'll look at these panels in depth when we talk about workflow. The Library panel, which opens by default when you first open A:M, is the first panel you see. If you look through the library you will immediately see what kind of data it represents for you: a library of models, textures, projects, tutorials, and more. This library is independent of any project context allowing you to move data from one to another with ease. These files live on your hard drive or the Animation:Master CD-ROM, and you can add files to the library yourself and build up a collection of reusable data.

The final group of interface elements is the first group, which we will explore in depth: the toolbars and the tools that each of them contains. There are a large number of tools in A:M (see Figure 1.1); you will find that they are grouped logically, and a number of them will probably be familiar to you already.

FIGURE 1.1 The A:M toolbars.

 For clarity, all palettes have been undocked in the figures of this book. For the most part, however, I recommend leaving them docked. Floating tool palettes can consume a lot of screen space. As you learn A:M and become familiar with the keyboard shortcuts, you might find that you rarely use some of the tool palettes, which allows you to close them and save on screen space. The exception to this is for Mac users with older hardware. Undocking your tool palettes can actually speed up the interface of A:M a great deal, and you might want to consider doing so.

Figure 1.2 shows the first group of tools we will be looking at. The standard tools palette contains globally accessible tools that primarily deal with file and data manipulation. Your experience on any type of word processor will help you instantly recognize these tools.

FIGURE 1.2 The standard tools palette, undocked for clarity.

From left to right, the tools are:

New: Creates an item. More specifically it brings up the catalog, which presents the types of items that can be created. The choices—model, material, action, and choreography—are the basic building blocks of every project.

Open: Brings an existing document from the hard disk into A:M. A:M can open any file type that it generates.

Save: Saves the current project to disk. If it is a new project, a dialog opens allowing you to specify where to save. If you learn nothing else from this book, take this with you: Use this button, use it often, and, more importantly, use it wisely! It is not enough just to save: save in versions. Learning not only to save often but to save wisely will do more than save files. It will save frustration and heartache as well.

Cut: Removes the selected portion of an object from the workspace, be it a selection of control points in a model or keyframes in the timeline. This removes the selection and stores it on the clipboard, just like text in a word processor.

Copy: Functions much like Cut, but instead of removing the selection from the workspace it creates a copy of the selection on the clipboard.

Paste: After putting a selection onto the clipboard via Copy or Cut, this tool inserts it into any workspace. This is data sensitive so that it won't paste the control point (CP) information from a model into the timeline for a bones rotation. It will paste information only into areas of the software that understand the information being pasted.

Delete: Removes the selection from the active workspace. This is unlike Cut, in that data cannot be pasted back in. Once deleted, the data is gone unless the deletion is undone.

Undo: Goes back one step in case of a mistake or a change of plan. The program allows for unlimited undos, but it is more efficient on memory and more conducive to stability to limit the number of undos. A setting of 10 or fewer is recommended.

Redo: A companion to Undo. Use Undo and Redo to toggle between changes before committing to, or discarding, one.

The standard functions are pretty much the same that you would find in a word processing application.

The next group of tools (see Figure 1.3) is focused on rendering in A:M. (Rendering is the term for the process of drawing the pixels of your scene. In most cases, this indicates a longer process than a real-time view.)

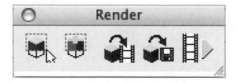

FIGURE 1.3   The Rendering toolbar.

Quick Render: Does a final quality render of either a window or a selected portion thereof. It is useful in gauging what an image will look like when rendered to a file and is the only way to preview certain render effects, such as volumetrics or *z*-buffer soft shadows. The downside is that you have to wait for the full render. You can press the Esc key to stop the render, but any progress made before stopping is not shown.

Progressive Render-lock: Renders the whole window, or a selection thereof, in progressive steps, refining the render in passes. In most cases, you get a good idea of what you are looking at long before the render finishes. Pressing the Esc key will stop the render, leaving the work that it has done visible on the screen until it is refreshed with the Spacebar, or other changes are made in the window. This option does not include many fine-quality render features such as volumetrics, *z*-buffer shadows, or antialiasing. It is particularly useful for checking materials or lighting, which may require numerous small changes. If you are adjusting a surface attribute (see Chapter 11) or lighting or any other aspect of an object or scene, then the progressive render will continue to interactively update as you work, until you escape out of it or click the Progressive Render button again.

Render to File: Once your animation or scene is finished and you are ready to output the product of your labor for the world to see, use the Render to file button to have the computer render a final image. This is also useful for doing quick tests to see how the animation is progressing. See Chapter 13 for more on rendering.

Play Animation: Allows the selection of an animation file from the hard drive for playback. This can be used to view renders or to view reference footage, but is not used very often.

Item Help (PC only): Toggles Help. Clicking another part of the interface (windows, buttons, or menus) brings up the related Help files for the selected item.

Most of these buttons have keyboard shortcuts (see Table 1.1), and getting used to them is the fastest way to increase productivity and spare you from carpal tunnel syndrome.

TABLE 1.1   Standard Tools Shortcuts

COMMAND	PC SHORTCUT	MAC SHORTCUT
New	Ctrl+N	Cmd+N
Open	Ctrl+P	Cmd+O
Save	Ctrl+S	Cmd+S
Cut	Ctrl+X	Cmd+X
Copy	Ctrl+C	Cmd+C
Paste	Ctrl+V	Cmd+V
Delete	Delete	Delete

→

COMMAND	PC SHORTCUT	MAC SHORTCUT
Undo	Ctrl+Z	Cmd+Z
Redo	Ctrl+Y	Cmd+Y
Quick render	Q	Q
Progressive render-lock	Shift+Q	Shift+Q
Render to file	None	None
Play animation	None	None
Help	F1	None
Item help	None	None

If a function you use often is unassigned, you can create your own hot key. Select Customize from the Tools menu, then find the command you wish to create a shortcut for on the Keyboard tab. Click Create Shortcut and press the key or key combination you wish to bind to that function. If it is not already assigned, the dialog will display (unassigned) and you can safely create the shortcut. If it is assigned, it will display the command tied to that key, allowing you to choose a different command. Be careful not to overwrite another command's key binding until you are familiar with the program, as it will make tutorials and documentation harder to follow.

Figure 1.4 shows the next logical set of tools. They are used to navigate in 3D space and are used often. Animation:Master is not a CAD program and as such eschews the standards of that environment (i.e., the quad view layout for windows). Instead, a single viewport into a model/choreography/action workspace is presented. Navigation tools are coupled with the numeric keypad on the keyboard to switch views, providing all the mobility and control needed to see any angle. Not having four windows open at all times is a very good way to optimize space, but if more than one view at a time is needed this is allowed—it is just not the default.

To open an additional view to the current workspace window, choose New Window from the Window menu.

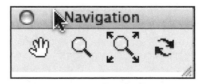

FIGURE 1.4   Navigation tool palette.

These tools (see Table 1.2 for navigation shortcuts) can have slightly different functions depending on the type of workspace you are in and what you are looking through. As you look at Animation in Chapter 10, you will see this in more detail.

The navigation tools are:

Move: Used for moving a view in two axes, as if pushing a flat sheet of paper around in the window.

Zoom: Used to move in or out of a viewport to either look at specific areas more closely or larger areas of the workspace than currently shown in the view. Control-clicking with the Zoom tool active (right-click on PC) draws a box around a specific area to zoom into.

Zoom to fit: Changes the zoom level to the point where all items in the window will fit in the view.

Zoom to selection: Zooms in or out to fit the selected object or objects in the viewport window. Use the Ctrl+Shift+Z keyboard shortcut to zoom to selection. There is no button for this action.

Turn: Rotates the view around the origin of the window or around the pivot of the current selection, be it a control point or bone in a model window or a model in the choreography or action windows. Turning the view also changes the setting for Bird's Eye view in the workspace.

At any given time you can see what the current settings for the active view are by looking at the lower right-hand corner of the screen where the View settings are shown (see Figure 1.5).

Clicking these numbers brings up the View Settings dialog, where you can type directly into this box to position the view anywhere you like. This is typically used to reset the Bird's Eye view back to its default rotation (30, 30, 0 in X, Y, and Z rotation, respectively).

Most of the keys on the numeric keypad (see Figure 1.6) correspond to one of the directional views. They are also accessible from any workspace window by control-clicking (right-click on the PC) in the workspace and selecting the desired view from the contextual menu.

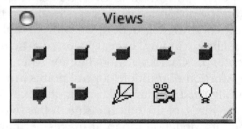

FIGURE 1.5   The View settings show the current position of the viewport.

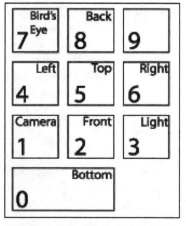

FIGURE 1.6   The numeric keypad on your keyboard changes the angle of view into any window.

Practice navigating through the views with the numeric keypad. If you are using a computer without a numeric keypad (a laptop, for example) get used to the contextual menu.

TABLE 1.2   Navigation Tool Shortcuts

COMMAND	PC SHORTCUT	MAC SHORTCUT
Move	M	M
Zoom	Z	Z
Zoom to Fit	Shift+Z	Shift+Z
Zoom to Selection	Ctrl+Z	Control+Z
Turn	T	T

The Mode tools (see Figure 1.7) change the work environment, as well as the tools that will be available and how many of them, such as the Standard tool, function. Briefly go through each mode, then look at each in depth.

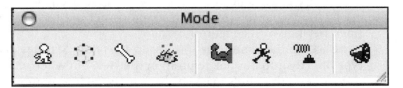

FIGURE 1.7   The Mode tool palette.

Modeling: Allows the movement of control points (CPs) at the model level, making permanent changes to the wireframe mesh that makes up an object. It is important to distinguish from muscle mode, which allows the manipulation of CPs on the action level. Access is available from almost any portion of the software, model, action, or choreography. Use this mode only in the modeling window, except in one particular example that is covered in Chapter 5, "Character Modeling for Animation."

Distortion: Allows the distortion of multiple control points at once. Similar to Modeling mode, but instead of manipulating individual CPs, a lattice box is used to distort the shape of the object inside. It has two contexts: If the selection was made in Modeling mode, it makes permanent object-level changes to the mesh. In Muscle mode, it creates keyframes for muscle motion to animate the mesh without changing it on the model level.

Bones: Adds bones to models and assigns CPs to them. This is different from Skeletal mode, which is used to manipulate bones that have already been added to the model.

Grooming: Gives access to the guides for a hair system associated with a model. Allows the manipulation of length, density, and direction of hair on a model's surface.

Muscle: Animates individual control points, termed "muscle motion" in A:M. Similar to Modeling mode but is only available in action, pose, and choreography, as it is an Animation mode. Movement of control points in Muscle mode is nondestructive and can change over time.

Skeletal: Gives access to the bones in a model. It is available in choreography, action, and relationships. Like Muscle mode, it allows nondestructive animated changes to a model.

Dynamics: Edits and creates spring systems: drawing in masses and springs used to manipulate mesh and bones with soft body dynamic simulations. These tools take some effort to master but can greatly improve an animation's realism.

Choreography: Allows the positioning of models and other objects in a choreography window to set up shots and animated scenes. For many objects, this is all the manipulation that is needed. Available only in the choreography window. Often referred to as direction mode.

By default, the mode buttons are tied to function keys (see Table 1.3).

TABLE 1.3   Mode Tool Shortcuts

COMMAND	PC SHORTCUT	MAC SHORTCUT
Model mode	F5	F5
Bones mode	F6	F6
Distort mode	None	None
Muscle mode	F7	F7
Skeletal mode	F8	F8
Dynamics mode	None	None
Grooming mode	None	None
Choreography mode	F9	F9

Manipulators (see Figure 1.8) are the tools that get the work done in the program. The first four tools in this grouping are used in almost every aspect of the software. Some uses for the tools change depending on the mode and what you are trying to accomplish. The brief discussion here will help establish a vocabulary from which to explore these tools in further depth. Table 1.4 shows keyboard shortcuts for the manipulators.

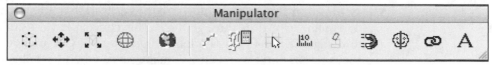

FIGURE 1.8   The Manipulator tool palette.

Standard mode: The default manipulation tool for all areas of the software typically used for the selection of individual items or the drag selection of multiple items. It can also be used to move individual items around in the viewport, rotate bones, or scale. Sensitive to what is being manipulated, it adjusts its function, as from mode to mode, and based on selection.

Translate mode: Limits the effect of manipulation to translation options. It also brings up the Translate manipulator in the viewport. The manipulator resembles a bounding box with red, green, and blue handles that can be used to translate in one axis only, and special two-color handles that allow an object to be moved in two axes at once. Simply clicking inside the manipulator and dragging allows free translation of an object in 3D space.

In A:M and most other 3D programs, red, green, and blue are used to represent the x-, y-, and z-axes, respectively. This makes sense, as RGB is the order of colors monitors use, and xyz is the order of axes alphabetically.

Scale mode: Changes the standard manipulator to the scale manipulator, which allows an object to be sized up or down in one or more axes. It functions much like the Translate manipulator. The important difference is the pivot. The origin of any scale operation is the pivot, which can be moved. This can be useful for distorting objects or scaling points of a model while keeping the same surface features.

Rotate mode: Limits the effect of manipulation to rotation operations. The manipulator for this mode makes it obvious what the base function of the tool is. Note that the overall yellow rings provide free rotation, so that clicking and dragging inside the manipulator other than on the red, green, or blue handles causes unconstrained rotation. The color-coded rings rotate in their respective *x-*, *y-*, or *z-*axis. All rotation is based around the pivot.

You can move the pivot while a group is selected. To do so, simply move the cursor over the center of the pivot until the pointer changes to the pivot manipulator cursor, and then click and drag the pivot to move it. To rotate the pivot, click and drag on one of the RGB color-coded pivot rotation handles. This becomes very important during the modeling discussion.

Show manipulators in world space: Moves an object with any of the previous manipulator modes but using the choreography's XYZ rather than the XYZ stored in the model file.

Show bias handles: Bias handles are the controls that manipulate the curve of a spline as it runs through a CP. This concept is very similar to vector drawing programs such as Adobe® Illustrator®. If you are not familiar with the concept, don't worry. It will make sense when we talk about this tool in context.

Show manipulator properties: This tool is used to toggle a user interface (UI) widget that presents a heads-up display about the selected item and its editable properties. It is sensitive to the manipulator mode so that different properties are presented for Rotate mode than Scale mode, for example. This movable widget can also accept text input that can precisely position control points in the model window.

Snap manipulator to grid: Forces the manipulator to move in grid intervals, meaning that a CP that is not on a grid point can be moved the distance of a grid space, but it will not snap to a grid point. Snapping control points to grid intersection is done with the contextual menu, and will be discussed in the section "Modeling Basics." This tool causes more confusion than almost any other function, as most people expect that it will snap control points to the grid intersections in the modeling window.

Show rulers: Toggles the visibility of the rulers in the current window. This also hides any guides but does not remove them.

Compensate mode: Creates, when used in conjunction with constraints, an offset for the current position, rotation, and scale of a bone in relation to the bone it is being constrained to, as needed. That may not make much sense right now but its value is immeasurable, as you will see when we discuss constraints.

Magnet mode: Takes the selected CP and creates an area of control around it. Points inside that area are moved along with the selected CP. The control has a linear falloff, which means points move less as they move farther from the center of control and eventually fall out of the controlling radius. Used while modeling or creating muscle motion.

Mirror mode: Manipulates points in a symmetrical model and keeps them symmetrical. It only works across the y-axis; most models that need it are constructed this way. Preserving the symmetry of a model ensures that commands such as Paste mirrored will function properly. It is important to remember to turn off this toggle when not in use. Leaving it on can cause problems, not to mention general confusion.

Relationship mode: This mode indicates that all changes will be recorded into the current relationship node. It is important that once finished editing a relationship that this mode is turned off. What a relationship is and why this is important will be explained in Chapter 8.

Animate mode: This mode is used in action and choreography to toggle automatic keyframing on or off. When this toggle is depressed, A:M creates a keyframe for any changes you make at the current frame of animation time. When it is inactive, A:M will not create any new keys for any changes you make; instead, it will *offset* all keys in the current property. This may not make a lot of sense to you now, but as you explore animation tools it becomes clear. How this works exactly is explored in Chapter 10, "Animation."

TABLE 1.4 Manipulators Shortcuts

COMMAND	PC SHORTCUT	MAC SHORTCUT
Standard mode	Esc	Esc
Translate mode	N	N
Scale mode	S	S
Rotate mode	R	R

That's the extent of the global toolbars. Familiarize yourself with them as much as you can. As you progress with A:M, their use will become second nature. The remaining tools are sensitive to the context in which they are used, or are only available in certain areas of the software. We will begin to explore these tools as we look at the various components that make up a project in A:M.

Modeling Mode Tools

Model is the term used to talk about the objects that are rendered to create a 3D scene. These objects live inside a project or an external file on your hard drive called a model file. Later, we will discuss project management and workflow and go a little more in depth about external versus internal model files. A modeled object can be just about anything—a character, a car, a prop, or a set. These are the pieces that will make up your virtual world. All objects, no matter what they may be, have one thing in common: They are constructed of splines using the Modeling mode tools.

To access the tools used in modeling mode, the correct 3D viewport must be open and set to the correct working mode. The most common site for working on models is the *Model window*. You can also create and manipulate models in the *Choreography window* but this is not commonly done in A:M. To create a model, click the New button on the Standard toolbar, or use the keyboard shortcut for that function (Ctrl+N on the PC, Cmd+N on the Mac). Once the catalog window is displayed, select Model in the item list and click Create. A new Model window looking in the "front" view will result.

There is often more than one way to go about things in A:M. You will learn all the various options as you go, and you can choose the one that best suits your working methods.

When you open a new model, the modeling window for that object will default to Modeling mode. Look at the buttons on the Mode toolbar, and you will notice that some of them are grayed out and others are not. This indicates the modes that are available in the current working window (specifically Modeling, Bones, Distortion, and Grooming). In order to work with Modeling mode tools, the window must be in Modeling mode.

Once a Modeling mode window is open, you will see a vertical toolbar on the right side of the screen that holds all the tools needed for modeling even the most complex objects (see Figure 1.9). These are the tools you use to create and manipulate models:

- Edit (Standard)
- Add
- Break
- Detach Point
- Peak
- Smooth
- Lasso
- Line Lasso
- Patch Select
- Hide
- Lock
- Extrude
- Lathe
- Make Five-Point Patch

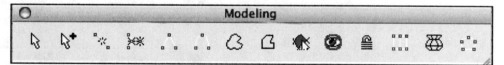

FIGURE 1.9   The Modeling toolbar, undocked for clarity.

Edit (Standard): The general-purpose selection and manipulation tool. Use it to select things or move them in a window. It can make selections of multiple items by clicking and dragging a selection box around them. Edit is the default tool, so it is active when not using another tool and can be returned to at any time by pressing the Esc key.

Add: The most basic model surface construction tool, it is used to draw a series of control points (CPs) connected by splines. Activate this tool with the Add button or by pressing A on the keyboard. Once active, each click of the mouse in the Modeling viewport will create a new control point, and between each point A:M will draw a spline. A single spline can (and often should) run through many points (see Figure 1.10). The Add tool remains active until you disable it. There are three ways to exit Add mode: pressing the Esc key (returning to Edit mode,) right-clicking (PC) or control-clicking (Mac with single button mouse), or clicking the first point you drew again. This last option will connect the beginning and end points to create a loop. You will learn more about connections later.

TRY IT NOW

Draw a spline in your model window. Activate the Add tool, and lay a few points down. If you accidentally double-click, it is possible that you can stack two control points and have it look like a single point, so be careful. Overlapping points can cause problems down the road. In order to stop adding points to a model, simply press the Esc key or right-click (PC) or control-click (Mac with single button mouse). Now you are back in Edit mode. Click a point and drag it in the window. Note how the spline moves through the points. Note the curve it has. All of these aspects are discussed further as you progress.

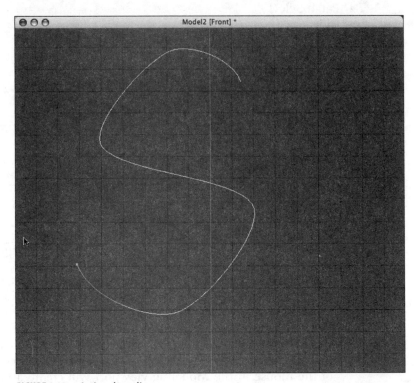

FIGURE 1.10   A simple spline.

 A set of points connected by splines is the basis for all A:M models. Models generally start with a single point and move out from there. This concept is sometimes hard for new users to grasp, especially if they have had previous modeling experience with polygon-based applications. There are no primitive shapes to start from; everything must be constructed from raw splines. Thankfully, once the tools and the spline mind set are learned, it's not that hard.

If further detail is needed in the middle of a spline, the Add tool can also "stitch" new points into an existing spline. Simply enter Add mode, and click on a spine between two control points to add a point (you can then continue to draw points as a new spline or press the Esc key to exit Add mode). This is a slightly advanced use for the Add tool, and it is covered much further in depth later.

Break Spline: This tool is for separating long splines into smaller segments by removing spline connections between control points. The Break Spline tool has a few rules for use that necessitate looking at another aspect of splines and control points: As a spline goes into and then exits a CP, there are rules that define how the spline behaves as it moves through the CP, and each part of the spline (in and out) can be separately selected and adjusted. A CP cannot exist without a spline, and likewise, a spline cannot exist without at least two control points to define its ends.

The Break tool can be thought to remove the spline that connects two control points, but each of those control points must have a spline that remains attached to it for this to happen. This means that the Break tool needs some information in order to perform its function. It needs to know which spline to break from which control point. This requires you to focus the modeling window with a selection. We have already said that the Edit tool is for general selection, and this is the perfect time to use it. The Edit tool has two modes of selection: direct selection and group selection. Use direct selection by clicking on a point or spline; use group selection by dragging a box around the points you want to select. Note that you can click on a point or a spline; this is critical. If you click on a spline, a control point will be selected, but it will also show a green selection leg on the active spline that indicates which spline from the control point is active in the selection and focused for any modifications or tool use. The Break tool remains grayed out on the toolbar until a selection is made that it considers valid for a break. Valid selections will not orphan any control points after the break has been made. Look at Figure 1.11. There are two selections on the same spline. Note that the Break icon is not active in the first selection but it is on the second, even though the same CP is selected for both. The difference is in the spline selections.

TRY IT NOW

Select a point on the spline you drew earlier and attempt to break it. If the Break tool does not activate, check your spline selection. Remember to click on the spline itself rather than the CP and to click without dragging the Edit tool. Learning proper selection techniques will come in handy later on.

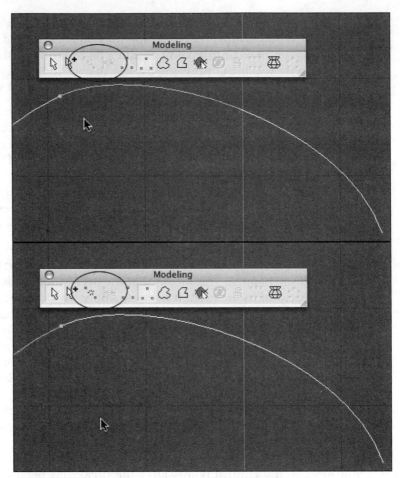

FIGURE 1.11   The Break tool requires a correct selection.

Detach CP: Used to detach one spline from another. At first, this might sound like the Break tool, but the operation of detaching a point is very different than that of breaking a spline. In order to understand this better, you need to learn about connections when more than one spline is in- volved. A single spline runs through a control point, but two or more control points can be joined or "welded" together so that the splines of each point seem to move in and out of a single point. This is a convenient way to look at what is going on, but in reality each spline moves through its own point. Those points just happen to be selectable and moveable as a single unit. If you don't want those points to move together anymore, you can detach them. Logically, this requires that there be more than one spline and that they be attached to one another. Like the Break tool, the Detach tool button remains grayed out until you make a selection that can be broken. This means you need to select a point that has more than one CP welded together. If there are more than two points joined at a given intersection, the tool will only detach one point based on the spline selection as with the Break tool.

TRY IT NOW

Using the Add tool, draw a spline with three points on it running from top to bottom in the modeling window (see Figure 1.12). Next, use the Add tool to draw a second spline with three points running right to left. As you lay down the points for the second spline, use the "stitch" feature off the Add tool to join the two splines together. Be certain that your second click for the left-right spline is exactly on top of the top-bottom spline. You should have a rough plus shape, as in Figure 1.13. Now select the point where the two splines meet, and use the Detach tool by clicking the button or pressing the Shift+K keyboard shortcut. The points will still sit on top of each other, but if you select one of them and drag it with the Edit mode tool, you can separate them easily (see Figure 1.14).

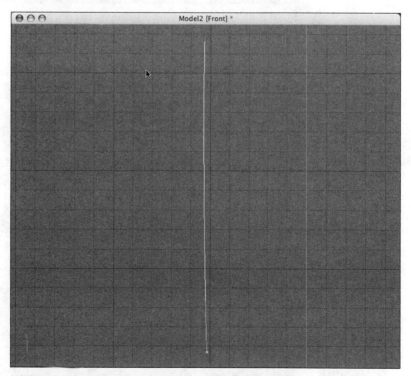

FIGURE 1.12   Lay down one three-point spline top to bottom.

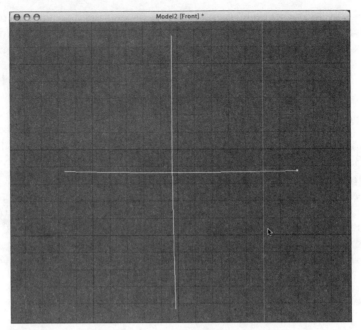

FIGURE 1.13   Lay down a second spline left to right being sure to stitch it to the first.

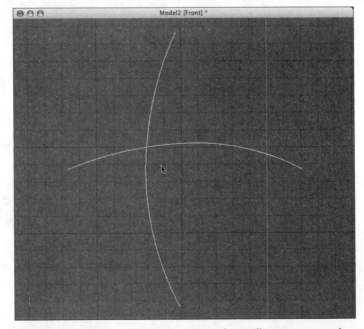

FIGURE 1.14   After you detach the points, they will move separately.

If you have two separate splines that you have drawn and later want to connect them without the Stitch tool, simply drag the point you wish to weld over the target point, and without letting go of the mouse, right-click on the PC or press the ~ (tilde) key on the Mac. This will weld those two points together just as if you had used the Stitch tool. The ~ (tilde) key might have a different mapping on non-American keyboards. You may need to map the join function to another key. If this is the case, do so with the Customize option from the Tools menu. The Keyboard tab allows you to change the keyboard shortcut for any tool or function.

Peak Spline: Overrides the default behavior of a spline so that it moves in and out of a control point at sharp angles (see Figure 1.15) rather than a smooth curve. It also provides advanced control over the curve of a spline. This is discussed further in Chapter 2.

Smooth Spline: Returns a peaked spline to its default smooth state (see Figure 1.15). Since splines are drawn smooth by default, this tool is used less frequently than Peak.

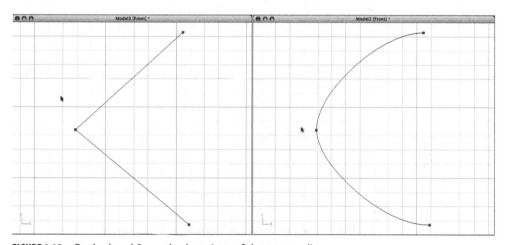

FIGURE 1.15 Peaked and Smoothed versions of the same spline.

TRY IT NOW

Draw a spline with at least three points that has a curve to it, similar to the one in Figure 1.15. Select the center point, this can be done by clicking the point or dragging a selection around it. Once you have the point selected, press the Peak button or press the P key. Note how the spline loses its curve as it moves into and out of the control point. If you have deselected the point reselect it, and click the Smooth button or press the O key to return it to its default.

The next three tools are selection tools, which, in modeling, allow the selection of control points for further manipulation and the creation of named groups in the model. Groups (either selected or named) are required before the rotate, scale, or translate manipulators or the Extrude tool can be used. A group selection is identified in the Model window by a yellow bounding box around the control points that have been selected (see Figure 1.16).

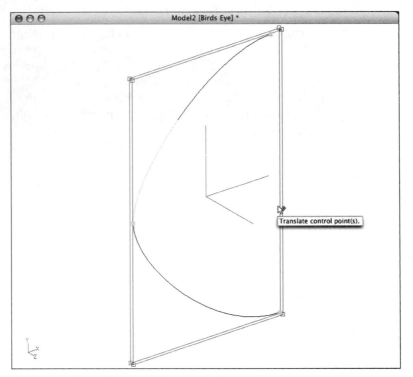

FIGURE 1.16   The yellow bounding box indicates a group.

Lasso: This tool allows the selection of points by drawing a flexible curving line around an area to select. It uses the same modifier keys as the Group Select tool.

Line Lasso: This allows a selection to be defined by drawing straight lines between points at each mouse click. In this respect, it is much like the Add Lock tool. To stop making lines and complete the selection, simply click on the point that the Lasso started again. All the keys from the Group tool apply for adding, subtracting, or toggling groups of control points.

Patch Select: This tool will select any rendering patch simply by clicking it inside the points it is comprised of. This tool is sticky, meaning it remains active until you click outside a patch or press the Esc key to return to the standard tool. The modifier keys for Group mode also apply here.

Hide: This tool hides any control points that aren't currently selected. This causes confusion for many new users who expect the tool to hide what is selected. To hide what is selected, simply invert the selection. You do this with the . (period) key, which invokes the Inverse Selection command. (There is no button to do this in the interface; it can be accessed by key command only.) Progressively hide more of a model by making a new group and selecting the Hide command while using the Shift key as a modifier.

Lock: This locks any control points that aren't selected, the same as the Hide tool. Unlike Hide, however, locked points are still visible but are not selectable. This is very useful for working on new areas of a model while keeping what is already done in perspective. Like Hide, you can progressively add to the locked portion of a model by modifying the command with the Shift key.

Extrude: This tool is named after a manufacturing process by which material is pushed through a shaped hole to "extrude" a product. In A:M, this is one of two patch-creation tools (the other being the lathe). Extrude duplicates any points in a selection (including any splines that may connect them) and then creates a set of splines that connect the original points with the new ones.

TRY IT NOW

Draw a spline across the top of a model window with the Add tool. Use at least two control points, but you can use as many as you like. Select all the points along the spline with the group functions of the Standard tool or any of the Group mode tools. Once you have a bounding box indicating a selection of points, invoke the Extrude tool by pressing E on the keyboard or by clicking the button. Presuming you have not changed any of the preference settings, this Extrusion is moved −10 pixels in the y-axis. Once one extrusion has been made, the next one will be moved in the same direction the same distance, instead of the default. The most important part of the tool is that it will create what is referred to as a Patch. While you learn more later about what a patch is and what makes one, what you need to understand at this point is that a model's surface is shown only where there are patches. Any area, even if it has points and splines in it, will not draw a patch that the software can see when it comes time to render. In fact, if you do a progressive render of the model window now (Shift+Q shortcut), you can see your first patches (see Figure 1.17).

Lathe: The second of the patch generation tools is also named after an industrial machine. A carpenter or a machinist uses a lathe to spin raw material and cut parts out of it. Due to the spinning nature of the lathe, it is ideal for creating things like cylinders, banisters, and the like. Similarly, the Lathe tool here revolves a point or group of points around the y-axis (by default, more on this shortly) creating a curved surface that looks as if it might have come off an industrial lathe.

FIGURE 1.17   The Extrude tool makes your first patch.

A single spline needs to be selected to activate the Lathe button. Draw a spline to one side of the *y*-axis. The shape of the spline and the number of points don't matter. Once you have drawn the spline, simply click on any point on the spline to select it and note that the Lathe button becomes active. (A:M will often let you know when it cannot perform a function by simply making a button inactive.) Click the Lathe button or press the L keyboard shortcut to lathe your spline. With any luck, you have something similar to Figure 1.19.

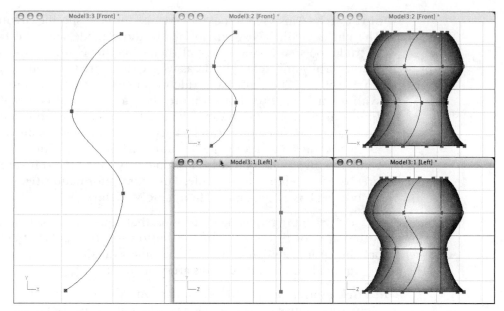

FIGURE 1.18   If your spline looks like it has fat lathe syndrome, check its position from a side view.

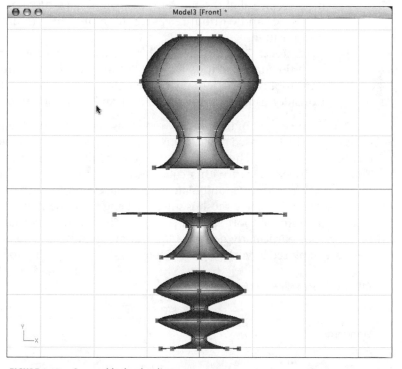

FIGURE 1.19   Several lathed splines.

5-Point Patch: This special tool was created for very specific circumstances. The patches you have seen so far are those made with the Lathe and Extrude tools, and if you look at them they have at least one common feature: They are created by areas where there are four control points on a few splines. The most basic rule of a patch is that it cannot be made without at least three but no more than four control points. There are times when an area in a mesh will have five points that you would like to be a patch, but five points can be very difficult to close cleanly. Selecting all five points and clicking the 5-Point Patch button defines this area as a rendering five-point patch. It's a simple way to tell the software that this area is an exception to the rule. For more information see Chapters 2, "Modeling Basics"; 5, and 6, "Inorganic Modeling."

There are a few more modeling mode tools that you can access from keyboard shortcuts that are not readily available as buttons on the toolbar (you can add them from the customize dialog) or only become available in specific instances. The more commonly used of these tools are as follows:

Add Lock mode: Similar to Add mode, with the exception that it will only draw two control points joined by a spline. It can be useful when creating certain types of nonorganic geometry; however, the results are the same as using Add mode and only drawing two control points. Using Add Lock mode is also slightly different. Instead of clicking to place each point, you click once and without releasing the mouse button drag the second point into position.

Group Select: This functions the same as simply dragging a selection group with the Standard tool; however, it forces Selection mode while the Standard tool can accidentally move a point when your intention is to select. Consider using this tool when a mesh is cramped with geometry.

This is the extent of the primary modeling tools. If you have previous 3D experience with polygon-based applications, you might be used to palettes upon mountainous palettes of tools. The elegance of patches is that you don't need all those tools. There is no need to start with a cube and attempt to arrive at a curve. Instead, you can start at a curve and manipulate your surface directly until it is the desired shape. Building an animateable mesh is still a challenge but one that can be easily met with just this handful of tools applied properly. There are tasks that the A:M modeling tools are not particularly designed for, but alternatives and solutions to these situations are explored as you progress. Table 1.5 shows modeling tool shortcuts.

TABLE 1.5   Modeling Tool Shortcuts

TOOL	PC SHORTCUT	MAC SHORTCUT
Standard	Esc	Esc
Add	A	A

→

TOOL	PC SHORTCUT	MAC SHORTCUT
Add Lock	Shift+A	Shift+A
Insert CP	Y	Y
Break Spline	K	K
Detach CP	Shift+K	Shift+K
Peak Spline	P	P
Smooth Spline	O	O
Group	G	G
Lasso	Shift+G	Shift+G
Line Lasso	None	None
Patch Select	None	None
Hide	H, Shift+H to hide more	H, Shift+H to hide more
Lock	None	None
Extrude	E	E
Lathe	L	L
5-Point Patch	None	None

Selection Tools

While they don't have buttons in the GUI, there are other important selection tools (see Table 1.6). These tools are there to let you expand your selection out from a current point or group of points into a logical selection. For instance, a model can consist of more than one set of control points and splines that are connected, and you might want to select just the points that are connected to the current selection. You can use the / keyboard shortcut to do this with the Group Connected command.

If you have a spline selected and want to select all the points along that spline into a group, you use the , (comma) keyboard shortcut to invoke the Complement Spline tool. (Complement in this case doesn't mean you tell the spline how nice it looks today, but rather that you want to select the *rest* or the *complement* of the spline.)

Sometimes you want to change the selection to the points that are not currently selected and simultaneously deselect those that currently are. This can be done simply with the . (period) keyboard shortcut and the Invert Selection command.

And, of course, there are times that you just want to select everything in the model all at once. This is done in the same way you would **Select All** in a word processor, with the Command+A (Mac) or Ctrl+A (PC) keyboard shortcut.

TABLE 1.6   Spline Selection Keys

FUNCTION	PC SHORTCUT	MAC SHORTCUT
Select All Connected	/	/
Complement Spline	,	,
Inverse Selection	.	.
Select All	Ctrl+A	Cmd+A

We can also use what are termed *modifier keys* to add, subtract, or toggle (into or out of selected states) points for a selection. These tools can be used to change the default behavior of any selection tool (see Table 1.7).

TABLE 1.7   Selection Modifier Keys

KEY	FUNCTION
Shift	Adds to the current selection
Alt (PC) or Option (Mac)	Subtracts from the current selection
Ctrl (PC) or Command (Mac)	Toggles the selection or deselection of the points

Distort Mode Tools

When you have a model, you often want to manipulate groups of control points quickly while maintaining the base shape already created. This mode of working is what Distortion mode is designed for. The tools for Distortion mode are very similar to those that we covered in the Modeling section, and as such, there is no need to go quite as in depth on them here. This section has only been separated to maintain the consistency with the interface that indicates distortion is a separate mode with a separate set of tools (see Figure 1.20).

FIGURE 1.20   Distortion mode tools are similar to the Modeling mode tools.

All the tools here are analogous to tools from Modeling mode. The only difference is that in this instance they apply to the distortion lattice instead of individual CP. Keyboard shortcuts are shown in Table 1.8. In brief:

Standard: Selects individual points on the deformation lattice. This tool can also select groups of points by clicking and dragging a selection rectangle around the desired points.

Group: Forces a group to be selected by drawing a selection rectangle around the desired points.

Lasso: Selects a group of points on the lattice by drawing a flexible line around the desired points.

Line Lasso: Allows a group of points to be defined by drawing straight selection lines between mouse clicks. To close the line, click the starting point of the selection.

Peak: Peaks the splines that make up the deformation lattice at the selected control point. It also allows the adjustment of bias settings of the splines for the lattice on either side of the peaked control point independently

Smooth: Returns a peaked spline from the peaked state to the default smooth state. It also returns the control of spline bias to a single manipulator handle.

TABLE 1.8   Group Tools Keyboard Shortcuts

TOOL	PC SHORTCUT	MAC SHORTCUT
Standard	Esc	Esc
Peak Spline	P	P
Smooth Spline	O	O
Group	G	G
Lasso	Shift+G	Shift+G
Line Lasso	None	None

TRY IT NOW

In order to truly understand what Distortion mode is and how it works, you need to try it out on a model. Start by drawing a spline and lathing it. The shape of it doesn't matter so much. Once the mesh is in place, click the Distort Mode button. If you selected no control points, the distortion grid will surround the entire model. If you wish to only distort a portion of the model, simply select that portion before entering Distort mode, and the distortion cage will be drawn around any group you have selected. The distortion grid (sometimes called a lattice) by default has a density of what we call 3 x 3 x 3, meaning that there are three points of control in all three axes for a total of nine points. Select any point in the lattice and drag it. Notice how the geometry inside of the area defined by that point distorts to maintain its shape and volume in that area. Continue to adjust the mesh until you feel you have a grasp on how the tool works. Once you are satisfied, simply click the Model Mode tool to exit the distortion cage.

Bones Mode Tools

Moving points around in a model gives us a lot of control and also can present an overwhelming amount of data to deal with. For the creation of objects, this is actually a good thing, where a fine level of control is what allows you to create anything you might want. In animation, however, it is much less desirable. To that end, you have tools that allow you to group sets of points together as a group for easy movement when animating. These groups are represented with objects called "bones." You place bones in a model and assign CPs to their influence with the Bones mode tools (see Figure 1.21).

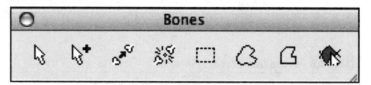

FIGURE 1.21   Bones mode tools are similar to Modeling mode tools.

The tools for bones are to a certain extent analogous to those used when modeling, and that makes sense because this is still manipulating things on a model level.

Standard: Selects and manipulates bones. The type of manipulation it performs to a selected object, however, is dependent on the context you are using it in. A:M gives visual clues as to what the tool will be doing by adding a badge to the cursor (see Figure 1.22). Clicking and dragging with the Standard tool does not select multiple bones (only one bone can be selected at a time). The grouping rectangle indicates that any control points that fall within its bounds will be assigned to the currently selected bone. If no bone is selected, they will be unassigned from any bones they have currently and reassigned to the model or to what is referred to as the Model Bone. This will be explained in further detail in Chapter 3, "Bone Basics."

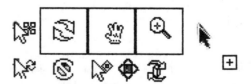

FIGURE 1.22   Badges and changes to the pointer can tell you what is going to happen.

Add Bone: Much like Add mode for splines, this tool draws new bones into a model, but it behaves more in line with Add Lock mode in that it only draws a single bone. There are a number of subtleties that can change the properties of a bone as you draw it, all of which will be covered in depth in Chapter 3. However, in order to understand some of the other bones tools you will need to know a few more things about bones.

TRY IT NOW:

You will find that many things in A:M rely on the concept of the hierarchy, where one object or property is the parent of one or more other similar items. A bone, for instance, can be a "child" of another bone and can itself have a child. Each bone can have only one parent but each parent can have more than one child. This is important to the way the bone will be controlled in animation.

Create a new model, and change the workspace to Bones mode, either with the Bones mode button or the F6 keyboard shortcut. Now add a bone to the model by clicking the Add mode button or pressing the A keyboard shortcut. Click anywhere in the workspace and drag without letting go of the mouse button. You should see a bone draw.

After you draw the bone, it should be selected automatically. You can tell a bone has been selected because it flashes from yellow to the color that is assigned to the bone. Bones have different colors to distinguish them visually and to assist you in determining which control points in a model are assigned to a given bone.

You can continue to add bones by clicking the Add button (or using the shortcut) and clicking and dragging in the workspace. If a bone is selected when you create a new one, it will be added as a child of the selected bone. If you click on an empty space in the workspace (or press the Esc key), you can clear any selection. If no bone has been selected when you create a new one, it will be created at the base of a new hierarchy. Bones that are children of the same parent or have no parent are called siblings.

A series of bones that are in a progressively deeper hierarchy are called a chain (see Figure 1.23). It might help to think of it like your own arm: The shoulder would be the parent of the bicep, which in turn is the parent of the forearm, which is in turn is the parent of the hand, which is in turn is the parent of the fingers, and while the fingers are all children of the hand they would be considered equal as far as hierarchy goes. Each bone can have one child that is attached to it, meaning that the bottom of the child bone is linked to the top of the parent. This is a very important concept and determines what type of chain you create with your bones. A series of attached bones form what is called an *inverse kinematic* (IK) chain, while a series of unattached bones will form a *forward kinematic* (FK) chain. We don't want to get too deep into this bit of jargon at this point, but we cover it as we progress. Keep those words in mind, though, as you will hear a lot about them when it comes time to animate.

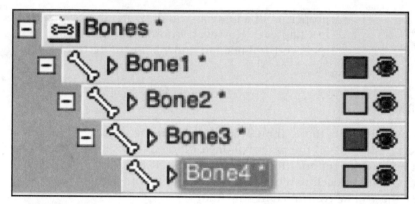

FIGURE 1.23   A series of bones that progress deeper into a hierarchy is called a chain.

Draw a new bone in your workspace; while it is selected, draw a second. Be sure that when you draw the second bone you start it by clicking the tip of the selected bone. Now when you move either the child or the parent, you will affect the position of the other. You have created an attached bone.

With the parent selected, draw a third bone. Click the tip of the parent bone again. Note that if you move the parent now, only the first child you drew will move with it. This shows that only one child can be attached to a parent at any given time. If you move the last bone you added, it will not affect either its sibling or its parent.

With that in mind, look at the next couple of tools.

Attach Bone to Parent: If a bone is not attached to its parent in a hierarchy, this will force it to attach itself, even if it must move its base to reach the tip of the parent. The tip of the bone will, however, remain stationary. This function is only available if the bone has a parent and only if the parent has no currently attached children.

Detach Bone from Parent: Detaches a child from the parent so that it may be moved without affecting the parent's position. Again, this is only available when the selected bone is a child of another bone and currently attached.

Lasso, **Line Lasso**, and **Patch Select:** Behave the same as the modeling tools of the same name, with the exception that the control points selected, instead of being turned into a group, are assigned to the currently selected bone.

When a CP is assigned to a bone, the color of the point is changed while in Bones mode to match its assigned bone. When viewing the model in Shaded mode, the patches are also colored to match the bones that they are assigned to, making it easy to see the area of control for all bones in a model. Shortcuts for the Bones mode tools are shown in Table 1.9.

TABLE 1.9   Bones Mode Tool Shortcuts

TOOL	PC SHORTCUT	MAC SHORTCUT
Standard	Esc	Esc
Add	A	A
Attach Bone	None	None
Detach Bone	None	None
Group	G	G
Lasso	Shift+G	Shift+G
Line Lasso	None	None
Patch Select	None	None

You've done pretty much all you can in the model workspace. Before you can explore more tools, you need to expand your knowledge of A:M's workspace windows.

Once a model has been created, you may at some point want to animate it, perhaps by using the individual CPs to change the surface of a model or by moving bones to control groups of control points. Before the tools you need to animate become available, an action window needs to be active. (In fact, you can work inside a number of windows, but for now stick with the action window, which lets you focus on just the tools you need at the moment.) To create an action, click the New button on the Standard toolbar, or use the keyboard shortcut (Ctrl+N on the PC, Cmd+N on the Mac). Once the catalog window is displayed, select Action in the item list and click Create. If you have exactly one model in your project, a new Action will open in Skeletal mode, looking at the front view of your model. If you have no, or more than one, models in your project you will be presented with one of two dialog windows.

If you have multiple models in your project you will be presented with a dialog that will list the models and ask you to choose one for your action (see Figure 1.24). If you want to use a model that is not in your project, simply click the Browse button, and a File Open dialog opens, allowing you to import any model into your project.

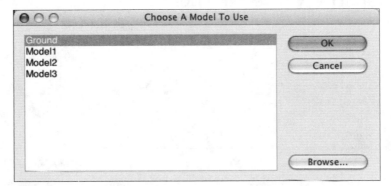

FIGURE 1.24   Select which model in the project to use in your action.

If there is no model in the project, a File Open dialog box is presented, and you are asked to select one from your hard drive. For the purpose of your explorations, any model with control points will do the trick.

Muscle Mode Tools

A new action window defaults to Bones mode because this is the most common type of animation. To change it to Muscle mode, click the icon for that mode on the Mode toolbar, or press F7. Once in Muscle mode, the model will be displayed identically to the way it is displayed in the model window, with one major exception. Changes made to the points of the model in this window do not change the model permanently; rather, they are stored as a sort of instruction that tells A:M to move the points to a given place at a given time. We explore this much further in depth in Chapter 4. The tools for Muscle mode are basically an abbreviated set identical in function to those used in modeling (see Figure 1.25). The tools that are missing are the ones that are used for adding, breaking, and splitting splines.

FIGURE 1.25   The Muscle mode tools.

These tools should look very familiar by now, as they are the same from the Modeling section, and their function here is identical. Refer to the section on modeling for detailed descriptions of each if you need to review. Table 1.10 shows Muscle mode tools shortcuts.

TABLE 1.10   Muscle Mode Tools Shortcuts

TOOL	PC SHORTCUT	MAC SHORTCUT
Standard	Esc	Esc
Lasso	Shift+G	Shift+G
Line Lasso	None	None
Patch Select	None	None
Hide	H	H
Lock	None	None

TRY IT NOW

An action has two elements that can be thought of most simply as What and When. In terms of our Muscle mode tools, where we move any control points becomes the What; the When is indicated with the tools located on the Frame toolbar (see Figure 1.26). There are a large number of tools here, and we will go into them with great detail in Chapters 4 and 10. For now, we are interested in the frame number box. An animation is nothing more than a series of still images played back one after another; each of those images is called a frame. You create motion in your animations by changing something (the What) across a number of frames.

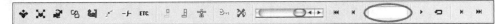

FIGURE 1.26   The Frame toolbar with the frame number box circled.

Click in the frame number box (circled in Figure 1.26) which has the current time listed as Minutes:Seconds:Frames. Highlight this text and type a number. This will move the Current time to the frame you typed in. Now select and move some points in the model. Note that when you deselect them they are shaded blue rather than the default red, which indicates that those points have been changed on that frame.

To see your animation, step back trough the frames either by clicking the button just to the left of the frame number box (each click moves the time back one frame), or press the – (minus) key on the number pad. You should see the points you moved slowly go back the their original positions.

Skeletal Mode Tools

The most common method for animating is the manipulation of an object's skeleton. This is a factor of convenience and power, as a bone allows the movement of all control points assigned to it as one unit. Bones can translate, rotate, and scale any associated control points, as well as the points assigned to any children that bone may have. Through IK, a child bone can also affect the rotation of its parent and points farther up the hierarchy. The base (large end) of the bone becomes the pivot for all manipulation, while the tip (small end) and roll handle become the rotational manipulators.

Bones and animating with them will be covered in greater depth in Chapters 3 and 4, but as you can see, with a complex set of tools like these (see Figure 1.27), it is better to take them in small bits! We're kidding, of course, and one of the strongest aspects of A:M is the simple and direct set of animation tools. Table 1.11 shows tool shortcuts.

Standard: Selects, translates, or rotates a bone; with a modifier, it can also scale a bone.

The pointer icon will indicate what the tool will do by the badge that is added as you roll over various parts of the bone. A bone moved by its base is translated. Selecting the tip of the bone allows rotation in the *x*- and *y*-axes, while the handle (see Figure 1.28) pointing off to the side (called a roll handle) rotates the bone on the *z*-axis. This tool defaults to free rotation, which allows the bone to move in all three axes simultaneously (except when the roll handle is moved explicitly). To constrain rotation to a single axis, use the Rotate Manipulation mode.

FIGURE 1.27 In spite of a small toolset, skeletal manipulation in A:M is second to none.

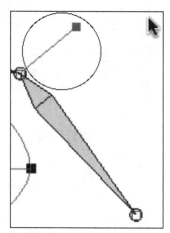

FIGURE 1.28 The roll handle has been circled for identification.

The Rotate Manipulator focuses the function of this tool by presenting three color-coded rings. Using a ring as a handle restricts the rotation to one axis.

The Translate Manipulator can be used to restrict bone translation.

A bone can be scaled by either using the scale manipulator or by holding down the Shift key or Option/Alt key while clicking and dragging the tip of the bone. The Shift key scales the bone in the *z*-axis only, while the Option/Alt key scales all three axes simultaneously.

Lock: The Lock tool allows you to change the way that a chain of bones is handled in an action. If you recall, we discussed some of the basic differences about chains of bones that are attached to their parents and chains that are not. Inverse kinematics is the type of chain that you get when you attach bones from parent to child. In an action, the entire chain will be controlled by the tip of the last bone in it, meaning that dragging the tip of the hand will cause the forearm to rotate to reach the hand, and the bicep will likewise reach the forearm. This is reversed from the direction you drew the bones (which is where the inverse part comes in). If you lock a bone, however, the rotations of the chain will stop at the lock. So if you lock the forearm, dragging the tip of the hand will still move the hand and the forearm, but the bicep will not rotate. The lock placed on the forearm blocks the movement up the chain—which is exactly how an FK chain would act normally. Use Lock instead of just making FK chains where you want the ability to turn on and off IK behavior for a chain; attaching or detaching a bone can only be done in the model and cannot be animated on or off.

TABLE 1.11   Skeletal Mode Tool Shortcuts

FUNCTION	PC SHORTCUT	MAC SHORTCUT
Standard Mode	Esc	Esc
Lock Bone	None	None

TRY IT NOW

Let's see some bone manipulation in action. Create a new action, and when it asks you for a model, browse to load the ikChain.mdl file from the CD-ROM. In the action, you will see two sets of three bones: the top set is attached to parent and the bottom set is not. Grab the tip of the last bone with the Standard tool off the top set and drag it. Note how the whole chain follows along.

Now grab the tip of the last bone in the bottom chain and drag it. Note that the other bones in the chain do not move. This is the difference between IK and FK.

Now select the second-from-last bone in the IK chain, and click the Lock button. Note that the base of the bone now has an X drawn through it. This indicates that the bone is now locked. Now once again select the tip of the last bone in the IK chain and drag it. Note how the rotations stop at the lock. In Chapter 10, we will look at practical uses and discuss when locking an IK chain is preferred.

These rotations we have performed on our chains can also be used to fill in the What part of the animation equation in the same way CP manipulation did earlier. If you type a frame number into the Frame toolbar and rotate either or both chains of bones, you can see the way the bones rotate around their pivots as you step through the frames.

Choreography Tools

There is only one more basic area of the software that has its own set of tools: choreography. (Dynamics mode also has its own toolset, but that is an advanced topic that is covered in Chapter 13, "F/X.") In general, choreography is the place where you compose all your bits into a cohesive whole. This broad and expansive topic will be discussed in stages throughout this book. There is, however, a small set of tools restricted to Choreography mode that needs to be discussed separately. Note that all the tools that are previously mentioned are also available in a choreography. It is possible to model, bone, and animate objects directly in the choreography window. This can be useful when modeling and has a wide series of uses, which will be discussed in later chapters.

To activate the Choreography toolset, a choreography window must be opened. Choose the new function as before, and from the catalog select the choreography item and click Create.

There are just two tools in Figure 1.29. Both have been seen in some form before, but in Choreography mode their application is slightly different. (Shortcut keys are shown in Table 1.12.)

FIGURE 1.29   There are important distinctions to Choreography mode tools.

Standard: Positions models, lights, cameras, and other objects in the choreography window while in choreography mode. The function of this tool in the choreography window changes based on the current mode in the Mode toolbar (modeling, muscle, bone, skeleton, and so on). Refer to the section for each mode for a full description of its functions. In Direction mode it functions the same as the Skeletal mode Standard tool, but it manipulates the base model bone rather than any individual bones an object may have. This coarse manipulation is used to place models in a scene or animate general positions of models over time.

Add Path: A special kind of spline exists in a choreography, not intended to create patches or models. It is meant to be a "path" for an object to follow. (See Chapter 7 for information on the Path constraint.) The Add Path tool is used to draw a spline in the choreography window precisely the way it is used in the model window. Once the Add tool has been exited (by pressing the Esc key or right-clicking), the choreography workspace switches to Model mode, and the Choreography toolset is replaced by the modeling tools allowing further manipulation.

It is possible to extrude or lathe a path into patches. This is not recommended, but the tools are available for it. Clicking off the path at anytime or using the Esc key returns to the Standard tool and the Choreography mode.

TABLE 1.12   Choreography Mode Tool Shortcuts

FUNCTION	PC SHORTCUT	MAC SHORTCUT
Standard Mode	Esc	Esc
Add Path	A	A

WORKFLOW AND PROJECT STRUCTURE

The buttons and tools examined so far are only half the power of Animation: Master. To get into the real guts of the program, you need to get a feel for the workflow.

Workflow defines how you move through the software and deal with data. In A:M, workflow encompasses the modes (modeling, action, and so on) as well as the windows available through the View menu. (Shortcuts to access all of the workflow windows are listed in Table 1.13 at the end of this chapter.)

Modes break up work into logical stages. Each has its own set of tools and rules for use, most of which have been discussed. To a large extent, the mastery of A:M lies in using the modes and workspace windows to their greatest effect, even using them in ways they may not have been originally designed for, or to augment another mode or tool.

The remainder of the power of A:M lies in the windows that let you look at and manipulate the data in a project, whether that data is the position of a single CP, the name of a bone or group, or a whole model. When you first launch A:M, the first of these windows—the Library—is open.

Libraries

Libraries are user-defined sets of data that are independent of any single project file and give access to all items contained in them for any project (see Figure 1.30). Libraries are used to store links to projects, choreographies, models, actions, materials, images, and sounds. If the tutorial data was installed along with the application, there is already a set of libraries, along with the default empty library, "my Library." Any file that fits one of the types listed on the tabs of the libraries window can be added to a library.

To add an item to a library, open one of the other workflow windows. Choose Project Work Space (PWS) from the View menu and the PWS will open. There is a lot to learn about the PWS, but for now just focus on how it is used in conjunction with the library. Upon starting A:M, assuming no preference has been changed, the PWS tree will look identical to Figure 1.31. To a certain extent, it resembles the file structure of a computer. Each grouping of file types exists inside

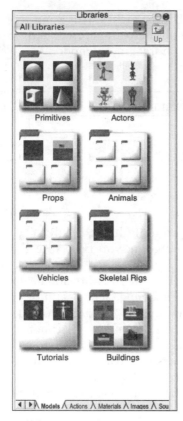

FIGURE 1.30   The library window allows easy access to existing data and a way to organize and sort new data.

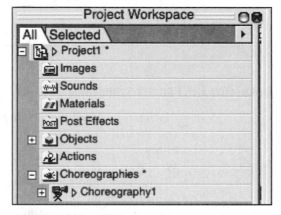

FIGURE 1.31   The PWS tree.

a folder that can be opened or closed by clicking the disclosure box for that category. To see the item that you are going to add to the library, expand the Objects folder to reveal the models and objects in the project. There should be a model called ground. This is the default ground plane in the choreography.

TRY IT NOW:

The simplest way to add an item to the library is by using the contextual menu. Contextual menus hide a lot of power in A:M and can make finding what you need as easy as clicking. On a Mac with the default one-button mouse, the menu is brought up by control-clicking; on the PC or a Mac with a multibutton mouse, right-clicking will do the trick.

The contents of the menu will vary depending on where you click, showing only items related to the context of the item you click. For example, bringing up the contextual menu for the ground model will show the functions available to all models. In this case, we want to bring up ground's contextual menu and choose Create Shortcut in Library from the presented menu. A dialog will pop up, explaining that ground must be saved externally to the project before it can be added to the library, and asks if you would like to save it externally. Click Yes.

Most items in a project can exist in one of two states: embedded or linked. Embedded means that the object is saved as part of the project file on the computer's hard drive. This keeps all the items for a project together in one place, but it also means that no other project can access the items. Linked items have their own files on the hard drive, each of which is linked to the project but also available to use in any other project. Any changes to a file that is linked will appear in all projects that use the same linked file.

When the Save dialog is presented, choose a place to put ground.mdl on your hard drive. When you finish, an icon will be added to the top level of the Models tab in the library that represents the ground model. You can place it into any already existing folder in the library by dragging and dropping, or you can create a folder by bringing up the library's contextual menu and choosing Folder from the new heading.

The other methods of adding a file to a library require that the file has been externally saved. Add the choreography to the library. To save the choreography to an external file, select the icon or name of the item and choose Save Choreography As… from the File menu. When the Save dialog appears, name the choreography, choose a location, and save it. The icon in the PWS is given a badge resembling a floppy disk indicating that it is now saved externally to the project.

Now simply drag and drop the choreography's icon from the PWS to the library. It will be added to the Choreographies tab in the library. Notice that the appropriate tab of the Library comes to the front, ensuring that files remain organized by type (i.e., it is impossible to add a choreography to the Models tab).

It is important to understand that the library just stores a static file path to the items it contains. If you move the items on your hard drive, the library will be unable to locate them.

The last way you can add a model to the library is from the library window itself. Bring up the contextual menu for the library, and from the New heading, choose Shortcut. The Open File dialog appears allowing you to browse your hard drive to add any externally saved files to the library.

You can create new libraries to keep individual projects organized or to make finding the correct set of data easier. Simply add an empty text file (empty means it has no text in it) into the Libraries folder, and make sure that you name the file with the three-letter extension .lbr (see Figure 1.32). The next time you launch A:M you will see a library added to your libraries window pull-down with the same name as this file. Setting one up for each major project or client lets you access all the data specific to that project in a snap.

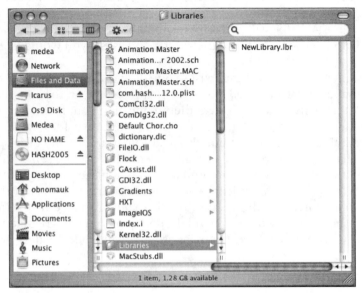

FIGURE 1.32   New libraries can be created by adding a text file to the Libraries folder.

The Project Work Space (PWS)

All of the data you work with is in one way or another stored in the PWS. On its most basic level the PWS tree is a visual representation of the project file that is saved to the hard drive. It contains a set of folders: Images, Sounds, Materials, Post Effects, Objects, Actions, and Choreographies. Each folder can be expanded or closed to reveal the items it contains. Double-clicking a folder will create an item of the default type for that category. (Images and Sounds import files from the hard drive rather than creating a new file.) Right-clicking the folder (control-click on the Mac) presents all the options available to that folder, including creating or importing the file types that folder can contain. The Objects folder, for instance, can contain any number of things: Models, Cameras, Lights, Forces, Nulls, Motion Capture Devices, Material Effects, Volumetric Effects, or Layers (see Figure 1.33).

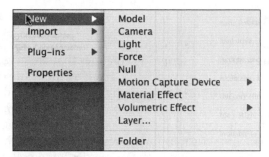

FIGURE 1.33   An object can be one of a number of items.

Other than the default item types for each folder, you are also able to create subfolders. Folders are used to group items together and organize the PWS. This allows a more flexible control over the structure of projects in the PWS. Ambitious projects can get very complex with hundreds of objects, materials, and images. An unorganized PWS would be difficult to navigate. Creating subfolders for different logical sets of objects makes it easier to find the data you need when you need it. A folder inherits the properties of the group it is in, so a folder created under objects will have the same contextual menu options as the Objects folder.

The PWS also shows project hierarchy. If you look at any of the folders, you will note that items inside those folders are indented, which indicates that they are children of that folder. The same applies for groups or subobjects within an object—bones, for instance. You will recall the discussion on hierarchy and parent-child relationships of bones earlier in this chapter. Care was given to explain how to draw a new bone as a child of an existing bone, but you can also adjust the hierarchy of bones directly in the PWS. For instance, if you had a bone called leg and a bone called foot, you might want foot to be a child of the leg; if you didn't draw foot correctly this might not be the case. Rather than deleting the foot bone and starting over, you can drag and drop the foot bone onto the leg bone directly in the PWS. Once you drop the bone, A:M will indent it as a child of leg.

There are also aspects of a project that will have a number of children that, while they are indented by the same amounts indicating equal hierarchy, in fact have a distinct order of precedence. You can order these items in the PWS with the same drag-and-drop techniques. Dragging an item onto a line that separates two other items will insinuate that item between the other two. Dragging an item onto the parent item will move it directly under the parent at the *bottom* of the hierarchy for that group. The order of items becomes important when you start working on texturing your models and using the A:M built-in composite tools. As you progress, hierarchy of items will come up again and again; so it is important that you understand this concept and how to adjust levels of hierarchy in the PWS.

Properties

The Properties window (see Figure 1.34) lists each property available to a selected item presented in a series of categories that are accessed from the disclosure triangles on the left of the window. Changing the value of a property is as easy as clicking on the current value in the Properties window. The nature of the value selection becomes apparent as soon as it is clicked, as the property's value becomes a list presented in a pull-down style menu, a dialog window, or a simple text box input. For numerical input values, the focal length of a camera for example, you can also click the value in the properties window and drag the mouse to the left or right to adjust the number (dragging left lowers the value, dragging right raises it). The Properties panel is also used heavily in creating relationships (see Chapter 8, "Relationships") where the manipulation of multiple values for a given driver is a common occurrence. We will cover each property available to the various aspects of a project as we work through the book.

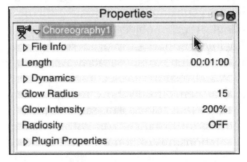

FIGURE 1.34   The Properties window presents only the information for the currently selected item.

Many of the more common properties, especially those associated with direct manipulation (translate, orient, scale, and so on) are also presented in a direct fashion in the workspace via the Manipulators Properties Widget. This floating dialog is overlaid in your workspace windows, giving immediate access to the most pertinent information in a given selection. It also allows you to change a property in much the same way you do with the Properties panel—clicking a value changes it to a text editing box. What properties are shown change, depending on the selection; any manipulators that are selected (the Rotate Manipulator, for instance, will have just the properties for rotation listed), as in Figure 1.35. The widget can be moved by clicking the semitransparent space at the top of its box and dragging. This is important as it can, on occasion, obscure the object in the workspace window.

FIGURE 1.35   The manipulator properties widget gives easy and immediate access to the most pertinent properties of a selection.

Pose Sliders

The Pose sliders window presents two types of user-defined properties specific to models: On/Off or Percent. These properties are presented as sliders or toggles (depending on type) that can be animated to change aspects of a model. The On/Off properties are typically used for applying constraints; percent type properties are used for animating aspects of a model over time. This can be as simple as making a character smile or as complex as dancing a waltz. (See Chapters 8 and 9, "Expressions," for more on Pose sliders.)

Timeline

The timeline presents information about frames that are created during the animation process and allows adjustment of timing, interpolation, and other aspects of animation. It has two aspects: the timeline and channels. The timeline displays the animation information for the currently selected items or for any pinned items associated with the current working viewport. Channels show the mathematical curve between frames, while the timeline represents keyframes in a strictly time-based fashion (see more on the timeline in Chapters 4 and 11). The timeline is so important to workflow that there are two of them. One is a separate window (accessed via the View menu) while the other is attached to the PWS window. When the PWS is first opened, you will not see its timeline, but if you click and drag the edge of the PWS window you can resize it. As you resize the window, the timeline will become visible. This attached timeline is useful for adjusting material properties that change over time or for viewing animation data in timeline format while the stand alone timeline is in channel view. We will go more in depth on both these windows in Chapters 4, "Action Basics," and 11, "Lighting."

All of the windows we have looked at can be moved on the screen either docked along a different edge or undocked and allowed to float, perhaps on a second monitor. Doing this is as simple as clicking and dragging the title bar of the window in question. As the window is dragged, it will attempt to dock with any edge it comes near, unless you hold down the Ctrl key.

There are also elements of the interface that simply provide assistance or information as you work. Along the bottom of the screen, for example, you will find the status bar (see Figure 1.36). The status bar provides hints as to what a tool will do or how modifier keys will change a tool's behavior. It also presents the current real-time performance of the interface in frames per second (fps). When you render a workspace window with the progressive render or the Render Lock tools it provides a progress bar. At the right end of the status bar the current settings for the view are shown, giving you the orientation, offset, zoom, and perspective settings. As you move a view or rotate in Bird's Eye view these numbers will change. If you like, you can enter any value you want (to return to a preferred viewing angle perhaps) by simply clicking on any of the boxes on the status bar. This will bring up the View Settings dialog (also available by pressing Shift+4).

FIGURE 1.36   The status bar will provide useful feedback and information as you work.

The Project Structure

Many years of hard-won experience lead to the recommendation that you develop a default Project Structure on your drive now. Before you so much as lathe a vase, get into the habit of breaking your projects down into their component pieces on your drive, as well as in the PWS. Figure 1.37 shows an example directory structure. Adopt it or develop your own. Down the road it will save sanity and heartburn, provide an easy way to transport projects with a friend or coworker, and make regular backups a snap. All projects on the CD-ROM follow this structure, as do all the author's professional and personal projects.

The directory structure starts with a Root folder named after the entire project. Keeping in mind that an animation project might involve a large number of individual project files (.prj), it is important to have a base directory in which to house all the separate pieces a large project might generate. This keeps the base of the structure clean.

Next, a set of directories holds all objects that can be saved externally from a project: Actions, Choreographies, Image Maps, Lights, Materials, Models, Project files, and Sound files. Each of these directories is composed of several subdirectories, broken down into logical chunks as best suits the project.

FIGURE 1.37   File management starts here.

Separate character models from props. Break props and other models down by scene and shot number, even if it means duplicating models in multiple folders. This makes it easier to share an individual scene of a large project without the worry of leaving anything behind. If a project only has one scene, this can be ignored.

It is very important that the project (and all files for that matter) is saved in versions. This is just a good work habit that will prevent a lot frustration. The mantra is "Save Early, Save Often," but should be more accurately stated: "Save Early, Save in Versions." Save to a new version any time it would take more than an hour to duplicate your current progress. That way, if a change is made that is not wanted, there is always a prior version to fall back to. Or if a crash or some other problem occurs with a file, the most work that can be lost is one revision. On an active project, there can be as many as 20 or 30 revisions in a day. Table 1.13 shows workflow keyboard shortcuts.

And, of course, back up all files once a week or once a day if you can.

Maintaining an organized file structure helps build work habits that will steer you through even the most complex project. Even an animated feature film can be easily managed by one person if strict naming and file structure rules are followed.

TABLE 1.13   Workflow Keyboard Shortcuts

FUNCTION	PC SHORTCUT	MAC SHORTCUT
Project Workspace	Ctrl+0	Cmd+0
Libraries	Ctrl+1	Cmd+1
Properties	Ctrl+2	Cmd+2
Pose Sliders	Ctrl+3	Cmd+3
TimeLine	None	None
View Settings	Shift+4	Shift+4

SUMMARY

In this chapter, we have covered almost all the interface elements of Animation: Master. You should now have a general idea what a mode is, how the tools function, and a basic feel for the workflow. It is not expected that you now go out and create a major motion picture on your own, but you should be able to locate any button indicated in the text or its keyboard shortcut equivalent in the following chapters.

You should also be thinking about how you want to structure your files on your hard drive. Proper organization of files and assets now will save you a lot of headache later. Of course, it really can't be stressed enough: Save early. Save in versions. Save a backup.

The information presented thus far is just the bare necessities to get you going. If you are unsure about any of the tools or their functions, reread the section on that tool and experiment with it until you have a decent grasp before moving on. The rest of this book will assume that you understand at least what is in this chapter.

MODELING BASICS

In This Chapter

- Tutorial: Creating Patches
- The Torus
- Spline Bias
- Common Surface Problems
- Tutorial: Spline Continuity
- Modeling a Flour Sack
- Using the Modeling Wizards in A:M

In this chapter, your goals are to learn what a model is and how to construct one. It covers the basics of splines and patches and how to manipulate them. Some of the information from Chapter 1 is also reviewed. Some intermediate concepts such as spline connectivity and continuity will be covered, along with important tips on what not to do when modeling. Rotoscopes and their use in the modeling process are also introduced.

ON THE CD

You can find the files for this chapter on the CD-ROM.

The plan of attack is to understand splines and the A:M modeling tools in the context of simple modeling projects before moving on to more complex things.

By the end of this chapter, you should have a model of a floursack (the sack of flour is a long-standing tradition for animators) that can be used to work through Chapters 3 and 4 (bones and actions). Hopefully, you will gain an understanding of what splines are capable of, and how to lay control points and manipulate bias settings to achieve surface topology.

SPLINE PATCH BASICS

What is a spline? Because A:M uses them exclusively in modeling this is a very good question. The nontechnical answer: A spline is a curved line used by A:M to define a surface. This line is defined by a set of points in a connect-the-dots fashion. These points are defined by you and are called *control points* (CPs). The math behind what a spline is and how it functions is complex and not something taught here. Luckily, splines can be used without knowing the equations behind them. Most importantly for us, splines are the most basic building blocks of the *patch*.

What is a patch? A patch is how A:M defines its rendering surfaces. A patch is defined in the software by a simple rule: three or four CPs on two or more splines. Every valid surface on a model must conform to this rule. Areas defined by more than four CPs or by points that lie on the same spline are considered holes in a surface and will not render.

Many 3D programs use the polygon as the basis for creating surfaces; this has some inherent problems that splines and patches avoid. Spline patches have an unlimited resolution, meaning that no matter how close you get to an edge, it will always be a perfectly smooth curve. Polygons, on the other hand, have a fixed resolution, and getting too close to an edge will reveal resolution-based faceting. Spline patches also animate deformations very well, in part due to their infinite resolution. The ease and power of the A:M animation tools are a direct result of this. Polygons are rigid by nature and can shear and twist at joints unless additional resolution has been added.

Are spline patches perfect? No. Surfaces that crease or get lumpy are some of the more common issues that spline patches have. Most of these problems can be dealt with by learning how patches work and how to adjust them properly. For those hard-to-fix areas, there are mesh-smoothing materials and methods that are discussed later. Due to the nature of patches, some of tools that you might be used to if you have a background in polygons, aren't there. This is a matter of acquiring the mindset required by patches. There are also certain modeling tasks that can be faster or more easily accomplished with polygon-based tools. This is one of the important lessons of 3D graphics: there is always some form of trade-off. For the ease of animation that A:M provides, you have to sacrifice some of the benefits of polygon modeling.

So put your modeling cap on and do this: Open A:M and create a new model (if you need to, go ahead and refer back to Chapter 1 on how to create new objects in A:M). Before you attempt something ambitious, learn how to make patches and get a feel for navigating the workspace. The following tutorial is designed to do just that.

TUTORIAL | **CREATING PATCHES**

Remember: three or four points on two or more splines. This means that before you can have a patch of any kind, you need at least two splines. Draw two splines. Using either the Add button or the A key on your keyboard, activate the Add/Stitch tool.

Make the first spline U-shaped with six points, as shown in Figure 2.1. Simply click in the modeling window six times, once for each control point you wish to lay down. A:M will automatically draw a spline through the points you create. Once all six points are drawn, press the Esc key or right-click to stop drawing points.

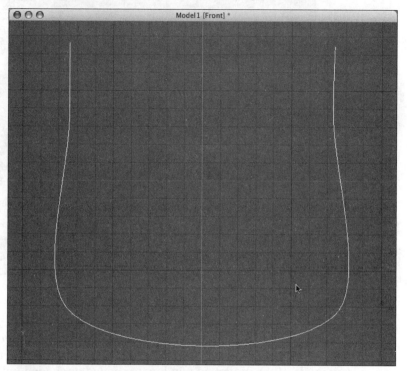

FIGURE 2.1   A U-shaped spline with six control points.

These six control points all lay on one spline, which is indicated by the curve that the spline takes as it moves through the points. It just also happens to be the default way A:M connects CPs when using the Add/Stitch tool. In order to make this spline into a patch it must have some of its control points connected to a second spline to form a "closed" area surrounded by at least three, but no more than four, CPs.

There are a number of ways to connect points along splines, but for now you are looking at the easiest and most direct way. Click the Add button again, and this time draw a four-point spline, as shown in Figure 2.2. Click once to the left of the shape, once on the control point circled and marked 2, once on the control point circled and marked 3, and once to the right of the shape. With the Stitch tool, clicking on a point automatically connects the point you are drawing to the existing point. You will look at how this works and some other aspects of the Add/Stitch tool in a moment.

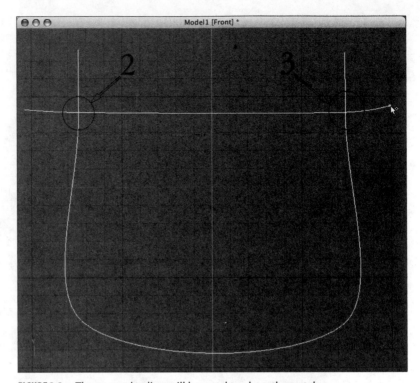

FIGURE 2.2   The second spline will be used to close the patch.

Verify that this is indeed a rendering patch before you go any further. Again, there are a number of ways to do this. The most direct method is changing the draw mode of the modeling window to shaded or shaded with wireframe. Do this by using the number keys along the top of the keyboard (not the number pad) from 7 to 0. Press 7 to set the mode to the default draw mode of the active window (this can be any other draw mode or a combination of them for windows with multiple objects in them). Press 8 to force wireframe drawing (typically the default for modeling; so you won't see much of a change from 7 to 8 most of the time) on all objects in a window, regardless of their default. Press 9 to change the draw mode to Shaded, which uses the real-time 3D of your computer's graphics card to display surfaces as if rendered. It is imperfect, but useful for getting a general idea. Press 0 to get the same shaded view with the wireframe of the model drawn on top. You will use this last mode frequently, while modeling, to see the surface more clearly as you manipulate the points that comprise it.

You can also change the draw mode of a window by control-clicking (right-clicking on the PC) inside the window and choosing the desired setting from the contextual menu under View > Render Mode. The keyboard shortcuts tend to be much faster; so it is recommended that you use them instead of the contextual menu in this case.

Choose either Shaded or Shaded Wireframe now. The space between the four control points that make up your patch should turn white indicating that there is a rendering surface (see Figure 2.3).

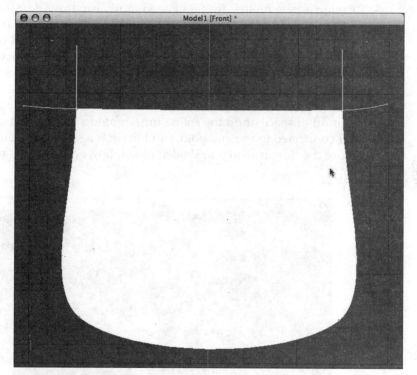

FIGURE 2.3   A rendering patch.

Before you go on to look at other ways to create patches, here is a little information about the nature of splines and the curve of patches. The curvature of the patch surface is determined by the points that define its edges and the points further along those splines. In your example, if there were no dangling end points there would be no easy way to introduce a curve into this patch: the surface would remain flat at all times. You could only change the orientation of the surface or shear it. (This is actually a very broad generalization and not technically correct, as there are other attributes of a spline that can contribute to its curvature; but those are a little more advanced than you need to worry about right now. We will get to them once you start modeling some actual objects rather than single patches.)

Change the view to Bird's Eye (using the 7 key on your number pad or the contextual menu), and select and move the points that were left dangling when the patch was formed. Once you get into things, understanding how one point can relate to another will be crucial to building surfaces that look good and animate well.

Before moving on, it might be a good time to take a peek at some of the other methods that you could use to make this same patch. When you model objects that are more complex, you will find you use each of these methods at some point or another.

Create a new model. In the new window, use the Add/Stitch tool to draw a four-point spline in the same rough U shape you had before. It will look slightly different due to the lower density. Now, if you simply wanted to close this into a surface, you might think that you could just draw a spline across the mouth of the patch; this would give you four points, but would they be on separate splines? Try this: Use the Add/Stitch tool and make a new spline by clicking on either of the two end points of your U. What happens? If you clicked on the points themselves and not off in space or on the spline further along, you would see that they have indeed connected to the end points and there is a spline between those points, as in Figure 2.4. If you switch to shaded mode, however, there is no patch here.

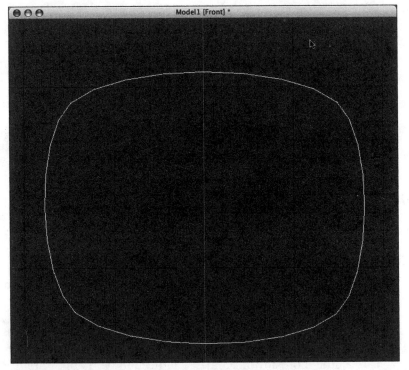

FIGURE 2.4   Four points on a single spline do not make a patch.

What happened? Instead of creating a new spline between the two end points A:M continued the spline: What you actually have here are four control points that lie along a single spline. While they enclose an area, they do not follow the

Patch creation rule because there is only one spline. If you want to add a new spline attached to an end point, you have to inform A:M that you don't want the default behavior. (Once you start talking about spline continuity, in modeling you will see how continuing a spline is a very helpful default.) You do this by modifying the default behavior of the Add/Stitch tool with a modifier key.

Select all the points (press Ctrl+A PC, Command+A Mac) in the model window and delete (press the Delete key) them. Draw the four-point U-shape again, and this time when you want to add the closing spline across the top of the shape, you will modify the tool. Click the Add/Stitch tool button or use the A keyboard shortcut. Before you click on anything, press and hold down the Shift key on your keyboard. Keep the Shift key down, and click on the end points of the U shape. When you have clicked on the second point, release the Shift key and press the Esc key to stop drawing points. Do you notice anything different about the shape? Compare the two shapes in Figure 2.5: One was created without the Shift key and the other was created with the Shift key.

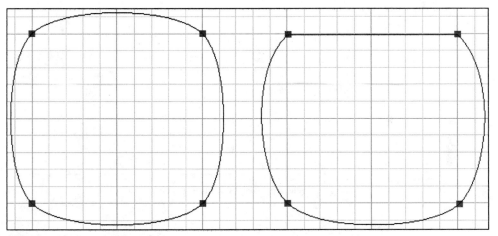

FIGURE 2.5   The difference of the curves shows that one spline is a continuous loop while the other is not.

Note that the spline continues in a smooth continuous curve through the un-shifted version, whereas the shifted version has a sharp corner on each of the end points. This sharp corner indicates, among other things, that the spline does not continue through the point; rather, there are two splines that abut here. If you are still in Shaded mode, or switch to it now, you will see that a patch was indeed created.

By holding down the Shift key, you have told A:M to override the default behavior of the Add/Stitch tool and to abut these splines, rather than continuing the original one. Now there are two separate splines and four points, which conforms to the rules of creating a patch.

Look at yet another way you can create this patch. Go ahead and create a new model. This time, create two separate splines and join them together manually, without the benefit of the Stitch tool. Start with the same six-point U-shaped spline that you created for your first patch. Then above or to the side of that spline, create a four-point spline that goes from left to right, as in Figure 2.6. It is important that you don't click the U-shaped spline or its end points. You have two distinctly separate splines, and in order to build a patch, you need to tell A:M that some of the points on these splines should be connected in order to form a patch. You do this by using the Weld function.

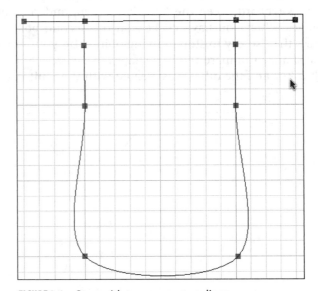

FIGURE 2.6   Start with two separate splines.

Click the point circled in Figure 2.7 in order to select it. Be careful that you just click it rather than dragging a selection box around it. In order to connect this point to the U shape, you must position it over the control point that you want to attach it to. Click and drag the point down until it sits over the point you want to attach it to (indicated with the arrow in Figure 2.7). Without releasing the mouse button press the *tilde* key (~) for Mac users, or right-click. This is the Weld command. The points are now connected. Go ahead and drag them around to make sure.

To connect the other side of the U and close up the patch, repeat the process with the CP circled in Figure 2.8. If your window is still in Shaded mode, you will see the patch form as soon as you close it. If it is not, change draw modes now to verify that your patch is valid.

Believe it or not, there is at least one more way to make this single patch, and for the sake of completeness we will look at it now. This is basically the same technique as the first patch you made in this tutorial, but instead of having the

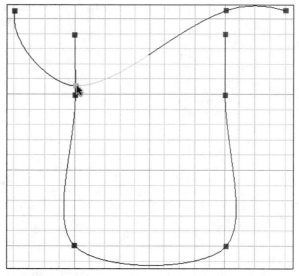

FIGURE 2.7   Start by dragging this point in and welding it to the U-shaped spline.

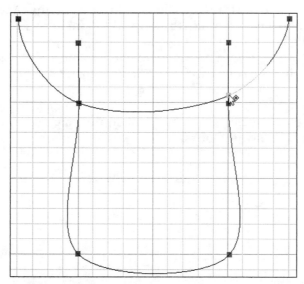

FIGURE 2.8   Close the patch by dragging and welding this point to the U-shaped spline.

six-point U shape to start, you will use the Stitch tool to create new points as you add the second, closing spline.

Either select all and delete or create a new model. In the window, draw a four-point U-shaped spline (see Figure 2.9) with the Add/Stitch tool.

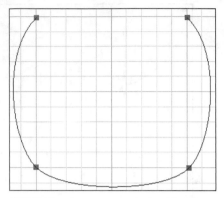

FIGURE 2.9   Start a new patch with a four-point spline.

So far, so good. You have seen how you can use the Shift key to close off this shape with a second spline and get a rendering patch. But what if you want to add a couple points to the U shape, so that the dangling ends remain? There are a number of ways to do this (which we won't get into for the moment), but the easiest is to use the Stitch functionality of the Add tool. Simply click the Add/Stitch button or use the keyboard shortcut (A); click once to the left of the U shape, then click on the original spline where you want to add a point (see Figure 2.10). This creates a new point on the U spline and welds the spline you are drawing to it, all in one easy step. Click the spline on the opposite side of the U (see Figure 2.11), then once to the right, and press the Esc key or right-click to stop drawing the new spline. If you are not already in Shaded Wireframe mode, change the window now and look at the patch you created. It should look like Figure 2.12, which looks exactly like Figure 2.3.

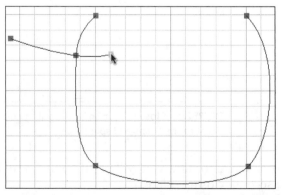

FIGURE 2.10   Clicking the spline between control points adds a new point.

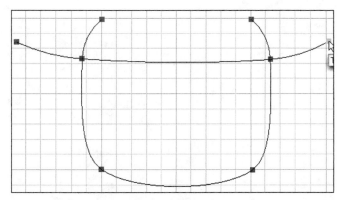

FIGURE 2.11   Clicking again on the opposite leg closes off your patch.

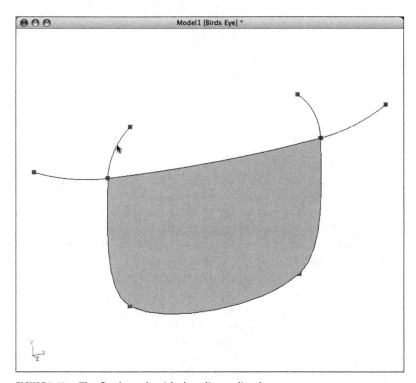

FIGURE 2.12   The final patch with dangling spline legs.

You should have the idea that there are a wide number of ways in which you can create new patches, and as easy as it is, there are preferred methods and spline layouts. While any three or four points *can* define a surface, there are optimal layouts of splines that give the most control over a surface. The most stable is a regular grid of four-point patches, as shown in Figure 2.13.

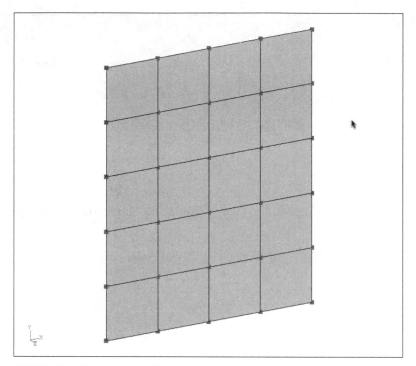

FIGURE 2.13   The basis for a "perfect" patch.

The basis for what makes this grid stable and ideal for creating surfaces in A:M lies in the construction of the individual patches in the grid.

The perfect patch is not just a component of the four points that mark its edges. Since A:M uses the points along the length of the spline to determine curvature, the points outside the patch are equally important. In fact, the perfect patch resembles a tic-tac-toe board (see Figure 2.14). The four points in the center define the bounds of the patch, and along with the eight points surrounding them, define the curve of the surface of the patch. A grid network then creates a set of interdependent surfaces that, when laid out properly, will create a smooth rendering surface. Of course, there are inherent difficulties with this, but for now it is just important that you understand the concept.

The regular grid of patches is so perfect, it is be the layout you will want to use whenever possible. We look at how this is done as you progress and explain the places where you can get away with less-than-perfect splinage. For the moment, however, the focus is on making models with as many perfect patches as possible. It all starts with being able to construct the perfect patch itself.

The Perfect Patch

Adding in the splines that create this patch happens the same way that you drew the patch in your first tutorial. However, what you want to create is a little differ-

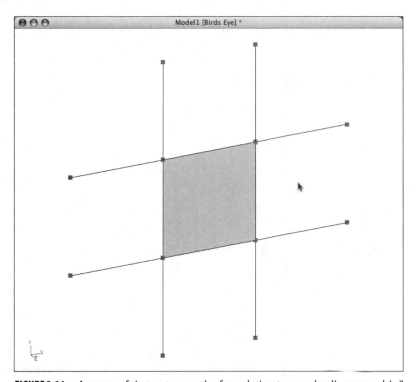

FIGURE 2.14   A game of tic-tac-toe, or the foundation to good splinesmanship?

ent. Start by making a single spline in a rough line from top to bottom with four CPs (see Figure 2.15).

This is one side of the perfect patch; there will be three more of these to build. The second one is simply a duplicate of the first, but spaced to the right or left (your choice). Start by selecting all the points in the first spline you drew, either with the bounding box drag, or the Select All keyboard command (Ctrl+A PC, Command+A Mac). While the points are selected, copy (Command+C Mac, Ctrl+C PC) and then paste (Command+V Mac, Ctrl+V PC). An identical version of the original selection should paste, slightly offset, from the original. While the new spline is still selected, position your cursor over the bounding box. It will change to indicate that you are about to move the selected CPs. Click and drag the copy to the side. Now all that remains is to fence in your patch. Again using the Stitch tool, create a spline exactly like the one you made in the first patch tutorial by clicking to the side and then on the two CPs at the top of the spline (see Figure 2.16), and finally one point to the other side, creating a sort of H shape. Once the fourth point is created, press the Esc key or right-click to stop drawing points. Repeat the process on the bottom of the shape, enclosing the four center points to form a perfect patch, as in Figure 2.17.

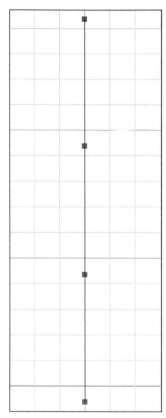

FIGURE 2.15   The single spline is often the start of a model.

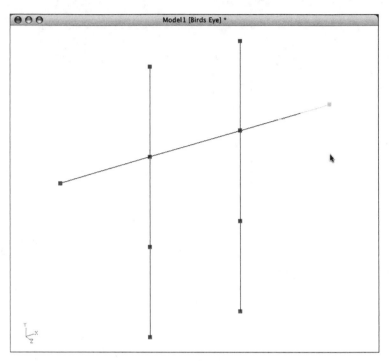

FIGURE 2.16   Lay in a new spline with the Stitch tool.

Play with this patch and its dangling splines to get a better idea of what patches are made of and what defines their curves. This understanding will be crucial to becoming proficient with patches. Notice that the closer the CPs that make up this patch are to an even plane, the flatter the surface of the patch. If you move one or more of the dangling CPs back or forward, the patch takes on a greater curve along that spline's edge. If you could build every surface entirely out of four-point patches exactly like this one, even in all aspects, then there would be few to no difficulties in modeling. The four-point patch, however, is not always a practical solution, and shapes often require uneven patch sizing and distribution. As you progress, we will explore techniques to minimize the problems that arise when straying from this ideal.

Single patches are, in and of themselves, thrilling (and no doubt you could make them all day and never tire of it), but most people have more ambitious creations in mind when they buy A:M, so let's take your knowledge of the patch and examine how to build basic primitive shapes. In the following tutorials, you are

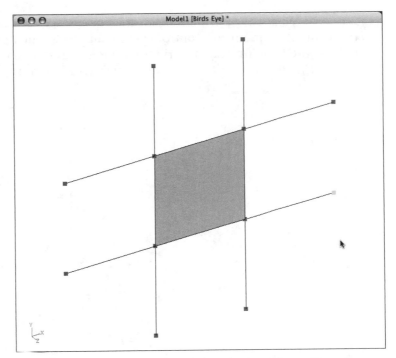

FIGURE 2.17   The 16 points in this patch make the perfect spline surface.

going to build a cube, a sphere, and a torus (doughnut). These shapes are all 3D solid primitives that will teach you a few lessons about how the tools work and will reintroduce you to the two fundamental modeling tools: Extrude and Lathe. You won't typically create these shapes often, but the knowledge behind them will help you understand how to build masses from splines.

The Cube

The simplest cube can be created from the perfect patch from the previous tutorial. This cube won't include beveled edges or other aspects of advanced modeling, but it will be a fast and easy way to introduce dimension to your patch.

If you have closed or deleted the model with the perfect patch in it, reopen it or create a new one in a new model. (Creating a new one just for practice wouldn't hurt anything mind you.)

In order for this to be a perfect cube, the points need to have some precision, meaning that the initial shape needs to be as close to a perfect square as you can make it. We will use the A:M grid to put the points into alignment. Start by selecting the four points that make up the corners of the patch, as in Figure 2.18. Notice that the eight dangling points are not selected. It really doesn't matter if you have them selected for this step, but later you will want to be certain that they are not included in any selections. Inside the bounding box of the selection, bring up the contextual menu by control-clicking on a Mac or right-clicking on a PC. Choose the function Snap to Grid from the menu. (You could also use the apostrophe (') keyboard shortcut and not bother with the contextual menu at all.)

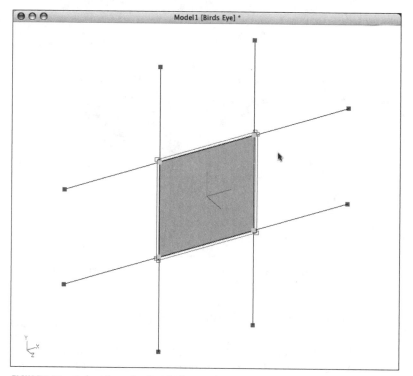

FIGURE 2.18   Select just the inside four points.

Snap to Grid will move any selected CPs in to the nearest intersection of the grid, which is displayed in the modeling window (presuming you haven't turned it off in the preferences). If they are spaced fairly evenly, they might be in a perfect square. If they aren't, simply deselect the group, turn on Snap Manipulator to Grid, and move the offending control points to the appropriate grid intersection. You have to use the Snap Points to Grid function first, because, as you may remember from Chapter 1, Snap Manipulator will only move points by grid units from where they happen to be positioned. Once the points have all been positioned, turn off the Snap Manipulator mode.

Now that you have established a square, proceed to a cube. Make a selection of the four center points again (if you had to deselect them in the previous step; but note that the eight dangling control points cannot be a part of this selection, or you will run into some problems). While the group is still selected, click the Extrude tool button or use the keyboard shortcut (E). This will extrude the points once, which, if the preferences for this are still at the default, will position the points –10 pixels in the *y*-axis (see Figure 2.19).

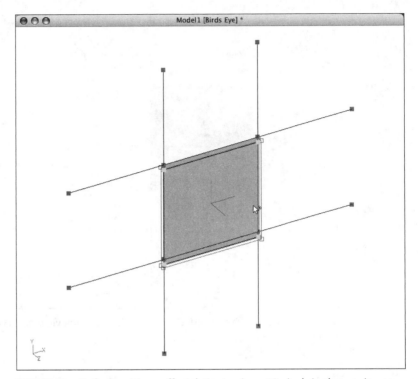

FIGURE 2.19   Default settings offset the extrusion –10 pixels in the *y*-axis.

When you extrude, A:M helpfully makes the newly extruded points the selection. In order to make your shape a cube you only have to move this selection into position. Move the extruded points up to match the original box by pressing the Shift key and the up-arrow key. This will move the selection up 10 pixels.

The arrow keys will "nudge" a selection 1 pixel at a time along the same plane as the viewport. Holding down the Shift key will nudge the selection 10 pixels.

Change to a right or left view by pressing the 4 or 6 key on your keyboard's number pad, and move the selection back (or forward if you prefer) in the *z*-axis until it is roughly as far back as it is tall (see Figure 2.20). If you want it perfect, of course, you can use the Snap Manipulator to Grid function, but it is preferable to just nudge the shape back with the arrow keys until the grid shows that it is roughly correct.

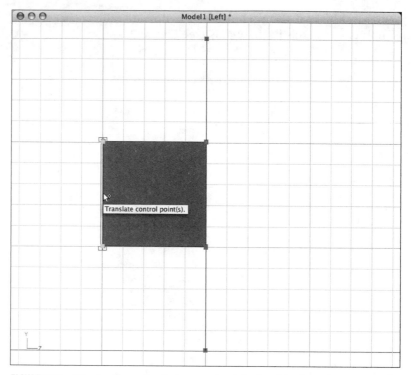

FIGURE 2.20   Moving the extruded group back in the side view gives your cube dimension.

If you had to move the front points much out of line with the dangling control points, the front edges might show some curve (see Figure 2.21).

To iron this curve out, you can either peak all the points on the cube or simply delete the dangling points. Peaking the points is done by selecting the entire object and clicking the Peak tool button (keyboard shortcut P). Either way you go about it, the result should look like Figure 2.22. If it isn't already, put the window in Shaded mode to get a look at your handiwork.

The simple six-patch cube teaches a lot about how patches are formed. Notice that the sides and rear of the cube were built as legal patches when you used the Extrude tool. This is because your extruded selection was in itself a patch. The Extrude tool creates a new group of splines and points with the same continuity as the original. If the extruded group had been a hole (four points along a single spline, for instance), the resulting model would have been a box-shaped tube with no end caps. Try extruding closed splines that are not patches, and notice how this behavior is different. When modeling, it is important to know exactly what the tools are creating; and when you look at internal patches, you will see a good example of why that is. Put your cube aside and examine some other primitive shapes.

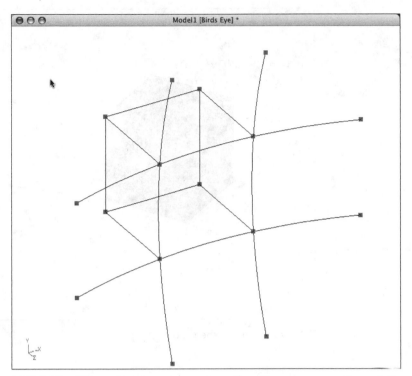

FIGURE 2.21   If the points are not on a plane, the splines may curve through them.

The Sphere

Creating a perfect sphere requires a perfect circle. Hand-drawing splines to achieve this is more likely to create heartburn than a sphere. Luckily, there are ways to create perfect circles without resorting to antacid.

Start with a new model window. Instead of the Add/Stitch tool, use the Add Lock tool to draw a two-point spline to one side of the *y*-axis at a slight angle (see Figure 2.23). By default, there is no button for the Add Lock tool, so use the Shift+A keyboard shortcut to invoke it. The Add Lock tool will only draw two-point splines, and it is used by clicking and dragging. The point you click becomes a point, and a spline is drawn out from that point in the direction you drag. When you release the mouse button, the second point will be positioned. If you simply click in the window you will see what looks like a single CP with no spline, but in reality, there are two points on a single spline exactly on top of each other.

A control point cannot exist without a spline. At bare minimum, you can have two control points with a spline between them. If you delete the CP at either end of the spline, then A:M would remove both points and the spline as well.

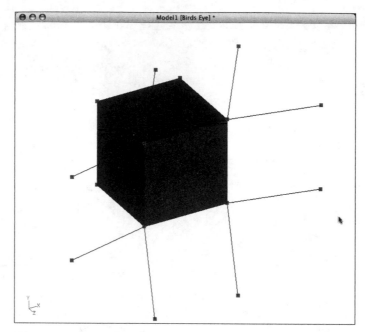

FIGURE 2.22   The finished cube.

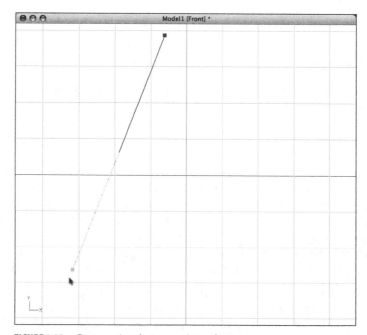

FIGURE 2.23   Draw a simple two-point spline.

Once the two-point spline is in place, you are going to Lathe it to make a rough conical shape: two circles, one above the other, with straight splines drawn between each CP to make the walls. The Lathe tool always creates circular spline rings, with, by default, eight cross sections. In order to use the Lathe tool, you need to give it something to work with. The Extrude tool, for instance, needs a group of points in order to work (try extruding a single CP; it just won't work). What the Lathe tool needs was discussed in Chapter 1, but now is a good time for a quick refresher.

A real-world lathe is a machine into which a piece of raw material is placed and spun along an axis, then cutting tools remove portions to create a profile. A wood lathe, for instance, might be used to create balusters for a handrail on a staircase; by using a pattern, a number of items can be cut to exactly the same profile. The Lathe tool in A:M uses the same basic idea to create shapes from spline profiles. You create the pattern (profile), and then use the Lathe to make the shape solid. The axis around which the material rotates is the *y*-axis of the modeling window by default. As your spline is set up to work from the default, there is no need to change that. (You will eventually want to lathe something not on the axis line; then the axis of the Lathe tool is explored further.) The only other thing that the Lathe tool needs to know is which spline you want it to work with. The key word here is *spline*. You tell A:M what the focus of any tool is by making it selected. This is true of all the modeling tools, as well as the data tools for the PWS, and so on. Therefore, with the Lathe tool, you need to indicate which spline is going to be used as your pattern. The easiest way to do this is to simply click a single point on the given spline. If you drag a bounding box around a CP (even if that CP exists on only a single spline) then A:M is not focused on the CP/spline, but rather the group that you indicated. This is not acceptable because a group selected this way can contain multiple splines on differing planes. A:M needs to know where the lathe "pattern" is in relation to the axis. (This can seem odd, but it is important to understand. As was quickly shown in Chapter 1, there are ways to select groups and still have the Lathe tool available. This is covered in more detail when you start working on complex models.) If the wrong type of data is selected, then the Lathe Tool button will be grayed out, indicating that lathing is not currently possible.

With this information in mind, simply click one of the two points on your spline, and then click the Lathe button (or use the L keyboard shortcut). A:M will use this pattern to create the conical shape we discussed (see Figure 2.24).

What you have are two perfect circles, but for your sphere, you only need one. Select and delete the top ring of CPs by dragging a bounding box around the whole ring, and press Delete on your keyboard to leave just one circular spline without any rendering patches. This will be the basis for your sphere. Effective lathe patterns describe only half of a profile. You need to get rid of half of this circle so that the Lathe tool can do its job properly. Change to a top view (press 5 on the number pad) so you can see the full circle. Select all the CPs on one side of the *x*-axis line (by clicking and dragging a bounding box around them), and delete

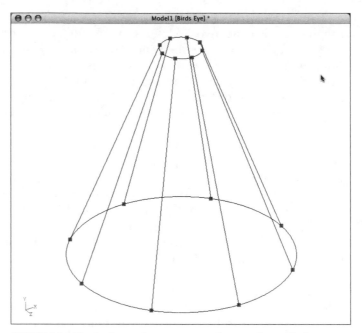

FIGURE 2.24 The Lathe tool creates a rough cone that will give you a perfect circle.

them, what remains should be a semicircular, almost gumdrop-like shape (see Figure 2.25). This is not exactly what you want, but it is close. What you need to do is to open the flat edge of the semicircle. For this, use the Break Spline tool. Select the point circled in Figure 2.25, and note on which side of the CP the spline is highlighted.

If the spline is highlighted on the flattened leg of the spline, then you are ready to break, If not, you need to change the selection. Do this by pressing the Tab key (if more than one spline passed through this point, you could select each of them by pressing Tab in succession). Press the Tab key once, and the green highlight changes from one side of the CP to the other. Once the correct side is highlighted, click the Break tool button or use the keyboard shortcut (K) to break the spline and open the flattened edge. What you have is an open semicircle, which will be the pattern you give the Lathe tool for the final sphere (see Figure 2.26).

Drag a selection around the whole spline, and bring up the Rotate Manipulator (by clicking the Manipulator button or pressing the R keyboard shortcut). Rotate the selection 90 degrees in the *x*-axis, using the red handle of the manipulator or typing the value in the group's properties (either on the Properties panel [see Figure 2.27] or in the Manipulator Properties Widget [see Figure 2.28]).

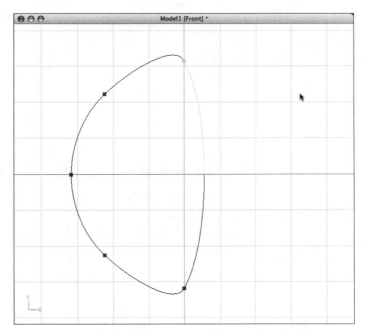

FIGURE 2.25   Select the circled point to prepare to break this spline.

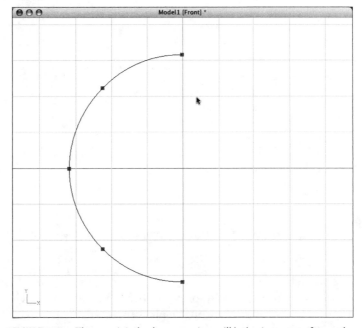

FIGURE 2.26   The semicircle that remains will lathe into a perfect sphere.

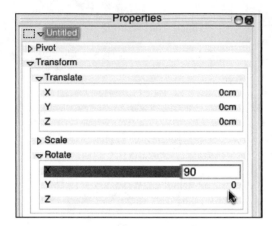

FIGURE 2.27 The Group properties in the Properties panel.

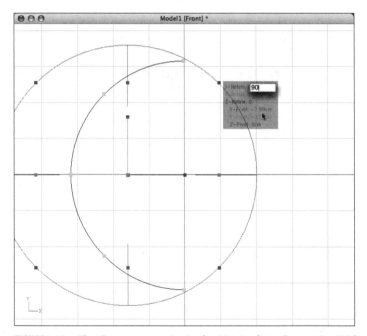

FIGURE 2.28 The Group properties in the Manipulator Properties Widget.

Switch back to the front view to get a better look at things and return to the standard manipulator by pressing the R key again (or clicking the Standard Manipulator button). Without deselecting anything, nudge the whole shape off the *y*-axis with the left cursor arrow (or use the right cursor arrow if you have deleted the left half of the original circle). This is done so that the points on the ends of the lathe don't overlap, which would cause a pinched or creased look at the poles of the sphere. After nudging the spline over, deselect it using either the Esc key, the Return key, or simply by clicking outside the bounding box in the modeling window. Select any single CP on the spline. Be careful to only select the CP by clicking on it. Dragging a selection around it or group-selecting it will leave the Lathe tool unavailable (as previously discussed). Simply clicking a CP selects a particular spline, and this is the information that the Lathe tool uses to do its job. Once you have a CP selected, click the Lathe tool. Insert the Lathe tool icon here or use the L keyboard shortcut to make the final sphere. The result should resemble Figure 2.29.

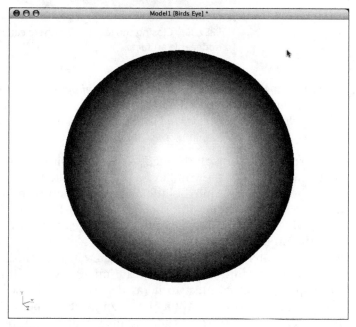

FIGURE 2.29   A perfect sphere.

As perfect as it looks, this sphere has one minor flaw. If you zoom in to the poles of the sphere you can see that there is a small hole at each end of the sphere. In most cases this is not a problem (and can even be helpful for some modeling tasks). If the hole is too large and can be seen clearly without zooming in, you can make it smaller. On the other hand, if you want or need to close those holes you can stitch in a couple a splines to close them. The problem here is that adding the points needed to close the top of this sphere will change the way the splines run through the existing points. This will cause a noticeable surface artifact at the pole of the sphere (see Figure 2.30). Masking this artifact is a two-step process that starts back at the half circle that you lathed to create the sphere in the first place.

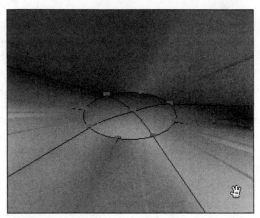

FIGURE 2.30   Closing the top of the sphere can lead
to noticeable artifacts.

*Surface artifacts are not indicative of a flaw either in you or in A:M. Rather, they are a
fact of life when working with patch surfaces that you must learn to deal with. At least
half the challenge of modeling with patches is coming to terms with, and conquering,
bumps, lumps, creases, and other anomalies.*

Start by repeating all the steps up to the point where you are ready to click
the Lathe button so that you have a semicircle like the one in Figure 2.26. Before
you lathe this shape, think a little about what you want to do in order to close it
and how that will affect the shape of the finished sphere. Look at Figure 2.30
again, which shows a sphere that was simply closed with the Stitch tool and indicates the problems you are trying to avoid. Notice how the splines that continue
across the center point have a different curvature than those that dead-end. This
is because the additional point in the middle is now influencing the shape of
those splines that connect to it (as discussed in the section about the perfect
patch). But you may ask: "What if we continue the points that dead-end through
the center as well? Wouldn't that change their curvature to match and alleviate
the surface anomalies?" The answer is: It *might*, but it will cause other problems
that are even more difficult to repair. The problem with this approach is that you
now have four splines crossing at one point, creating an area of three-point
patches. For the math behind a patch, this creates some areas of uncertainty on
how the patches should be smoothly rendered. The result is creasing, and in addition to the original four splines that had changed their shape, the remaining four
have now joined them in their oddness (see Figure 2.31).

What this situation calls for is an increase in the density of the control points at
the poles of the sphere. This is something you will need to add in manually before
you lathe the shape. In order to buffer the transition from side to poles you will
need two extra points at each end of the semicircle. You can add these points by
simply clicking on the existing spline with the Add/Stitch tool (keyboard shortcut
A). But you want to modify the behavior of how A:M deals with adding points to

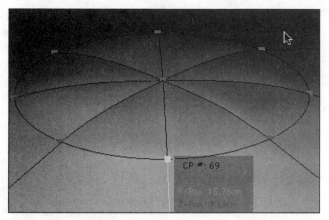

FIGURE 2.31   Continuing the remaining splines across the pole causes more problems than it solves.

a spline. Without getting to far into the complexities at this point (you get to them soon enough), look at how adding a point to the spline changes the spline itself. In a new window, a three-point spline has been drawn (see Figure 2.32), which can be thought of as an arc from your sphere. Some adjustments have been made to the bias to make it mimic the sphere more closely (we discuss bias in great depth shortly, but for now you need to be aware that something has been changed).

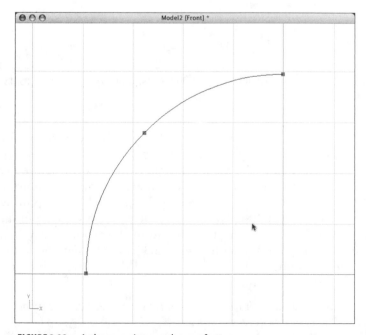

FIGURE 2.32   A three-point mock-up of your arc.

When you click the spline with the Add Lock tool and stitch in a new point, what happens is that the bias does not remain consistent. indeed, the shape of the spline is altered (see Figure 2.33). You want to tell A:M not to alter the shape of existing splines when you add in a new point. This is a modification of the default behavior, which you may guess requires the use of a keyboard modifier. When you want a spline to maintain its curvature, use the Shift key to modify the Stitch tool's behavior (in the same way it modified the way the tool handles connectivity).

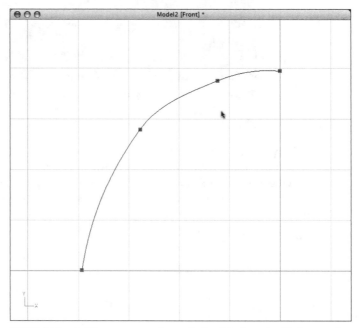

FIGURE 2.33   Adding a new point with the Stitch tool will change the curvature of the spline.

With this knowledge, go back to the semicircle and add in the points you need. Click the Add button or use the A keyboard shortcut (before clicking the spline, hold down the Shift key). Now click the spline near the pole of the semi-circle template. This will add a new point and maintain the curvature of the current spline. Press the Esc key (or right-click) to stop drawing points, and use the modified Stitch tool one more time to add a second point to the top pole. Now repeat this process for the bottom of the semicircle. When complete, you should have a spline similar to Figure 2.34. Now when you lathe this template you have more spline density at the poles of the sphere, which helps maintain the shape when you continue the splines across them.

Dead-end splines can be a major source of creasing and other artifacts. It is best to avoid them whenever possible.

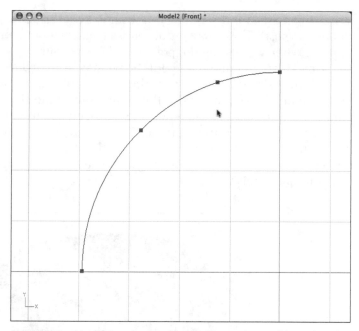

FIGURE 2.34   Modifying the Stitch tool allows you to add a point to the spline and maintain its curvature.

Go ahead and lathe the semicircle to make the basic sphere, and close the top. Once lathed, zoom in close to the top of the sphere so you can see the hole in the pole. At this point, closing that hole is a simple application of the Stitch/Add tool (which you should be familiar with by now). Your resulting splinage should look something like Figure 2.35. Note that the splines do not cross across the top of the

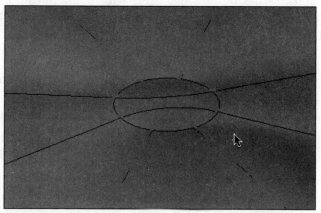

FIGURE 2.35   Changing the spline layout across the top of the sphere solves most of your problems.

pole. The reason for this is that you want to avoid as many patches with dead-end splines as possible. This layout of splines creates only two patches with dead-end splines, whereas crossing the pole would create four.

Now, if you zoom out and put the window into Shaded mode, you will notice some artifacts on the surface near the pole, as in Figure 2.36. This is a direct result of the splines that dead-end rather than continuing through the pole, but you don't want to continue them because that would cause other problems. So what should you deal with these artifacts? A:M has a special material called Porcelain that is used to tell the renderer to smooth out surfaces. It is an extremely useful material, and you will use it more than once as you progress through the modeling tutorials in this book.

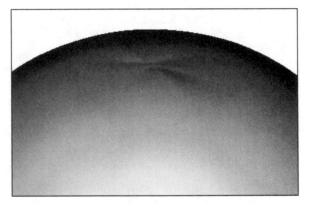

FIGURE 2.36 Even with new spline layouts, dead-end splines cause artifacts.

First, add the material to your project. This is done by right-clicking on the PC or control-clicking (for Mac users with single-button mice) the materials folder. Choose Import Material… from the contextual menu. The File Open dialog will appear. Navigate the A:M CD-ROMto Data/Materials/Geometry/Porcelain.mat, and click OK. Once the material is loaded into the project, all you have to do is drag and drop it from the Materials folder onto the Model name in the PWS. If you are in Shaded mode, you should see immediate results, as in Figure 2.37. With the application of the Porcelain material, the closed sphere is complete.

The Porcelain material is used so often you might want to consider adding it to your library for quick access. Just drag and drop it from the project workspace into the library window. Then in the future all you need to do is drag and drop the material from the library directly into the model window.

The sphere is one of the more useful primitives, as it lends itself to organic-shaped characters well. The techniques you just practiced will be used extensively in the creation of characters. In addition, you have already covered the basic use

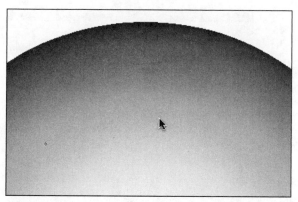

FIGURE 2.37   The Porcelain material will smooth out the remainder of our surface irregularities.

of just about all the major modeling tools that A:M has to offer, but there are some twists, turns, and slightly more advanced topics that need to be discussed before you can have a complete understanding of splines. Continue your exploration through the creation of primitive shapes.

THE TORUS

Torus is the technical name for a doughnut shape. You will be building one in A:M as a way to demonstrate the use of the group pivot. Start exactly as you did with the sphere: Lathe a cone and delete the top. You should have something resembling Figure 2.38.

From here, use the Lathe tool to fill out the remainder of the torus. In order for the Lathe tool to create a torus, you need to override its default behavior. If you were to simply select a point of this circle and lathe it, it would look like nothing had happened, but selecting a spline and translating it reveals Figure 2.39. The Lathe tool took your circle and lathed it around its own center point creating a many overlapping CPs, splines, and patches. Not at all what you want.

There are two ways you can handle this situation. First, move the splines into a position that allows the default lathe function to create the shape you want. Second, change the defaults the Lathe tool uses in order to create the shape you want without altering the splinage. For the this shape, either would be fine; however, since the learning focus here is on the pivot, opt for the second method.

Adjusting the pivot is an essential modeling technique, giving control not only of the lathe but also the way manipulators behave when using them to affect the mesh. Pivot is a property of a group (visible in the Properties panel or by showing the Manipulator Properties Widget), and requires a group selection in order to be set. This presents a problem as the Lathe tool, by default, is a function performed on a single spline as indicated by one CP, meaning that it is unavailable to groups.

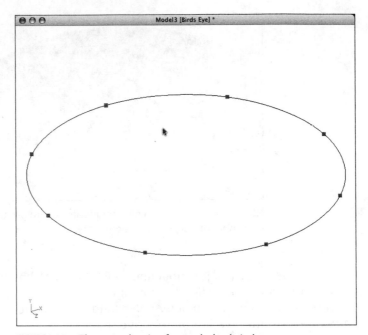

FIGURE 2.38   The torus begins from a lathed circle.

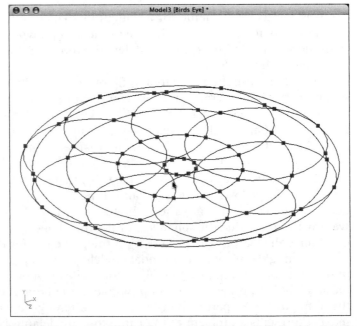

FIGURE 2.39   Letting the Lathe tool decide how to handle this situation created more of a mess than anything.

However, you can select a group in such a way to preserve the spline information that the Lathe tool needs in order to do its job. Make your initial selection by simply clicking a control point. This selects a spline (indicated by the green highlight along the spline), which provides the lathe its information for the template. You can maintain this information (and expand your selection) by using the Spline Selection tools—complement, spline, and select all connected, represented by the comma and backslash keys, respectively. This creates a group selection that allows the Lathe tool to function, while at the same time allowing you to adjust the pivot and alter the way the lathe functions.

Select any control point on the circle you made earlier, and use either the comma or backslash keys to create a group. Once the bounding box indicates that a group has been selected, the next step is to gain access to the pivot point of the group and move it to a more desirable location. The pivot can be seen in any group selection indicated by the Y-shaped RGB axis indicator, initially located in the center of the selection. The axis indicates the local axes of the current group and can be changed; when the mode is set to one of the manipulators other than standard, such as rotate, the pivot can be manipulated without altering the position of the control points. You can use Translate or Scale as well, but rotate is more intuitive. When a group has been selected, the Lathe tool will use this pivot to determine the axis of rotation rather than the default axis of the Modeling window.

Bring up the Rotate Manipulation tool and switch to a Bird's Eye view to get a good look at the pivot. Look at the axis indicator at the center of the manipulator. Note that the ends of each axis and the center of the indicator have square "handles" (see Figure 2.40) called pivot manipulation handles. If you place your cursor over any of the handles it will change from the standard arrow to one of the pivot manipulation icons, either rotate or translate.

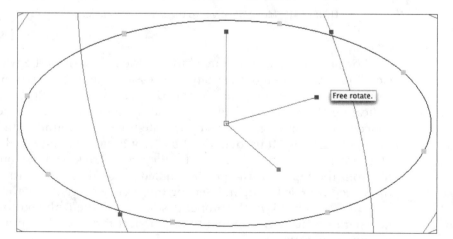

FIGURE 2.40   The pivot handles give control over many modeling operations.

Remember what these icons look like so you can know from any view when and how you will be adjusting the pivot. The handle on the end of each axis will rotate the pivot in the axis corresponding to the color of the handle. The yellow handle in the middle of the pivot will translate the pivot. The pivot can be translated two ways—by hand or by numerical precision. Numerical precision can be given to the pivot by using the manipulator's properties box or the Properties panel. For your purposes here, simply clicking the yellow pivot translation handle and dragging it to the left of the circle spline will suffice. You will want to move it far enough that the pivot completely clears the circle (see Figure 2.41). Notice that the Rotate Manipulator expands as the pivot is moved, indicating the new range that it will turn. Lathing this ring now still won't give you the nice doughnut shape you are after. Since the Lathe tool uses the y-axis to perform its rotations, we would instead get a very confused flat disk shape.

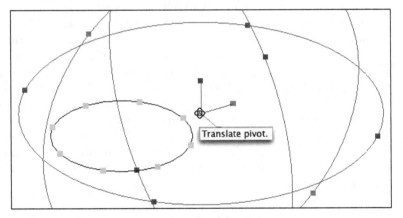

FIGURE 2.41   Move the pivot to the side of the circle.

The pivot must also be rotated so that the axis of the lathe will sweep the circle around as the hull of the shape. The easiest way to picture how the lathe will work is to imagine the green-handled y-axis ring of the Rotate Manipulator as indicating the future hull of the object, meaning that the lathe will function concentric to that ring. You need to rotate the pivot around so that this ring is in the right position. Mouseover the Blue Pivot Rotation handle and rotate the pivot 90 degrees in z. Then do the same for the x-axis. Looking down on the manipulator from the top view, the green-handled y-axis ring should run straight across the screen from left to right, bisecting the circle you want to lathe.

Once the pivot is in the proper position, click the Lathe button or press the L keyboard shortcut. You should have a perfect torus, as shown in Figure 2.42. If not, undo and try again.

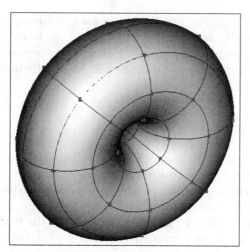

FIGURE 2.42   The finished torus.

The pivot has more uses than adjusting the Lathe tool, although that is one of its most important. Depending on the active manipulator, it changes the way the current group behaves. For the Rotate Manipulator, the connection is easy to make: The pivot changes the arc that defines how the current group will move. The Scale Manipulator moves all selected points toward or away from the pivot; so moving the pivot changes the vector that the points will follow during a scale operation. Also, points closer to the pivot will move less than those farther away, which maintains a basic approximation off the curve of splines as they scale. This allows scale to maintain a basic shape but "flattens" it as points approach the pivot.

The Rotate Manipulator can also be used as a *Skew* tool when used in conjunction with some more modifier keys: the axis limit keyboard modifiers. When manipulating a group or object, the 1, 2, and 3 keys across the top of the keyboard (not to be confused with the numeric keypad, which is used to switch views) limit movement to the x-, y-, and z-axes, respectively. If you hold down more than one key you will be able to move the selection in all the axes you have activated (i.e., pressing 1, 2 will allow x and y; pressing 1, 3 will allow x and z). When using the standard manipulator this generally means that the selection will translate in only the selected direction (or directions, if more than one modifier key is held down). This is used frequently in Choreography mode to constrain the movement of an object to one or more axis. When used in Modeling or Muscle mode, along with the Rotate Manipulator, these keys will cause the selected control points to be skewed as they slide along the constrained axis. This skewing is, as might be expected, centered on the pivot point.

Creating simple shapes, such as these geometric primitives, can be thought of as breaking down the surface to its basic shapes (a circle, a square, and so on) and determining the optimal shape for that surface in splines, then following through with the tools.

Unfortunately, not all shapes are this simple. When striving for realism, even cubes require more than an extruded box. Bevels and other surface irregularities require an understanding of how splines behave, going through control points and across surfaces before they can be convincingly executed.

SPLINE BIAS

The way a spline moves through a control point is determined by several factors. You have already discussed how adding points affect splines and examined how peaked or smooth control points can change a surface. Here, how peaked and smooth control points relate to spline bias is explored, which no doubt raises the question: "What *is* spline bias?"

Simply put, the bias of a spline defines the mathematical parameters that A:M uses to define the curvature of a spline in and out of a control point. That sounds complex, and in reality it is, but you don't need to understand the math behind bias in order to be able to use it to affect a spline. Bias consists of three numbers that you can edit: *magnitude*, *gamma*, and *alpha*. Each of these numbers controls a different aspect of a spline's curvature as it passes through a point. All three types of bias can be adjusted by typing numerical values into the properties of a control point (more on how you can show and select those properties later) or adjusted by the use of interactive handles in the Model (or action in Muscle mode) window. Here are some simple definitions you need to learn before you progress to a simple example of their use.

Magnitude is the most commonly used bias adjustment for models. It defines how strong a curve may go through a point: At a magnitude of 5, it may appear almost peaked, while a magnitude of 300 produces a stronger, rounder curve (see Figure 2.43).

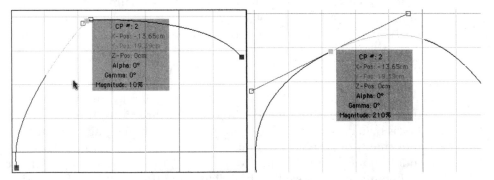

FIGURE 2.43   The magnitude of a CP affects the "strength" of a spline's curve.

To adjust the bias of a CP, use the bias handles. Turn them on with the Show Bias button. Pulling the handles to make them longer or shorter will adjust the magnitude of the CP. To get numeric precision, type a value into the Properties panel or PWS for the selected CP under the bias disclosure triangle. Often, it is more convenient to use the Manipulator Properties box, which presents data on the selected items in a Model window, changing its context based on the current manipulator. The Standard Manipulator gives the *xyz* coordinates for the selected CP, and if the Show Bias Handles button is depressed, the current bias settings.

The Lathe tool automatically adjusts the magnitude for points that make the circumference of the rings to make each ring a smooth circle. Magnitude can smooth corners or it can create a bulge in a surface.

Gamma can be difficult to understand, yet it is crucial to have an understanding of why it behaves the way it does before it can be used effectively in modeling. Once mastered, however, gamma can be a potent tool in your arsenal.

The why of gamma isn't very complex, but unless someone tells you how it works, it can be an impenetrable mystery. Recall that a spline going through a CP has its curve determined not only by the control point that it passes through (by the bias settings of that point), but also by the control points on either side of it, along the spline. Look at Figure 2.44. Here is a simple three-point spline with bias handles showing on the middle, selected CP.

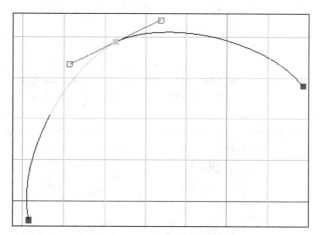

FIGURE 2.44   The bias handle has a logical point of reference.

Note the angle of the bias handle in reference to the spline. At first, this seems to be arbitrary, but it has a logical point of reference. If you draw a line between the two CPs on either side of the selected point you would see that the bias handle at a gamma of 0 runs parallel to that line. Call this the gamma reference line (see Figure 2.45). Any adjustment to gamma is an expression of how far off parallel the bias handle is moved in degrees. Gamma can be changed simply by dragging the bias handle, or you can specify numerical precision by the methods discussed while talking about the magnitude (Properties panel or Manipulator Properties box).

If you want to adjust just the magnitude and avoid accidentally tweaking the gamma (or alpha) of a spline, hold down the Command key (Mac) or Ctrl key (PC). This locks out the gamma and alpha. Likewise, holding down the Shift key will lock the magnitude to one side of the CP.

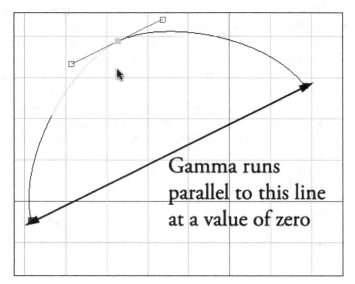

FIGURE 2.45 The gamma of the bias handle is related to the parallel line between the adjacent CPs.

Alpha indicates how far off the centerline a bias handle is when compared to the gamma reference line (see Figure 2.46). Its use is more difficult to grasp than gamma or magnitude, though, and it is used less frequently.

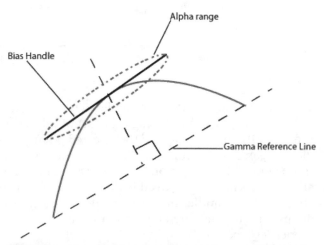

FIGURE 2.46 The alpha/gamma reference line relationship.

Alpha is used to turn the direction of a spline, to control the shape of a leg muscle, for example. Sometimes a large gamma adjustment can make splines running though them play out to one side or the other; alpha can be used to counter this side effect and bring the splines back in line. (This is used primarily on mechanical models and to maintain lower patch counts on curves.) Note that alpha's rotation is tied to the gamma, and the greater the gamma the less movement the alpha seems to have. To understand this phenomenon, look at how alpha works in relation to gamma.

Imagine that perpendicular to the gamma reference line, running straight up through the control point being adjusted, is an axis. This axis is immoveable and always remains perpendicular to the gamma reference. The tip of the bias handle describes the radius of a circle around the axis, which represents the rotational path of the alpha (360 degrees given as −180 to 180). This circle also remains parallel to the gamma reference line. As the gamma raises or lowers the bias handle, this circle is narrowed.

Therefore, when manipulating alpha on a CP with a high gamma setting, the effect seems limited but is actually just moving in a smaller circle. Indeed, a gamma of 90 would make the alpha appear to not move at all.

Let's put some of this to work. You have already modeled a simple cube (emphasis on simple). Take that example to the next level, and at the same time introduce an important concept in mechanical modeling: the beveled edge. Bevels are important in that they help define a shape by giving light a surface to interact with along the edges of an object. Without bevels, your models will look less realistic (which is fine if that is what you are going for) because they will lack crucial specular highlights.

The Beveled Cube

The simple six-patch cube is easy enough, but modeling for realism requires the use of beveled edges; A:M has no automated beveling tools (well, that's not 100% true; when discussing modeling wizards, ways to introduce automatic bevels will be shown). Plan and lay down your splines with the bevel in mind.

Start by laying down a rough, rounded, square-shaped loop (see Figure 2.47), using the grid points as a guide. Don't worry about making it perfect yet. That will be taken care of later with judicious use of the Scale tool. Simply draw nine points with the Add Lock tool, connecting the last point to the first.

Select the loop and extrude it. Move the extrusion back up in *y* to line up with the original shape. Without deselecting, switch to the side view and move it back in the *z*-axis to give it depth. So far, this is pretty much what you did for your fist cube, except that the ends of this cube are not capped off (because you did not start with a rendering patch). You still have to cap the ends of the shape manually (see Figure 2.48).

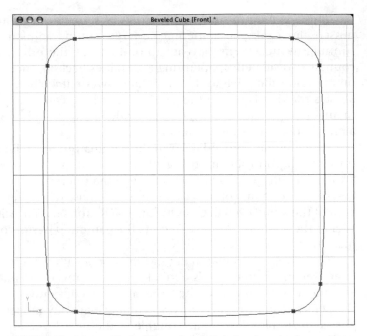

FIGURE 2.47 The outline of the cube already has bevels planned into its spline layout.

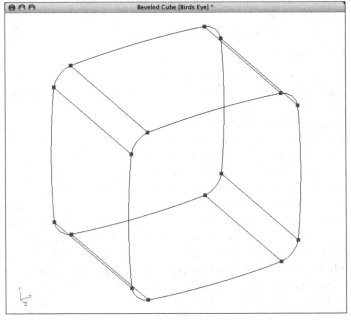

FIGURE 2.48 After extruding, move the new ring back to form the sides of the cube.

Now make a single four-point patch with eight loose CP ends as you did earlier. Make the spline ends roughly match the points of your original loop. Select the new patch and all its CPs, and move it forward in the *z*-axis. Copy it and paste it, and move the new patch to the back of the cube. These will be the end caps (see Figure 2.49).

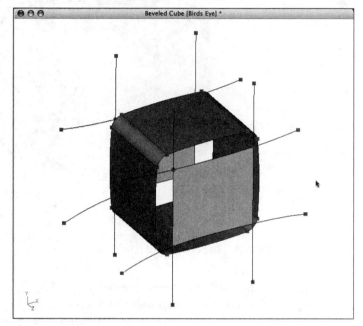

FIGURE 2.49   Two four-point patches will cap the ends of your cube.

Take each of the points dangling from the four-point patches and attach them to the corresponding points on the tube you extruded earlier. This is your rough cube shape (see Figure 2.50).

It's a basic cube, but not perfect. You need to introduce precision to clean this shape up. Simply select all the points on the cube and snap them to grid (via the contextual menu or the ' key).

Depending on why you need the beveled cube, you might want the bevels to be flat or rounded. To flatten out bevels, simply peak the entire shape and leave the bias handles alone. This simple shape is the basic building block for many objects: office buildings, tables, chairs, and so forth.

If a more rounded bevel is desired, the gamma and magnitude of each spline must be adjusted. Since the sides need to remain flat, it makes sense to peak the splines for this operation as well. A peaked spline gives control to the bias on either side of the control point independently of one another, allowing you to set different curves in and out of a point.

Start with the gamma. Make sure your bias handles are visible and select any point that comes off the face of the cube onto the bevel. You want the selection to

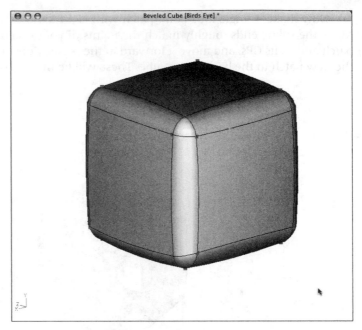

FIGURE 2.50   The completed rough cube.

be along the spline that runs across the bevel; if it is not, use the Tab key to move through the splines that pass through that control point until you have the correct spline selected. Right now the bias handle should be running right along the spline. You will want to pull it up so that the gamma runs parallel to the face of the cube instead (see Figure 2.51). For this cube, a gamma of about 45 will do the trick (or a −45 gamma depending on the spline). Once the gamma is in place for all of the splines, you can adjust the magnitude to round out the edges as much as you need.

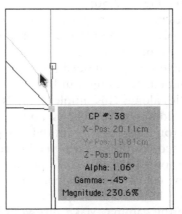

FIGURE 2.51   The gamma should be parallel to the face of the cube.

Throughout your gamma and magnitude adjustments, it is important to notice that the sides of the cube shape remain perfectly flat, thanks to the peaked control points. This technique of peaking points and adjusting gamma is used quite frequently in mechanical modeling. When you are finished, you should have cube similar to Figure 2.52.

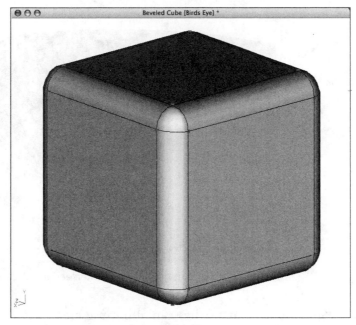

FIGURE 2.52   The finished beveled cube.

COMMON SURFACE PROBLEMS

While learning how to model, you will encounter problems with creasing, artifacts, and lumpy surfaces. These are often because the result of incorrect splinage or bad patch-making decisions. This section will cover some of the more common problems and offer some general solutions to overcoming them.

Three-point patches are best to avoid, if possible. They have their uses but if the area they are placed isn't ideal for them, they can cause creasing. If an area seems to need a three-point patch, reconsider the splines to see if it cannot be resolved with a four- or five-point patch (more on five-point patches later). There are times when you want a crease—in the corner of a mouth or an eye, for example—and three-point patches can do the job nicely.

Connecting *more* than two splines at any junction of a mesh will also crease (see Figure 2.53). Considering that a patch takes its curvature from the CPs that make up the ideal patch sheds a little light on why this is the case. When there are more than two splines crossing at a single control point, the math must estimate the surface, which lets creases slip in. If a set of splines must cross like this, either find a good place to hide them or rethink the mesh.

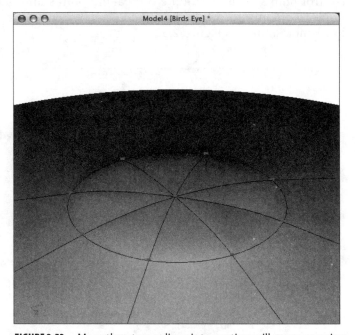

FIGURE 2.53   More than two splines intersecting will cause creasing.

Some four-point patches can also cause creases (see Figure 2.54). A spline that doubles back on itself can create a legal four-point patch, for instance, but any splines that come off of it are going to cause creases. It is better to continue a spline until it terminates.

Four-point patches that are too close together can also cause creases and lumps on the surface of the model. Careful adjustment of the bias of splines that are bunched closely together can help eliminate this creasing. However, that is a long and tedious process. Radical changes in the proportions of patches will cause lumps and creases. Areas of small dense patches must transition into areas of larger patches gradually.

Splines that are not connected by the ending control points maintain their separate nature, allowing noncontiguous splines in modeling. Deleting the tails and continuing to model will guarantee creasing. Ideally, splines should terminate only at radial holes in the mesh. Care must be taken with the Extrude tool as it preserves continuity (or lack thereof), making for a lot of potential work to fix creasing models.

Avoid internal patches. An internal patch causes render time errors on the outside of a model, which can be particularly frustrating and difficult to understand. To avoid internal patches, it is necessary to know what causes them. Remember: any three or four points on two or more splines define a patch. This can include areas *inside* the model. For example, when a surface has been built with

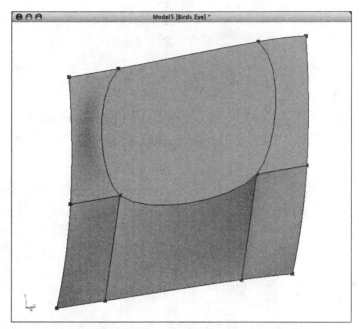

FIGURE 2.54   Some legal four-point patches can cause creasing.

valid patches, extruding that surface will generate valid patches in the extrusion. This is to be expected and can be used to advantage in some instances. If, however, you extrude a surface more than once, the first extrusion forms a valid patch that is retained when the second extrusion is made. This creates a patch that exists entirely inside the surface of the model. It is impossible to see this unless the model is in Wireframe mode (8) and the surface normals are showing (show normals with the Shift+1 keyboard command). Look at Figure 2.55. See those little lines? Those are surface normals. What a surface normal is and how it works is more than a little complex. For the purpose of this example, if you see a normal, that means there is a surface connected to its base. If you look closely, you can see one in the center of the object, indicating the surface of an internal patch (circled for clarity). To get rid of that internal patch, make the splines that form the middle ring a single spline. Or, if the density of splines there is not necessary, delete it.

These are some of the most common issues that cause creasing, or other render artifacts. Avoid them and your models will get smoother and smoother. There is, of course, the whole art of learning how to optimally place your points and splines to generate smooth surfaces, but that's what years of practice are for. Right?

Spline Continuity

Often, you will have portions of a model to join: arms to a torso, for example. How do you run the splines to achieve the best layout, maintain the animatabil-

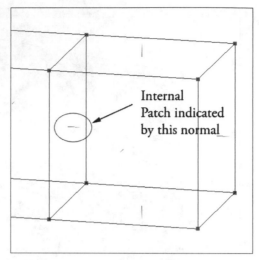

FIGURE 2.55   Internal patches like this can cause rendering artifacts.

ity, and avoid surface creasing? Spline continuity is your guide in making these decisions: Splines should continue as smoothly and naturally as possible.

Joining separate splines is as easy as joining the two by the control points at their ends. In some cases, a CP can pick from two splines to continue. The logic behind which spline will continue is sometimes hard to predict. To determine which spline you are continuing, add a single two-point spline to the model and attach it at the questionable joint. If it extends the spline you had intended, great. Attach the new end to the continuing spline, and delete the extra point. If, on the other hand, it continues the spline you did not intend, attach the continuing spline to the junction. It will now continue the other spline as you had wanted. Delete the extra point and continue modeling.

TUTORIAL **SPLINE CONTINUITY**

In this tutorial, you are going to attach two perpendicular cylinders, forming a sideways T shape (this is a common joint and can represent a shoulder, for instance). You start with the tools we have discussed here and finish it in the next section.

Start by lathing two tubes, as shown in Figure 2.56. Note the number of sections the first tube has. The three in the middle are intended to allow enough density to join the second tube to it. The second tube was lathed where it sits by moving and rotating the pivot.

Your next step is to find splines that can continue as easily as possible. Look for splines that line up from one object to the other. Figure 2.57 indicates your ideal candidates. These splines can continue across the surface without changing direction drastically and will maintain a continuous spline layout.

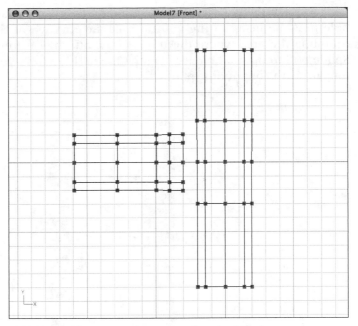

FIGURE 2.56   These two tubes are ready to be joined.

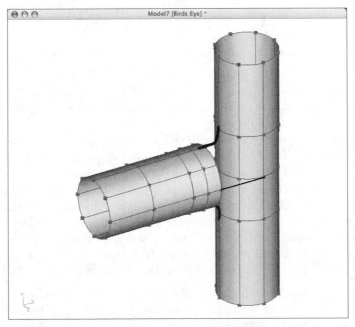

FIGURE 2.57   Look for splines that can easily continue.

To attach the horizontal tube without creasing or causing internal patches, a hole must be made in the vertical tube. Select each of the control points surrounding the area where the tube will be attached in turn, and use the Break Spline tool to open a hole (see Figure 2.58). This allows you to tie the horizontal tube in, with continuous splines.

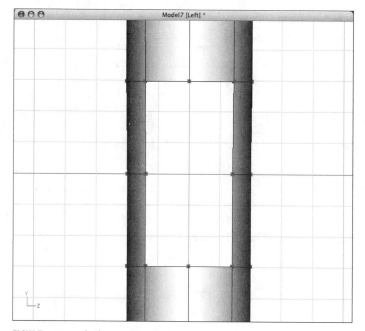

FIGURE 2.58   A hole is opened using the Break Spline tool.

To tie the two together, use the Add tool to draw single splines, and join each end of the spline to the two points you decided to continue (see Figure 2.59). They are now a single spline.

But you still have holes in the mesh, instead of a smooth transition. Make a decision as to what to do with the splines in the horizontal tube. You can tie them around, by drawing splines and adding control points around the horizontal tube. You could delete the remaining splines. You could run the splines down the tube, but all of these still leave holes in the mesh. What to do? For now, run the splines down the tube, as shown in Figure 2.60. Do this by inserting a CP along each ring where you want your new splines to run. Then draw a three-point spline with the Add Lock tool, and attach it to the two new control points and the appropriate spline end on your horizontal tube. Do this for each spline that is to be continued.

The 5-Point Patch is a specialized tool to close holes that would otherwise require lots of spline rerouting or potential crease-causing splinage. The tubes in your tutorial present just such a problem. Where the two tubes intersect, the splines will always create holes of five points at the junction.

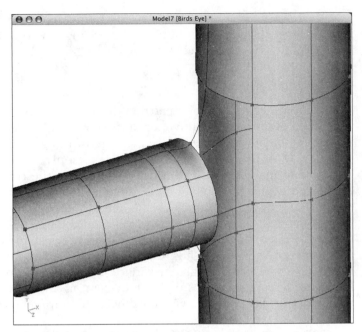

FIGURE 2.59   A simple spline can tie the two shapes together.

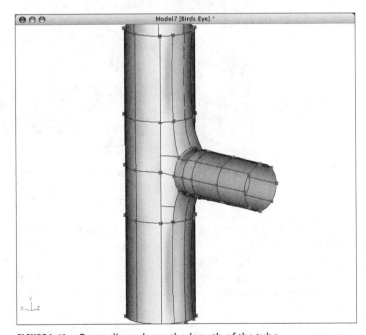

FIGURE 2.60   Run splines down the length of the tube.

To finish your model, simply select the five points that make up the holes, and click the 5-Point Patch button. The hole is now specified to be a rendering patch. Do this for each hole.

Five-point patches and hooks

"Wait a minute . . . five-point patch? Where did you come up with that? Isn't the rule three or four points on two or more splines . . . what gives?" Okay, that was a little fib to get you started, but as with most things there are exceptions to the rules. In A:M, the exceptions come into play only when you explicitly tell the software to make them. In this case, you except the rule when you select five points that would normally indicate a hole, and click the 5-Point Patch Button.

While they are extremely useful, and in some instances practically required, there can be disadvantages to using five-point patches. In order to use them effectively, it's important to understand how they are best implemented.

When a five-point patch is rendered, it is broken up into five areas that are individually tessellated to create the surface. This process is not as informed about the curvature of your surface as typical four-point patches. Five-point patches tend to flatten out or crease when given a highly curved surface to cover (see Figure 2.61).

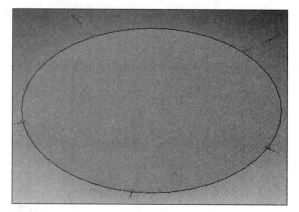

FIGURE 2.61   Five-point patches tend to flatten out on a highly curved surface.

In addition, it is important that the patch is as close to a regular pentagon as possible. Flattening out any edge of the area can cause problems with creases when the patch is rendered. When a five-point area is encountered that is more square than pentagonal, as shown in Figure 2.62, a hook is a better choice. This doesn't always mean for certain that it will artifact at render time, but why take the chance?

You can also create a patch by dead-ending a point into a spline in what is called a hook. Hooks are typically used to ease a mesh of higher density into a mesh of considerably lower density. You create a hook by attaching it to any

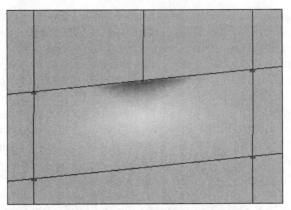

FIGURE 2.62   This five-point patch would be better served as a hook.

spline between two points, rather than connecting it to another point or stitching it onto the spline. You can't just click on the spline and be done with it. That would stitch the point to the spine, creating a new point. What you need to do is click to the side of the spline just off in space, and then escape the Stitch/Add tool. Now that you have a point hanging in space doing nothing, drag it over the spline and weld it in place as you would to connect to points (press the ~ key on the Mac or right-click on the PC while dragging).

There are three points that can be hooked into: the ¼ mark, the ½ mark, and the ¾ mark between two CPs. After the hook is created, it will maintain its relationship between the two control points on either side of it. This makes hooks animateable to a certain extent. Up to three hooks can be attached to a spline.

Like five-point patches, hooks need to be used with some amount of caution. While they can average themselves between control points easily, they are problematic for rotations at joints. Hooks should not be placed on areas that will twist or bend excessively in one direction.

MODELING A FLOUR SACK

In traditional animation, the flour sack is used to teach animation because it is a simple, unintimidating form that most people can draw without difficulty. This simplicity allows the student to focus on creating the illusion of weight and convincing movement. In the grand tradition of animators everywhere, you are also going to start with a flour sack for very similar reasons: its shape is easy to model and will give you an object to work with as you progress.

Rotoscopes

Animation:Master gives you a tool that you can use to trace over images to get models working quickly. This process is called rotoscoping, after the traditional animation term for tracing animation based on live footage. Rotoscopes, like most things in A:M, can be assigned to the model in a number of ways. You may add one with the contextual menu. Choosing New > Rotoscope will allow you to use any image already in the project or allow you to browse your hard drive for any image you like by choosing the Other… option. If there are no images in your project, the Rotoscope menu item will be followed by ellipses indicating that an open file dialog will let you browse for an image to use. If you already have a rotoscope image in the project, simply drag and drop it to the Model window from the PWS. You can do the same from the Library window's Images tab. A dialog will ask if you would want add the image as a decal or a rotoscope. Select rotoscope, and click OK. This adds the image to the model window as a rotoscope for the current view. If you dropped the image on the front view, it will be visible *only* in that view; switching to the right, left, top, bottom, or back views will not show the image. Once you have an image added, there will be an item added under the model object in the PWS. This is the rotoscope object (see Figure 2.63) It is named Rotoscope 1 by default, but you can change its name to something more recognizable if you want. More importantly, though, are the two icons that follow the name in the PWS: the hand and the eye indicate pickability and visibility, respectively. These are actually toggles in the PWS, and clicking them will change the state of the rotoscope. The status of the toggle is indicated by either being crossed out or not. A red X through the hand icon, for instance, means that the rotoscope is not pickable (cannot be selected with the default selection tool in the Modeling window). Similarly, a red X through the eye icon indicates that you will not see the image in the window at all.

FIGURE 2.63   The rotoscope item in the PWS is followed by visibility and pickability toggles.

If you select the rotoscope item in the PWS and look at the Properties panel, you will see the properties that define the rotoscope (see Figure 2.64): where it is located, what size it is (translate, scale), what image it uses, as well as the properties of that image (most of the image properties are not used for rotoscopes; you will look at them more when surfacing is discussed). Some of the more important properties are the ones that define what view the image will be shown in and how it will be shown. If, for example, you dropped the rotoscope for the front of your model into the left view, you can simply change the view property to place it into the correct viewport. Transparency allows the background to be seen through the rotoscope, or if you enable the On Top property (placing it above any objects in the workspace window), it will allow you to see the model through the rotoscope. The final property—Include in Alpha Buffer—is used for rendering and is not typically something you need to worry about with rotoscopes for modeling. The alpha buffer is discussed more in Chapter 14.

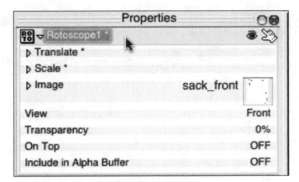

FIGURE 2.64   The properties for rotoscopes.

Start modeling your flour sack by adding a rotoscope to a new Model window. Open the CD-ROM that accompanies this book and import the sack_front.tga file in the images folder into the model as a rotoscope. Once the image is in the window, select it, and open the Properties panel (press command+2 Mac, or Alt+3 PC.) The front flour sack image should be visible in the front view; if for some reason it isn't already, set the view property to Front. You may notice that if you switch to any other view you will not be able to see the rotoscope. This is because it has been assigned to only be viewable from the front view. You want to look at the image as your reference, but you don't want to accidentally pick it or move it in the view, so you need to change its properties. Click the gloved hand and it will change to have a red X drawn over it, indicating that the rotoscope is not pickable. Add a second rotoscope this time for the left view using the sack_side.tga image, also on the CD-ROM. In order for these two images to work together to provide an accurate reference, make certain that they are lined up and the same size in the model window.

To test this:

- Go to the front view.
- Click in the ruler that runs along the side of the Model window. A guide (called a marker) will be drawn across the Model window; in the ruler you will see an arrow-shaped marker handle. Click and drag the handle in the ruler to adjust the position of the guide.
- Place one marker on the bottommost line of the drawing and another on the topmost portion of the rotoscope (not the "ears" of the sack, though), then switch to the side view (see Figure 2.65).
- The corresponding parts of the drawing in the side view should line up with the established guides (which will be visible in both views). If they don't, adjust the position and/or scale of the drawing, using the bounding box handles until they do. (Holding the Shift key down while scaling a rotoscope will maintain its proportions as it scales.)

Once the side-view rotoscope is lined up, make it nonpickable and switch to the front view. It is time to start laying down our splines.

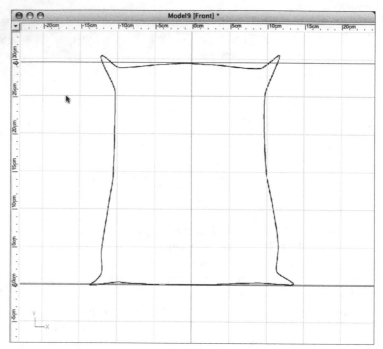

FIGURE 2.65 The guides should rest along the top and bottom edges of the rotoscope drawing in the front view.

Splining the Flour Sack

Draw one spline in a loop using as many points as needed to trace the shape of the rotoscope image. This line will be your outside guide, and in a way, dictates the final density of your mesh. (But you can, of course, remove or add points later if the model needs them.) Keep the number of added points to a minimum. Overly dense meshes cause lumpy surfaces and are difficult to adjust later on. Make certain that one point at both the top and bottom of the spline is on the centerline of the model, and try to have points on both edges in the same number and in roughly the same places. This will make filling in the mesh easier as we add depth to the flour sack.

Once the outline in the front is complete, do the same for the side view. There are a couple things to think about and be aware of when you draw the side-view loop. First, you want to give the loop the same amount of detail as the side of the front loop. Remember how you were told to keep the density from top to bottom on the first loop the same and positioned in the same place? Same thing here, except front to back; and you need to consider the first loop's density. If you have five points down the side of the front loop, then you should have five points across the front and back of the side loop. Second, make sure that you don't inadvertently stitch the side spline onto the front. In this instance, you want to weld the connections between the front and side yourself. You should have two splines similar to Figure 2.66

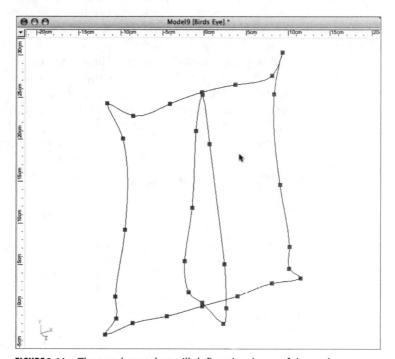

FIGURE 2.66   The two loops that will define the shape of the sack.

The CP that you are connecting will jump to the same position as the one to which you are welding it. This is normal and something that can be used to your advantage. Drawing any arbitrary spline can be placed onto an existing set of splines by merely selecting the point that is not in line and connecting it. When working from a Bird's Eye view, splines are almost never drawn in place, but rather to the side, so you can see where you want them. The danger exists of connecting a point that was in the proper place to one that was not. This is something that must be considered as points are connected.

Once these two splines are drawn, go to a Bird's Eye view and connect them. Since the first spline was drawn in front view and the second in side view, the shapes should meet exactly at the middle of the object. The topmost and bottommost CP of each shape should come close to overlapping. Select one of them and weld it to the other.

Now all that you need to do is to route the splines that will fill out the patches for your shape. Thanks to the magic of computers, you only worry about filling in splines for half of your sack. Your number-crunching friend will take that half and make it a whole later.

Building any mesh breaks down to simply adding splines, attaching them, and inserting control points as needed. Rather than always drawing in every spline, sometimes you can reuse an existing spline in other parts of your model. Since the first vertical section is already in place, has the necessary basic shape, and the correct number of control points, using it to fill in the other sections makes a lot of sense. Select any CP along the vertical loop and use the comma key to select all points along that spline. Copy it to the Clipboard (Command+C on the Mac, Ctrl+C on the PC) and paste it back into the Model window. Presuming you haven't changed the default settings in the Options panel, the new ring will be –10 pixels down in the screen and will be an exact duplicate of the first ring, with the important distinction that it is not attached to the mesh. Move the new ring up and over to the next control point on the main body loop similar to Figure 2.67.

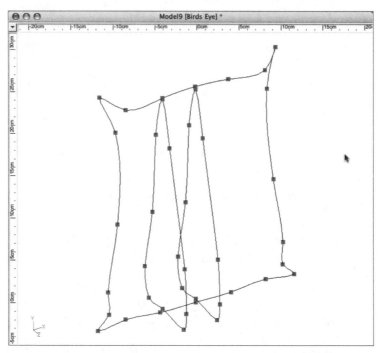

FIGURE 2.67 Move the second ring up and over to the next point on the main body loop.

Repeat the process to add enough rings to go from the middle to the last control point before the ear of the flour sack. The result will look something like Figure 2.68.

From this point, it's very much like a connect-the-dots puzzle. With the Stitch tool, simply click the points along each vertical ring that lines up, going from the middle of the shape in the front to the middle in the back. This can be done entirely from the Bird's Eye view, and that is often the simplest way to go

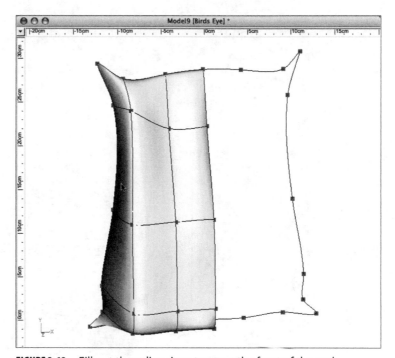

FIGURE 2.68   Fill out the spline rings to cover the front of the sack.

about things, as it allows you to stay in one view to stitch in all the points. Activate the Stitch tool either with the Add button on the Modeling toolbar or press A on your keyboard. Choose one cross section of the sack and, starting from the back center point, click each point that marks that cross section until you reach the front center point. Press the Esc key to exit the Stitch tool, and then repeat the process for the remaining cross sections.

When finished, you should have a rough half flour sack shape, as shown in Figure 2.69. Tweak this half a sack until pleased with its shape. You might want to make some broad changes to the shapes in the sack. If so, you might find the Distortion box helpful.

If you want to distort just an area, group-select the control points and enter Distortion mode. If you want to distort the entire model, then just enter Distortion mode without making any selection. The control points and splines in the model will now be drawn as if they were locked with a 3 × 3 × 3 (this is the default; you can change this on the Modeling tab of the Options panel) control lattice drawn around them. By pulling this grid around, the model underneath it can be sculpted to a better shape. The lattice pushes and pulls all the CPs in the mesh to follow along. Any operations that can be performed on a normal model can be performed on the lattice: bias adjustments, Scale, Rotate, and Translate manipulators all work the same.

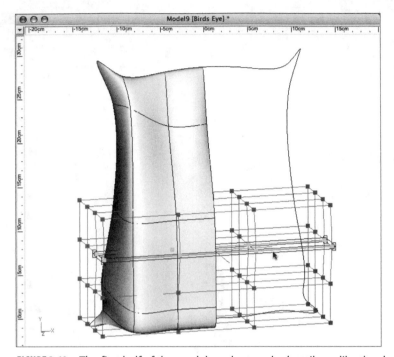

FIGURE 2.69   The first half of the model can be tweaked until you like the shape.

Say, for instance, you want to plump out the belly of the sack. To do this, se-lect the lattice points that surround the belly, including the ones inside the model, and bring up the Scale manipulator. Position the pivot inside the body in line with the lattice there and scale the lattice up in the z-axis. This pulls the points that are already furthest from the center of the body forward, first bulging out the belly just as you want. Shape the lattice until satisfied with the shape of the model. Exit Distortion mode by clicking the Modeling Mode button (or press the F5 hotkey).

Once you are done modeling the first half it needs to be prepared to copy/flip/attach to make the whole model. For this, you need to get the centerline of the model to run along the y-axis and to be as even in the x-axis as possible.

Before worrying about that though, get rid of the extraneous bit of spline that made the outline loop in the front of the model. Because you modeled just one half of the sack, you have half a loop that is not used, and would cause nothing but trouble if left in place for the copy/flip/attach (C/F/A) operation. You could delete the points on that side of the model but that would leave a spline to be bro-ken before you could continue. Believe it or not, there is a faster and easier way to remove that bit of spline without deleting it. If you recall, when you started with the vertical loops of the sack when you copied and pasted the first loop, it came into the mode not attached to the mesh. You can use that same behavior to your advantage here. Simply group-select all the points that you want to keep (whichever half of the model you filled out but not including the empty front loop). Copy this section (press Command+C Mac, Ctrl+C PC). Before you paste it anywhere, group the remaining points with the '/' key (group-connected). Now all the points should be selected. This might sound a little crazy, but delete all the points. Don't worry; you still have a copy of the part you want in the computer's clipboard. Simply paste the half you copied back into the Model window, and you will have the sack sans the empty front loop with no splines to break.

This might seem an odd way to get rid of a single spline loop, and for a model like the sack, you could probably remove the spline by hand without any problems. However, if you were working on a larger, more complex model and needed to remove one or more splines to prepare for a C/F/A, then this technique would save you a lot of time and frustration with stray splines. Now to finish up the sack:

Select any control point on the vertical centerline loop of the model. Be sure the spline leg that is selected runs along the centerline loop. If need be, use the Tab key to move through the splines, which pass through the control point. Once the spline is selected, use the comma (,) keyboard shortcut to select all CPs on this spline. This will have just the centerline of the model selected. If you find that one of the cross sections was selected instead, that means you had the wrong spline leg selected at that CP.

When this group has been selected, look in the Properties panel for the scale properties, and scale the group to 0 in the x-axis. This aligns all the points on that spline. Alternatively, you could show the Manipulator properties with the Show Manipulator Properties Widget, and press S to bring up the Scale Manipulator (or click the button on the Manipulator toolbar). The Manipulator Properties widget will change to reflect the numeric values of the current manipulator allowing you to type a scale value directly into the Manipulators Properties panel.

With the group (and spline leg) still selected, check the pivot for the group. Take note of the X value for the pivot and enter its opposite value into the X translate property. If the pivot is at negative .12, translate the selection to a positive .12 in the x-axis. This places the selected group exactly on the X0 mark. Again, if you are using the Manipulator Properties Widget, you can see and manipulate all this information directly in the widget.

Note that you can avoid the Translate step entirely. It is done here to show you how to ensure that the centerline is x-0 and how to adjust it if it isn't. To avoid this whole issue, set the Pivot to 0 in the x-axis before scaling the center loop down.

It is important to note that during this entire process the original spline leg that was used to select the first ring was never deselected, which is why the comma and backslash keys were used. This spline leg indicates to the program which axis and along which spline the copy/flip/attach operation should follow. One of the more common problems with copy/flip/attach operations is not having this spline leg selected or deselecting it somewhere during the process. Select the entire model with the backslash key. Bring up the contextual menu inside the bounding box for the new selection and choose copy/flip/attach. If the splines are set up correctly, the operation should result in one whole model of a flour sack, as shown in Figure 2.70. If copy/flip/attach didn't work, undo, set it up, and try it again.

Modeling half a model and then applying copy/flip/attach is a common method. It not only speeds up your modeling work, but also gives you mirrored control points that are used for pasting mirrored data when setting up muscle poses and Smartskin. (See Chapter 8 for an in-depth discussion of Smartskin.)

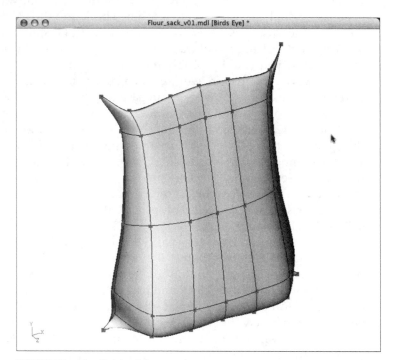

FIGURE 2.70   The finished flour sack.

Finally, prepare your model for bones and animation by moving it so that the bottom of the model rests along the *x*- and *z*-axes in the Model window. This will place the model on the same level as the ground in Action and Choreography windows. If this character were a human or animal you would want the feet to be on the ground. So select all the points in the model (Ctrl+A PC, Command+A Mac) and nudge them up with the up-arrow key until the base of the sack rests on the red axis line in the front view. Be careful not to move it in the Y axis as that will put the points out of mirrored alignment and can cause problems later. This is why you use the arrow key rather than just dragging the group in the model window (although there are ways to constrain a drag operation on points, but that is explained later.)

USING THE MODELING WIZARDS IN A:M

Modeling in A:M can be simple, but there are also repetitive tasks and tasks that are complex and require numerical precision that only a computer can achieve.

These types of tasks are encapsulated into wizards. Only the wizards that ship with A:M are discussed here. There are third-party plug-in wizards that you might look into on your own; or if you are a programmer and there is a task that you feel a wizard would be perfect for, the A:M software development kit (SDK) can give you all the information you need.

A:M has six wizards: Sweeper, Grid, Font, AI, Extruder, and Duplicator. The wizards are broken down into two basic categories: those that are used primarily to generate meshes from nothing, and those that are used to manipulate existing mesh.

The mesh generators are Grid, Font, and AI. These are accessed by control-clicking (right-clicking on the PC) the model in the PWS and choosing wizards from the Plug-ins heading. You will see Extruder in this list as well but it is actually a mesh manipulation wizard.

The Grid Wizard (see Figure 2.71) generates mesh grids. The wizard can be used to create flat mesh grids or (by adjusting the scale and magnitude settings) wavy, undulating, terrain-like grids.

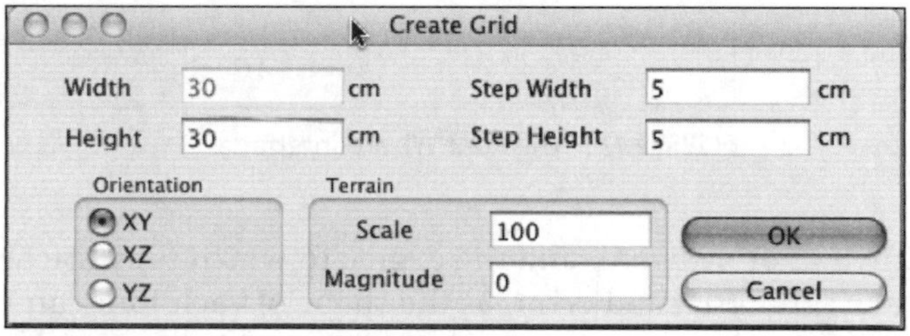

FIGURE 2.71   The Grid Wizard interface.

The settings for the wizard are self-explanatory. A width and height in the unit of measurement that A:M is currently using (cm by default) is specified. The step width and height are set, indicating how far apart the grid will space the splines. The axial orientation of the grid is indicated—*xy* indicating a top view, *xz* a front view, and *yz* a side view orientation. The terrain group's magnitude settings will increase the undulation amount, and the scale will adjust the height of the peaks. Setting magnitude to 0 will keep a perfectly flat grid.

The Font Wizard (see Figure 2.72) creates 3D letters for use in logos or titles, or if you build custom fonts, it can be used to speed modeling of things like nuts or other precise mechanical items.

The use of the Font Wizard is straightforward. The letter or letters to be generated are typed in the text box. Select the desired font, from the available true type fonts on your system and any desired formatting styles.

The pieces settings indicate which portions of the font are created. Fronts, sides, and backs can each be created independently of one another, or together to create a fully enclosed font. The bevels settings specify which portions of the font, if any, are to receive beveled edges and whether those bevels are to be round, flat,

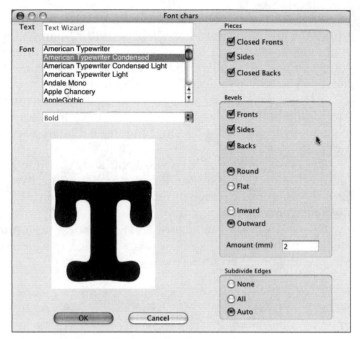

FIGURE 2.72 The Font Wizard interface.

inward, or outward, and the degree to which they are beveled. The bevel settings take some trial and error, as the shape of each font can have different effects.

The subdivide edges settings can provide increased spline density for complex fonts ensuring that the shape generated is accurate. None creates no subdivision and uses the fewest control points to describe the shape; all forces all edges to be subdivided and increases density in curves; auto setting allows Font Wizard to decide how to subdivide any given edge.

The AI Wizard (see Figure 2.73) functions identically to Font Wizard, except you must browse in a previously created Adobe® Illustrator® file for the shape. This allows any shape that can be drawn in a vector graphics program to be converted into an extruded mesh. For complex mechanical shapes this can be invaluable.

The pieces, subdivide, and bevels settings all work exactly as they do for the Font Wizard. If you are not getting good results, you might want to look online at Jeff Cantin's Font and AI Wizard Tutorials. Jeff has been an active tutorial writer in the A:M community and has created a number of beginning-level tutorials that are recommended reading. You can find the URLs for his tutorials and many others at The ARM (*http://www.lowrestv.com/arm*).

The second group of wizards—Extruder and Duplicator—requires that there are splines in the model to manipulate. Extruder can be called from either the model's contextual menu or a group's contextual menu. Duplicator can only be called from a selected group's contextual menu.

The Extruder Wizard (Figure 2.74) takes a single spline and extrudes or copies it along the length of a second spline, following the second spline as a path. This requires that there are at least two named groups in the model. To name a group of CPs, select them and look in the PWS. Note the Groups folder under the model has opened and an item called Untitled has been created. This is the default named group that will disappear once the group is deselected. To keep the group in the PWS, allowing it to be easily selected later by simply clicking its name, select it in the PWS and press F2 and type a new name for the group. This named group is saved with the model.

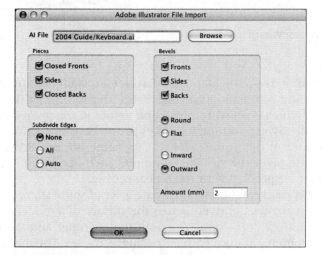

FIGURE 2.73   The AI Wizard interface.

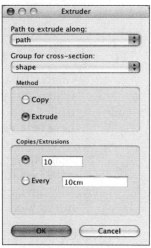

FIGURE 2.74   The Extruder Wizard interface.

The two groups that must be named for the Extruder Wizard are one describing the shape to be extruded (e.g., a ring or star), and one indicating the path the extrusion is to follow.

These groups are indicated in the two pull-down menus on the Extruder's panel. Method indicates whether the cross section is to be extruded or copied. A copy would be used to get a series of spheres to array along a path. The copies/extrusions settings indicate how many times the cross section is to be copied or extruded: either a set number of times or a number of times based on the length of the path.

The Duplicator Wizard (see Figure 2.75) can also extrude or copy a group, but instead of working on named groups and following a path, the duplication is performed on a selected group in the Model window.

The options for the Duplicator Wizard indicate how the duplicates are to be placed. Duplication method indicates whether a selection is to be copied or extruded. In general, single splines would be extruded and shapes (such as spheres) would be duplicated. Sweep, translates in a particular axis a particular distance,

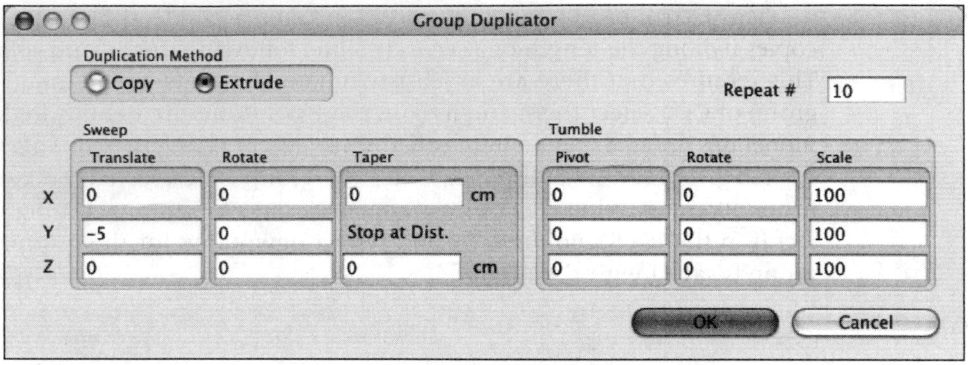

FIGURE 2.75   The Duplicator Wizard interface.

rotates on a particular axis a particular degree, scales a certain amount until a particular distance, or any combination of the three. The tumble settings are controlled by the pivot, which is set with translation values in the pivot boxes. Rotate here behaves as in the Sweep section, but takes the pivot as the center of rotation rather than the center of the group. Scale, as its name implies, scales the item, again in regard to the pivot the specified amount. Each operation is carried out once per duplication as specified with the repeat setting.

The Duplicator Wizard can be used to create a set of spiral stairs or a pyramid out of blocks, or to space a set of rivets across the surface of a model evenly.

Sweeper (see Figure 2.76) is similar to both the Extruder and the Duplicator wizards. It moves geometry along a path extruding as it goes. The main difference is in the ability of Sweeper to take the points of the extrusion path into account.

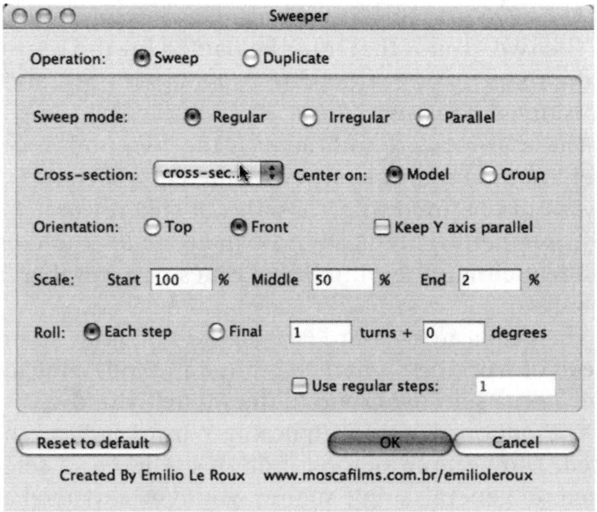

FIGURE 2.76   The Sweeper Wizard interface.

Sweeper is similar to Extruder in that it takes two groups to work with. The first is the cross-section group, which can be any spline shape or a solid piece of geometry (although if you use solid, you will most likely want to duplicate rather than extrude). The cross section must be named in the PWS. The cross section is then duplicated or extruded along a spline path. The wizard is used by selecting the path you wish to extrude along and bringing up the contextual menu. From the menu, simply choose Plug-ins > Wizards > Sweeper. In the Sweeper interface, you select the type of sweeping you want the plug-in to do (either extrude or duplicate) and the method you want it to use (regular, irregular, or parallel). Each type of sweep has its own unique way of handling the spline that will be swept along. Regular adjusts the splines off the cross section to maintain volume and shape as it moves along the path. Irregular does not adjust the cross section and allows distortion to happen as the extruding spline changes. Parallel keeps all the cross sections parallel to one another. The Cross Section pull-down is where you choose the named group that will be swept along the path. Note that, unlike the Extrude Wizard, there is no selection of the extrusion path. Instead, sweeper will use whatever path was selected when you invoked the wizard. You have the option of setting the center of the extrusion on the Model window or the group. This is used to determine the pivot for sweep operations. If you draw your cross section off the origin of the Model window, you will want to use the group setting. Orientation is the view you drew the cross section in. You can choose either top or front, and you must draw your cross section in one of these two views. Keep Axis parallel forces the cross section to remain parallel to either the *y*- or *z*-axis (depending if it was drawn from the top or the front). This does not affect the other axes like the parallel type would. Scale and Roll allows you to change the orientation or size of the cross section as it is swept along the path. This can be very useful for organic shapes like vines. Use Regular steps allows you to override sweeper's default behavior, which is to place a cross section at each CP on the path it is swept along and to use a specific number of steps evenly spaced along the path instead.

SUMMARY

This chapter covered a lot of material and moved pretty quickly. These simple modeling tools can take you months of work to get the hang of completely, but you should have learned enough about splines and how they work to take on more complex modeling than our little flour sack.

We have gone over some of the more common mistakes and problems that you might encounter when modeling, which should arm you with the knowledge to avoid these problems or to find solutions to them. More design-specific modeling is covered in later chapters, focusing on mechanical objects and characters in their own sections. Those chapters will build upon the skills introduced here.

A:M has one of the simplest and most intuitive sets of modeling tools around. Now that you have an understanding of how they work, you are well on the road to creating your own models with them. All that you need now is lots and lots of practice!

BONE BASICS

In This Chapter

- What is a Bone?
- Assigning Bones
- Tutorial: Adding Bones

This chapter looks at bones: what they do, how they work, and how you use them in your models. We investigate bone hierarchy, control point weighting, bone properties, and inverse kinematics. By the end of this chapter, you should have a complete skeleton in your flour sack model, ready to animate in Chapter 4, "Action Basics." You should have already read and understood Chapter 1, "Interface," particularly the section on Bones mode tools, and you will need the finished model from Chapter 2, "Modeling Basics," to complete the tutorials in this section.

The plan of attack is to first learn what bones are, their various parts, and how you place them in models, assign control points, and determine falloff for weighting. Then you will develop a workable animation structure for your character. This will require a single control to move the entire object easily in action; a way to move the top and bottom of the model separately from each other, yet retain a smooth middle; and a way to animate each corner of the sack to emulate hands and feet.

WHAT IS A BONE?

In real life, a bone gives structure to vertebrate creatures like you and me. Without them, we'd be lumps of tissue. Muscle drives that structure to let us walk, grasp, and type long books about Animation:Master. Similarly, in 3D bones are used to give structure to the movement of models. Bones provide the structure that animators use to control a model.

In A:M, bones have several parts, as shown in Figure 3.1. As the use and properties of bones are discussed, knowing the names of these parts will become important. The parts, as indicated in Figure 3.1, are:

A. The bone's tip
B. The bone's base
C. The bone's roll handle
D. The bone
E. The inner falloff
F. The outer falloff

These terms will be used frequently when discussing bones and later constraints and relationships. When you draw your bones, typically you will not see the inner and outer falloff, but these can be turned on and controlled on a bone-by-bone basis.

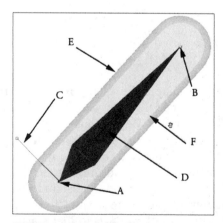

FIGURE 3.1   Parts of the bone.

Placing bones properly is perhaps the most important step in gaining control of a model. For characters and complex objects, this can require layered systems of bones, each with separate functions that are linked with constraints, expressions, and relationships. This can be a complex topic and will be covered in Chapters 7, 8, and 9.

Each bone has its own set of properties and attributes that you can use to place them with precision, to visually identify one from another, or to hide them to keep your workspace from growing cluttered (see Figure 3.2). Some of these properties can be accessed directly in the PWS by the toggles that follow the name of the bone. Specifically, you can change the color and visibility of a bone directly in the PWS. Depending on the hierarchy of a bone, you may not see all these properties on every bone. If a bone is at the root of a model, for example, you will not see the option to attach it to a parent or to lock IK at that bone. More on this in a moment. First, let's go through the attributes of bones.

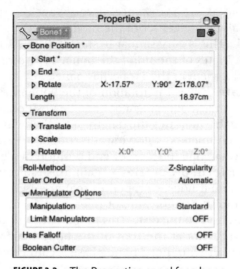

FIGURE 3.2   The Properties panel for a bone.

By default, a new bone is named Bone followed by a number, starting with 1 and increasing with each new bone. Renaming bones (or anything in the PWS) is done by selecting the bone in the PWS, then pressing F2 to edit the name. Double-clicking the bone's name in the PWS allows the same function but is less predictable, since double-clicking can also be used to group all the points assigned to a particular bone in the PWS. You may also use the contextual menu for the item, choosing Rename.

All bones in a model must have unique names.

The properties that can be accessed by the Properties panel are as follows:

Color chip. Immediately following the name of the bone in both the PWS and the Properties panel, the color chip allows you to change the color of the bone as displayed in the Model window. Clicking this will bring up the standard system color picker.

Visibility icon. Directly following the color chip, this toggle will show or hide a bone. Hiding the bone on the model level hides it throughout the interface, meaning you can't see it in an action or choreography. This is commonly used to hide bones that are not directly manipulated but rather controlled by a pose or constraint.

Bone position. This is a compound group that holds the properties that define where the bone is and how it is oriented in the model. A:M will often group a set of properties together when they are closely related.

Start. This gives the X, Y, and Z coordinates of the base of the bone. If the bone is attached to its parent then it will start at the same point that the parent ends. Most commonly, this property is used to align a bone along an axis. For instance, if you want the spine of a character to be exactly along the center of the model you could enter 0 into the start X position

End. This is very similar to start, except that it indicates the X, Y, and Z coordinates of the tip of the bone. Type directly into these values by clicking on them in the Properties panel.

Rotate. Gives the rotation of the bone in reference to the axis of the model window allowing a bone to be positioned at a precise angle in a model.

Length. Indicates the length of the bone in units of measurement (default is centimeters), allowing adjustment or exact duplication of a bone's length. Changing the start or end position of a bone will change its length.

Transform properties. Again, this is a compound group of properties. This time it houses properties that are used only when in an action, choreography, relationship, or referenced by an expression.

Attached to parent. This property is only available when the bone is a child (i.e., not at the root of the bone hierarchy for a model). This indicates whether or not a bone's base is connected to the tip of its hierarchical parent. While each parent bone can have a number of children, only one of those children can be attached. Attaching a child to a parent forms a *kinematic chain* between those two bones. This property serves the same function as the Attach and Detach bone buttons on the Bones mode toolbar.

Lock IK. Sets a global lock on a bone, meaning that the bone, while attached to its parent, does not affect the position of the parent as it would in an IK chain. This property performs the same function as the Lock button from the Skeletal mode toolbar. Note that it is available directly in the Model window. This will set the *default* state of the bone to locked. If you find yourself locking a particular bone in an action frequently, then you might consider changing its default state to save yourself some time.

Has Fall-Off. This is both a toggle and a compound grouping. When it is off there are no further properties available to a bone. This is the property that shows the falloff envelopes (items E and F from Figure 3.1). When it is active, the attributes that describe the falloff envelope of the bone are grouped underneath it.

Pivot/End Outer. Determines the outer size of the envelope at the base or tip of the bone (pivot is the base, end is the tip). This will adjust the inner envelope as well, which will be discussed in a moment. Even though the value is expressed as a percentage, it can have more than 100% as a value. In fact, it can run from 0 to 100,000%.

Pivot/End Inner. Determines the percentage of distance that the inner envelope at the base or tip (depending on which property group it belongs to) of the bone will cover in relation to the outer envelope. The area inside the inner envelope is more strongly affected by the bone (more on weights later in this chapter.) This property can go from 0 to 100% meaning that the "firm" control zone can either not exist at all or exist to the full extent of the falloff envelope.

Scale X, Y, and Z. The properties that shape the envelope. By reducing the scale in an axis, you can take the capsule shape at the end of the bone and distort it. In this way, you can have bones not overlap in one axis while sharing others, or simply focus the falloff more accurately for the splines that you are attempting to control.

Boolean cutter. Indicates that the CPs attached to this bone are to be used to cut away the surface from another portion of the model. This cut is made at render time and does not affect the actual surface of the model permanently. There are, of course, rules and limitations to the use of booleans. The surface that is to be cut must belong to a different bone than the cutter, and both the surface and the cutter must be completely enclosed surfaces.

Each bone has its own inherent set of personal axes. A local coordinate system is used in action or choreography, which is determined by the direction of the bone and the roll handle. In an action or choreography window, the axis indicator (found in the lower-left corner of every workspace window) will change to indicate the axis of the currently selected bone (unless the Show Manipulators in World Space button is clicked, in which case the window's axis is always indicated).

The axes are determined as follows:

The z-axis runs up through the center of the bone. The tip is positive; the base is 0.

The y-axis runs through the roll handle. Toward the tip of the roll handle is positive; the base is 0.

The x-axis runs perpendicular to the bone, with the roll handle indicating front. Positive runs to the right-hand side and negative runs to the left; the base is 0.

For rotations, the tip rotates the x- and y-axes, and the roll handle rotates the bone in the z-axis (along the length of the bone).

Nulls are similar to bones and look very much like them in the interface. Unlike bones, they cannot have control points assigned. Nulls are used commonly as animation controls because they tend to be easier to select and find.

ASSIGNING BONES

Assigning a bone to a model first requires that you have a model and be in Bones mode. In the following tutorial, some bones are laid down in the flour sack modeled in Chapter 2, and the ways by which you can assign CPs to them are discussed, giving some thought to creating a manageable and animateable skeleton.

TUTORIAL ADDING BONES

Open the flour sack model and switch to Bones mode (press F6 or click the Bones mode button). The first step to creating any rig is analysis: What do you want to move on this model and how do you want to move it? Imagine this sack of flour as a character. Anthropomorphizing it, make the ears at the top hands and shoulders, the bottom ears feet. The top half of the sack is to be like a torso, and the bottom half like the pelvis and legs. You want some kind of control for each section of the sack, either independent or in conjunction with the others. That means at least six controls, plus there should be a way to move all the bones at the same time. So, you have at least seven bones that you will need: one as a parent for the whole model and six for controls.

Most motion starts at the waist and moves outward from there. When laying out bones, the same methodology applies. The torso and the pelvis of your flour sack must move independently of each other and often in opposition. You can break the bones needed down into two sets of three bones: one for the upper body and one for the lower body. The seventh bone will be the root of your character, but you will add that in last, after the surface is under control.

If your sack looks like the model in Figure 3.3, the placement of bones for the control you need is logical. The center of the sack is clearly defined by the central splines. They meet right in the belly of the character.

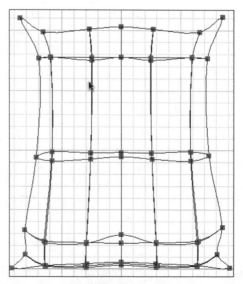

FIGURE 3.3   The splines in the character indicate where bones might belong.

To control each of the sack's ears and torso, simply make a Y-shaped set of bones. Start from the middle of the model and go up to almost the top ring of splines with each arm of the Y extending to each ear (see Figure 3.4).

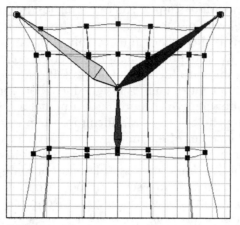

FIGURE 3.4   The three bones that make up the character's upper body.

Likewise, the pelvis and legs can be made by an upside-down Y shape, as shown in Figure 3.5.

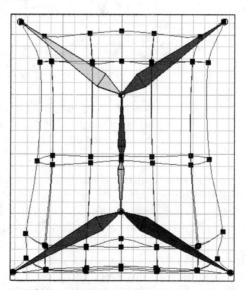

FIGURE 3.5   The six major control bones for the character in place.

Right now, don't worry about the hierarchy. Focus on getting bones in place. If the hierarchy isn't set properly, that's okay. We'll go over how to adjust that. For now, get your bones assigned, and then add your seventh control.

Any of the group tools can be used to assign selected control points to any given bone. More simply, you can bring up the contextual menu anywhere inside the model window and choose "auto assign bones". This function takes the control point in the model and roughly assigns them for you. It makes decisions based on the proximity of a bone to a given point. This process can be influenced a little by the introduction of bone falloff (more on that shortly).

When a control point is assigned to a bone, it takes on the color of that bone, quickly showing which portion of a model a bone controls. In some areas of a model, the choice of CPs is difficult for the program to select cleanly, such as the area in the center of the model where two bones meet end to end.

When this happens, use the selection tools to clean up the control point assignments. This is a simple process: Select the bone you wish to add the CPs to, and while it is selected, change to a selection tool (Group, Lasso, Line Lasso) and "group" the points you want to be specifically assigned to the selected bone. If you wish to unbind control points from any or all the bones in a model, you must assign them to the default bone for that model. This is done by selecting the model name in the PWS. This makes the default bone visible (it is colored black by default) (see Figure 3.6); grouping any points will bind them to this bone. All CPs are *always* assigned to a bone, if not one of the user-specified bones then to the black default bone.

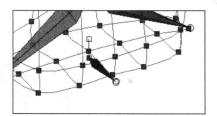

FIGURE 3.6 If a control point is not assigned to a user-defined bone, it is owned by the default black bone.

The seventh bone will not directly control any CPs in the model. It will instead hold all the bones under it in hierarchy, providing a convenient handle with which to move all the points in the model at once. Since it will be used to move the entire model around the action window, it needs to be easily selectable from any view. This makes a *null* ideal for the job. A null is very similar to a bone, both in appearance and in how you select and manipulate it in an action. The major differences are that nulls have a larger selection zone and are easier to select from any view (bones can get buried under other bones or become hard to select in certain situations). Nulls also cannot have control points assigned to them (they are called nulls because they can hold no, or null, control points). In a practical sense, nulls are used most often as targets and controls. Nulls can exist either inside a model, alongside bones, or as an object all its own.

To add a null to the model, control-click (right-click on the PC) the model name in the PWS, and choose New > Null in the contextual menu. Your new null will be drawn at the origin of the Model window. In a side view, select the null and translate it up to where the two y's meet (see Figure 3.7). Depending on the scale of your model, you might need to adjust the length of the null to a more reasonable size. Do this by dragging the tip of the null.

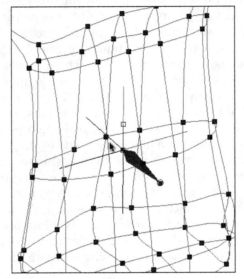

FIGURE 3.7   The null is the last control bone
your model will need.

Before moving on, it is a good idea to name the bones something that makes sense while animating. Get into the habit of keeping your PWS organized and clean at all times; stray bones with no logical names will cause confusion later.

Rename the base of the upper section of bones "torso"; each of the two ear bones can be "arm", left and right, respectively. For the lower portion call the base "pelvis" and each of the ears "legs", left and right, similar to the upper body.

It is important to maintain left and right naming conventions. By prefacing a bone name with the word left or right, it is prepared for paste-mirrored functions, which can drastically reduce the time it takes to animate later on.

Since the null is going to be the root of model controlling all the bones in the model, "Root" is a logical name.

Parent-Child Hierarchy

Adding bones to a model and assigning control points will do very little good unless the hierarchy is in place to ensure that the bones themselves behave properly. The first rule of character setup, regardless of how complex, is that hierarchy is king. All bones take their cues from their parent as to where they should be and how they should orient. If bones are in a chain and attached, then the entire chain will move to reach the tip of the chain.

Knowing how hierarchy should work is a fairly logical process based on how you expect the character to move. In your flour sack, for example, it is fairly obvious that the arms should follow the torso as it rotates. You wouldn't want to have to translate the arms every time the body rotated, which you would have to do if the arms were not children of the torso. So, the arms need to be children of the torso. Likewise, the legs should logically be children of the pelvis. Since you want your root null to control the whole model at once, both torso and pelvis should be its children. As you learned in Chapter 1, a bone can have more than one child, but only one attached child. For your purposes, you don't want any of the bones in the sack attached to their parents. This will allow you to animate the character with forward kinematics, avoiding the need for a complex character rig.

Adjust the parts of a hierarchy to suit by dragging and dropping them into the PWS. Almost everything in the PWS has some sort of hierarchy. As you learned in Chapter 1, a good deal of its function is to represent hierarchy visually. Dropping one bone on top of another tells A:M that you want to make that bone a child. Likewise, you can move a bone up in the hierarchy with a simple drag and drop. As you change hierarchy, A:M will indicate a bone's level in the chain by the indentation of that bone's name in the PWS.

Adjust the flour sack's hierarchy to match Figure 3.8.

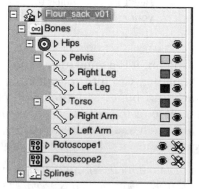

FIGURE 3.8   The hierarchy for the flour sack character should look like this in the PWS.

For a simple character like a flour sack, this is often enough to begin animation. However, you want the sack to remain smooth as you move it about; so there is one more step and one more concept to cover.

CP Weights

As mentioned, you can influence the behavior of the auto select function, and you can also have A:M assign control points in a model to more than one bone. This blending of influence from bone to bone is called *CP weighting*. In order for A:M to perform these calculations, first turn on and adjust up the falloff radius for each bone in the model you want to contribute to the assignments (bones that have no falloff are not considered when A:M performs its calculations). For the flour sack, you want all the bones to contribute to the control; so select each bone and toggle its falloff property on. As you do, the Fall-Off envelope for each will become visible. This envelope indicates the area of influence for a given bone. You can change the size, and to a certain extent the shape of the Fall-Off envelope, by adjusting the properties for the falloff in the Properties panel (see Figure 3.9).

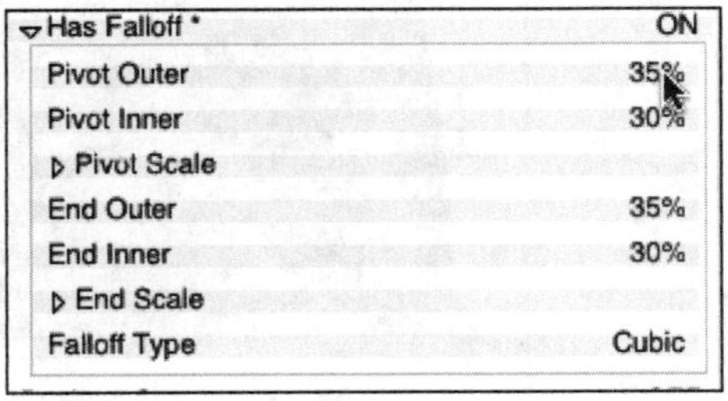

▽ Has Falloff *	ON
Pivot Outer	35%
Pivot Inner	30%
▷ Pivot Scale	
End Outer	35%
End Inner	30%
▷ End Scale	
Falloff Type	Cubic

FIGURE 3.9   The falloff properties are used to shape the area of influence a bone has.

For the flour sack, you won't need to get too involved with complicated shapes for the Fall-Off envelope. You just need to adjust the area of influence of each bone so that it covers the correct area in the model. The amount of control that CP weighting gives to each control point is determined by the falloff area around the bone. Each CP that falls into the capsule of the Fall-Off envelope is given at least in part to that bone. The closer to the center of the envelope a CP is, the more weight is given to a particular bone. The inner falloff indicates the area in which the bone has "absolute" control. The area between the inner and outer Overlapping envelopes gives the bones a share of control over the CP in question.

Once you have the bones falloff set to on, have A:M compute the weights for the entire model. Bring up the contextual menu in the workspace window and choose Compute All CP Weights. To see how much control a particular bone has on any area of the model, simply change the Draw mode to Shaded Wireframe, and the shading will take on the color of the controlling bone (see Figure 3.10). For the sample flour sack, the numbers in Table 3.1 give good results. There is no magical formula applied to arrive at them. Adjusting falloff is primarily a trial-and-error process. Giving it at least enough falloff to control the CPs immediately surrounding it and to blend into the adjoining bones produces the best results. You can recompute falloff as many times as you need to. Or if you want to start over, you can have A:M remove all the CP weights from a model through the same contextual menu.

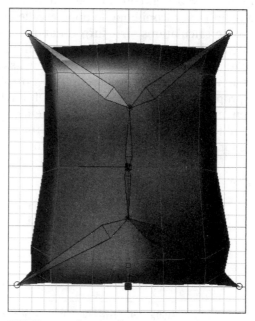

FIGURE 3.10 The weight of bones on a model is graphically represented in Shaded mode.

TABLE 3.1 Example CP Weights

BONE	INNER	OUTER
Torso	55	65
R and L Arms	30	50
Pelvis 5.15	55	65
R and L Legs	30	50

The root null gets no falloff (in fact, it doesn't even have a falloff property), as it cannot control any CPs on its own.

If you did not want to calculate all bones for CP weighting or were making minor adjustments to the falloff of a single bone, each bone in the model has the option to compute the weight for just that bone. This is accessed through the bone's contextual menu. Some of the control points assigned manually may change bone assignments when CP weighting is computed. This is to be expected, as some bones will have almost total control of a CP when weighting is calculated. In terms of weighting, the bone with the greatest level of control is the owner of a CP.

Selecting a bone in the model or PWS makes the control points that it controls flash. If any other bones share control of the CP, they are indicated by secondary outlines around each CP in the color of the sharing bone (see Figure 3.11).

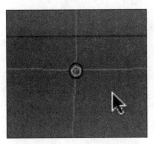

FIGURE 3.11 Control points will have secondary outlines for each of the bones that contribute to their movement. The closer to the actual point the more control a bone has.

SUMMARY

This is all there is to bones on the most fundamental level. They are drawn, assigned CPs, and weighted. There are, of course, more complex setups that are used for characters, and those will be covered in Chapters 7 and 8, but all setups, no matter how complex, start with getting geometry bones set up and ready for animation.

In this chapter, you learned how to assign bones to a simple model. Now we can deal with models that are more complex. You should have a fully boned version of the flour sack ready for animation in Chapter 4.

4

ACTION BASICS

In This Chapter

- Keyframing
- The Frame Toolbar and Keyframe Filters
- Poses
- Tutorial: Animating a Hop
- Timeline and Channels
- Keyframe Interpolation

This chapter explores the action window using the flour sack character that you modeled and boned in the previous two chapters. Examining the tools at your disposal, you will animate this character. Also discussed is what a keyframe is and how it is important to animation, and you will look at the channels and timeline, and talk about timing. You may want to review Chapter 1, particularly the section on Skeletal mode tools, as you will be using them throughout this chapter.

The plan of attack is to navigate the action window and to learn some of the fundamental concepts behind character animation. By the time you have finished this chapter, you should have created an animated action of your flour sack taking a small hop.

KEYFRAMING

In traditional animation, an animator draws *key* poses that define the action, the *breakdowns* that define the arcs and secondary movement, and then passes the drawings to an assistant to clean them up and draw the in-betweens. If it were action that required careful in-betweens, he might draw all the frames leaving the assistant nothing more than the cleanup. In 3D animation, the computer is the assistant that fills in the space between your key poses. Those key poses and the breakdowns are termed *keyframes*.

When you move a bone, control point, or make any changes to any animate-able property, Animation:Master automatically sets a keyframe for the changed attribute and interpolates through each change smoothly.

If the first component of action is change, time is the second. Time in anima-tion is measured in *frames*, spaced at various intervals of a second. This is termed *frames per second* (fps) and is dependent on the animator's preferences and the in-tended format for the work.

Most professional animators work to 24 fps. This is the standard speed for film and is frequently used in studio environments. The default for A:M is 30 fps and is used primarily for NTSC television. (The actual speed of NTSC is 29.97 fps, but 30 is generally considered close enough. PAL-formatted television uses 25 fps.)

As you learn to animate, you should choose one fps and stick to it; 24 is rec-ommended not only because it is the standard for most animation studios (if you study old animation it will invariably be timed to 24 fps), but also because it is six fewer frames per second of animation for the computer to render. Working to a single-frame rate, whatever it is, helps you develop timing. The fps is a property of the project and can be changed in the Properties panel (see Figure 4.1). Select the Project (the root of the PWS tree) and change its property to whatever rate you prefer. You can set the default to whatever rate you like through A:M's pref-erences (see Chapter 16, "Miscellany").

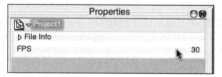

FIGURE 4.1   Change the frame rate in the properties of the project.

Before overcomplicating things, here is the secret to animation—all anima-tion. It's actually quite simple, Animation consists of only two things: *Pose* and *Spacing*. You may have heard talk of 12, or more, principals of animation. Even *The Art of Animation:Master* lists 10 "ingredients" to animation. The truth is that all those principals and ingredients are actually one or more aspects of pose and spacing. We will talk about all these aspects at one point or another, but you need to keep them in the context of Poses and Spacing.

The pose will establish the character and the action it is performing. You set up these poses in keyframes, and the spacing of those poses will establish the *feel* of the actions. The classic example is the turn of a head. If a head turns from left to right over 12 frames (half a second) it looks like the character heard something and turned quickly to see. Over four frames the same the character appears to have been slapped. Over two frames it might look as if the character took a brick to the face. The feeling of a set of poses can be completely changed by the spacing of the keyframes. The keyframes are the poses of the head as it changes position from left to right. The spacing is how many frames you allow those poses to take.

THE FRAME TOOLBAR AND KEYFRAME FILTERS

Spacing in an action refers to how much time passes from one pose to the next. To advance or retreat in time, there are several tools that first need to be discussed. Most action tools can be found on the frame bar at the bottom of the interface (see Figure 4.2).

FIGURE 4.2   The frame toolbar.

These tools are all used regularly when setting what are called *forced* keyframes, when viewing and editing the information for action in channel form. This is also where you find the tools for navigating the individual *frames* of your actions. All of these tools are also available to us in the Choreography window (see Chapter 10).

The first two groupings of buttons are called Key Filters. They are combined to specify what aspects of the current selection will be affected by any keyframe operations.

Key translation. Filters operations to either include or ignore bone translations.

Key scale. Filters operations to either include or ignore bone scale.

Key rotation. Filters operations to either include or ignore bone rotations.

Key constraints. Filters operations to either include or ignore constraints.

Key muscle. Filters operations to either include or ignore CP or "muscle" motion.

Key bias. Filters operations to either include or ignore spline bias.

Key pose sliders. Filters operations to either include or ignore pose sliders. (For more on pose sliders, see Chapter 8.)

The second group of buttons indicates how much of a skeletal hierarchy is affected by keyframing operations. This is used in conjunction with the bone filters from the first group.

Key bone. Filters to the currently selected bone only. This does not affect any other bones in a hierarchy and will paste any skeletal data onto the selected bone, even data from dissimilarly named bones. This overrides the normal naming requirements for pasting in A:M.

Key branch. Filters to the currently selected bone and all its children. When using this filter to copy or paste data, the name of the bones themselves also act as a filter.

Key model. Allows manipulation of all the bones in a model. In a choreography, this is limited to the currently selected model. The name of the bones in the model further filters keyframe copy and paste operations, only pasting data onto bone channels that have the same name as the copied data.

The next small grouping of buttons sets, deletes, or edits keyframes, based on key filter settings. Shortcuts are shown in Table 4.1.

Set keyframe. Forces a keyframe channel to be set on all filtered keyframes at the current time.

Delete keyframe. Removes all keyframe channels at the current time based on the keyframe filter options.

All of which would do us very little good if we couldn't advance and retreat in the timeline of an animation. The frame controls resemble those of a VCR and have very similar functions. You can step through the animation's time one frame at a time, or jump from keyframe to keyframe. If your computer has a fast enough video card, you can even get a real-time playback of your animation.

Previous/Next key frame. Advances the time to the next or previous keyframe in the timeline, based on the key filter settings.

Previous/Next frame. Advances or retreats exactly one frame in time.

Frame counter. Shows the current frame in the format selected in the preferences. Type a specific time into this box to jump directly to a frame. You can also use the keyboard shortcut Command+F (Mac) or Ctrl+F (PC), which will bring up a dialog to jump to a particular time.

Time in A:M is represented by what is called SMTPE (simp-tee) time. This universal time format is easy to understand. Each segment of time is represented by a number and separated by a colon—Hours:Minutes:Seconds:Frames—though most animations don't use the hours field.

Play/Loop. Moves through a range of frames defined by the Timeline window (more on that in the next section). If the Loop button is on, it will play through the range and start again. This is good for looking at cycles in real time (or as close to it as your computer's graphics card will allow) and to get a handle on how timing and poses are working.

With practice, using these tools will become second nature.

TABLE 4.1   Keyframe Shortcuts

COMMAND	PC SHORTCUT	MAC SHORTCUT
Next Frame	+	+
Previous Frame	-	-
Next Keyframe	Shift +	Shift +
Previous Keyframe	Shift -	Shift -

POSES

Before you actually animate something, we need to discuss poses. A pose is the smallest unit of animation, indicating the way that a character or object is positioned on a given frame.

The pose determines how well any action or animation reads to the viewer. Consider the pose the basic building block for every action. If a pose is weak, confused, muddled, or otherwise not executed well, then the action as a whole suffers. What makes a good pose is based partially on personal preference and partially on a set of guidelines.

Poses are inherently tied to their actions. They must be considered as a unit. Any pose that does not lend something to the action as a whole, that does not clarify some point, should be rethought. A pose expresses intent, motion, direction, and emotion. Even simple characters, like Flour Sack, can appear to be tired, happy, or scared. Figure 4.3 shows a few poses for Flour Sack. The emotion each one demonstrates is readily apparent.

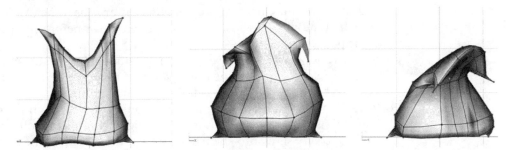

FIGURE 4.3   Flour Sack looking angry, incredulous, and sad.

An understanding of body language, weight, composition, and motion are the most important things when building a strong pose. Observing people around you as they move and react to things, watching classic animation or film, frame-by-frame, and acting in front of a mirror are all time-honored techniques for animators. The basic rules, however, remain the same regardless of the emotion or goal that you are trying to portray:

Establish the line of action. Every action should have a line that defines its motion. This curved line indicates the spine and center of gravity and helps establish strong convincing motion. A weak line of action will make poses muddled and confused. But the line of action should fit the pose; extreme curves do not indicate that a character is simply standing in place.

Establish a strong silhouette. Every pose should be readable without any internal detail included; its outline alone should convey all the needed information. Watch great animation and you will see this rule applied religiously. If a pose reads strongly in silhouette, then it will read even stronger when the internal details are rendered.

Avoid "twins." *Twinning* is the term given to a pose that is symmetrical on both halves of the character. Each body part should be positioned differently than its mirrored companion.

Be natural. The way people hold their bodies is very natural. Gravity pulls joints down, and the body flows into place. When you are building poses for a character, you want to be sure that you don't sacrifice the natural, *comfortable* feeling that a character should have. This cannot be stressed enough. Too often in the pursuit of the perfect pose, we forget to make the character look as if it is comfortable and affected by gravity.

These principals are in place in most good animation you see. They are the keys that a pose is built up from. Each pose has a role in an action and an action is composed of many different types of poses. Many of the principals of animation that you may have heard of are nothing more than descriptions of the rolls of poses and the spacing used to implicate them.

Anticipation. A type of pose that comes prior to a motion. It is a sort of winding up to get ready to move. This can be as simple as leaning back slightly before taking a step or moving an arm back before swinging a punch. Typically, it is spaced out a frame or two before the pose that it anticipates.

Overshoot. A pose that goes *past* the final resting point for the action. Overshoot can be considered the anticipation of rest. Similar to anticipation it is spaced a couple of frames before the character hits its settled pose.

Follow-through. Indicates that motion should carry through in relation to the intensity of the action and the weight behind it. Follow-through poses are very similar to Overshoot, except they come in the middle of an action rather at the end of it. Follow-through can be a single pose, with any variety of spacing, or several poses where individual elements of a character follow through in succession.

Weight. This is more a subset of all poses, rather than a pose type in and of itself. Simply put, the character and the objects it interacts with should appear to possess weight. This is more difficult than might first be assumed, and along with improper spacing, lack of weight is a key contributor to "floaty" animation. When you animate your flour sack, we will explain practical ways to introduce weight into your characters.

Secondary motion. Sometimes called *overlap poses*, secondary motion describes action that is not in line with the main animation of the character. Hands, for example, will lag a frame or two behind arms as they move. Clothes, hair, and other loose-fitting or flowing items also exhibit secondary motion.

Armed with these principles of what makes a good strong pose, you are ready to move on into some actual animation!

You are finally ready to give Flour Sack some life. You will be using everything you have learned in this chapter to create an animation similar to the one on the CD-ROM. It's a very simple animation to be sure, but it possesses all the principles we have discussed and builds on them to make a convincing animation of a sack of flour hopping along. It involves the animation of bones and CPs. For the most part, it will be an exercise of building poses and adjusting timing.

ON THE CD

TUTORIAL   ANIMATING A HOP

Start by opening an action with the flour sack model in it. The window opens in Bones mode and Flour Sack will be in its default position. Since this action is intended to work as a cycle, the first frame and the last frame need to be the same. At the end of the action, your sack will have just landed from his hop. This places him at the bottom of the cycle. He needs to be squashed down, ready to recoil into his next hop.

A bird's-eye view gives you the best approximation of what you are looking for camera-wise. Once the bird's-eye has been set, leave it there. It is to be your frame of reference, and you must make sure that your poses hold up to this view.

Squash and Stretch are tools used to indicate weight.

For the first pose (see Figure 4.4), the sack needs to be squashed down. The mass of the object needs to be maintained; so if an object is flattened by 20% it should spread out 20% wider. With that in mind, select the root null, and if the Properties panel is not open, open it. On the Properties panel, open the section of properties for the scale. Since the root is the hierarchical parent of the entire model, any operations applied to this bone will propagate through the entire hierarchy. The sack needs to be squashed down in the *y*-axis and stretched out in the *x*- and *z*-axes. How much squash is best determined by eye. Many of the decisions made about keyframes and poses are aesthetic ones. A squash of 90% in the *y*-axis and 110% in both the *x*- and *z*-axes might work in this instance.

This lifts the sack off the ground as indicated by the *y0* point in the action window. To counter this, translate the root down so that the base of the sack sits on the 0 point of the action window. A bit of weight has already been added to your model. Squash is one of the key contributors to weight. Set the keyframe filters to filter translation, rotation, and scale the whole model, and click the Make Keyframe button. Advance to Frame 24 (assuming the project has been left in

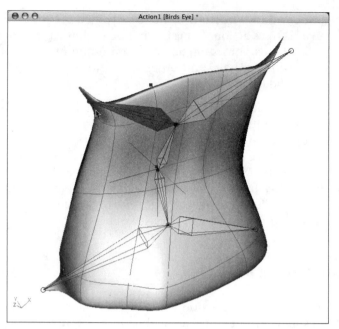

FIGURE 4.4   The first pose of the hop.

24 fps), and click the Make Keyframe button again. These 24 frames represent one second of time, but time in actions is flexible in relation to a choreography and can be changed. (This will be discussed in depth in Chapter 10.) The two keyframes you have made do absolutely nothing yet. Stepping through the action frame by frame will show that the sack just sits there. To introduce motion, move to Frame 12, where you will establish the top of the arc for the hop (see Figure 4.5).

More than simply lifting the sack up in the y-axis by the root, the top arc is the point where the character should be stretched out. Currently, it remains squashed from the first frame. Stretch it out by changing the scale values on the Properties panel to 110% in the y- and 90% in both the x- and z-axes. Now translate the root up, until the sack is a reasonable distance above the ground. Stepping through this animation shows that you have a sack hopping in place. Bland though it may it be, it hops. This is your basic motion, what is often referred to as the blocking pass of animation. Look at this motion and determine if the spacing and the poses work well together. If the sack hops very high it will need more time to complete the action. If the hop is very short it won't be in the air as long. The only way to know when you have it right is experience. Make some changes to the poses and the spacing to see if it looks better. What if the sack hopped higher at frame 12? What if the full extent of the hop lasted 12 frames (with the top of the hop at frame 6)? Only trying these variations will show you what is possible.

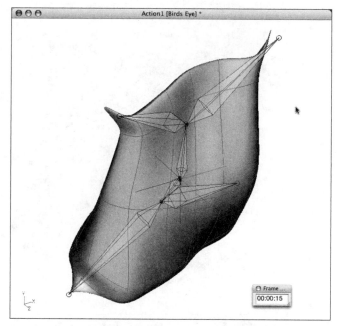

FIGURE 4.5   The top of the hop.

Currently, there is no variation in the hop. If it were looped over time, it would be a rhythmic and regular up-down motion with little or no weight and even less interest. Arcs of motion and breakdowns need to be added to keep this interesting. For Flour Sack to hop, it will need to throw its upper-body weight forward, dragging the heavier bottom off the ground and into the air. This is in part what will make the stretch appear natural. The bottom of the sack, being heavier, will lead the top as the sack descends. Start with the top of the sack.

On frame 12, the sack is at the top of the arc. The thrusting motion that the torso and arms did paid off, and the bottom of the sack is in the air. However, the bottom of the sack hasn't moved forward enough to drag the sack down yet. The torso and arms should be thrust forward. So, starting with the torso, rotate the bone forward. Each arm also comes forward and up toward the middle of the sack, but slightly asymmetrical. The pelvis and the legs of the sack should be trailing behind as if they had just thrust off the ground establishing a line of action for this particular pose (see Figure 4.6).

Make sure to adjust the legs and arms to remove any traces of twinning, and this is a convincing pose.

Back to frame 0. This frame is supposed to be the landing of the sack after its hop, but it's very stiff-backed and not indicating it has landed at all. The current line of action for this frame is a straight line, not a curve. This can definitely be better. The feet would be the first part of the character to land. The torso and arms would trail behind (try jumping and see how this works). On top of that, the

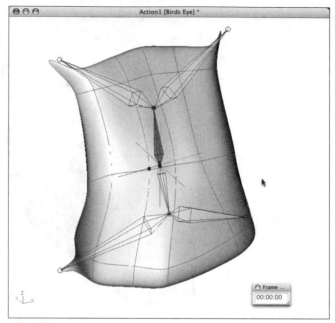

FIGURE 4.6   Establishing the line of action.

dreaded twins are all over this pose. Lean the torso back a bit to establish the line of action as a nice subtle curve (see Figure 4.6). Adjust the hands and feet to get rid of the twins.

Copy this frame by using the copy keyboard shortcut (Command+C Mac, Ctrl+C PC) and paste it (Command+V Mac, Ctrl+V PC) on frame 24 to ensure that they are the same. Stepping through this action looks a little better already, but it's still too linear and artificial. It needs some breakdown poses to help the action along.

After landing, you have to recoil, adjust your weight, and thrust out again for the next hop. So, a character should spend a little time on the ground—more than one frame in any event. Copy frame 0 and advance to frame 3 and paste. This establishes the base from which you need to work. This gives the sack three frames on the ground, but all in the same place and position. When landing, the body compresses and recoils. The pelvis moves forward, thrusting the weight in preparation for the next jump. The upper body folds down with the momentum of the jump and is leveraging the weight of the body for the next jump. Push the pelvis bone back and pull the legs in just a bit to arch the lower body. The torso should come forward, making a nice line of action for this pose (see Figure 4.7).

The same thing can be said for frame 24. You hit the ground evenly right now, just a flat stop on the ground. If you jumped like this, your feet would come down in front of the rest of your body (or you'd fall over). The upper body would just be following along at this point and would flow back from the legs.

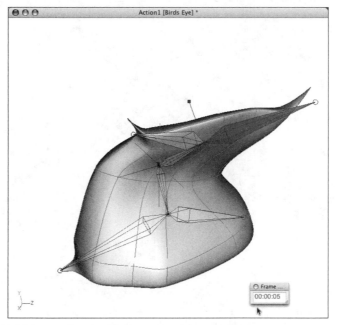

FIGURE 4.7   The recoil pose.

Go to frame 24 and copy the frame. Step back to frame 20 and paste. To counter the weight of the pelvis that is coming down, the legs would be forward. Move the pelvis forward now, adjusting the legs to remove any twins and to keep the feet in contact with the ground. This establishes the line of action for this pose and gives the sack a little more weight. The momentum of its lower body seems to carry the weight forward now (see Figure 4.8).

There are a couple more breakdowns to do yet: The weight in the air needs to be more apparent, and the sack would thrust its legs forward at the top of the arc to maintain velocity forward and to position the legs to catch its weight as it comes down. Prior to the jump, the body needs anticipation. The upper body would bend down more to give more thrust to the jump, and the body would have an extreme line of action immediately after the jump.

First, the anticipation of the jump. Go to frame 6. The sack should still be on the ground or close to it. If it isn't, translate the root down until it is. When people jump, they thrust their upper body out to pull the weight off their hips, as the legs thrust to push the whole body into the air. The animation needs to anticipate this by pulling the upper body farther forward. Rotate the torso bone until the line of action is more like Figure 4.9.

To show the weight in the air and the force of the thrust from the upper body, establish a sharper line of action prior to frame 12. Advance to frame 8 and rotate the torso back until there is a nice strong curve in the character (see Figure 4.10). The legs may also need to be pulled back.

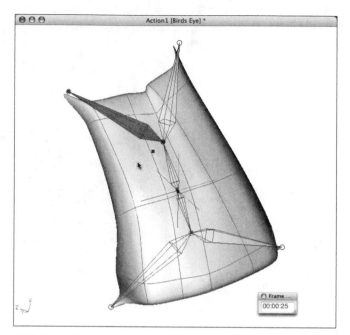

FIGURE 4.8   The landing pose.

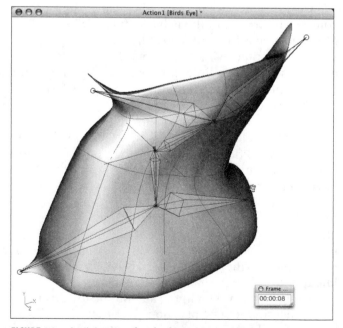

FIGURE 4.9   Anticipation for the hop.

FIGURE 4.10   Adding weight in the air.

Past the top of the arc, the legs of the sack should come forward in anticipation of the landing and to swing the weight forward to extend the jump. Advance to frame 16 and pull the pelvis bone forward. The legs could move forward, too. You should have something similar to Figure 4.11.

Now go to frame 0 and step through it using the +/- keys on the numeric keypad. It should be a reasonable facsimile of a hopping sack of flour. You have used anticipation, squash, stretch, pose, and timing to get this far, and a little overlap would do just the trick to make the action ultimately believable. Looking at the model as it moves, the ears of the flour sack stand out as a likely candidate for secondary motion and overlap. Muscle motion can be used to drive the motion of the loose parts of this character.

Change to Muscle mode (press F7) and switch to a front view. Select the CP that makes up the tip of the ear with the Group tool. This is so that the Rotate Manipulator will move just this control point. Selecting a single point, while allowing the manipulators to be used, will not have its rotation affected from changes to the pivot. (A group, even though it contains the same single CP, will.)

Once the group is selected, bring up the rotation manipulator and position its pivot at the base of the ear. Check from the side view to be certain that the pivot is lined up there as well. Now step through the animation frame by frame: Look for points where the motion of the torso is drastic, moving from front to back over the course of just a few frames.

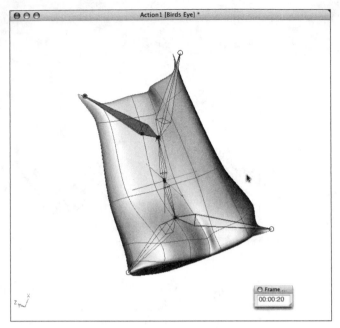

FIGURE 4.11 Anticipating the landing.

At the start of such motion, rotate the ear CP opposite to the motion of the body, so that it appears to lag behind the rest of the torso. After the torso comes to its new position, rotate it in the same direction a bit further. This establishes this part of the mesh as lagging behind the rest of the body and adds a lot of credibility to the motion. Do the same for each motion of the torso.

It is very important to bring the ear control point to rest at some point as well. If it remains constantly in motion, it will become floaty instead of adding to the motion. To make the point come to rest, set a keyframe shortly after the torso comes to rest in the same position that the ear was in at the last key. Do this with the key filters set to just muscle action and using the Set Keyframe button.

Once the motion of the ear lags behind the rest of the body, copy and paste frame 0 to frame 24 again to ensure that the CP is in the same position on both frames and repeat the process with the other ear, remembering to avoid twinning the motion. Think about offsetting the second ear by a frame one way or the other temporarily to give the motion some breakup.

Go ahead and step through this motion. Congratulations! You have completed an animation exercise as old as animation exercises themselves: the hopping sack of flour! We will come back to this action and explain how to get it into a choreography and out to a final render in Chapter 9, "Expressions."

TIMELINE AND CHANNELS

You may never need to look further than the Action (or Choreography) window for creating animations. But there are times when either you want to access the raw components of motion to change a specific aspect of an animation, or you want to change the way your assistant (the computer) handles the in-between drawings without specifying a new key pose. You do this through the channels and timeline.

The timeline is accessed from the window of the same name (see Figure 4.12) or from the project workspace (review Chapter 1 if you need a quick refresher). The timeline is made active by choosing Timeline from the View menu. Once open, this window presents the currently selected object, bones, groups, driver, or any other item in the PWS, in either Timeline or Channel format (see Figure 4.13).

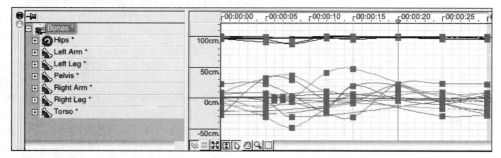

FIGURE 4.12   The Timeline window.

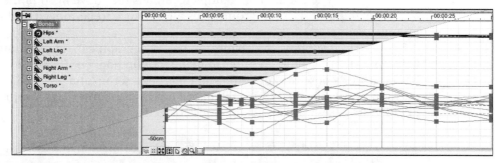

FIGURE 4.13   Data can be presented in either Channel or Timeline format.

The left-hand pane shows the currently selected item or items (select multiple items by shift-clicking them in the PWS). Once an item is deselected, it is removed from the timeline unless it is pinned by clicking the Straight Pin icon at the top-left corner of the Timeline window. When the window is tacked, its contents remain in the timeline and will be visible even after you select a different object.

The right-hand pane indicates the time along the top and presents either a Timeline view or a Channel view of the current data depending on the selection and the toggled states of the buttons along the bottom of the Timeline.

From right to left along the screen they are: Channel view, Timeline view, Scale to Fit, Fit all values, Standard, Move, Scale, and Group (see Figure 4.14).

FIGURE 4.14   The Timeline toggles.

When a single bone or any attribute in a model is selected, all keyframes for that bone are shown in Timeline view, allowing adjustments to the timing of all channel data for a model on any given keyframe. You can toggle into Timeline view to adjust the timing of a keyframe without relation to the values it represents.

The Scale to Fit button zooms the window to show all the information for the currently selected items inside the Timeline window.

By default, the *y*-axis (values) of the Channels window is zoomed to fit the full range of values of the data that is being shown. If you turn off the Fit All Values toggle, you can change the zoom to show a section of the values more closely.

Move in the Timeline window works similarly to any other viewport with the Move tool. Unlike Model windows and other 3D workspaces, the timeline also has a set of scroll bars that make it more akin to a word-processing document (you will find that A:M always presents 2D data in this type of standard window).

Group draws a bounding rectangle in the Timeline window, selecting multiple keys from a single channel or multiple channels that have been pinned. Clicking and dragging also selects a group. This allows keys to be moved and edited as a group.

The *Timeline* view (see Figure 4.15) is a graphical representation of the keyframes that we build in order to make motion happen. Each red block on the bar indicates a pose (or keyframe) that has been set up and gives you a visual indication of the time between each of them. This is a great way to adjust the spacing of your poses until an action reads correctly.

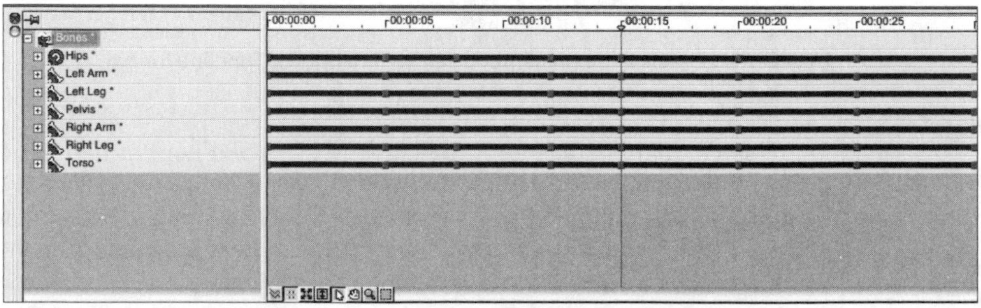

FIGURE 4.15   This view shows the data for the animation created in Timeline mode.

The *Channel* view (see Figure 4.16) represents not only time, but also motion and interpolation between frames. The values for each keyframe are plotted graphically with control points, connected though time by splines. The *x*-axis of the chart indicates time, which is shown at the top of the Timeline window in the same SMTPE code used in the frame number box. The *y*-axis shows the value of the animated properties. The values for your poses will change along time as the graph plots them out. The spline in the graph indicates what the value for a property will be at a given frame.

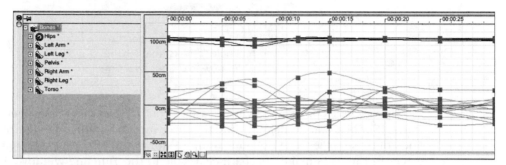

FIGURE 4.16   This shows the data for the animation created in Channel mode.

How the computer decides how a bone or any animated property will change (or move) between the key poses that you set is determined by the *interpolation* of the channel that you create when you animate. Channels default to *spline* interpolation and can be manipulated just like the splines in a model. Bias handles allow the manipulation of gamma and magnitude directly in the Timeline window. As you adjust a curve, you change the way the computer will draw the in-between frames.

All information that is animated generates channel data, which is expressed in these charts. Finding some of that data can be a challenge. In order to bring forward a particular piece of channel data, look to the PWS.

Each item that is changed in an action or choreography is a change from the cache (or default) value of the model or object that was originally created. In the PWS, this information is stored in drivers. Bones, materials, and properties respond to requests like a car, following the driver's instructions for speed, direction, and other attributes.

In A:M, these drivers can be found in the folders (see Figure 4.17) under the shortcut to the original object (both in chor and action.)

A:M uses the concept of the shortcut for animation. When you use a model in an action or a choreography A:M calls this a shortcut, meaning that the original model is only being referenced, not changed. You can use more than one shortcut of the same model in a scene, which allows you to use one character to fill out a crowd.

FIGURE 4.17   The folders under the Shortcut hold "drivers" that tell the properties how to change over time.

The folders represent the various aspects of the object that have been animated. Bones, Splines, and Model Bone are the three most common types of driver folders. Each of these folders can hold one or more storage drivers. Selection of any storage driver in the PWS makes its channels visible in the Timeline window. The storage driver also houses the interpolation settings and end methods for each animateable attribute, which is discussed in the next section.

Storage drivers are a very important concept in A:M. They allow the powerful manipulation of properties based in relationships or expressions, and have many practical and innovative uses. For action, their primary function is to hold the changes that are made to any property. There are properties that do not spawn drivers in the PWS but their use is less complex and rarely requires a driver (such as ease on an action).

KEYFRAME INTERPOLATION

A:M uses four methods to change values between keyframes. Each has its own uses and is set on a driver-by-driver basis.

Spline. The default interpolation between keyframes. This behaves similarly to and obeys the same general rules as the splines that make up models. Often leaving the interpolation as spline produces clean, smooth action that needs little or no adjustment of the individual channels. On some actions, however, the interpolation will benefit a different setting.

0-slope. Enforces a flat peak and valley by locking the gamma parallel to the 0 value of the channel. It is used to smooth out overshoot on channels and to set up looping motion such as walk cycles. The downside of 0-slope is that control points not on a peak or a valley in the channel have the same gamma-locked settings, which can add unwanted adjustments to the spacing of in-betweens our assistant draws for us.

Linear. Draws a straight line from keyframe to keyframe in the channels, allowing for no curve. This makes motion look very robotic and artificial, which is useful when animating robotic and mechanical things. Since the motion is so artificial, this is the least-used type of interpolation.

Hold. Forces the value of a keyframe to remain constant until a new value is encountered. Then it is automatically changed with no intervening motion. This is more useful than it seems. When blocking animation, it helps to focus attention on timing and poses rather than having those masked by interpolation. It is also used sometimes when changing a camera position, making it behave as if it were a cut.

Each driver has its own setting for its default interpolation, located in the PWS next to the name of the driver (see Figure 4.18). There are actually three pull-down menus located under that image, the first and last of which look ghosted out and are for extrapolation methods (which we discuss next) while the center is for the interpolation of the channel in question. Changing the interpolation method affects the entire channel. If you do not want that, change individual points or groups of points to any interpolation method by bringing up the contextual menu for a selected group or single control point in the Channel view and choosing a method from the interpolation method heading.

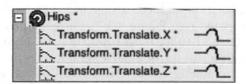

FIGURE 4.18 The three icons indicated here are actually pull-down menus that give access to a channel's interpolation and extrapolation methods.

Pre- and Post-Extrapolation

A:M has a secondary set of methods called *extrapolation methods*. These methods indicate what will happen in an action either *before* or *after* the time that you have defined with keyframes. Again, these are set on each storage driver individually. There are six types of methods:

Hold last. The default. It keeps the value of the last set keyframe for the channel as a constant. This is most commonly used when, after the last keyframe, an object is normally at rest and has no further motion.

Reset. Returns the value to the default value regardless of where it is at the end of the action. This is not to be confused with returning the value to the start of the action. If a keyframe is set that is not at the same values as the original model at the beginning of the action, the reset will snap back to the values of the model, not the first keyframe.

Repeat. Cycles through the action forever. The channel will repeat through all the keys that have been set on it in a loop from the last keyframe back to the first. If the last keyframe is not exactly the same as the first, there may be a pop or jump. Even if they are the same, careful adjustment of gamma (or use of 0-slope) is often needed to smooth out looped motion.

Ping Pong. Cycles back and forth through the action. This could be useful for cyclical action that moves back and forth—swaying grass or the pendulum of a clock, for example.

Accumulate. This method takes the total change across the keyed portion of the channel and offsets the action by the total change in the value before repeating the channel. A channel that translates an object 10 cm over 10 frames would, for example, translate that same object 1,000 cm over 100 frames at a constant rate when using this method. You might use this to make an object roll along at a continuous rate, like a tumbleweed, for instance, as it goes across a desert plain.

Linear. Takes the slope of the channel from the first (or last) two control points and extends it infinitely into the time before or after the keyed portion of an action.

Extrapolation methods are great for extending an animation past what you had anticipated (see Figure 4.19.) For example, you may have a shot to which you need to add 10 seconds. You may have animated some background elements in the shot for just the original length. Rather than having to animate those items to cover the additional time, you could use an extrapolation method to extend the poses you already animated.

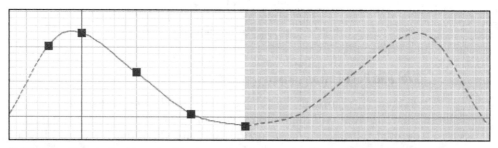

FIGURE 4.19   The dashed lines in this channel are being extended with extrapolation methods.

SUMMARY

We covered a lot of material and moved quickly through it, but by now, you should be comfortable creating skeletal motion in the Action window. You should also be acquainted with the basic principles of animation.

And you created some animation! The hopping sack of flour is a simple exercise in weight and understanding motion. Before you move on to Part II of this book and its intermediate coverage of these topics, try your hand at animating your sack of flour through some other actions. Here is a list of ideas to get you started:

- Walking
- Skipping
- Sneaking
- Falling over
- Walking while sad or tired

See how many actions you can come up with for the sack. Make it express emotion. Don't be afraid to make mistakes. Someone once said, "Every animator has a million bad frames in them." Take this time to get some of them out.

Finally, we took a peek behind the curtain to see the powerful tools that are behind your animation. The channels and timeline can, at first, be a little intimidating, but you don't need to dig into them as you just start out. There will be a time when you need to adjust something and will be glad those channels are there; but they actually have very little to do with what makes animation good. So don't let them overwhelm you too much right now.

PART I SUMMARY

Congratulations; you have finished Part I!

You have become familiar with the interface and conventions of Animation: Master. You then applied the tools to modeling, boning, and finally animating a character. Before you move on to Part II, you should be familiar with all the tools covered here. It will be assumed you know them when we move on.

The discussions in Part I focused on the broadest, most general concepts of 3D animation, and they should carry you through the rest of this book. If there is a concept you don't understand, or a tutorial that you didn't finish, go back over it now and make sure you have it down. Then take a break. See you in Part II.

PUTTING IT TOGETHER

5

CHARACTER MODELING FOR ANIMATION

In This Chapter

- Spline Density and Joints
- Starting a Morgue
- Tutorial: Modeling Legs
- Spline Layout
- Tutorial: Modeling the Face
- Tutorial: Modeling Shoulders
- Modeling a Character

This chapter explores how to apply the A:M modeling tools for making characters that not only look good, but also that *animate* well. It is easy enough to make a good-looking model, but care must be given to the layout of the splines if you want a model to deform well during animation.

We begin by looking at how density affects deformation and cover techniques for creating optimal joint density. We talk about the layout of splines and how they can affect your ability to animate, discussing techniques for splining to achieve muscle tone and other character features. This knowledge is then applied toward the creation of a character.

ON THE CD

All the project files referenced throughout this chapter can be found on the CD-ROM. Copy each project to your hard drive and work along with the tutorials in this chapter.

By the time you finish, you will have a character designed and modeled to animate, an understanding of some common pitfalls of character modeling, and some solutions to help you overcome them.

SPLINE DENSITY AND JOINTS

Few things have as direct an impact on the animateable properties of a model than the density of its splines. This is most evident in a character's joints.

As an example, open the Spline_Density_01 project from the CD-ROM. This project has two models and two actions that could be a character's knee or arm; one is too dense, and one is of a lower, more manageable, density. The control points in both models were auto assigned and CP weights calculated. Looking at the action for each model (see Figures 5.1 through 5.4) the bunching and overlapping in the denser model is evident. Bone and constraint techniques can be used to fix these problems, but the best solution is to avoid the issue in the first place.

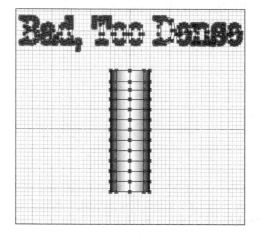

FIGURE 5.1   The density of this model will cause problems when animating.

FIGURE 5.2   This model's more conservative splinage will animate smoother.

There are times—fine details, muscle tone, and other nuances—when heavy spline counts are needed (see Figure 5.5). This trade-off must be made very carefully. Open the Spline_Density_02 project in A:M and look at the "Legs to Compare" model. When building in density, it is important to use as few cross sections or rings as possible, especially at the joints of the character. Adding even one more spline ring at the knee joint can make animating the mesh problematic. Whenever possible, the bias of control points should be adjusted to avoid the addition of splines. Knowing this, you can build any style of character from the most cartoony to one bulging with realism, and you can do it with the appropriate level of density.

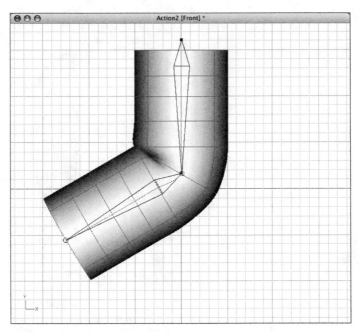

FIGURE 5.3   The bunching and overlapping mesh is a direct result of the modeling.

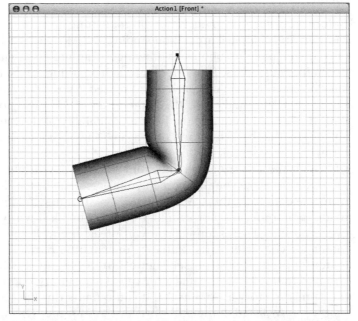

FIGURE 5.4   The lighter the mesh, the less work it will be to animate.

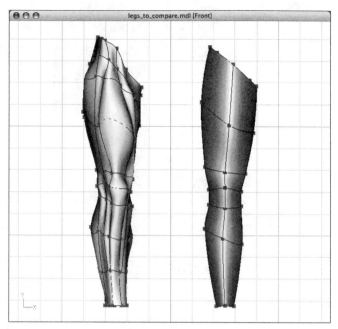

FIGURE 5.5 Design will dictate the necessary spline density.

STARTING A MORGUE

Before you get into modeling is a good time to introduce the concept of the Morgue. In traditional animation studios, the Morgue is a flat file storage of reference material, either photos or drawings, from projects that are long-completed or preliminary exercises. The concept is that if anything can be of even a little bit of use later on, then it should be saved and reused if possible. With 3D, this concept can save a lot of time and effort. If you model a hand at some point, and you are happy with the spline layout and the basic animatability of the hand, then you should be able to use that hand over and over again. The most effective way of doing this is to set up a library specifically for the task.

Open the Library panel and from the pull-down select My Library. This will force A:M to place your Morgue in your personal library, keeping its data separate from the data from the A:M CD-ROM. Create a new folder on the Model tab and name it Morgue. Inside this folder you can break down your model parts however you like. For example, you can break them down by the type of part—a folder for character parts, a folder for machine parts, a folder for set pieces, a folder for props, and so on(see Figure 5.6). After you add files to this Morgue, you will find that A:M has created a file called My Library.lbr in the Libraries folder (in the same directory as A:M itself). If you rename this file Morgue.lbr, you will find that it is now listed in the pull-down list as Morgue. This will allow you to isolate just the files for the Morgue (and frees up My Library for the creation of a new library, perhaps for a project). As you progress through the tutorials in this chapter, you are instructed to put parts into your Morgue; and later when you build a character, we will look at how a fully stocked Morgue can really speed the process of creating new models. This mentality of reusability is at the core of A:M.

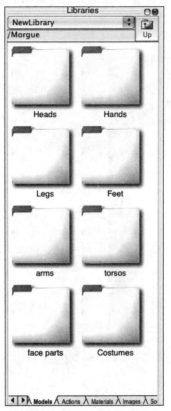

FIGURE 5.6   Organize your Morgue as you see fit. As an example, you might choose to organize by part.

TUTORIAL   MODELING LEGS

Like most limbs, legs are simple tubes. They can be shaped and tweaked to create any desired shape. The most basic example of a leg remains a tube (see Figure 5.7). Most of the time, this is fine for cartoon characters and even for pants on more detailed characters. Making this leg is as simple as lathing.

Toon Leg

First, draw a seven-point spline with the Add tool. This will be the basis for the lathe. Place two of the points at the top of the spline, three in the middle, and two at the bottom (see Figure 5.8). Since this leg will remain a basic tube, you can reduce the lathe settings to produce a lower resolution.

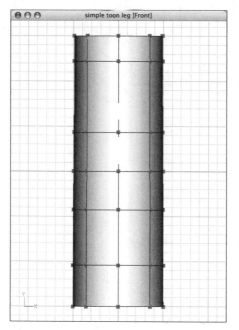

FIGURE 5.7   The most simple leg that can be modeled.

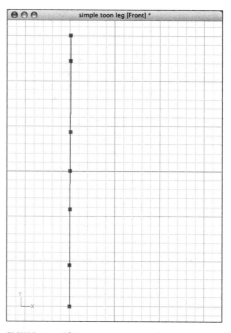

FIGURE 5.8   This seven-point spline describes the parts of the leg.

Open the Options panel by selecting Options from the Tools menu. Click the Modeling tab and note the lathe cross sections option in the Modeling mode group (see Figure 5.9). This number sets the density of splines that the Lathe tool will produce. In most cases, a setting of 8 is fine, but for your simple leg, it could be more density than you need. Change the setting to 4, and click OK.

You can also call up the lathe settings by holding down the Shift key while clicking the Lathe button. Many tools in A:M allow you to access the settings they use this way.

Back in the model window, select any point along the spline and click the Lathe button (or use the L keyboard shortcut). The resulting tube makes a fine leg. Note the extra density at each end and the knee.

The splines at the knee will ensure that the leg maintains its volume when animated, while the extra splines at the top and bottom prepare the splines to be stitched into a hip or ankle respectively. Go ahead and save this model to your

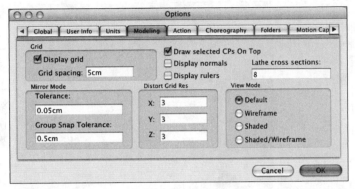

FIGURE 5.9   The cross sections option controls the density of the Lathe tool.

hard drive (start a directory for your library of models not associated with any given project) and then add it to your Morgue.

Most humanoid legs begin from this point. Legs that are more detailed are merely a further step along this process.

Semirealistic Leg

A slightly more complex leg might indicate the thigh and calf muscles and have some variation at the knees to indicate the location and direction of that joint. For this variation, your starting point is the same. A simple seven-point spline, but a more detailed lathe setting of 6 will give you the splines needed to shape the leg. Open the Options panel from the menu or use the shortcut (Cmd+P on the Mac; Ctrl+P on a PC). The Modeling tab should still be forward. If it isn't, click it to bring it forward. Change the lathe settings to 6 and click OK. Back in the Modeling window, click any control point and lathe the spline (see Figure 5.10).

Start by selecting the spline ring that defines the wide part of the thigh muscles. This ring will define the muscle masses on either side of the thigh, which are offset at an angle higher on the outside of the leg than on the inside. Bring up the rotate manipulator (R) and hold down the 2 on the keyboard while rotating the selection around the z-axis. This will skew the ring into position, while keeping the shape consistent in the y-axis. The same can be done to the top ring of splines. Pull out the CPs on the side of the thigh until you have a shape similar to Figure 5.11

The same technique can be applied to the calf splines. Skew them the same direction as the thigh. If they are too close to the ankle, they may also need to be translated up and scaled a bit (Figure 5.12).

Now, it's just a matter of tweaking the shape of the knee splines. From the front view, this is a presentable leg, but from the side view (see Figure 5.13) there is still a lot of work to be done. The majority of it is just pulling and pushing CPs until the shapes look right (see Figure 5.14). There are no hard and fast rules for what works and what doesn't at this stage; your own skill and aesthetic taste

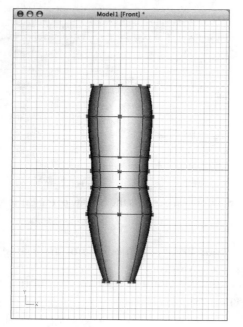

FIGURE 5.10 A simple lathed tube can be shaped to build definition.

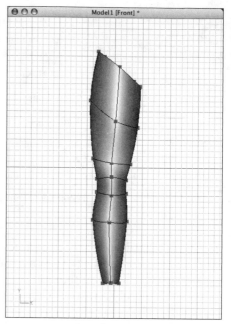

FIGURE 5.11 The thigh masses are pulled out after skewing the spline rings.

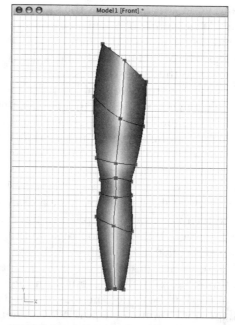

FIGURE 5.12 Adjusting the calf in the same manner as the thigh brings us closer to the desired results.

must guide you. When you are satisfied with the overall shape and proportions of the leg save it out and into your Morgue.

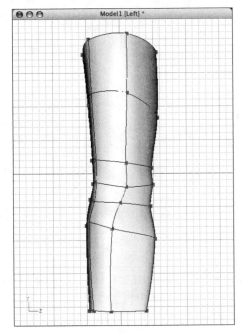

FIGURE 5.13   From the side view things are still a bit flat.

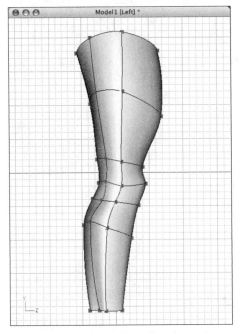

FIGURE 5.14   After tweaking the shape, it resembles a leg.

Realistically Muscled Leg

The legs you have looked at so far are simple, lack a lot of definition, and require little or no tweaking of CP bias to make them work. The last leg that you work on has more defined muscles (see Figure 5.15) and will need bias adjustments to form the muscles without resorting to excessive splinage.

Start with a 10-point spline roughly shaped like a leg (see Figure 5.16), and lathe it with a setting of 6. This will provide most of the density that you will need and allows you to decide where you need to stitch in more. It is almost always better to start out with less density and work your way into the details of a model. Like the previous leg, start by shaping the front view to define the muscle tone. It may help to hide the splines on the back of the leg while doing this, or to work in Shaded mode.

Once the rough shape is there, it is time to think about where to add density to bring out the details. Focus on the front of the leg, and see how the main thigh masses will need additional splines if you are to pull them out from the leg.

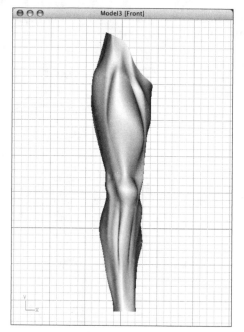

FIGURE 5.15 A more complex leg requires bias adjustments.

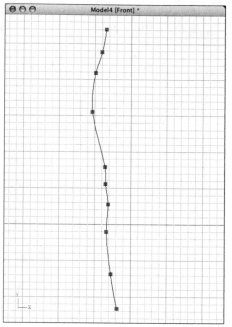

FIGURE 5.16 More CPs are needed to build definition.

Rotate the leg to a position where you can see what is going on. For each spline ring, stitch in a CP, starting at the top of the leg and working your way down. Do this for each side of the knee (see Figure 5.17). These two splines add enough density on the front of the legs, but the sides and the back will also need attention if they are to hold up. One additional spline down the leg in the left view will help flatten the front-to-back transition (see Figure 5.18). Again, rotate the view so you can clearly see where you are working, and stitch in the new spline.

Looking at the back view of the leg, you will need additional splines to assist with shaping the calf muscles. One additional spline down the middle of the leg should do the job. Add in the spline and do the needed shaping of the mesh (see Figure 5.19).

With this spline, your leg's density is in good shape. With the density in place, you start the process of sculpting the shapes. In this way, the A:M modeling tools are very appealing to the artistic mindset. Creating a surface is a matter of just grabbing a point and moving it until the shape is correct. There is certainly no rush if you are after quality, but speed comes with time. The best advice this book or anyone can offer you as you learn the tools is to take your time with them. The focus for the shaping portion is to get the splines to flow as close as you can to the actual muscles that you are trying to emulate. The flow of the splines is very important. Look at Figure 5.20, and see how the splines have been adjusted.

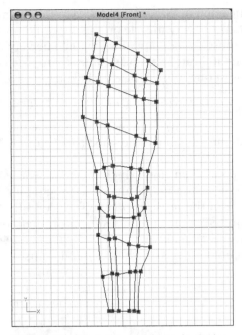

FIGURE 5.17   Stitch in two splines down the front of the leg.

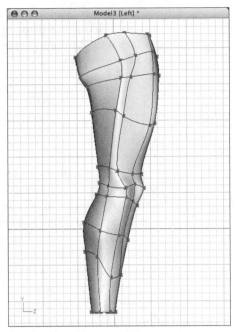

FIGURE 5.18   Additional splines need to be added to the side of the leg.

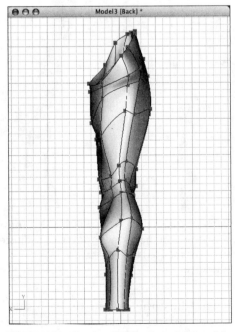

FIGURE 5.19   The back of the leg also needs a little more density.

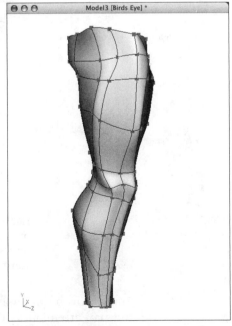

FIGURE 5.20   The splines should flow along with the surface.

In some cases, this might be enough, but take it one step further and develop the muscle masses using bias. Almost every muscle on this leg could use some form of bias adjustment to make the muscle tone stand out. It would be very dry and not to the point to list each point and indicate exact bias values to duplicate the results of the example. Instead, we look at one muscle mass and explain the process.

In order to adjust the bias, you need to be certain that the Show Bias Handles toggle is on.

Hide the back of the leg. You will be working with the muscle mass above the knee. Starting with the two CPs directly above the knee (see Figure 5.21), look at the magnitude.

This area needs to be more flat than not, which means that the magnitude values need to be relatively tame. If the magnitudes are much over 150, lower them. In order to pull the shape of the muscles off the surface of the rest of the leg, the gamma needs to be adjusted to lift the splines (or push them down as the case may be). Again, because this is a relatively flat area, a gamma of 40 or 50 degrees will probably do the job. Hold down the Shift key and adjust the bias until you are happy with the shape of the muscle mass (see Figure 5.22).

Move up to the next CPs along these splines (see Figure 5.23). This is one of the more prominent muscles on the thigh, so it will need to be pulled up from the thigh a good deal.

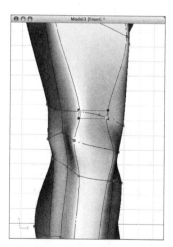

FIGURE 5.21   Start your adjustments at these two points.

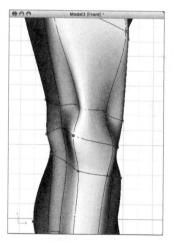

FIGURE 5.22   After adjusting the magnitude and gamma of the points the muscle has started to come up off the knee.

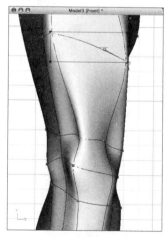

FIGURE 5.23   These points are next to be adjusted.

Start with the gamma this time. Adjust the gamma on each side of the muscle and pay attention to the way the splines move. Change views to bird's-eye and watch the direction the gamma adjusts the flow of the spline. Be sure that it comes up out of the leg rather than pushing it back into it. Depending on your mesh, a gamma value of 60 or 70 degrees might do the job (see Figure 5.24).

The extra density you added earlier to the leg will keep these adjustments from wreaking havoc with the sides of the leg. You could (and indeed might want to, at some point on the leg) peak the points you are working with and adjust the bias in and out of the point individually to create the best curve on both sides of the CP.

The muscle has likely not pulled far enough from the thigh with only the use of gamma, so your next step is to increase the magnitude. The muscle should be larger in the center of the leg than it is on the inside of it, so keep that in mind and give the CP toward the inside of the leg a higher magnitude. On the example leg, a magnitude of 250 on the inside and 130 on the outside works out well.

This process continues up the leg to the next set of control points, but on a lesser scale as the muscle should be flattening out to tie into the hips here. Remember, the hips will likely need to be animated later, so to avoid problems only adjust the magnitude on the next couple of rings. Your leg might now resemble Figure 5.25.

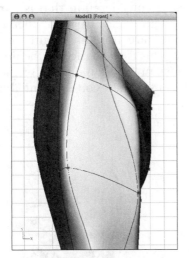

FIGURE 5.24   After adjusting the gamma on the second set of points, the muscle is pulled up off the leg.

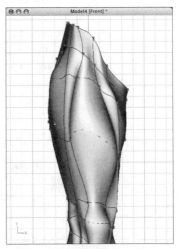

FIGURE 5.25   The thigh has more definition to it after careful bias adjustment.

ON THE CD

This is simply repeated for each muscle grouping on the leg. As you work, you will likely have to adjust the bias for the muscles you have already worked on to make the model work as a whole. Since space here is limited and you still need to cover many more techniques, it is left to you as an exercise to finish this leg. If you need help, examine the muscled leg model on the CD-ROM. This leg is still quite dense and will require some tricks to make it animate smoothly, but using bias instead of adding splines reduces the amount of work that it will take. Once you have finished the leg, save it into your Morgue and move on to other body parts.

These same techniques work for all appendages. The detail needed dictates the density of the splines, but in any event, the density should be kept as low as possible.

SPLINE LAYOUT

The shape of the model, in part, dictates the layout of splines across its surface. There is a wide range of spline solutions that will achieve the same basic surface. Some spline solutions will create better results than others, but there are very few rules as to what makes one layout better than another. Nevertheless, there are a number of successful layouts that solve particular problems elegantly.

Faces can be quite a challenge to model accurately, while remaining easy to animate. Yet, this is usually one of the first things the beginning user of A:M attempts to model. While there are as many methods for modeling the face and head as there are A:M users, a common solution that works well is the *concentric mask paradigm.*

The concentric mask paradigm is based on the layout of the features of the face and how they need to be animated, a consideration that is part of what makes it such a popular solution. Look at Figure 5.26. This simplified illustration of a face has a series of rings laid over it: one starts from the mouth, one from the eye, and one encompasses the whole face. This is the basic idea behind the concentric mask paradigm. The holes in the face mesh are the basis for the layout of the splines. This arrangement also makes sense when you examine the layout of the muscles in the face (see Figure 5.27).

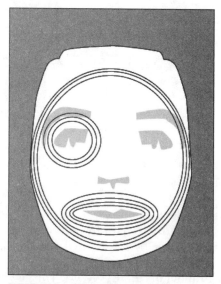

FIGURE 5.26 Concentric rings mimic the muscles in the face and aid in animation.

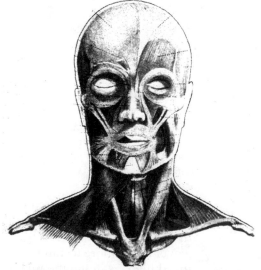

FIGURE 5.27 When building models, referring to real anatomy can be a big help.

TUTORIAL   MODELING THE FACE

Before attempting to model a photorealistic version of your neighbor, it is a good idea to start on something simple. Figure 5.28 shows the model that you should end up with at the end of this tutorial. As you can see, it is very simple (little more than a mask), but it shows all the techniques that are used in modeling faces.

Open a new model and get started. Where you begin the model is a matter of preference, but with the concentric mask paradigm, it makes sense to start from either the mouth or the eyes and work outward.

The mouth can quickly be started with the Lathe tool. Draw a six-point spline in the front view as in Figure 5.29. This shape will be lathed to form the mouth and part of the face. Set the lathe cross sections to 8 (shift-click the Lathe button to access the lathe settings), select any point on the spline, and lathe it.

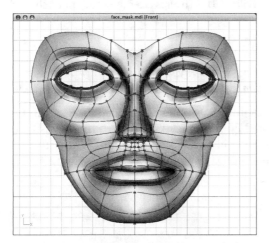

FIGURE 5.28   You will be building this simple face.

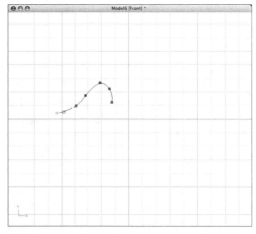

FIGURE 5.29   Lathing this spline forms all the geometry needed for the mouth.

Select the entire shape and bring up the Rotate Manipulator (shortcut key R). Rotate the shape 90 degrees in the *x*-axis (it may be easiest to do this by typing directly into the Manipulator Properties box or the Properties panel). Turn on the *Mirror Mode* toggle and pull the corners of one side of the shape out. Be careful that you select only one-half of the model when in mirrored mode, as it can give unexpected results otherwise. As you manipulate the points in the model, you should see the points on the opposite side follow. This is because the surface was created with the Lathe tool on the default axis, which places the points symmetrically. Switch to a side view and pull the same corner back in the *z*-axis. It should already look a lot like a mouth (see Figure 5.30).

Now it is a simple matter of pushing the lips into shape (see Figure 5.31). Once you have the lips in good shape, turn the Mirror mode tool off.

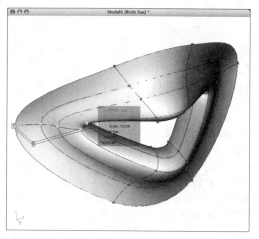

FIGURE 5.30 Using Mirror mode, you can move both sides of an object at the same time.

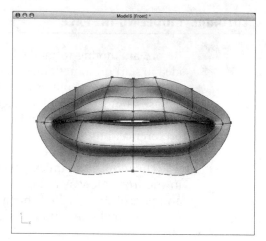

FIGURE 5.31 The lips after they have been shaped.

 It is important to always turn off Mirror mode when you are finished working with it because it can cause trouble when selecting areas that span both halves of the model.

The eye begins the same way as the mouth. Draw a four-point spline (see Figure 5.32) and lathe it with eight cross sections. Rotate this 90 degrees in the *x*-axis, and move it into position on one side of the face. In the same way that the mouth was shaped, merely tweak the rings until they resemble an eye socket (see Figure 5.33).

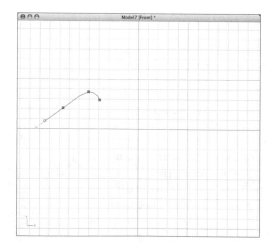

FIGURE 5.32 The eye will be lathed from this spline.

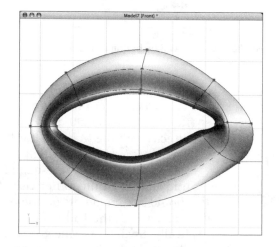

FIGURE 5.33 The finished eye socket.

Move the eye into a position relative to the mouth and roll up your sleeves for a real challenge. Switch to a side view and start by drawing the profile of the nose (see Figure 5.34). Switch to the front view and make sure that the spline you drew is at zero in the *x*-axis.

Select the entire spline for the nose and extrude it. This will, by default, put the extrusion –10 pixels in the *y*-axis. Move the new group up (using Shift+⑦ will move the selection 10 pixels up on the screen) and to the left to start building the nose mesh. Now extrude it a second time. This time the extrusion should automatically be placed to the left the same distance and direction you manually placed the first (see Figure 5.35).

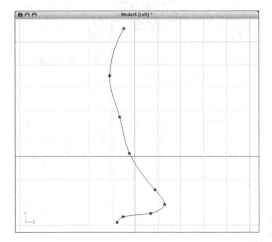

FIGURE 5.34   The nose begins with the profile.

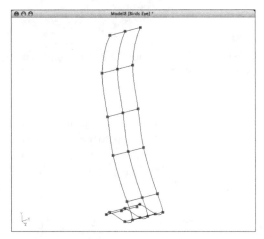

FIGURE 5.35   Extrude the spline twice to start building mesh.

Shape these three splines to look roughly like the bridge and tip of a nose. There are no formulas to follow and no shortcuts to take at this step. Once you have a decent shape, it is time to start working on the nostril (see Figure 5.36).

The nostril is simply a hole that goes up into the nose. Our mesh at this point is solid, and any further extrusions would also be solid. The most elegant solution for making a hole is to create a loop similar to a cursive "l" in which all the points run along the same spline. How this spline gets plotted into the nose is very important. First, clear out some of the splines under the nose to make connections easier and clearer. Imagine this as the nose on your face. Trace a line down the bridge of your nose, across the tip, and down to your nostril. When you reach the nostril, trace the outside edge of the nostril: first going down toward the mouth, out to the side of the nose, then back around and across the bottom of the nose to the opposite nostril, where the same path back up the bridge of the nose is mirrored. Now look at our spline nose again. Figure 5.37 shows this path traced onto the nose you are modeling. Notice the traced line crosses over itself and describes a loop around the nostril. Arrows have been drawn in to indicate the flow of the spline.

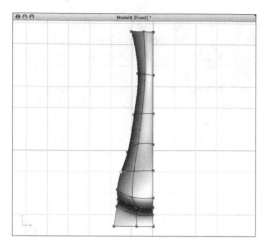

FIGURE 5.36 Once the nose shape in roughed in, start on the nostrils.

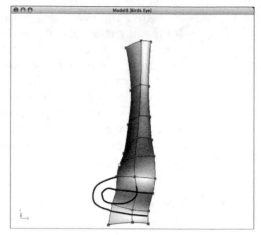

FIGURE 5.37 Tracing out splines before you stitch them in is often helpful.

With the plan for your spline in place, you still need to decide how to implement it. Right now, the spline from the bridge of the nose runs down and toward the mouth. You want it to curve back in. In order to do this, break the spline across that patch (see Figure 5.38).

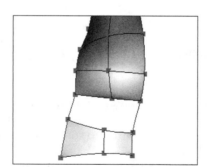

FIGURE 5.38 Start by breaking the spline you need to loop around the nostril.

This sets you up to stitch in the nostril loop. Activate the Add tool and continue the spline from the bridge of the nose by clicking the end point of that spline. Now stitch the loop in place using Figure 5.39 as a guide.

Now you have a loop but you also have some splines that run across and close off parts of the nostril. Simply break those splines to make the inside of the loop a hole in the surface (see Figure 5.40). This hole can later be extruded back into the head.

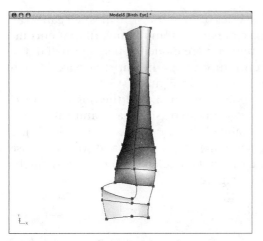

FIGURE 5.39   Stitch the loop into the nose, being sure to come back around across the same point you started from.

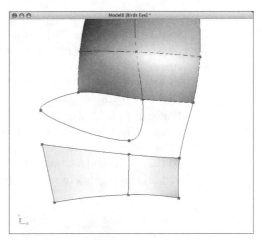

FIGURE 5.40   The nostril is made by creating a hole in the bottom of the nose.

Now tie the nostril into the splines that continue down the center of the nose. When you are finished you will have something similar to Figure 5.41. Notice that you have a hole here, due to the fact that you have two areas where separate concentric rings will meet. The bottom spline will be a concentric ring around the mouth. When two concentric rings meet, there will be an area that can only be closed by a five-point patch. This is true of almost every joint on a character's body and certainly in several places on the face. Go ahead and close the five-point areas now with the Five-Point Patch tool (see Figure 5.42).

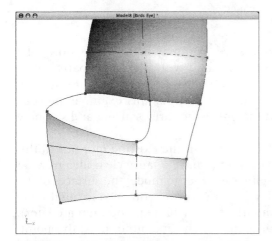

FIGURE 5.41   After you stitch the nostril back into the splines of the nose, you still have some holes.

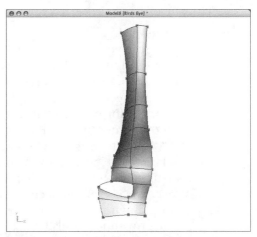

FIGURE 5.42   Those holes are closed simply with the use of the Five-Point Patch tool.

The nostrils form fleshy wings on the sides of the nose. The most elegant way to create these are with concentric loops emanating from the nostril that encompasses both halves of the nose (even though you are modeling just one-half of the nose, you need to consider the spline continuity across the entire surface). Stitch in a new spline and shape it to form the wings, as in Figure 5.43.

To finish the nose, simply select the points that make up the nostril and extrude them. While it is still selected, nudge the extrusion back and inside the head. When you are satisfied with the shape of the nose, it is time to tie all the various parts of the mask together. If it is not already, position and scale the nose so that it fits in place with the mouth and eye you modeled earlier. Start by stitching together any obvious connections (see Figure 5.44).

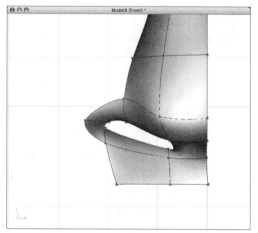

FIGURE 5.43   Shape the wing of the nose to round out the nostril.

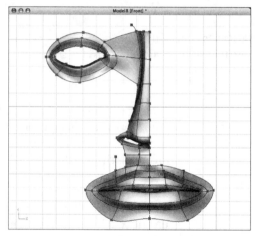

FIGURE 5.44   Start by connecting any obvious splines.

How you proceed is a matter of preference. You may prefer to lay down the spline ring that will encompass the entire face and work the other parts out to meet it, or you might prefer to flesh out the connections and build out until you can connect the outer ring. Both are valid methods. For this example, proceed with the former. Draw a spline around the entire face area starting and stopping on the centerline (see Figure 5.45).

Now stitch the obvious spline connections from the existing face out to this spline (see Figure 5.46). At this point you should have a fairly clear idea of what areas in the mask area will need more splines in order to model the surfaces of the face. The cheek will need an additional spline or two, and you need to build some rings down from the nose under the mouth (these will help you animate later). The brow line will also need a couple of splines to give it definition. At this point,

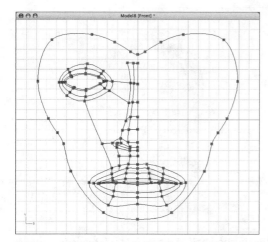

FIGURE 5.45   Lay down the final ring for the face first.

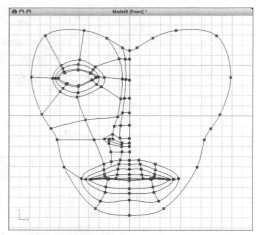

FIGURE 5.46   Stitch the existing parts of the face out to the last ring.

however, the process is one of adding a spline and sculpting the shapes of the face. Use the spline layout in Figure 5.47 as a guide, and Figure 5.48 as a reference to the shapes you are trying to build.

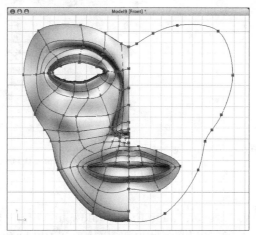

FIGURE 5.47   Use this as a guide for stitching in the necessary splines for your face.

From here, a simple copy/flip/attach will give you the finished mask. Start by selecting and deleting the half of the mouth that is not part of the finished half of the mask. Be careful not to delete the center spline. This will leave behind splines that join the top lip and the bottom lip. Go through each spline and break that stray connection. The result should look like Figure 5.49

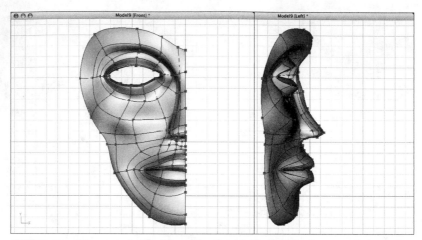

FIGURE 5.48 A front and side view of the finished half of the face as reference for the shapes.

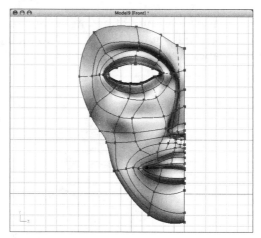

FIGURE 5.49 Start by cleaning up the model into one half.

Now center and align the middle spline of the face on the 0 point of the *x*-axis. Click any part of the spline at the top of the face and press the , (comma) key to select that spline. Notice that the selection is just the top half. The portion of the centerline from the bottom lip down is not selected because that is not a connected spline. Without deselecting anything, hold down the Shift key and click anywhere along the lower half of the center spline. Note that the bounding box should expand to include the point you clicked nearest, as the Shift key has added to your selection. Now press the , (comma) key again and notice that the selection automatically adds the remainder of the spline. Bring up the Scale Manipulator with the S keyboard shortcut (or click the Scale Mode button). If the Manipulator Properties Widget is not showing, toggle it on. Directly in the Manipulator Properties Widget set the *x* pivot to 0, then scale the selection down to 0 in the *x*-axis. This will place the selected spline exactly on the axis. Without deselecting anything, press the / (backslash) key. This will select the entire connected set of splines (in your case the entire model). With this selection made, simply bring up the contextual menu for the group (right-click or control-click inside the bounding box for the selection) and choose Copy/Flip/Attach from the menu. The result should be a full mask, as in Figure 5.50.

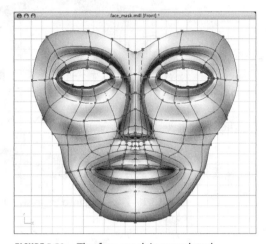

FIGURE 5.50   The face mask is completed.

If your first attempt doesn't look like the example, don't panic. Modeling faces takes time and patience. If you stick with it and practice your splining, you will get the hang of it in no time at all. Once you have a face that you like, save it and add it to your Morgue.

TUTORIAL **MODELING SHOULDERS**

Faces lead to heads, heads lead to bodies, and bodies lead to frustration when you are trying to figure out how to model shoulders that will animate.

There are two basic approaches to shoulders: bring the arm rings into the shoulders, and take the chest splines out onto the arms.

Let's look at both and how they are modeled, as well as the pros and cons of each.

Simple Shoulders

The ring into torso shoulder (see Figure 5.51) is primarily used on clothing and very simple characters where muscle tone is not needed. The major benefit to this method of building shoulders is the ease of creating it. The T-tube you built in Chapter 2 has all the basic techniques that are used to build this shoulder. Rigging and animating this style of shoulder is also a relatively simple affair.

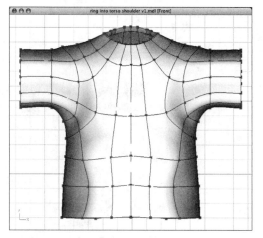

FIGURE 5.51   The ring into torso shoulder is the easiest to model.

However, the lack of detail and the way the mesh runs makes this shoulder unsuitable for musculature. If your character design requires accurate anatomy or super heroic proportions, a more complex shoulder might be needed.

Building this shoulder starts with three lathed shapes.

For the arm, draw a four-point spline horizontally on one side of the y-axis and lathe a horizontal tube (see Figure 5.52). Remember to adjust your pivot. If you want to add thickness to this model, do it here before you lathe the tube.

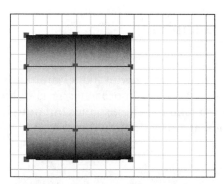

FIGURE 5.52   The arm is a simple lathed shape.

The neck and abdomen are also simple lathe shapes. You could lathe them as a unit, but the amount of work that will be done to them makes it easier to lathe them separately now and stitch them together later (see figure 5.53).

Much like the two tubes covered in Chapter 2, the most straightforward connections are made first. The top three splines on the arm tie easily to the neck, and the bottom three tie to the abdomen (see Figure 5.54).

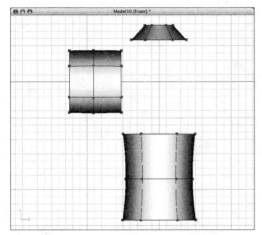

FIGURE 5.53   The neck and abdomen are the last of your lathed building blocks.

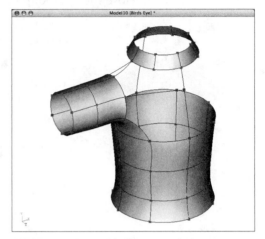

FIGURE 5.54   Start with the most obvious connections first.

The centerline between the neck and abdomen pieces can be attached. With the center point of the arm easily connecting to the centerline, leave two five-point holes in the torso (see Figure 5.55).

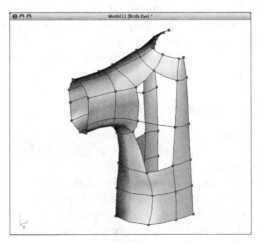

FIGURE 5.55   Connecting the neck and abdomen sections leaves five-point holes.

You could use the Five-Point Patch tool to close these holes and be done with it, but that might cause some problems with animation later, primarily because the five point areas lie close to the flexible area of the arm. Additional density down the arm, into the neck, and down the torso will make this shoulder animate better. Stitch in a spline down the front of the torso and down the front of the arm. Then do the same for the back of the model. With this density added, you can close the five-point patches (see Figure 5.56).

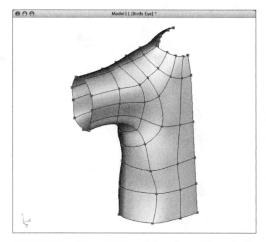

FIGURE 5.56 The additional density will head off many problems when animating.

From this point, it is simply a matter of shaping the mesh to your needs. It could be shaped to be used as a short-sleeved shirt, or with a little bias tweaking, it could make a fairly simple torso. Either way, use the same procedures you used on the face mask and the flour sack to copy/flip/attach your half to make a whole torso. When you are pleased with its shape and layout, save it into your Morgue. It might even be a good idea to develop the shapes a bit and make two variations for your Morgue.

Semirealistic Shoulder

The muscle into arm shoulder is more complicated to model but more accurate (see Figure 5.57). The benefit of this layout is the detail that it gives to a character and the accurate muscle tone that it affords.

The downside of more complex spline layouts is the difficulty in modeling. In order to get the same amount of ease in animation and setup, much more care must be given to the layout of the splines.

At its most basic level, the muscle into arm layout is the same as the ring layout already discussed (see Figure 5.58). But here the rings run with the underlying muscle structure rather than parallel to one another.

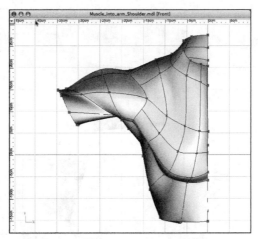

FIGURE 5.57   More detailed anatomy requires a different approach.

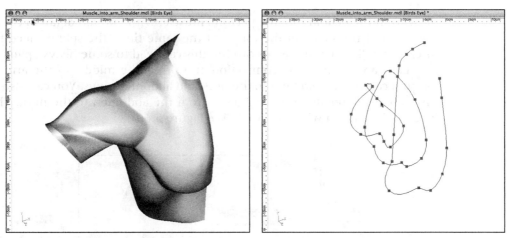

FIGURE 5.58   Even though the modeling looks very dissimilar, the muscle layout is based on rings as well.

The basic starting point for this shoulder is the same as before: three lathed tubes. The arm and neck tubes are the same as before, but for the abdomen, all that is needed is a single ring. So, lathe a two-point spline for the abdomen and delete the top ring. You should now have a starting point similar to the previous example (see Figure 5.59).

Rather than simply make the obvious connections and proceed to shape the mesh as you did before, some consideration needs to be given to routing the splines to achieve muscle tone and maintain animateablilty. The splines need to

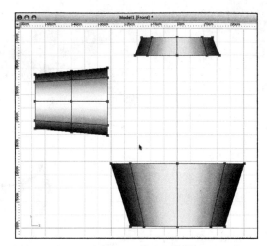

FIGURE 5.59   As before, a simple collection of lathe shapes starts you out.

flow from the deltoid into the pectoral muscle, with enough detail to cut the pectoral out of the shape of the torso. At the same time, the splines need to retain their flexibility. If you are not careful, this can lead to some heavy splinage.

Let's approach it one connection at a time. The middle of the arm top and bottom can connect straight to the neck and abdomen rings. You can also connect the centerline points, front and back, from the abdomen to the neck. This gives you a wire cage in which to work (see Figure 5.60).

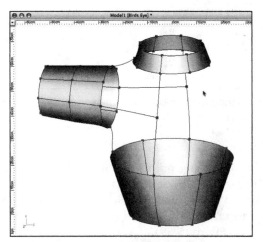

FIGURE 5.60   The middle points of the arms and body connect to make a cage.

While you work on the front, hide the back half of the model. You need at least two splines to build the definition of the pectoral muscles, and those splines need to run into the deltoid muscle. Select and extrude the two points on the arm tube center and down that are not connected. This makes a ribbon of splines out from the arm that we can shape into the pectorals. Add two points to the spline on the centerline, and connect the pectoral ribbon to them. You should now have something like Figure 5.61.

Before moving on, take time to sculpt what you have into a more finished shape. This may require that you pull the center spline on the front of the arm shape down, easing its transition into the pectoral. This move, unfortunately, also flattens the shape of the arm and makes the shoulder joint questionable for animation (see Figure 5.62).

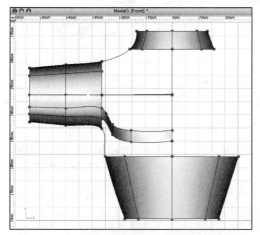

FIGURE 5.61   A ribbon of extruded CPs gives the mesh needed to define the pectoral muscle.

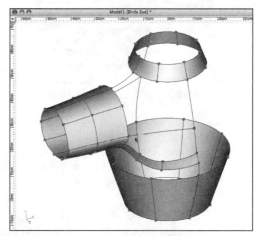

FIGURE 5.62   Some modeling to make muscle shapes work can make the model questionable for animation.

To counter this, the last unattached spline on the arm tube needs to be pulled forward and down. This spline would otherwise have connected to the neck, but that would disturb the muscles, so continue it to the centerline instead. After another round of shaping, you will have something similar to Figure 5.63.

While this is better, it lacks definition in the neck area. The pectoral is also a little flat. These symptoms tell you that the model needs more definition. Dragging that definition all the way into the arm can make other problems when modeling the elbows and hands. So, look to hooks to add definition without continuing the density. The spline on the side of the neck can continue down the torso and hook into the ring that forms the top of the deltoid. This may cause issues when animating but can be fixed with a minimal amount of effort, so the trade-off works. A third spline to define the front of the pectoral muscle would be easy enough to stitch into the mesh. You can hook this new spline into the deltoid with no worry about animation problems. You may as well connect the remaining pectoral spline up into the neck and down to the abdomen to fill out the torso. After a little more tweaking, you should have something similar to Figure 5.64.

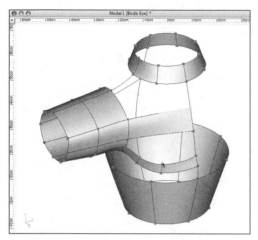

FIGURE 5.63 Adjusting the splines to maintain animation.

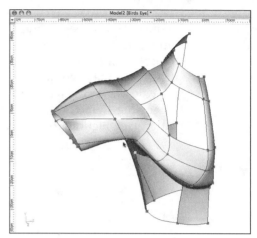

FIGURE 5.64 Looking much better, this mesh will still animate well.

You have two five-point areas left on the front of the mesh that you could close up, but before you do, look to see if there are any outstanding problems with shape or animateability. Looking to the serratus muscle, under the arm at the side of the body as it goes back, the taper into the abdomen is too flat to be convincing and a five-point patch this large here will almost certainly lead to trouble when you set this torso up for animation. Additional density is needed again.

You have the option of running a spline around the torso; that would work, but before you do that, look to see if the added density can aid the shape anywhere else in the model. The pectoral could use additional shaping at the bottom, and at the same time, the remaining five-point patch on the neck could be made smaller. All three of these tasks can be handled with the addition of one spline. Think about its placement for a moment. In order to bisect both the five-point patches and add definition to the pectoral, the most likely way to add in your new spline is diagonally up from the side of the torso to the neck. This has been indicated in Figure 5.65.

Following your guide, stitch in a spline. After closing the five-point areas that remain—and minor additional tweaking—you should have something similar to Figure 5.66.

Now that the front of the mesh is in good order, unhide the back. You will want to be able to see the front as you work on the back of the mesh to get proportions correct and to maintain your spline continuity. You don't, however, want the front getting in your way, so select the back half of the model and lock the CPs by clicking the Lock button. Begin by shaping the mesh that is already in place to more closely match the front of the model.

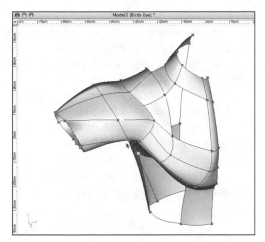

FIGURE 5.65   Adding a spline along this path will solve three problems at once.

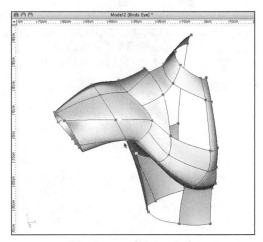

FIGURE 5.66   The front of the mesh completed.

The back is simpler in many respects, as it is made of larger muscle masses than the chest. This allows a simpler geometry overall to achieve good effect. The latissimus dorsi and trapezius muscles predominate the back. The latissimus dorsi (lats) muscle forms the "wing" shape under the arm and the trapezius covers from the back of the neck to the deltoid muscles, tapering down to the spine. The spline on the arm that would easily route up into the neck then, in this case, will serve better defining the trapezius muscle. Continue it across to the middle of the back. The same can be done for the other two splines on the arm. With a little shaping, you will have something similar to Figure 5.67.

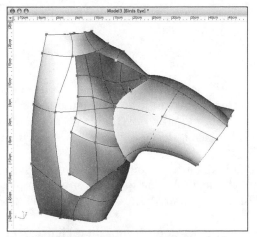

FIGURE 5.67   The initial stages of the back roughs in the basic muscle structures.

This leaves broad areas of flat mesh across the back, but more density is needed to pull out the shapes. We can continue the spline on the side of the torso up and to the neck, similar to the way it was stitched in on the chest (see Figure 5.68). This continues the spline nicely, gives density where it is needed, and will help when you are trying to animate the torso as it twists.

The two main issues with this back now lay in the lack of definition on the lats and the large six-point hole next to the spine. There are no tools to close a six-point hole, so additional splines will be needed. You can break the six-point hole up into a four-point patch and a five-point hole that can be closed easily. At the same time, though, you should be looking to address the definition issue with the lats. Never add splines without first considering all the purposes they may serve. After closing up the five-point patches and doing some tweaking you should have something similar to Figure 5.69.

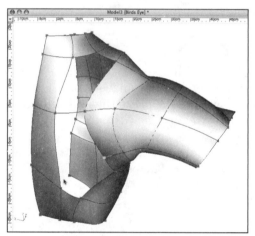

FIGURE 5.68 Additional density can be added by continuing the spline from the front of the mesh.

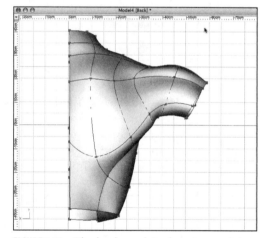

FIGURE 5.69 The back mesh is almost complete.

The mesh at this stage is decent, would even animate well, but it could use some further definition in the deltoid muscle. The easiest way to accomplish this is to simply extrude the ring that leads down toward the arm. Keep it close to the deltoid and scale it down a little bit, just to cut some definition into the arm (see Figure 5.70).

Extrude the arm a couple more times just to give the start of an arm.

Unlock the mesh. The splining is now complete, and all that remains is to shape the mesh until you are happy with the forms. Then copy/flip/attach it to complete the torso model.

If your model doesn't look like Figure 5.71, don't worry. It takes time and practice to model, and shoulders are the most difficult area of a character to get right. Shoulders are complex, but once mastered, there is nothing you can't take on. Once you are happy with your shoulder, save it into your Morgue. After all that work, you will most certainly want to use it again.

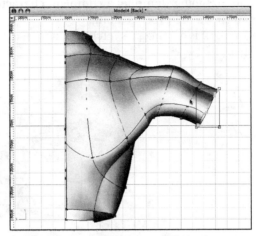

FIGURE 5.70 Extruding the arm a little gives us a spline to work with for the deltoid.

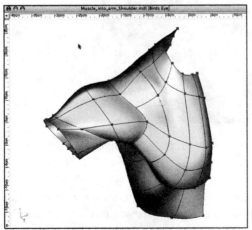
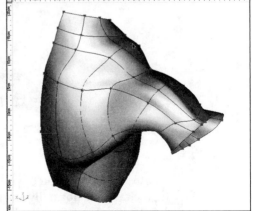

FIGURE 5.71 The finished shoulder.

MODELING A CHARACTER

Modeling a full character is merely an application of all the various methods that you have learned from modeling pieces. In fact, characters are often started from pieces of other characters or particularly good modeling experiments. Never throw away your work. You never know when you will need a piece of mesh. Also, look to the CD-ROM and library that came with A:M. Some of the characters on there may have just the perfect body part that you need. Half the point of working with digital 3D models is the reusability of the meshes. With that in mind, you are going to model a complete character. You will use all available resources to speed the process along.

Figure 5.72 is a concept sketch of a character called Captain Splines.

FIGURE 5.72   A concept sketch of Captain Splines.

Based on this sketch, you can create an entire character. The process of building a character normally starts with creating rotoscope images from the character sketch. If you have difficulty with spline layout or if you feel that there might be some problem needing a special solution, then you might want to sketch out a rough spline layout as well. When drawing rotoscopes, it is important that they match proportionately in both the front and side views and that the features of the character line up properly. Graph paper can aid in this process.

Rotoscopes for Captain Splines have been included on the CD-ROM. Begin modeling by creating a model and adding the rotoscopes for the front and side views.

Even though the basic structure is quite different, the mask you have modeled and stored in our Morgue is actually the perfect start for the character's face.

Open the mask model. From the library, select all the points in the model and copy and paste them into the Captain's model window. You will need to position and scale the points to roughly match the rotoscopes of the character (see Figure 5.73).

Once the mask is in place, turn on Mirror mode and adjust the points to match the shapes defined by the rotoscopes (see Figure 5.74). Be sure to work back and forth from a side view to the front view. Without adding a single spline you should be able to come very close. In some cases, you might need to add points or adjust the spline layout of the mask. Either way, be sure to save your new version of the mask to your Morgue. This new version might be closer to a character you design in the future. Building up a library of subtle variations makes a Morgue more useful.

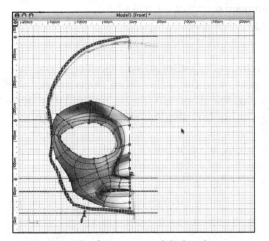

FIGURE 5.73   The face you modeled earlier pastes in and saves you work.

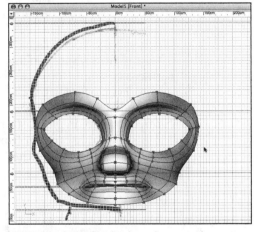

FIGURE 5.74   The finished mask.

The Captain wears high-tech, space-age clothing that keeps him warm even at the highest altitudes, but they are loose around his body and you will want them to move dynamically when the character moves. To this end, you will be modeling the arms and legs as if Captain were wearing a set of long underwear. A full unibody model will be needed when you fashion the clothing that you want him to wear. It will give the structure that the simulated cloth will hang on and interact with. For your needs, bring in the simple torso and semirealistic leg Morgued earlier, open each, and copy and paste them into the model. After you have the pieces positioned and scaled, you might have something similar to Figure 5.75.

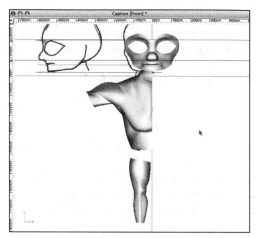

FIGURE 5.75 All the Morgued parts that will make up the foundation for your character.

Now simply start looking for the obvious connections from the face mask. The chin easily splines into the front of the neck, and the spline from the corner of the mouth fits particularly well into the side of the neck. Go ahead and add any density needed to the neck (see Figure 5.76) to define the jaw line. Once the straight connections are in place, start to sculpt the neck shapes.

A spline ring can run from the neck hole up and around the top of the head. This forms the ring that the forehead can tie into (see Figure 5.77).

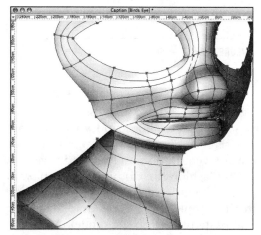

FIGURE 5.76 The chin ties into the neck easily, and the additional splines can be shaped to make the neck of your character.

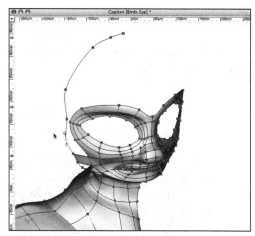

FIGURE 5.77 Run a spline from the middle of the neck up, and form the forehead with it.

Tie any splines from the face mask back into the forehead spline. From a side view, continue the centerline of the face back and shape out the cranium. While the Captain does wear a helmet, you will want a basic skull in place to indicate the proportions of the head later. You can tie this spline into the back of the neck hole (see Figure 5.78).

Continue to stitch the splines from the face mask back into the cranium, being sure to shape them into a nice round shape as you go. Soon you will have a full head and neck stitched into your torso, as in Figure 5.79.

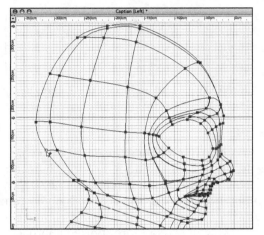

FIGURE 5.78   Continue the centerline back to form the shape of the cranium.

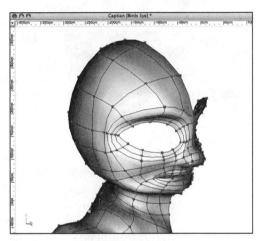

FIGURE 5.79   The head has been built by stitching the face mask into the torso.

Go over the mesh now, and be on the lookout for weak transitions—for example, along the jaw. If necessary, an additional ring can be added to the mask to harden the edge of the jaw (see Figure 5.80). These details are what allow you to give the character form later.

Before you go too much further, look at the features you have in place and the rotoscopes you are trying to match. The splines are all there; all you need to do is move them to match the drawing you have. Work from the front and side views of the model. Be sure to move your shapes into place as units first. The eyes need to line up before you shape them, the mouth needs to be in the right place, and so on. Once the features are roughly positioned, shape them one at a time until they match the features of the rotoscope as closely as possible (see Figure 5.81).

The face still needs the details that make it a face: eyes, teeth, and tongue. At this point, it becomes easier to model the details separate from the face as a whole. It also allows you to easily save out these parts to your Morgue and reuse them in other models later.

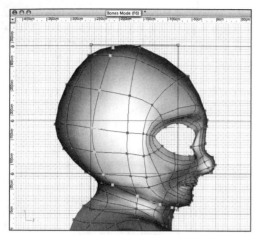

FIGURE 5.80 Watch for any details that can be firmed up as you work.

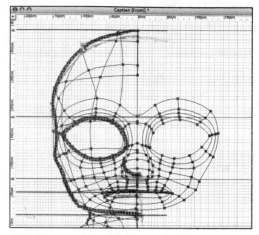

FIGURE 5.81 Adjust and sculpt the features to match the rotoscope drawings.

There are a number of directions you can go in modeling the details in a character's face. Which one you choose is dependent on the design of the character itself. All eyes are typically the same in their construction: three spheroid shapes nested inside one another. The major differences come in the details that you can include. Scientifically accurate corneas and iris muscles are fine for characters that might need them, but for the Captain we will take a more stylized approach.

In a new Model window, make a simple lathed sphere. This will be the basis for the entire eye. Select the entire sphere and change the name of the group untitled in the PWS to pupil by selecting the name either in the properties panel or the PWS and pressing the F2 key. Copy and paste this sphere. Move it back on center (up 10 pixels in y with Shift+↑) and scale it up about 120% to cover the first sphere. Notice that a group called pupil2 has been added to your PWS. This, the second sphere, will be the whites/iris layer, so rename it white. Copy and paste this layer and again move it back to center and scale it up 120%. This layer will be the cornea for the eye, so go ahead and rename the white2 group in the PWS to cornea. You should now have a set of three nested spheres similar to Figure 5.82.

Before you do much manipulation to these spheres, make a group that will allow you to move them all at once for positioning in the head. In the PWS, shift-click the first and last named group, and notice that every group in between is also selected. This ability to multiselect in the PWS becomes very important later. To make a noncontinuous selection of items, you can Command-click on the Mac or Ctrl-click on the PC. Notice that a new "untitled" group containing all the points in the eye is added to the PWS. Rename this group *whole eye*, and continue with your modeling.

The iris will need to open and close in reaction to light and to give your character some life. At the same time, the cornea will need to be unbroken, or there will be some obvious artifacts. The most logical place for the iris to open is at the pole of the sphere you lathed, which is technically a hole anyway. In order for the iris to function properly, move the pole of that sphere to face forward. Select the named group for the iris, and hide the CPs in the model to let you focus on just the mesh you need. First, rotate the eye 90 degrees in the *x*-axis so that the poles point forward (see Figure 5.83).

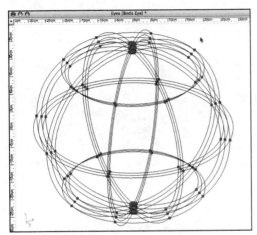

FIGURE 5.82   Three nested spheres make up the eye.

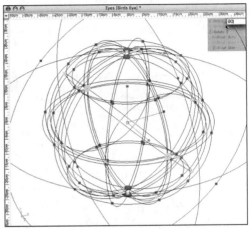

FIGURE 5.83   Rotate the whites group to start the iris.

Select the pole splines on the front of the sphere and scale the opening up in the *x*- and *y*-axes. How much you need to scale depends on how tight you lathed the original sphere to the pivot; for the example, 500% did the trick. This makes a very large opening in the front of the eye (see Figure 5.84).

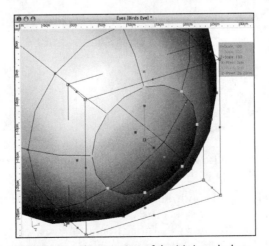

FIGURE 5.84   The opening of the iris is scaled up.

To let the light play across the iris more interestingly, simply translate the selection back into the eye to make a dish-shaped iris. The issue with this is that it distorts the shape of the eye and will further distort it every time you animate the iris dilating. To counter, there needs to be an additional spline ring at the edge of the iris.

You could add points, adjust them, and try to maintain the curvature of the eye, but that would be more work than necessary. Instead, you can use the spline that already exists at the edge of the iris to maintain the curvature while adding detail. Select the spline that makes the edge of the iris. Copy and paste it into the model and scale it down slightly. This makes a spline ring that is unattached to the rest of the eye, but retains the magnitude adjustments to make it the proper curvature. In order to attach this ring to the eye, you will need points along the cross sections of the eye. You could set them up with the Add tool, but there is a keyboard shortcut that will insert a point along a spline that will do the job easier. Select any of the splines that you need to add a point to, so that the green "selection" leg is on the inside of the iris area, and then simply press the Y key to insert a new CP. Do this for each of the cross section's splines. With these new control points in place, you will want to weld them to the ring you made earlier. Select any of the added points from the cross section and drag it so that it is aligned with the point on the ring that we want to weld it to. Without releasing the mouse button, right-click (PC) or press the ~ (*tilde*) key on your keyboard. The point you were dragging now attaches to the point you held it over. The result of this operation should look similar to Figure 5.85.

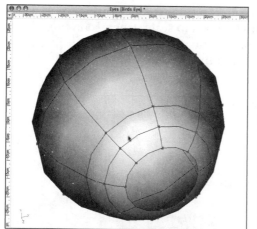
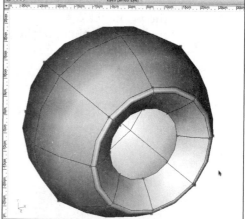

FIGURE 5.85   The added spline to the iris will stop the eye from deforming as you animate the pupil.

Before you continue, add the new CPs that were created on the eye model to the whites group. Select the whites group in the PWS and use the backslash (/) key to select all attached CPs. Since the group was selected, A:M assumes that you want to add the points to that group. Unhide the mesh and select the whole eye group.

While it is still selected, again use the group connected tool (/) to add the new points to the group. Select the cornea group, invert the selection with the period key, and hide the cornea with the Shift+H keyboard command. Notice the pupil shape penetrates through the iris mesh. To make the pupil only hide the back of the whites and enforce the black area in the eye, simply delete the front portion of the mesh and break the remaining splines to make an empty semisphere (see Figure 5.86).

Unhide the whole mesh, move the whole eye to position, and scale it to fit the eye socket. Copy and paste a second eye for the other half of the head (see Figure 5.87).

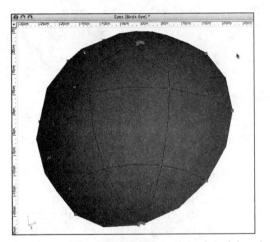

FIGURE 5.86   The front of the pupil mesh is deleted to avoid intersection with the rest of the eye.

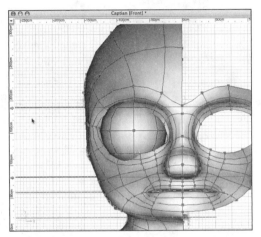

FIGURE 5.87   The eyes are positioned in the head.

At this point, you may be concerned that you cannot see the iris and pupil because the cornea is opaque. We will take care of that when texturing the model so don't worry about that right now. Save this eye out to your Morgue, and then copy and paste the mesh into the Captain's Model window. Undoubtedly you will need to adjust the position and scale of the eye to fit inside the Captain's eye socket. When you are finished, you should have something similar to Figure 5.88

Eyes without eyelids are disturbing and would be uncomfortably dry for the Captain, so model him a set. Select the last spline ring of the eye socket and the cornea of the eye and hide the rest of the model. Add some splines to the eye socket that will allow us to open and close the eyes without disturbing the overall shape of them. This is simply accomplished by extruding the last spline ring of the socket and shaping to fit over the cornea. You will need a couple extrusions to aid with animation and to allow you to curve the splines around the surface of the cornea. Start by selecting the spline ring for the socket and locking the mesh. Now you can adjust the socket and any new splines (such as our soon-to-be-extruded extrusions) without disturbing or accidentally changing the cornea. Extrude the eye socket spline three times. Each time scale the new extrusion down so that it fits inside the original. You won't be leaving the splines there but this will keep them out of the way. You should have something like Figure 5.89.

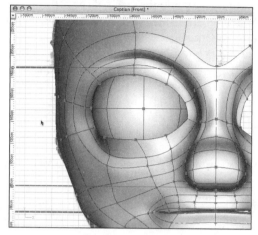

FIGURE 5.88   Paste the eye model into the main character and position it to fit.

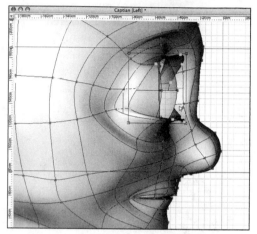

FIGURE 5.89   The eyelids are started with simple extrusions.

Now shape the lids to form over the eye and meet in a closed position. This is a simple matter of pulling the points of the lids so that they meet in the center, ease back into the socket, and cover without intersecting the cornea. You should have something similar to Figure 5.90.

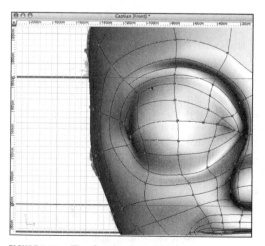

FIGURE 5.90   The finished eyelid.

Teeth, as with eyes, can be highly detailed models of orthodontic perfection, or they can be simplified and stylized. The choice of which method to use should be dictated by your character's design. The Captain's design dictates simple teeth, but even so there are still several options: You can model individual teeth, not a full set but enough to show some detail; you can model the entire set of teeth as one object with that tinsel-town gleam to them; or you could choose a method somewhere in between. For the Captain, either method could work but the individual teeth will give him something to grit later on. He is, after all, no pretty boy.

Each tooth is a simple lathe shape. Since you won't be animating them at all, it makes sense to lathe them at four cross sections to keep down the number of patches. In a new Model window, draw the out line of one tooth and lathe it at 4. Scale it down in the z-axis to flatten it out a bit. After some tweaking, you should have something similar to Figure 5.91.

In order to place the teeth properly, you need to see inside the character's jaw. Select the entire lower jaw and hide the rest of the head. Copy the tooth from its Model window and paste it into the Captain model. While it is still selected, lock the rest of the model so you can see the jaw and the inside of the mouth but won't accidentally change it. Position and scale the tooth. It should be fairly large but not overwhelming for the size of the mouth. When you are happy with this first tooth, copy and paste it to fill in one-half of the character's mouth (see Figure 5.92).

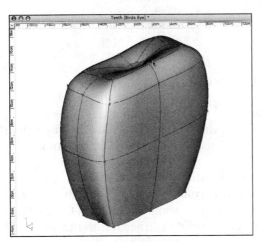

FIGURE5.91   This single tooth can be copied and pasted to fill an entire mouth.

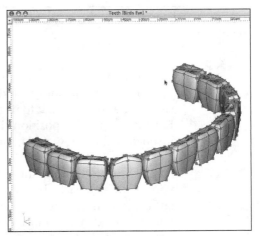

FIGURE 5.92   Half the teeth positioned in the mouth.

Select all the teeth and duplicate them via copy and paste. Bring up the new group's contextual menu and choose x-axis from the flip heading. This will invert the mesh along that axis. Translate the teeth over to fill in the other side of the mouth. Now duplicate the entire set of teeth by copying and pasting; this time choose y-axis to flip the entire set of lower teeth into a set of upper teeth (see Figure 5.93).

While you have them all by themselves, copy and paste the whole set of teeth into a new Model window and save them out to your Morgue.

Before unhiding the rest of the head, let's model the tongue. The tongue, like the teeth, is a simple lathe shape. Simply lathe the profile of the tongue with four cross sections and shape it to suit. Place it in the mouth, and you should have something similar to Figure 5.94.

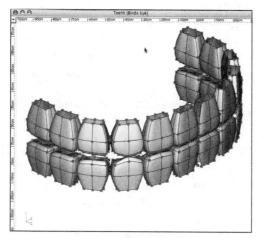

FIGURE 5.93   After flipping, you have an entire set of teeth.

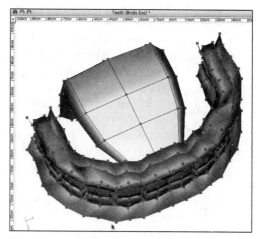

FIGURE 5.94   The mouth with tongue installed.

Congratulations, you have finished the head.

Arms, not including hands, are also very simple. Just select the last ring of the shoulder and extrude it to just above the elbow shape and scale this ring as needed. Extrude again and position the spline where the elbow will bend one more time just below the elbow and finally to the wrist. This should leave you with something like Figure 5.95.

If you were modeling a bare arm and needed the hands to mesh perfectly you might approach things a little differently, perhaps modeling the hand first and lathing an arm to suit the density of the more complex appendage. But for the Captain, his hands will be inside gloves and a direct spline connection to the arms will not be needed.

Make a new model to build the hands in, remembering that you will probably be able to recycle this body part for other characters later.

The fingers are a good place to start, as they are simple and will help determine the splinage needed to build the meat of the hand. The Captain will need a relatively simple hand, a variation on the three-finger cartoon hand. Start with a seven-point horizontal spline and lathe it with a cross section of 8. You can reduce the geometry later if you need to. This is one of the few cases where it is better to start off a little dense than to have to stitch splines into all the fingers to maintain continuity. Close one end of this tube in a similar fashion to the perfect sphere you modeled in Chapter 2. Push these points up to flatten out the top of the tube slightly. Adjust the splines until you have a basic finger shape, as in Figure 5.96.

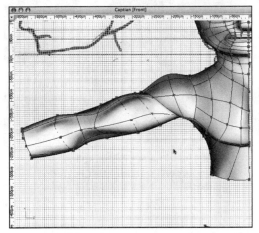

FIGURE 5.95   Extrude the arms out of the shoulders.

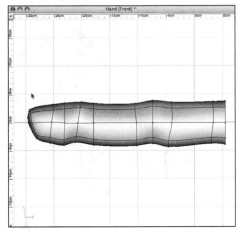

FIGURE 5.96   A basic finger.

Select the finger and copy it. Paste a copy, move it to position for the second finger, and paste again for the third. Select the middle finger, and scale it up in the *x*-axis. Then do the same for the first finger, making it slightly shorter than the middle finger. Paste a third copy of the finger and move it into position to be the thumb. Since the thumb has fewer joints than the fingers, delete the last spline ring from the base of the thumb. You should have something like Figure 5.97.

Now it is time to start stitching the fingers together. Start with the webbing between the fingers; this can be done easily with the three points on the side of each finger. Simply joining them with a spline across the web would let the movements of one finger affect the shape of another when animating. In order to isolate the fingers from the CPs on the splines of its neighbor, a stable center needs to be established. Connect the points on the three adjacent CPs with three-point splines, leaving three CPs floating between each finger. Stitch a spline in between each finger to close up the patches (see Figure 5.98).

Next, tie the fingers together into a single hand. For this, you need to draw a 16-point spline loop and stitch all the fingers into it. The thumb and first finger can use the end of the loop as the webbing between them, much the same as the fingers did. This will make many five-point patches across the fingers that will need to be closed. When you are finished, you should have something like Figure 5.99.

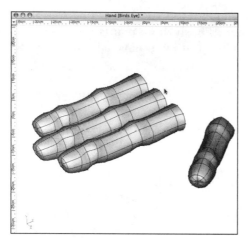

FIGURE 5.97   Copy and paste the first finger to fill out the hand.

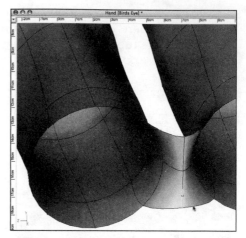

FIGURE 5.98   The additional spline between the fingers will stabilize the CPs during animation.

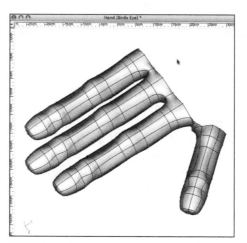

FIGURE 5.99   The fingers are connected into the hand via five-point patches.

Start looking for ways to trim down the splines at this point. For now, you can extrude the points from the fingers out into the palm. Don't include the thumb in this extrusion or you will wind up with some ambiguous patches that could cause creasing. Instead, extrude the three points on the outside of the thumb separately. The shape of the hand, and the way that the thumb in particular needs to animate, means we stop at least one spline from continuing to the wrist. The spline from the first finger can be connected to the extrusion from the thumb giving flexibility at that joint (see Figure 5.100).

Extrude the palm and thumb splines separately again and stitch them together as a wrist. As you can see, this creates a large five-point patch area on the top of the hand. This close to the wrist you can expect a five-pointer of that size to behave poorly during animation; so consider some alternative splining to move it back toward the thumb or to make it much smaller.

Bisecting the pad of the hand and moving the spline from the first extrusion of the fingers to the side of the hand solves this problem nicely. Break the splines on both sides of the hand that connect the first extrusion into the thumb splines. These can then move toward the side of the hand under the thumb; stitch in the splines needed to attach this area. The spline from the top of the thumb can then be extended down the hand and tie into the wrist, which pushes the five-point area nicely out of the danger area (see Figure 5.101).

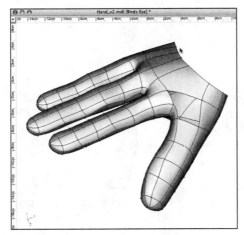 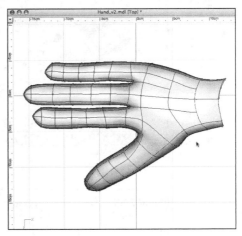

FIGURE 5.100   As you patch the hand together, look for ways to stop splines from continuing to the wrist.

FIGURE 5.101   Changing the routing of the splines on the surface makes the model more animateable.

This closes up the mesh, but the wrist is way too dense with splines. Extrude the wrist out one more time, and look for some opportunities to reduce the geometry with hooks. With the hook layout in Figure 5.102 you can reduce the wrist down to a much more reasonable seven points. Be sure to look at the hand_v3.mdl on the CD-ROM to see how it was done. As a challenge, try to reduce the wrist to six points without losing animation ability. With a little tweaking of the shapes, the hand is finished and ready to be saved to your Morgue.

Copy and paste the finished hand into the Captain's Model window. Position and scale it to match the character's proportions. Now that you have the basic hand, you can add the details that will make it specific to this character. Looking at the concept drawing of the Captain, the fingers and the top of the hand are protected with thick plates that are attached to the gloves. For these, it is a simple matter of importing your beveled cube from the Morgue and scaling it down to fit the part. There is no need to attach the splines to the glove underneath as the bones you add later will do that job for you.

The leg that you imported needs to be joined with a simple pelvis, which then needs to stitch into your character's torso. It is easy to think of the legs and pelvis as a variation on the method you used to make fingers earlier.

The two splines that run down the inside of the leg will be used to model the webbing across to the opposite leg. Select the two points at the top of the inside of the leg and extrude. Translate them over to the centerline of the model. This spline has now become the centerline of the pelvis (see Figure 5.103).

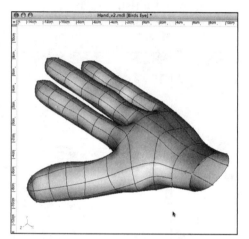

FIGURE 5.102 This layout of hooks will reduce the splineage.

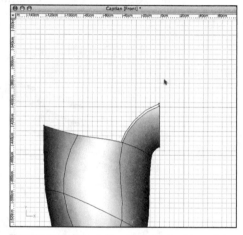

FIGURE 5.103 Extruding the two inside points of the leg sets up the centerline of the pelvis.

The remaining four control points on the leg will form the outside edge of the hip. While you are here, extrude the rest of the leg up and build the five-point patch that will finish off the leg-to-hip transition (see Figure 5.104).

Extrude the whole hip up one more time to the waist and the hips are done (see Figure 5.105). Shape them to form the basic shape of the legs. You don't have to define any muscles here, but the shape needs to approximate the masses of the muscles. The most important area is actually the crotch. Build it so that there are no intersecting areas. If one leg passes into another then the cloth simulation is likely to become very confused. We take a closer look at these areas when you set up the clothing solutions later, but a good base will save you work down the road.

The Captain has a fondness for steel-toe boots, which, like all of his design, are stylized to a certain degree. Start with the sole by lathing a four-point spline like the one in Figure 5.106 with a cross section of 8. This can then be molded

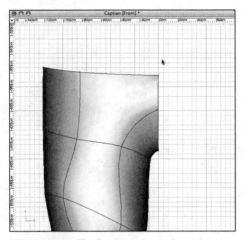

FIGURE 5.104   The legs can extrude up into the hips.

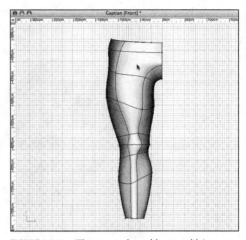

FIGURE 5.105   The completed leg and hip.

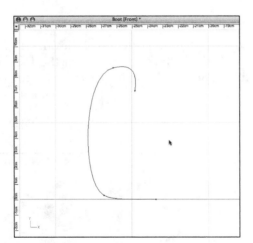

FIGURE 5.106   Lathe this spline to start the sole.

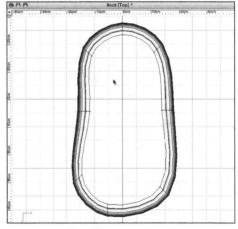

FIGURE 5.107   Arranging the lathed points to make a foot shape.

into a foot shape, which is easily closed on the bottom. The spline arrangement shown in Figure 5.107 allows the bottom of the sole to be closed off with the addition of two splines (see Figure 5.108).

Toes for these boots are nothing more than a quarter of a sphere. You have two options: lathe a new sphere in the boot model and delete the unwanted portions, or copy and paste one-quarter of a sphere from your Morgue. Both methods will result in something similar to Figure 5.109.

Place the quarter-sphere in the toe of the foot shape and adust the splines to your liking.

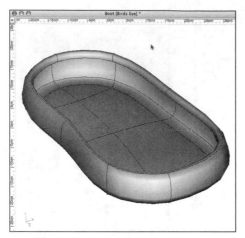

FIGURE 5.108   Careful placement of the splines in the foot shape makes closing the bottom of the mesh simple.

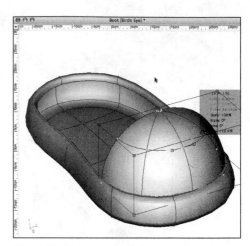

FIGURE 5.109   The toe cap is a quarter-sphere.

The main portion of the boot is started from the top of the ankle. Draw an 11-point spline in a rough circle with the splines open toward the toe (see Figure 5.110). Make the opening tight, and double the splines back inside the circle. This will give some thickness to the edge. Extrude this twice, and shape it as you go to start the sides (see Figure 5.111).

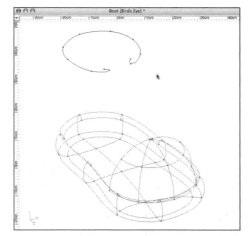

FIGURE 5.110   Start the leg of the boot with this spline ring.

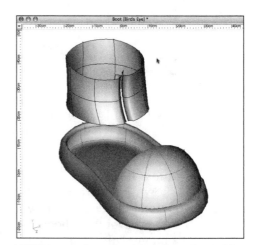

FIGURE 5.111   Start the sides of the shoe with two extrusions.

The top of the boot needs to run along the area the foot would be in and finish up at the toe, while the sides need to run down and around the heel area. To do this efficiently requires that you "split" your extrusion at the point where the leg of the boot meets the ankle. This means that you make two separate extrusions with only partial selections of the spline ring. For the top of the foot, select just the points at the front of the leg around the split. These eight points will be extruded three times down to the toe of the boot. Adjust the position and scale of each extrusion before moving on to the next. The back of the boot will be the three points at the rear of the leg. (Note that we do not select any of the points included in the first set of extrusions. Doing so would cause creasing, as it would create an extra spline at the point where the extrusions met.) Simply extrude this set twice to form the back of the heel. Finish the sides of the foot, extruding the top area (both left and right) down twice to meet the sole of the boot. Stitch and fill the gap between the heel and foot with a five-point patch, as in Figure 5.112.

For your boots, you will use thick leather straps in place of laces. These straps are built by extruding a four-point spline loop over the top of the foot (see Figure 5.113). You could model the stitching and very specific details in the boots spline by spline, but for the most part those types of things are more easily accomplished with texturing. That alternative is covered in Chapter 12.

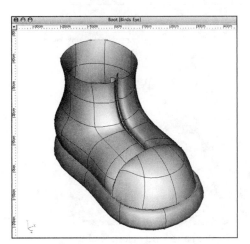

FIGURE 5.112   All this boot needs is a set of laces.

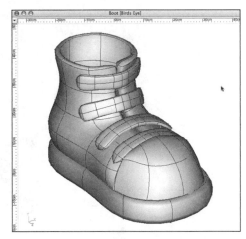

FIGURE 5.113   The finished boot.

You moved quickly there and should already be comfortable with all these techniques from the previous exercises. If you are confused at all, watch the demonstration video for modeling this character. For now, copy and paste the boot into the Captain model, position it at the base of the leg, scale it to fit, and finally, save the original boot model into your Morgue.

If your modeling and sense of proportion were perfect all the time, you could duplicate the leg and arm to the opposite side of the character and be finished.

But proportions often stray, and adjusting the character after both sides have been created is generally more work than making adjustments to just one side. However, it is also difficult to gauge the proportions of the figure without both halves of it in place. To counter this, use a special technique that involves the use of the choreography. If you have portions of your model on both halves of the character, hide the second half, or delete it and create a new choreography.

Drop the half version of your model into the choreography twice. To make certain they are aligned exactly, drop the model onto the choreography item in the PWS rather than into the Choreography window. This stacks both instances of the character exactly on top of each other in the workspace window. Select either shortcut to the character and open the transform disclosure triangle on the Properties panel. In the x-scale, transform property type –100%. This should flip your character, giving you an approximate full version (see Figure 5.114). While you have the shortcut still selected, change the mode to modeling. Now any changes you make on either shortcut will be reflected on the other side of the character. This allows you to gauge the proportions of a character and make adjustments as needed. Once you are satisfied with the proportions of the character go back to the modeling window for a copy/flip/attach.

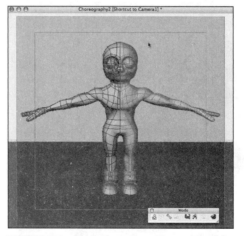

FIGURE 5.114   Scaling a second instance of the model to –100 in a chor lets you get a feel for the completed model without committing to a full model.

Congratulations! You have completed the basic structure for a character. In the process, you have learned all the most important aspects of modeling in A:M. Armed with this knowledge you should be able to design and create characters of your own. But this is not the same character that was in the concept drawing, That character wore a helmet, body armor, and pants, and you will need to add those elements to this character before you can call him complete. Go ahead and get the helmet modeled, and then look at what you need to accomplish for the costume on this character.

Modeling the helmet starts with the skull of the character. Select the area of the head that will be covered by the helmet and copy and paste it. Simply scale this group up around the Captain's head to make the basic shell for your helmet, as in Figure 5.115 (name your group helmet while you still have it selected). Now lock the rest of the model so that you can work exclusively with the helmet.

As a starting point this is pretty good, but you need to make the outer rim of this shape a single continuous spline loop. The easiest way to do this is to break and reconnect the splines that make up the front and back of the helmet (the back of the skull and the forehead line on the original head). Look at Figure 5.116. Break the splines as indicated by the circle.

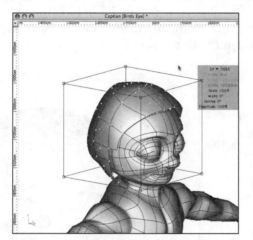

FIGURE 5.115   The skull of the character can be copied to produce the basis for the helmet.

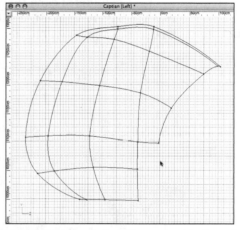

FIGURE 5.116   Break the splines where indicated.

Now connect the two front and rear splines to make a continuous loop. Once that is accomplished, simply stitch in the rest of the splines from the helmet. Now you can work with the helmet edge, extruding it out and shaping it as needed. Extrude once and pull the points forward at the front and down at the back and along the sides to fill out the rest of the helmet's shape, without covering the face of the character. You will need to do some adjusting of the existing splines to make the shapes work correctly, but it shouldn't take too much. To add thickness and hide the interior of the helmet, extrude again and scale in toward the skull. Extrude one final time, and tuck it under and against the head, making it a nice tight fit for Captain. The radio antenna, visor, and other elements of the helmet are what are commonly referred to as nurnies: those little bits that make a shape look detailed and complex. For your needs, just look at the shapes and put them into place. The base of the radio antenna is a simple cube. Import your beveled cube from the Morgue, and scale and position it. Just jam it inside the helmet; there is no need to attach it or worry about clean connections. The antenna itself is a simple lathe shape. If you have a cylinder in your Morgue (hint: look in the library that came on the A:M install disc from Hash, Inc.) you can import it, and scale and position it to fit the bill (see Figure 5.117).

The visor is quickly made by copying and pasting the front spline of the helmet's leading edge. This is scaled up and out to form the bottom of the visor, then simply extruding it to make the visor. You can add thickness to the visor in the same way that you did for the helmet by selecting all the points along the outside edges and extruding them. If you expect to see close-up on this visor at any point, you might want to completely spline the back side of the glass. But since it will be mirrored instead of clear and will have no need for complete accuracy, this should be enough. To hide the corners of the visor (which are just dead-ended splines) place a cylinder at each side of the helmet, which makes it look hinged. The result will look very similar to Figure 5.118. Some of the finer details (seams in the plastic, for example) will be added later with textures.

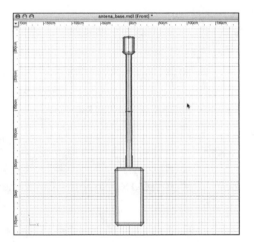

FIGURE 5.117   The radio antenna and base are just simple "primitives" imported from your Morgue.

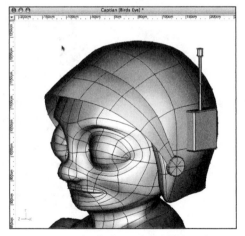

FIGURE 5.118   This helmet should keep the Captain's noggin safe from harm.

Preparing Solutions for Cloth

Right now, the look of Captain isn't likely to inspire confidence in any damsels in distress. He's in his longjohns and combat boots. Sure he's got that helmet there, but that's not very inspiring. What Captain needs is a set of body armor and some pants. But if you look at the concept drawings, portions of the uniform that he wears are not rigid. In fact, they are cloth. The armpits, the underside of the arm braces, the joints in the torso are all cloth areas that you will likely want to deform when you animate the character. In order to have this work later (when you learn about dynamic cloth), you will need to set up the geometry to give you the look you are after. This starts with the geometry already in place. The body you have modeled is called a "Deflector" (more on this in Chapter 13), and in order for it to do its job properly you need to tell A:M which side of this surface is "out." Patches represent hollow objects with two distinct sides. One of these sides is the front of the patch and the other is the back. In may instances, it doesn't matter which side is which. A:M will render both without difficulties, and both will accept materials and decals later without many issues unless the material you are working with is "Normals Aware." You may recall normals is touched on in Chapter 2 in only the most passing way (a warning to avoid internal patches). As discussed, you can toggle the visibility of normals in a model with the Shift+1 keyboard combination. This shows you the model's normals, which indicates a rendering patch, but it also indicates which side of that patch is *front*. When a material or dynamic effect is said to be normals aware, it simply means that it takes some form of useful information from the direction the normal is facing on a surface. In the case of cloth, it says "stay outside of me," and in order for it to work correctly you need to ensure that all the surfaces of your character have their surfaces pointing outward. For the most part, A:M does a good job of keeping normals facing the right way, but in the course of your splining, you will undoubtedly make some patches that cause a normal to face inward. You could scour all the patches of the character with a fine-tooth comb and seek out and fix the few normals that are not in line, but it would be easier to let A:M do that. Simply right-click (PC), Command-click (Mac) the name of the model in the PWS and from the contextual menu choose "refind normals". This will align all the normals on your model in one direction or the other, and more often than not it will point them outward. There are some things to watch out for, specifically five-point patches and hooks, which can sometimes have their normals reversed from the rest of the model. But knowing this helps you find them and fix them. Refind the normals in the Captain now. Zoom into the face on one of the five-point patches and rotate the view so you can see which direction the normal on that patch is facing. If it is in line with the rest of the surface, then move on to the next five-point patch. If it is not, flip it so that it is. First, select just that patch. You could select each point or draw a group around the five points that make up the patch, but it is much simpler to use the Patch Select tool (Shift+P), which allows you to select a patch just by clicking inside of it. Once the patch is selected, flip the offending normal by using the F keyboard shortcut (remember F for flip). Go over all the five-point patches and hooks on your character and flip them to the correct side.

 If all the normals are facing inside instead, simply select all the points in the model (Command+A Mac, Ctrl+A PC) and flip them at once with the F key.

Once the model's normals are in line, it is ready to start clothing. You can hide the normals with the Shift+1 key if you like, or you can leave them visible while you work. Before moving on to the actual costume, create a group that you can assign a deflector material to later. Simply group the points in the model you have so far, and rename the untitled group to "deflector" or something similar.

Now you can move on to the costume. Start with the portions of the costume that will be rigid. Building these sections show us where to set up dynamic groups and give you the chance to set up your "attach" groups before the mesh gets too complex. (Properly setting up your groups is arguably the most important part of the process.)

With the exception of the breastplate and gauntlets, most of the armored portions of the costumes are simply beveled squares (not cubes, as you want to use these to stitch cloth into). Start with a single eight-point spline loop in a square, as in Figure 5.119

Now patch up the interior of this patch to form a surface. Then select the outside spline, and extrude it and position to give the armor some depth. Once you have the single plate built, simply copy, paste, move, and scale to cover the shoulders, arms, and back of the character. You might end up with something that looks like Figure 5.120.

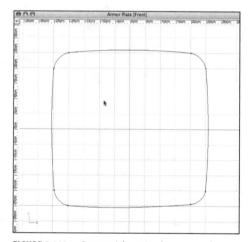

FIGURE 5.119 Start with a single square for the body armor.

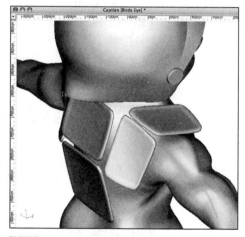

FIGURE 5.120 Start with the body armor by placing simple squares over the character's arms, shoulders, and back.

The gauntlets cover the forearms of the character and are roughly cylindrical. Simply draw the cross section of the shape, including points for thickness, and lathe around the forearm. This shape can then be copied and flipped to the opposite side of the character leaving you with something similar to Figure 5.121.

The breastplate is slightly more complex than the rest of the armor pieces, but you have the perfect starting point already in the model. In much the same way you created the helmet from the skull of the character, you can copy and paste the chest area of the character's torso to give you a foundation to work from. The breastplate is a more mechanical, sculpted version of the character's own chest. Start by simply peaking the points that define the lower edges of the pectoral muscles. Then shaping the outside edges to fit inside the other parts of the armor, you might have something similar to Figure 5.122. A simple extrusion gives the edge a little depth, and the breastplate is finished.

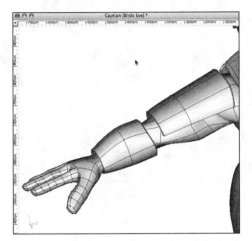

FIGURE 5.121   The gauntlets are simply lathed around the forearms.

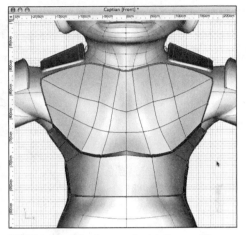

FIGURE 5.122   The breastplate is formed from the underlying character model.

Before you stitch the plates together, set up the plates as a group so that you can exclude them from the simulation later. Simply group all the plates together and name the group "armor_attach". Now you just need to fill in the gaps between the armor plates. This is one of the rare instances where denser meshes can be considered better. With a little extra density, you can expect to see more realistic simulation of the folds and shears for your cloth. Start by connecting the obvious joints between each plate, then stitch in splines to add density between each plate. Look at Figures 5.123, 5.124, 5.125, and 5.126 to see this in progress.

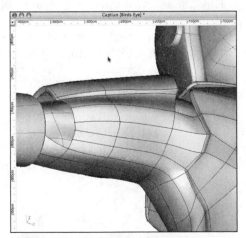

FIGURE 5.123   The cloth in progress.

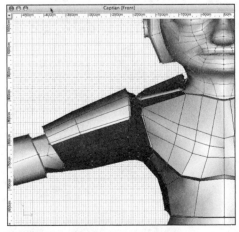

FIGURE 5.124   The cloth in progress.

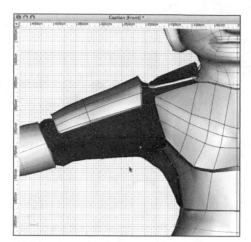

FIGURE 5.125   The cloth in progress.

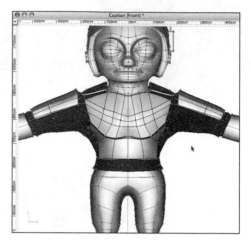

FIGURE 5.126   The cloth in progress.

Once the plates are stitched together, make one more group for your character: the Sim-Cloth group. It needs to hold all the dynamic parts of the cloth *and* all the "attached" group. Select all the work you just did into a single group including the plates, and name this group "torso_simcloth".

Now the Captain just needs some pants. Pants are a simple extension of the legs, and a copy and paste will get you most of the way. Copy the legs from the waist down to the ankles and paste them into the model. Scale this up and position it so that it covers the legs, but doesn't touch any part of them. This is particularly important in the crotch area.

The crotch is a danger zone (as are armpits) for cloth in that you have two opposing deflectors that get really, really close to one another. If the cloth is pushed into a position where it cannot stay outside both deflectors, it enters what is known as an "insolvable" state. This can and will cause the cloth to behave in an erratic fashion. In addition to ensuring that the cloth doesn't sit inside the mesh or get crushed, prepare it so that it can figure out where it stands before it comes into contact with a surface. To this end, the cloth will need to be a minimal distance from all surfaces that it can collide with. Look at Figure 5.127 to see an example of properly set-up cloth. In order to make these pants fully functional, you need to get them named into a group and set up an attachment point. Name the whole set of pants "pants_simgroup" and the topmost waistband spline "pants_attach".

Now you just need to hide the seam of the pants to the upper body. For this, Captian wears a belt. This is a simple lathe shape with a beveled cube belt buckle. Once in place, you should have a character that more or less resembles Figure 5.128.

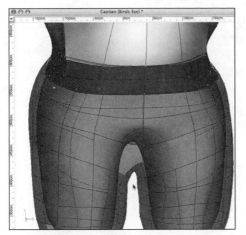

FIGURE 5.127   The surface of the cloth must be positioned to allow it to come to rest without hitting a deflector.

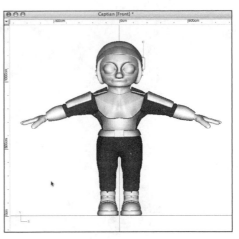

FIGURE 5.128   The completed character model for Captain Splines.

SUMMARY

Modeling characters is a challenging aspect of A:M, especially characters that animate well. The techniques learned for modeling here also happen to apply to almost every aspect of modeling in A:M.

The density of splines and the layout of those splines more directly affect the quality of your work than any other factor. A well-modeled character is easier to animate, texture, rig, and often renders better than poorly modeled characters. The time spent now improving your modeling skills will help bolster the quality of your work as a whole.

The character modeled in this chapter teaches the importance of reusing parts. A Morgue—or collection of pieces—of experiments and good splinesmanship will give you a foundation from which you will be able to build more and more complex models quickly and easily. Save all your models and experiments.

Finally, we looked at some interesting solutions to some common challenges. While the modeling was not revolutionary the ideas behind the techniques are effective and battle tested in real-life productions. Use these as a springboard for finding your own creative solutions to the challenges you face.

INORGANIC MODELING

In This Chapter

- Shot Planning in Modeling
- Tutorial: Basic Mechanical Modeling
- Buildings and Urban Landscapes
- Building the Perfect Robot

Now we turn your attention to building sets and props for our characters to use. We will also look at some general timesaving and patch-saving techniques.
As if that weren't enough:

1. We will discuss planning your modeling based on shot composition to save work.
2. You will learn to use bevels and the A:M modeling wizards to achieve believable mechanisms quickly and easily.
3. You will apply those techniques to modeling a street set, including a brownstone apartment building.
4. Finally, you will apply your mechanical knowledge to create a robot character.

SHOT PLANNING IN MODELING

One of the most common mistakes made in modeling sets and props is to expend a lot of time and effort creating highly detailed objects that wind up not being in the shot, or they are so small that all detail is lost. There are times when this cannot be avoided, but with planning, you can put the detail where it will count and save the patches where it will not. One of the best ways to plan is to visualize the shot you are working on before you begin work. Storyboards, sketches, and reference photographs can show you where to add detail and where to skip it.

For most props, the level of detail depends on whether or not a character uses it and how close the camera gets to the item in the course of the animation.

 Without knowing how close the camera gets to the object during animation, it is impossible to know how much detail is needed and how much would be lost.

It is important to move from the Modeling window to the Choreography window as soon as possible—the choreography is where models and animation come together into a completed scene. Until you see the models together in the choreography, you have very little idea how they work together. Choreography also contains the camera. This allows you to see what will be lost off-frame in an animation and to trim detail.

Set building in 3D is very similar to painting: You lay down the broad strokes first, and come in to refine the details as you work, modeling new items or refining existing models as needed. Later in this chapter, when you proceed to model full sets, this procedure will be used.

Roughed-out sets will show where particular areas of detail can enhance, while at the same time giving you a base from which to start. When working on a production with more than one artist, starting with low-resolution models allows the modelers and texture artists to work on refining the models at the same time that the animators and lighting artists work.

To make a complex object, model to the camera. Start with a simple base and combine small sections of a larger item from small models in choreography. When you build the brownstone apartment building later in this chapter, you will use this technique to build the set in modular chunks.

Before you get into modeling sets, however, look at techniques that these sets will employ.

Mechanical Modeling

Modeling mechanical items takes a certain amount of patience and an eye for detail. The tendency is to attempt to create models to real-world levels of precision, but most of this detail will be lost on the audience. A relaxed stance can be taken to precise dimensions as long as when the object is rendered it looks "right." In many ways, modeling mechanical items is easier than modeling characters and organic objects, as most of the time unibody construction is not necessary. More than any other type of modeling, mechanical items are rooted in the process of breaking an object down to its basic shapes.

Start with a basic object and look at how it is modeled. Figure 6.1 shows a simple remote control for a television set. Before you start laying splines for this object, we need to discuss a couple of the more important features of its modeling.

FIGURE 6.1   A simple remote control.

One of the most important things to note here, and for any mechanical or man-made object, are the bevels. Beveled edges are everywhere in real life, but in 3D they must be added. We add them to create a greater feeling of realism that comes from the added specular highlights that beveled edges provide. These highlights add an amount of solidity that an object without them would not have.

Notice, too, that the model has holes built into the case for the buttons and a seam where the parts join. This is not done with booleans, as A:M has no model-level booleans. Instead, this detail has to be modeled into the object at the spline level, which can be difficult if you do not take the time to plan for it.

With those points in mind, you can begin.

TUTORIAL   **BASIC MECHANICAL MODELING**

Punching holes into the model for the buttons after you have already modeled the top of the remote would be a serious chore and one that, generally speaking, would not give the best of results. A better approach can be taken from the methods used to model the face in Chapter 5: start with the holes. A single hole can be modeled with a lathed tube, setting your cross sections to 4 to keep the geometry down. Don't worry about animation here; every consideration can be given to low patch counts. Reducing the number of patches helps reduce render times. Start by lathing a two-point spline with four cross sections. You could copy and paste this to make holes for each of the buttons, but the spacing would vary unless you are careful. Instead, use the Duplicator Wizard. Select all the CPs for the hole and bring up the group's contextual menu. Set the Duplication method to copy and the Repeat setting to 3. The offset you will need for your holes will depend on the scale to which you lathed the first hole. For the example, an *x*-translate setting of 20 was used to get the first row. Select the three holes that you have now, and run the Duplicator Wizard again. This time use a *z*-translate setting of 20, and put the *x* value back to 0. You should have a regular grid of nine holes (see Figure 6.2).

The holes can easily be connected to start splining the top of the remote. Start by connecting the facing CPs on the top of each hole. The space between each set of four holes can then be broken up into five-point patches by simply adding a grid of splines between each set of holes. Close these five-point areas with the Five-Point Patch tool, and you have a good start (see Figure 6.3).

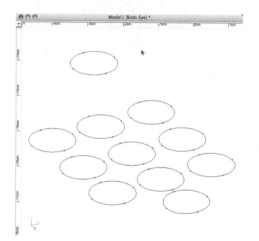

FIGURE 6.2 Start with the holes.

FIGURE 6.3 A lot of five-point patches close the surface.

You need two more round holes, one for the power button and one for the zero number button. These can be copied and pasted into position. You also need to spline in holes for the three rectangle function buttons. Start by lathing a two-point spline with a cross-section setting of 8. Deform the rings into a roughly rounded square, and place it inline with the first of the round buttons. Use the Duplicator Wizard to make three rectangular holes with the same spacing that you used for the round buttons. Stitch these new parts to the original holes, adding points to the square holes as needed (see Figure 6.4).

The difficult portion of the faceplate is now done. Now simply tie the entire thing into a rectangular plate (see Figure 6.5).

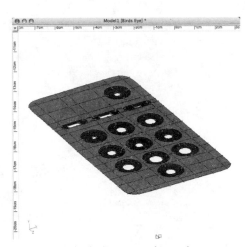

FIGURE 6.4   The rest of the holes are added and stitched in. Note the large number of five-pointers.

FIGURE 6.5   The holes are tied into the faceplate.

At this point, you may also want to pull each hole in at the bottom to cover where the buttons will sit. This part will remain separate from the rest of the model, allowing a much less dense spline layout for the rest of the model. To make the transition into the main model more believable and to give the faceplate some depth, extrude the spline ring that makes up the outside edge of the faceplate, push it down, and scale it up slightly. This will make a bevel where the two parts meet.

Copy and paste the last spline ring from the faceplate to provide a starting point to model the top half of the remote. While the new spline is selected, lock the mesh. Now you can work without disturbing what you have already done. Delete the extra detail in the spline ring, make any needed gamma adjustments; when the shape is correct, extrude this spline up and scale it out to form the bevel that will inset the faceplate. The remainder of the top can simply be extruded out and splined together from this ring (see Figure 6.6).

The bottom of the remote is simply a duplicate of the top that has the faceplate inset and unneeded detail deleted from it (see Figure 6.7).

The infrared (IR) lens is also exceptionally simple. A four-point spline is extruded with each extrusion scaled and positioned to match the shape of the opening that you modeled into the handset (see Figure 6.8).

All that remains are the buttons. The round buttons are easy enough to build as a lathed shape. You can build in all the rounded bevels with a single S-shaped spline. Lathing the button with a cross section of 4 allows you to close the top with one additional spline. Take this button and place it in the first hole on the faceplate. As you did earlier, use the Duplicator Wizard to accurately place the buttons (see Figure 6.9).

FIGURE 6.6   The top half of the remote is built using the last spline from the faceplate.

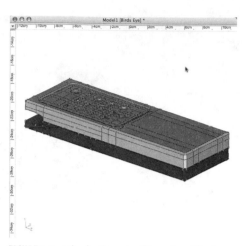

FIGURE 6.7   The bottom half is a simplified copy of the top.

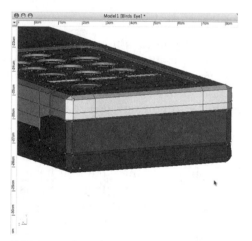

FIGURE 6.8   The IR lens is simply an extruded four-point spline.

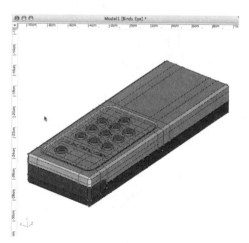

FIGURE 6.9   The buttons are simple lathe shapes placed with the Duplicator Wizard.

The rectangle buttons are a perfect place to reuse a previously modeled object. Import the beveled cube from Chapter 2, and scale it to fit in the rectangular holes (see Figure 6.10).

That's all there is to it. The concepts to model this remote are all variations on techniques already covered. An important thing to note here is that the various parts of the model do not have to be connected. Also, note how important modeling out from the holes is. If you had started this model and tried to put holes in later, the work would have been double that of planning and laying the holes down first.

Granted, remote controls are not typically the first things that come to mind when people think of mechanical modeling. A more expected example might be gears (see Figure 6.11).

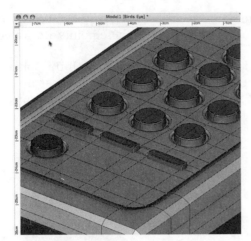

FIGURE 6.10 The square buttons are simple beveled cubes.

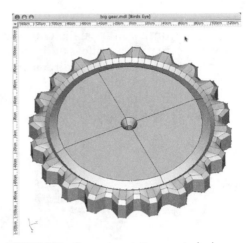

FIGURE 6.11 Gears are more expected when thinking of mechanical modeling.

While gears look complex, their construction is very simple. The secret to making them without excessive patch counts lies in building them in two pieces.

The teeth of the gears are built by determining how many teeth are needed and lathing at four times that number. For example, to make a gear with 20 teeth, lathe at a setting of 80. The teeth for the gear start with a C-shaped splinc that you lathe, as shown in Figure 6.12.

When lathed at a cross section of 80, you have a very dense mesh that must still be shaped to give you the teeth on your gear (see Figure 6.13). Making the teeth is a simple, if time-consuming, process of grouping the points that will make

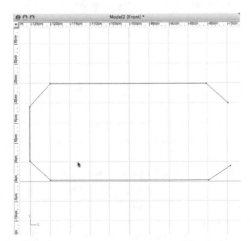

FIGURE 6.12 This shape will be used to lathe the teeth on the gear.

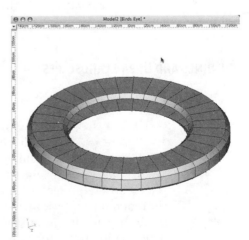

FIGURE 6.13 A mesh this dense is rare, but mechanical models often require more patches than organic ones.

up the valleys between the teeth—a process of select two CPs, skip two CPs—until you have the entire set of valleys selected. These points are scaled down to make the valleys of the teeth (see Figure 6.14).

Select the entire gear and change the magnitude of all the splines to 10, to tighten up the shape as needed. The center portion of the gear needs nowhere near this level of complexity, though. So simply lathe the centerpiece at 4 (see Figure 6.15).

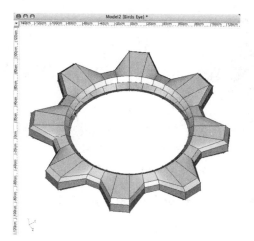

FIGURE 6.14   The valleys are scaled down to reveal the teeth of the gear.

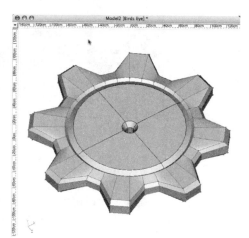

FIGURE 6.15   The center is lathed at a lower setting to conserve patches.

Most mechanical modeling tasks can be broken down in this manner, and with a little creative thinking, the most elegant solution to any problem will present itself.

BUILDINGS AND URBAN LANDSCAPES

In this section, you are going to build a very complex set based on a model originally created by James Poulakos for the storyboard sketch in Figure 6.16. This sketch is a street scene with an old brownstone apartment building as the focus.

Before investing a lot of time in building models, you can create a simple mock-up of the set to determine how much of it will show in the camera view. You can also use this time to block out the composition of the shot.

In a new project, create a new choreography. A:M will load in the default choreography, which includes a ground object and some very basic lighting. Leave these in place for now. The Choreography window, aside from being the place where animations are assembled, can also be used to do modeling tasks, as you learned in Chapter 5. You can tweak existing models, or create new ones in the Choreography window. Switch to Modeling mode and change to a top view. Bring up the window's contextual menu and choose Model from the new heading. Build a simple cube shape. This is to be the stand-in for the apartment building. It is not intended to be a full model, merely a basic indication of what and where. Adjust the points on the model just as you would in the Modeling window.

FIGURE 6.16   Set modeling often starts from a storyboard sketch.

Scale and place the cube in the choreography, and position the camera so that your shot loosely matches the layout of the building in the storyboard sketch. If you find a composition that works better than the storyboard, use that instead.

Given the position and scale of your cube, you can now start roughing in the other objects that will make up the set. Let's add the sidewalk first. Switch back to Choreography mode and make another new model. This time, rough in a sidewalk shape. Wrap it around the building in the chor. Because we can see both the building and the sidewalk in the choreography window, it makes it easy to model the sidewalk to the same scale and to match the shape without having to put both in the same model window. At this point you should have something like Figure 6.17.

Your shot also calls for a street lamp and a fire hydrant. Model two simple tubes to represent the lamp and hydrant based on the storyboard sketch. The story-board artist didn't fill in all the background details in the sketch though, and the empty space behind the main building leaves the scene looking odd. Add a building across the street and another sidewalk. Instead of modeling a completely new building and sidewalk, simply use a second instance of the models you are currently working with. Drag and drop the building model under the objects folder in the PWS—which unless you have already changed its name is called Model1—onto the Choreography window. You should now have a shortcut to Model 1 (2) listed under the choreography. Select this second shortcut, and move it into position across the street. Do the same for the sidewalk and streetlamp models. You should have something similar to Figure 6.18.

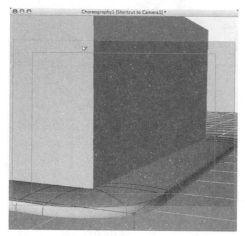

FIGURE 6.17   Modeling disparate elements in the chor helps maintain scale between them.

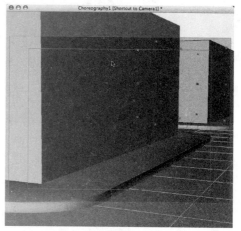

FIGURE 6.18   Use instances of existing models to block in the rest of the shot.

If the camera doesn't move, this shot now gives you all the information you need to create the set. The amount of each model that you can see is determined, and the proximity to the camera is set. The fire hydrant, for example, is far enough from the camera that it would not make sense to model individual chips of paint on its surface; details that small would simply be lost.

From here, move to the model windows for the individual elements, and work on the details that will make them believable parts of your set. Due to space restrictions, detailed tutorials on each of the set pieces can't be placed in this book. Instead, we will focus on the largest piece, and the one with the most lessons: the brownstone apartment building.

At first glance, the brownstone looks to be a huge undertaking (see Figure 6.19), and if it were modeled in one piece, it would be. But a modular design can be used that reduces the amount of work that has to be done.

FIGURE 6.19   The level of detail in this building would make it a challenge to build in a single piece.

Before any modeling, a great deal of research into the structure and design of brownstone apartment buildings was done. The Internet can provide a large number of images and references for almost any subject. The easiest way to get the basic building blocks into A:M is to use the Illustrator Wizard. If you have access to a vector graphics program such as Adobe® Illustrator® or CorelDRAW® you can simply draw out the shapes for the bricks you will need and save the result as an Illustrator file (see Figure 6.20). If you do not have one of these programs, use the keystone.ai file from the CD-ROM.

ON THE CD

FIGURE 6.20   These shapes were drawn as an Adobe Illustrator file.

Once the Illustrator file has been created, use the AI Wizard in A:M to produce a set of bricks. Create a new model and bring up the AI Wizard. Browse in the file that contains your brick shapes. Set up the Wizard to close the fronts and sides of the shapes, but not the backs. The patches on the backs of the bricks won't be seen so better to conserve them. Use flat bevels on the fronts of the objects and let the Wizard go to work. You should now have a set of brick shapes, as shown in Figure 6.21.

Leave the bricks Model window open and create another model. Start by working on the front stoop of the apartment building. Copy and paste bricks into the new model and arrange them to form half of the top arch of the doorway. Once the bricks are in place, select all the bricks except the keystone, and duplicate them via copy and paste. Use the Flip command from the contextual menu to flip the new bricks in the *x*-axis and move them to the other side of the model. You should have something similar to Figure 6.22.

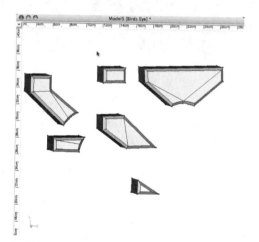
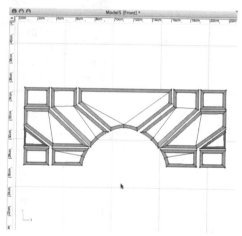

FIGURE 6.21   After the AI Wizard does its job, you have a set of bricks.

FIGURE 6.22   Arrange the individual bricks to form the arch.

The remainder of the bricks on the stoop are merely copy-and-paste versions of the rectangular brick. The rows by the door are scaled slightly up in the *x*-axis (see Figure 6.23).

The mortar can be modeled simply by placing a plane into the bricks. If you were doing a study of brickwork, you might model the mortar to bevel to each brick, but that is not needed. The only other consideration you need to make is to leave an opening for the doorway. You do this because the door has glass panels in it, and you will need to see through them. If it were a solid door and the script never called for it to be opened, a single patch would do. Extrude a four-point spline down from above the bricks to where the arch ends. Select the two points on one side, and extrude that down to the end of the bricks; do the same for the opposite side. This leaves the doorway open (see Figure 6.24).

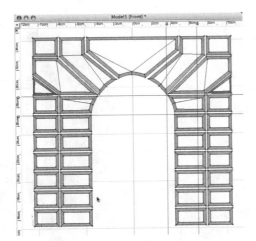

FIGURE 6.23   Copy and paste the rectangular brick to fill in the remainder of the wall.

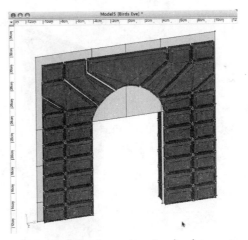

FIGURE 6.24   The mortar is a simple plane, set into the bricks.

The stairs are next. First, draw the steps and extrude them to the width of the doorway. Position this appropriately under the door. The handrails are extruded from a four-point spline with the two points toward the wall raised to the level of the second brick and the two points toward the street lowered. This shape is then extruded to give it thickness. Copy and paste a duplicate for the other side of the steps. You should have something like Figure 6.25. All that remains is to model the detail pieces on the handrail.

The end caps of the rails are made from two pieces. The base is a four-point patch that is extruded and shaped from bottom to top. Reposition and scale each extrusion to shape each cross section. Lathe a sphere and place it on top of this to finish the cap. For the planters on the tops of the rails, draw a spline in a rough inverted U to form the wall of the planter. Extrude this spline to form the walls of the planter. Seat the base in the handrail, and push the unclosed end into the wall. You should have a finished stoop, much like Figure 6.26.

This model looks very detailed and complex; but, as you can see, when broken down to its basic components and with the help of the AI Wizard, its construction is actually very simple. This is your first module for the building. You could continue the construction of the building in this model window, but this has some disadvantages that will become apparent. Check this model for scale in the choreography in which you started the set layout.

Drop the model onto the choreography and position it next to the proxy-building cube that was modeled as a placeholder. Your model might be much larger or much smaller than the size of the building. If so, do not scale the model in the Choreography window. Scaling models up or down by a large amount in the Choreography window can cause problems, such as artifacts in the final renders and much longer than normal render times. Instead, scale the model down in the Model window until it fits the scale of the scene (see Figure 6.27).

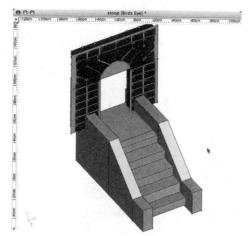

FIGURE 6.25 The steps and handrails are made from simple extrusions.

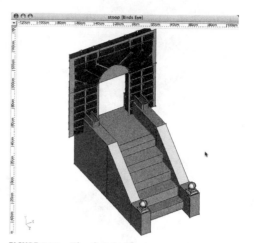

FIGURE 6.26 The finished stoop.

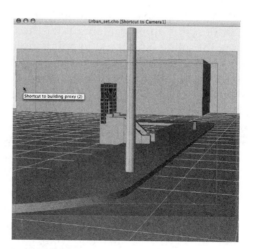

FIGURE 6.27 The stoop had to be scaled down to match the scale established for the shot.

You only need once instance of this model in the scene, which is why you do not build the entire building as one model. Since the foreground building covers over most of the background, much of the detail in the second instance of a large uniform model would be wasted. Creating small modules for the various sections of the model and assembling them in the choreography lets you use just the visible portions of each building.

The second module for the building you need to make is a window set into the wall of the apartment building (see Figure 6.28).

The bricks for the wall are simple rectangular bricks, which you already have modeled from the stoop. Use the Duplicator Wizard to place them in a grid. Delete the extra bricks from the center of the wall to allow room for the window (see Figure 6.29).

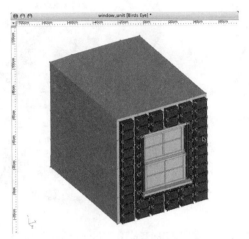

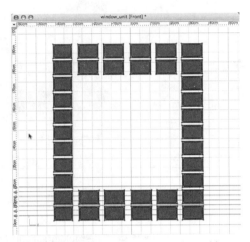

FIGURE 6.28   The next module for building the apartment.

FIGURE 6.29   The Duplicator Wizard quickly builds the grid.

This is a double-hung window with a wooden frame. You could model it as one piece of glass, but allowing windows to open, and by opening several windows different amounts, lets you break up the regularity of the building. Using the techniques you already know, modeling the windows is a snap. The glass in each frame is made from a single four-point patch. The frame could be a single extruded piece around the glass or a manipulated lathe object, but the simpler solution is to extrude the shape of the wood once to form the board and then simply place a copy around each edge of the glass.

You can make this molding as complex as you like, but looking at the choreography for this shot tells you that any small details on these windows will not be seen. Rather than strive to model perfect replicas of the molding used on windows, set a higher priority on conserving patches. A simple four-point spline loop can be swept around a simple square path and have all the detail your windows will need. A copy of this frame can be scaled down to break the glass up into four separate panes (see Figure 6.30).

Once the first window is finished, the second frame is simply a copy and paste. The sill comes under the same considerations as the window frame, and the same simple Sweep can be used in modeling it. Window hardware and other fine details can be skipped over unless the camera gets close enough to one of the windows to require more. Place the completed window into the hole in the wall. The hole may be wider than the window. If so, a row of half bricks on each side of the window can be added to close the space. You should now have something similar to Figure 6.31.

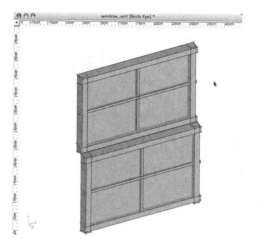

FIGURE 6.30   The molding around the window is a good place to conserve patches.

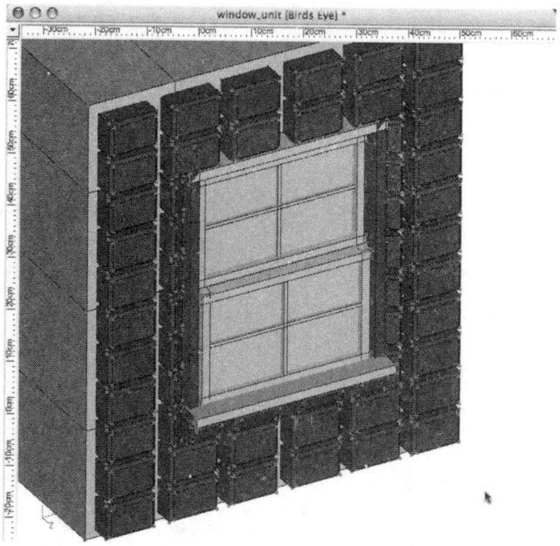

FIGURE 6.31   The completed window and wall.

In the same way that you did for the stoop, a layer of patches can be added as mortar for the wall. For this approach, you will also need a hole in the mortar where the window sits. The problem with having windows is that they allow the camera to see into the apartment building. You won't likely want to have to model the entire building, so a simple three-sided box can be built to give the room beyond some area. Later, you can texture this box to look like an apartment without having to model any of the interiors.

This finishes this module. Drop it into the choreography next to the stoop that you modeled, and make the scale match the rest of the scene. Once that is done, use it to stack the front of the building together (see Figure 6.32). Note that all of the background building that is visible is one corner; so a few of these modules give the impression of a much more complex scene without requiring the renderer to calculate the extra patches.

The remaining portions of the set are built in the same fashion. Remember: spend your patches wisely, don't waste detail on hidden or small objects, and build things modularly as much as possible.

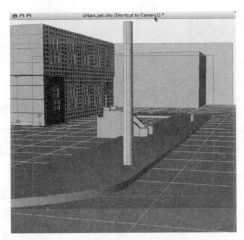

FIGURE 6.32   Stacking the modules up in the
Choreography window quickly adds
definition to a set.

BUILDING THE PERFECT ROBOT

The fun stuff isn't limited to organic character modeling, though. Take your
knowledge of mechanical splining and build yourself the perfect robotic character! This is Polygozmo (see Figure 6.33).

FIGURE 6.33   Concept sketch for Polygozmo,
the evil (yet perfect) robot.

Polygozmo is an evil robot that will play counter to our beloved Captain Splines in a short animation (the focus of Chapter 10). He was built perfect—too perfect—and his own ego has led him to a life of crime! Good thing Captain Splines is out there to protect us.

This character is built from a number of parts that you have already looked at. If you look closely at the concept drawing, you may even find part of your remote control in there. Again, this is an exercise in modeling from your Morgue. Start with pieces you already have and go forward from there. There is no need to respine the wheel.

ON THE CD

Start your model by laying out our rotoscopes. You will find a front and side drawing for Polygozmo on the CD-ROM in the images folder. Once the drawings are in place and lined up (refer back to Chapters 2 and 5 if you need a refresher), you can look over the design for parts that can be pulled out of other models. For instance, there is a button plate on the robot's chest that looks a lot like the top plate and buttons for the remote control you built. You will need the gears for the clockwork torso parts of the model. You can even go back to Chapter 2 and pull in some of the simple models you made. The various fitting rings on the arms and legs of the character are calling out for some toruses. Go over the rest of the drawings and see if you have any models or parts of models that can be adapted. Make a list of the parts you want, and import them into your project (which should be a snap if you have maintained an organized asset library). Here is a list just from objects you have modeled so far in this book:

- Beveled cube
- Perfect sphere
- Cog
- Remote control
- Torus
- Cylinder

Okay. Now you need to decide where to start with your robot. This is slightly different than a character and more akin to a set piece. You don't want to start with the details so much as you want to rough in the big shapes first. Block out the main portions of the robot, and then come back for the details.

Start by copying in a cube, align this with the drawing for the torso, and scale it into the correct trapezoidal shape (be sure to adjust from a side view as well). Paste in a second cube to fill in the "hips" of the character, again positioning and scaling to match the drawing. Copy in a sphere and position it below the hips. You should have something similar to Figure 6.34

The head is a cylinder, but you will want to lathe a new one here so that you have the proper splinage to form the mouth later. While you could stitch in a new spline, lathing produces a cleaner result. Start by drawing a nine-point cross section in the shape of a large C (see Figure 6.35). Then lathe this shape to form the head. If it is not already, position it and scale it to match the top of the body area, in position with the drawing. Go ahead and move the splines on the side and front of the head to match the demented smile that gives Polygozmo so much of his character.

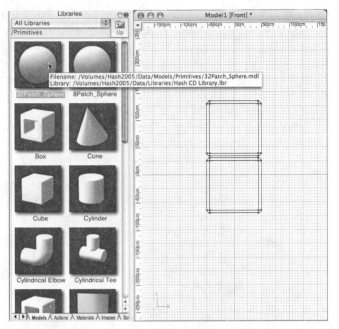

FIGURE 6.34   Two cubes and a sphere block in the body of your robot.

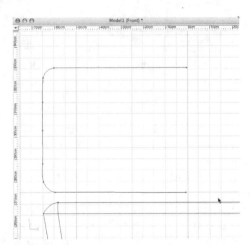

FIGURE 6.35   The head is lathed from this cross section.

Once the smile is more or less represented, you can start to get some of the details modeled into the head. Begin by breaking all the splines that will be inside the smile area. This leaves a large hole in the front of the head. You could stitch a spline in around and make a clean ring for the mouth area, but because you aren't planning to animate this shape and most of it will be peaked later, that would be more work than is needed. To make some depth to the mouth shape, select all the points around the hole you just made and extrude. Move the resulting group back up and in line with the original points, and bring up the scale manipulator. Scale this group down in the *y*-axis and then down in the *x*-axis. The result will be similar to Figure 6.36.

You could stitch the mouth area as a complete unibody mesh from the mouth opening, but it is just as easy to extrude and shape a few patches to fill in without having to worry about continuing the splines (see Figure 6.37). The details seen in the drawings are accomplished with textures later.

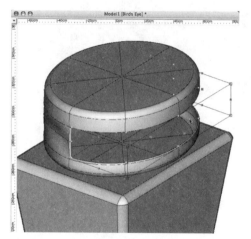

FIGURE 6.36   The mouth is first broken out then extruded for depth.

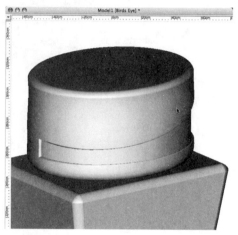

FIGURE 6.37   Three patches can fill in the mouth area.

The eyes of the robot are actually just simple hollow cylinders. Lathe them with a U-shaped cross section and "jam" them inside the head mesh. The lenses? Your perfect sphere from Chapter 2 scaled down will fit the bill nicely. Paste it into the Model window, and scale it so that it fits the diameter of the inside of the eye tube.

Now is a good time to add the details to the chest of the character. Cut two holes into the cube: one for the window that reveals the gears inside the robot and one that is filled with buttons and lights to make the robot look all science-fictiony. Start by defining the area that will be the hole. This means lay out the splines that will define the edge of the holes. These splines will tell you how you need to proceed and what density needs to be added. Both holes can be defined simply with an eight-point loop in a rough rectangle shape (see Figure 6.38). Go ahead and draw one of these now in about the area where you want the chest window to be located.

Position this spline loop in the chest and align it with the front of the torso. Now stitch the "hole" into the chest with the Add/Stitch tool, and take the splines all the way around the torso to have them connect with the opposite side of the hole. This leaves you with something similar to Figure 6.39.

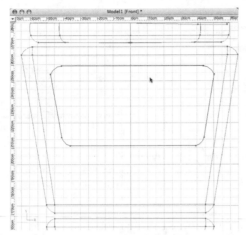

FIGURE 6.38   Start to set the details of the character by laying out an eight-point spline loop.

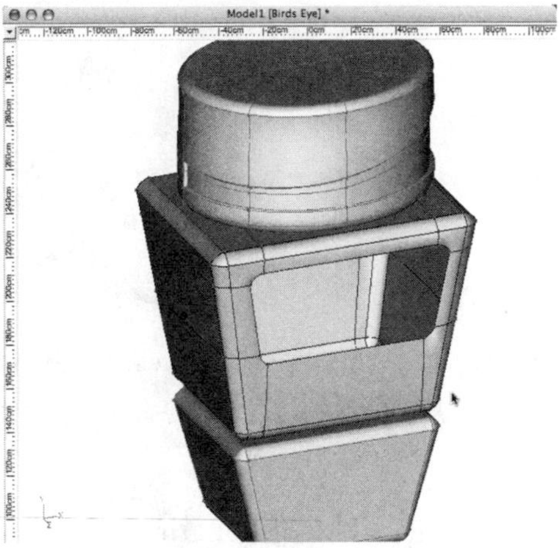

FIGURE 6.39   After stitching the hole into the torso.

Select the loop that makes up the hole and extrude it. Scale and push this group back into the torso to give the cutout some depth. While the new ring is still selected, copy and paste it to make a new unattached loop. Move this one under the first, and scale it to match the button panel on the rotoscope. Stitch this loop in, just as you did the main chest cavity, until you have something similar to Figure 6.40.

Extrude this panel back into the torso, just as you did for the main chest panel.

The chest panel is covered by glass and filled with interlocking gears. The glass is made by simply covering the hole with a single four-point patch. Group and name this patch so that you can make it transparent later. The gears are simply instances of the gear model from earlier in this chapter. Copy in as many as you like, and position them inside the chest cavity.

The button panel starts with the top of the remote control that you modeled earlier in this chapter. Copy it, buttons and all, and paste it into Polygozmo's Model window. Position, rotate, and scale to fill most of the hole you made. When it is close, adjust the outer spline ring on the face to fill in the remainder of the space, leaving the buttons intact. You should wind up with a fairly detailed torso, similar to Figure 6.41.

All that remains for your character are the arms and hands. The arms are just tubes and are easily lathed. But you do need to make them fairly dense to give them the flexibility you need. Start with a straight spline with 20 CPs evenly distributed

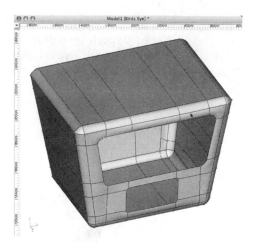

FIGURE 6.40 Stitch in a second hole for the button panel.

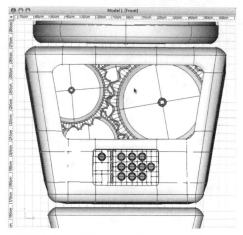

FIGURE 6.41 With some clever reuse of previous models, you have added a good amount of detail to your character.

along its length. Lathe this spline to form a simple tube (see Figure 6.42), and position it abutting the torso of the character. You will want to hide the joint of the arm and torso, as indicated in the rotoscopes, and this is the perfect place for a torus. Paste a torus into the Model window, and position, rotate, and scale it to match both the surface of the robot's torso and the diameter of its arm. When you have this torus in place, duplicate it and move the copy to the wrist area (see Figure 6.43).

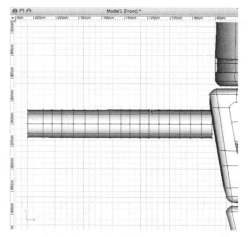

FIGURE 6.42 Start with a dense spline to lathe this tube, which will give you a lot of flexibility later.

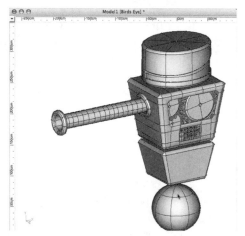

FIGURE 6.43 The torus from Chapter 2 covers up the joints of the arm nicely.

The hand is actually a fairly complex shape. Each finger has three distinct segments that need to be smoothly jointed, and each finger needs to have a smooth joint into the hand. You could model this to be a unibody mesh, but that would look out of place with this character. Instead, you are going to build distinct segments. A good place to start might be with a pencil and paper to get the design of the hands correct. One possible design is shown in Figure 6.44, where a set of ball-and-socket-style joints are made from each finger segment to the next and from the fingers into the hand. The challenge here is in making the sockets fit correctly into the hand of your robot.

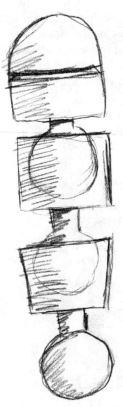

FIGURE 6.44   One possible solution for the design of the hand.

Each finger segment can be broken down into one of two types: the fingertip where the end is closed, and the finger segment where the top is left open to form a joint with the next segment of the finger. Regardless of the part of the finger, you can create it with a single lathe operation. Simply draw the outline of the shape, perhaps using your design drawings as a rotoscope.

If you need additional rotoscopes in your model window, set them up in the top or bottom view where you can see them without disturbing the rotoscopes for the rest of the character.

Once you have the two basic segments lathed, simply copy and paste them to assemble a whole finger. Then copy and paste that finger to make three for each hand (see Figure 6.45).

Place the fingers first, as they will aid in constructing your hands. The most challenging part of the hands is getting the joints for the fingers to line up correctly, so that they appear to "house" the joints. This challenge is easily met by selecting the ball ends of each of the fingers and making a duplicate of them. Once duplicated, simply scale each up slightly to form a bowl where the finger can sit. Now spline the rest of the hand in place with the same techniques that you used for the Captain's hand in Chapter 5. Start by making a spline ring with enough points to tie the finger holes to, and then stitch the fingers together. The major differences between this and the Captain are that this hand will not need to flex at all, so you don't need to worry nearly as much about the layout of the splines. Any arrangement that produces a clean surface is acceptable.

Extrude the hand back, and tuck it inside the torus at the wrist to finish up the model (see Figure 6.46).

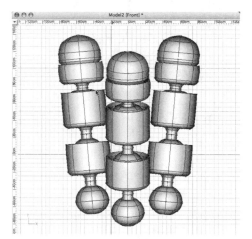

FIGURE 6.45 Paste and position the fingers for the hands according to the rotoscopes drawings.

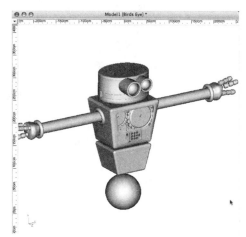

FIGURE 6.46 The finished Polygozmo model.

SUMMARY

You should now have a firm grasp on the techniques involved in modeling anything.

Each type of modeling has its own unique challenges. Sets require a lot of detail and an eye to making elements sit together properly. Characters require an eye for spline layout, and mechanical objects require knowing where patches can be spared and where it is best to work detail in.

Remember to model your sets to the camera so that you don't waste detail on things that will never be seen. Keep your surfaces simple, and use textures to fill in the tiny details as much as possible. You will see how this works when you learn about surfacing in Chapter 11. The time you invest here, though, will be rewarded when you finally render the scene.

If you are not very interested in modeling sets and props, don't worry about it. You can either go simple with plain backgrounds, or you can look on the Internet for free or for-pay model collections that you can modify to your needs. The Web site *http://www.eggprops.com* has models of very high quality for sale, and A:M user sites such as *http://www.hash.com/freemodels/* often have free model collections you can use. Don't forget the A:M CD-ROM. There are some very good models provided there for your use.

This is the last we will talk about modeling because the remainder of the book will discuss the other features of A:M. You should continue to practice modeling as you learn the rest of the software. Start building your own collection of set pieces and props.

CONSTRAINTS

In This Chapter

- Constraints Concepts
- Character Rigging
- Fan Bones and CP Weighting

In this chapter, we start to uncover A:M's ultrapowerful character constraint system. First, we go over each constraint, learn how they affect bones in a model, and examine some situations where they might be used in practical applications. Then we will look at a simple constraint system for a character, explaining why particular constraints and tools are useful, covering the concepts of fan bones, control bones, and geometry bones, and how they apply to a model. We also look at how to make your rigs reusable and fast to apply.

By the end of the chapter, you should have a basic rig installed into the character from Chapter 5.

Constraints Concepts

Regardless of their type, all constraints are designed to make an aspect of one object fall under the control of another object, or remain in a specified area of operation. This is normally a bone operation, but also strays into the realm of dynamics.

The types of constraints, or the aspects that can be controlled, are broken down into logical groups in the interface based on the attributes they are intended to control.

Primarily, constraints are used to build simple sets of control bones that can drive complex skeletal rigs in a character or any other type of object.

Each constraint in itself is typically very simple, forcing one bone to rotate like another, for example. Each simple constraint can, however, be mixed, layered, and blended with other constraints. It is through this blending that you develop sophisticated, transparent, and most importantly simple-to-use and intuitive controls.

Constraints can be applied to a model in choreography, action, or pose relationship windows. Applying constraints is accomplished via the contextual menu for the bone (either in the workspace window or the PWS/Properties) you wish to affect. Once the constraint has been selected, in most cases the cursor will turn into the eyedropper icon allowing you to select the target of the constraint.

In order to have constraints, an object must have at least one bone; but for most constraints, two are necessary. The hierarchy of the bones you are trying to constrain is very important. Hierarchy limits the possible application of constraints. A parent, for instance, cannot be the targeted by a constraint to any of its children; doing so would result in what is called a "circular" constraint error. Orienting a bone like its child, for instance, would be a circular constraint: The orientation of the child is dependent on the parent. If the parent were constrained to the child there is no way to determine which bone should define the orientation. A:M prevents you from setting up constraints that are circular, but if you set up a constraint and then change bone hierarchy, problems can creep in.

Hierarchy is also important to the application of multiple constraints to a single bone. Because a bone may have many constraints that are similar when applied (such as translate limits and translate to constraints), the order in which they are applied is critical. Like most things in the PWS, constraints take hierarchical precedence from the bottom of the list to the top. This means that if you constrain a bone and then apply a limit constraint, the limits will only allow the constraint to function within its limiting area (rotate like, but only within a given range). If, on the other hand, you have the hierarchy of the constraints reversed, then the bone will translate to the target without regard to the rules of the limits.

This does not apply to constraints of the same type. Two or more constraints of the same type are termed blended constraints, and A:M will apply them in proportion to the enforcement percentage of each constraint. Enforcement totals 100%, even if all constraints are 100% or the total of all constraints' enforcement values is greater or less than 100%. If all enforcements are the same, they are averaged and have equal control over the bone being constrained. Constraint blending in this matter is useful for a number of applications, most notably joint smoothing.

By default, when a constraint is applied to a bone it will move immediately to comply with the constraint. This is often the correct behavior, but sometimes it is desirable for the bone to remain stationary when the constraint is applied. This is accomplished by offsets. Think of a hand reaching for a glass. As soon as the hand is in position to pick up the glass, you would want the glass to stick to the hand. If the bones were not lined up and positioned for just this circumstance, and they aren't normally, the glass would jump and likely not be in contact with the hand as you had wanted.

Offsets can be generated in two ways:

Select the newly constrained bone and manipulate it until it is in the position in which it is to be offset (the difficult way).

Click the Compensate Mode button before selecting the target for the constraint (the easy way).

Offsets, enforcements, and all other aspects of constraints can be animated. If the character has picked up the glass and the glass has been constrained to its hand, then when the character sets the glass down the enforcement of the constraint can be lowered until the glass no longer moves with the hand. When you do this, it is important that you set a keyframe for the translation and rotation attributes of the glass, or when its constraints are turned off, it will move to the coordinates of its last keyframe.

Constraints can be applied with bones in two or more different models: when in the choreography or when using action objects. This allows a character to convincingly interact with its environment.

 Constraints are one of the more difficult aspects of A:M to understand, but their power and the control they afford when animating more than makes up for this.

In A:M, all of your constraints are accessed from the same contextual menu for the sake of discussion in this chapter; however, they are broken up into loose categories: Rotational, Translate, Scale, Limits, and Other. Each of your constraints can be thought to fall into one of these groups.

Rotational Constraints

Rotational constraints are:

- Orient Like
- Aim At
- Aim Like Two
- Aim Roll At
- Roll Like
- Roll Like Two

Orient Like forces a bone to rotate exactly like its target. An enforcement percentage can make the bone orient like the target to a lesser amount, but it cannot force it to orient like the target more than 100%. This is often used in conjunction with additional Orient Like constraints to blend portions of a mesh (often referred to as fan bones). The enforcement is set on the Properties panel for the constraint (see Figure 7.1).

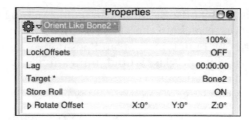

FIGURE 7.1   Orient Like properties.

Enforcement is the amount that the bone will orient like the target. When blending constraints, this indicates the enforcement a particular constraint will contribute to the final orientation of the bone. All blended constraints total 100%.

The target property indicates what bone will drive the constraint. This can be changed by clicking on the name of the target bone; doing so will reveal a pop-up list of all bones in the project and the eyedropper icon. Selecting a bone from the list will change the target to that bone; selecting the eyedropper will allow you to click any bone in the current workspace to indicate the target.

Lag is useful for creating automatic overlap and follow-through on soft objects, such as ears on a dog. It indicates that the constraint will enforce a number of frames behind the target, so that the constrained bone will seem to follow it. Think of the ears on the flour sack you animated in Chapter 4. Instead of using muscle motion to animate them, a bone could have been added to each and an Orient Like constraint used to force the ears to lag behind the arms of the sack.

The roll handle is also controlled by the Orient Like constraint. If you need the roll to be controlled by some other constraint, or manually, or not at all, change the Store Roll property to off. This is typically done when the target has a different roll orientation than the constrained bone.

Rotate Offset shows the offset the constrained bone has in relation to the target. This number can be entered by hand or generated automatically by use of Compensate mode. In addition, any movement of the constrained bone will generate offsets here.

The Translate Offset shows any offset that the target bone may have. These may be entered by hand, or any manipulation of the target after the constraint is applied will generate them.

Aim At forces the constrained bone to aim its tip at the base, or pivot, of the target bone. Multiple Aim At constraints on a single bone are blended based on the enforcement percentage of each. The properties for the Aim At constraint are shown in Figure 7.2.

Enforcement is the amount that the bone will point at the target from its default position. When blending multiple Aim At constraints, this is the value that each constraint uses to contribute its weight to the bone.

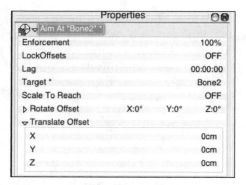

FIGURE 7.2   Aim At properties.

- Lag is the same as for Orient Like constraints.
- Scale to Reach forces the bone to scale to touch the base of the target bone as it moves through 3D space. By default, this scaling is in all three axes.
- Z-axis Only forces the Scale to Reach option to only scale the bone along its z-axis (length).
- Rotate and Translate offsets are the same as for the Orient Like constraint.

Aim Like Two is one of two motion capture-related constraints and is not used very often otherwise. It is used to control the aim of a bone along a line defined by two motion capture data points. Its properties are similar to those for the constraints already discussed (see Figure 7.3).

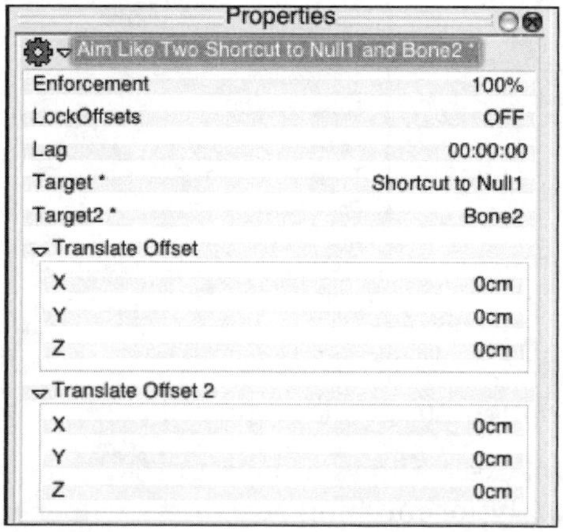

FIGURE 7.3   Aim Like Two properties.

Aim Roll At behaves the same as Aim At, with the exception that it forces the roll handle of the constrained bone to aim at the base of the target. The roll handle is limited to a flat disk of rotation and cannot always point directly at a target, but will aim as close as its limited rotation will allow. Two or more Aim Roll At constraints can be blended exactly as for the Aim At constraint. The properties for Aim Roll At are the same as discussed for Aim At (see Figure 7.4) with the exception that rotational offsets are replaced with the roll offset.

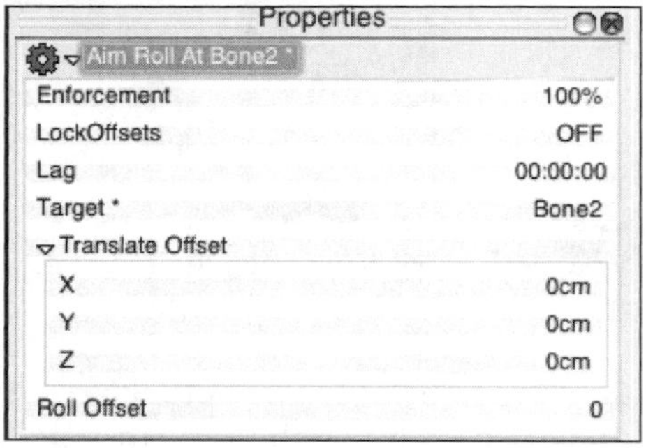

FIGURE 7.4   Aim Roll At properties.

Roll Like forces the roll handle of the constrained bone to move exactly like the roll handle on the target. Note that unlike the Orient Like and Aim At constraints, this does not force a bone's roll handle to move from its default position. It moves relative to the rotation of the target, but does not mirror it if the target is in a different default position. This constraint also supports blending. There are also some unique properties for Roll Like (see Figure 7.5).

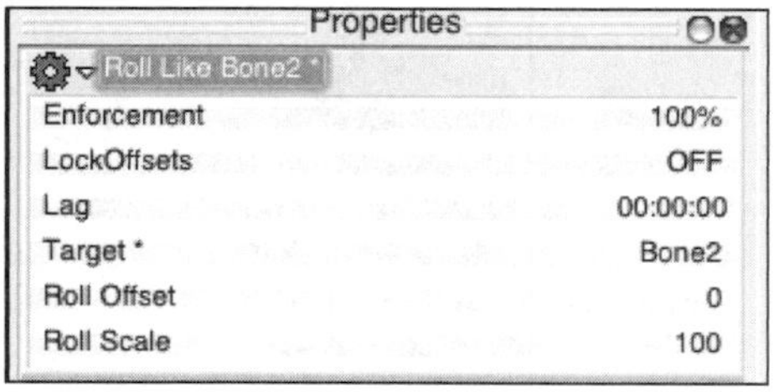

FIGURE 7.5   Roll Like properties.

Enforcement, target, lag, and roll offset all function as already discussed.

- Roll Scale allows a bone to roll faster or slower than the target. This is handy for meshing gearworks where a larger gear may need to drive a smaller gear.
- Roll Like Two is the second motion capture-oriented constraint type. Where Aim Like Two orients the bone, this constraint orients the roll handle along the vector defined by two motion-capture data targets. It is not used outside motion capture. Its properties are identical to those already discussed (see Figure 7.6).

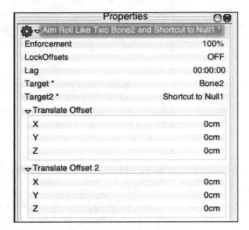

FIGURE 7.6   Roll Like Two properties.

Translate Constraint

The Translate To constraint translates the base of the bone to the base of the target bone. This is regardless of, and isolated from, rotation on either bone. Multiple Translate To constraints are blended together based on the enforcements of the constraints as set on the Properties panel (see Figure 7.7).

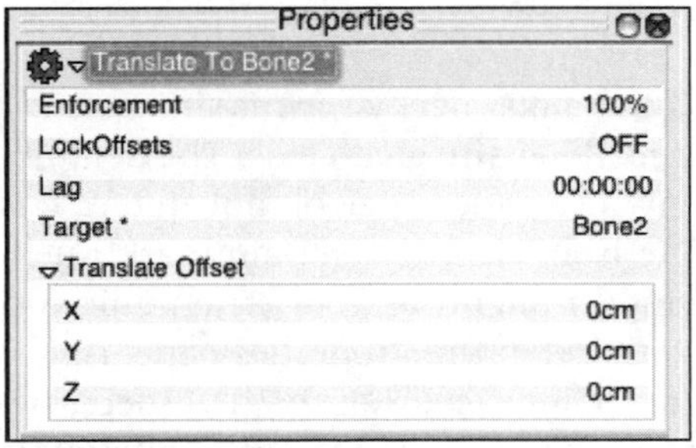

FIGURE 7.7   Translate To properties.

Enforcement, target, lag, and translate offset all function the same here as for the properties already discussed.

Scale Constraint

Scale Like forces the constrained bone to follow the scale operations performed on the target bone. Using the enforcement property on each constraint, you can blend their effect on the constrained bone (see Figure 7.8).

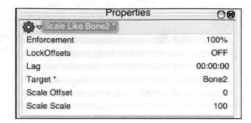

FIGURE 7.8   Scale Like properties.

Enforcement, target, and lag all behave the same as for other constraints. Scale Offset is similar to rotate and translate offsets, but applies only to scale channels. The odd-sounding Scale Scale property can be set to make a bone scale to a higher or lower percentage than the target—to keep a bone twice the scale of the target, for example.

Limits

Limits are a general category of constraint that restricts the movement of a bone, specifically in translation and rotation. Each of the limit constraints works by specifying a valid range of movement for the bone. Any movement outside that range will not be allowed. Limits cannot be blended.

There are three Limits constraints:

- Translate
- Spherical
- Euler

Translate Limits specify the maximum and minimum ranges that a bone may be translated along any given axis. The default settings allow 1000 centimeters in any axis, giving a wide range of movement. It is common to use this constraint to keep a bone from passing a certain mark, such as keeping the feet of a character from moving through the floor. The minimum and maximum values for Translate Limits are set in the Properties panel (see Figure 7.9).

Spherical Limits (see Figure 7.10) specify the maximum area that a bone may rotate. This is expressed in degrees of rotation from negative 180 to a positive 180 in three axes: latitude, longitude, and roll. It can be difficult to gain a firm understanding of what these numbers mean and how they function. However, they are used less frequently in real-world applications than most of the other constraint types; so a passing understanding of their concepts is often all that is needed.

Looking at the Properties panel for the Spherical Limits constraint you see the same basic setup you saw from the Translate Limits. The minimum and maximum properties are broken down into three numbers, and it is tempting to simply use latitude, longitude, and roll to stand in for *x*, *y*, and *z* rotation. But try this for an experiment: Create a model with one bone in it, make the bone point straight down, and point its roll handle back. Open an action with this model and

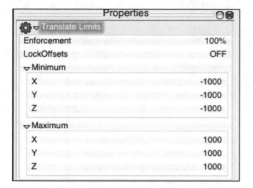

FIGURE 7.9   Translate Limits properties.

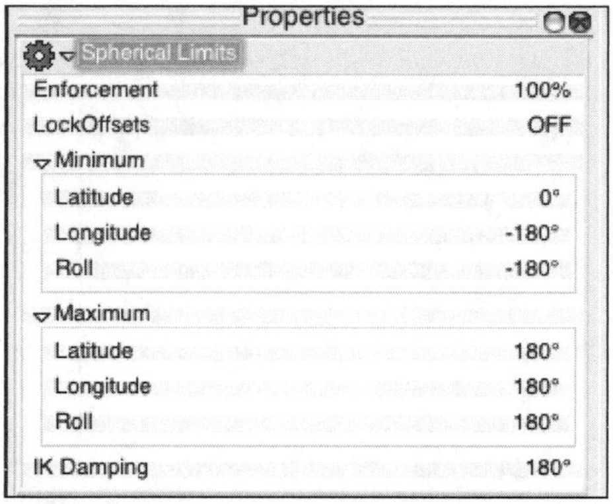

FIGURE 7.10   Spherical Limit properties.

apply a Spherical Limit to (by control-clicking on a Mac or right-clicking on a PC) the bone and choosing Spherical Limits from the limits heading of the new constraints option of the contextual menu. In the Properties window, change the minimum longitude to 0 and the maximum longitude to 90 degrees. Move the bone by rotating the tip.

If the latitude and longitude settings were equal to the axis of rotation for the bone, you would have expected to limit the bone to rotate 0 to 90 degrees in the *y*-axis; but with a little experimentation, you can see that the bone has almost unrestricted rotation in the *y*-axis. So what did you do?

The rotation of an unconstrained bone can describe a sphere, the base of the bone being at the center, and the tip indicating a given point along its surface. Adding a spherical limit describes a smaller area of the sphere that the bone's tip is required to remain within. In the case of longitude, think of an orange. The longitude setting describes how wide of a slice the orange has, so a 90-degree slice or one-quarter of the orange is what you have now. Latitude is best described by imagining a bowl, the lip of which is as far as the bone can travel along a surface. The default position of the tip is 0, so you can limit the bone to a bowl 50 degrees from bottom to lip or any other area you like. Together, latitude and longitude describe the 3D area of the bones' rotation that is allowed. Roll is very easy to understand, as it merely limits the roll handle, as you might expect.

Not only are spherical limits difficult to explain, they are difficult to use consistently. It is recommended that you use them sparingly, if at all. The other constraints offer as much control over bones with less trouble.

Euler Limits, the second type of rotational limits that A:M supports, are generally easier to use and understand. Each axis of rotation is given a minimum and maximum rotation in degrees. A bone does not have to be using Euler rotations to take advantage of this type of limit. The properties of Euler Limits, as shown in Figure 7.11, are identical to those found on the Spherical Limits: enforcement allowing movement beyond the range of the limit; apply before action; and IK damping, stiffening the rotation of the end of an IK chain when the limit is applied.

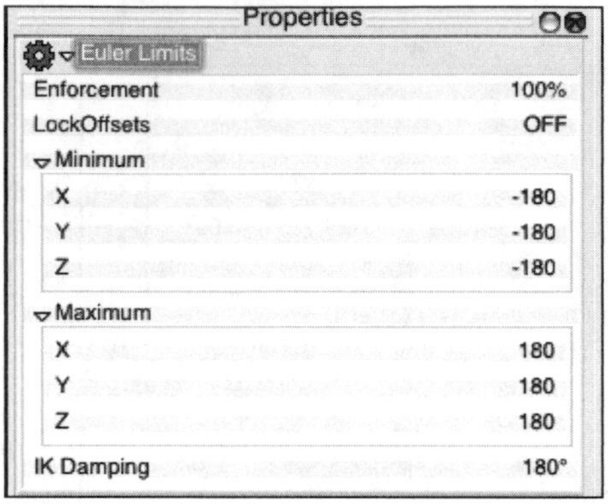

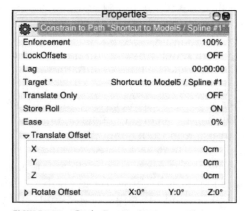

FIGURE 7.11   Euler Limits properties.

Other Constraints

In addition to the constraints (Path, Kinematic, and Surface) listed in this section, there are constraints specific to dynamic simulations that are discussed in Chapter 13, "F/X."

The Path constraint places a bone on any spline, even one that is part of a model. The constrained bone will aim along the length of the path as best as it can, and as the ease of the constraint is animated, it will move along the length of the path. It is common to use a Path constraint on a chain of bones to allow the simple manipulation of the path to control a complex object such as a phone cord or a tentacle. The properties for an Ease constraint (see Figure 7.12) have some similarities to the constraints already discussed. Path constraints support blending, and the enforcement percentage indicates the amount any particular Path constraint will affect the bone. Applied before action, lag, target, store roll, translate, and rotate offsets all behave as has been discussed for other constraints. The two new properties are Ease and Translate Only.

FIGURE 7.12   Path Constraint properties.

Ease indicates how far along the path the base of the bone is to be placed. It is a percentage ranging from 0 to 100.

Translate Only lets the bone maintain its own rotation and does not allow the constraint to affect the tip. This can be useful for objects such as curtains or accordions, where the rotation of the bone may need to be controlled separately from the translation.

Kinematic constraints allow you to place a bone that is typically out of the hierarchy of a kinematic chain at the tip of a chain. This is commonly used as a method to build control bones where IK is desired, such as in the feet of a character. This does not make the target a fully functional member of the chain by any means. It merely establishes the base of the target bone as the kinematic goal of the constrained bone, extending the tip of that bone, so to speak. The behavior of the Kinematic constraint very closely resembles that of the Aim At constraint, but the important distinction is that the Aim At constraint only affects the constrained bone's rotation. The Kinematic constraint propagates through the entire chain. In addition, because Kinematic constraints establish the new kinematic goal for the chain, they have properties that allow them to affect the behavior of the chain (see Figure 7.13).

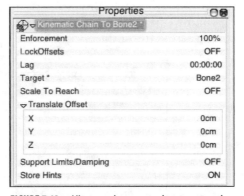

FIGURE 7.13 Kinematic constraints properties.

The majority of the properties are the same as those found on Aim At constraints. Support Limits/Damping tells the computer to enforce any rotational limits (such as Spherical or Euler) as it solves the IK chain. This ensures that the target will be reached if the constrained bone is able to do so within its limits. Without this option checked, the target, in some cases, may not be reached even if a possible solution exists.

This option also activates the IK damping of the rotational limits. Damping changes the preferred behavior of the IK solver (giving preference to the bone at the end of the chain when solving) to let the tip of the chain behave more stiffly and give the preference in solving to the next bone up the chain. This is useful for rotations on things like fingers where the last digit is stiffer than the ones that precede it.

Compute Roll allows the kinematic target to also affect the roll handles of the IK chain, within the range of their limits, to arrive at a solution. This is only truly on if the Support Limits/Damping property has been turned on.

Surface constraints are used to let a bone move across the surface of an object. This can be used to keep the wheels of a car in contact with an uneven surface or to place the pupils of a cartoony eye on the surface of the whites. It is one of the more complicated constraints to use, requiring at least three bones. The first bone that is needed is obviously the one to which the constraint is applied. This bone will keep its base along the surface that it is being constrained to at all times and will orient like the normals of that surface. The other two required bones are used to indicate the surface and to point where the constrained bone should sit on that surface. The surface bone must have been assigned the CPs of the surface to which you wish to constrain. The pointer bone aims at the surface the constrained bone will target. Specifically, the constrained bone will place its base on the surface at the point where a ray drawn along the aiming bone intersects the targeted surface.

The properties for surface constraints are similar to the other constraints (see Figure 7.14); Translate Only is the only unique property. The bone that is constrained will orient itself like the normals of the surface to which it is constrained, unless you turn the Translate Only property on. In which case, it maintains its own orientation or can be controlled by other constraints with the base of the bone translating across the surface.

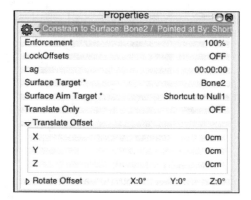

FIGURE 7.14   Surface constraint properties.

CHARACTER RIGGING

Rigging a character is the process of adding bones and constraints to make animation easier. It is a methodic procedure that requires logical thinking and planning. Not everyone enjoys or is particularly good at rigging; but without a solid rig, animation is less intuitive and more prone to problems. You start all rigs from a foundation of Geometry bones and move up from there.

Geometry Bones

The constraints we have discussed are all designed to give you more control over your characters and to make the task of animating them easier. However, that does you no good if you are unable to easily apply them to a character. Developing a rig, as it is termed, is a long process that is ruled by your knowledge of constraints, and how to combine them, and how you like to animate. It is recommended that you start simple. If you find that a more complex set of constraints suits your needs better, it is easier to build upon a simple rig than to have to tear apart a complicated rig to add control. Something important to keep in mind is that while rigging a character is at its core a technical endeavor, the results are as artistic as any other aspect of 3D. You are not just dropping bones in a character; you are also developing a user interface. Think about your favorite piece of software, A:M perhaps, and consider how the tools are laid out in a logical fashion and how they function the way you want them too. That is your goal here as well. You need to have access to the tools you need, when you need them. Those tools need to be in the right places, and their functions need to be self-evident.

You can proceed much as you did for the flour sack, first deciding what controls are needed and then building the rig to match. For this section, you will be building a constraint rig for the Captain character. The Captain is a simple character, but even he offers some challenges.

Like most humanoid characters, the most basic set of controls are relative to the parts of the body that will need to be animated: arms, legs, head, spine, hands, and feet all need discrete controls. In addition, mechanisms for eye, jaw, and finger movement are also important to character animation.

But characters like the Captain offer more challenges than your simple flour sack did. Sets of secondary, or "fan," bones to blend geometry through ranges of motion are needed, as well as relationships (see Chapter 8) and expressions (see Chapter 9) to simplify your controls and make the motion provided more robust, and to offer the ability to deform the overall shape of the model with Squash and Stretch.

These base controls then act as your goal in rigging this character; as with the flour sack, start with the geometry bones. Deciding where to place and orient geometry bones as well as their basic hierarchy is your first step.

Open the Model window for Captain and switch to Bones mode. Make sure that you have the Manipulators Properties Widget toggled on, as you will use it a lot in the boning process. For humanoids, and indeed most characters, the skeleton starts from the hips and moves out, making the hips the root for most of the geometry. For animation purposes, however, and for simplicity of organization in the PWS, a different root bone is sometimes desirable.

In the Model window, draw a bone from the base of the character's feet to the top of the character's head (see Figure 7.15), and rename it "root." It should run as close to the center of the character as possible. Use the Properties panel to put it on the center of the model with numerical precision. In the properties for the bone, set the start and end position of the bone to 0 in the x- and z-axes.

The root bone indicates the character's height, which, if you share actions between characters, will be a ruler A:M can use to scale the action to the proportions of the character. It is also useful when animating, as it gives a simple control to move the entire character in an action or choreography window. This bone has no control points assigned to it.

Once the root has been established, it is important to keep all bones under it in hierarchy.

Next, the basic geometry skeleton can be laid down, starting from the pelvis and working out. The pelvis in this character would be a bone that starts at the waist and points down, leading naturally into the legs. Place the pelvis bone along the centerline of the character in both the front and side views and point the roll handle backward (see Figure 7.16). In many cases, the position of the roll handle is critical to the constraints that will be applied later. Getting in the habit of adjusting your roll handles for consistency is a good idea.

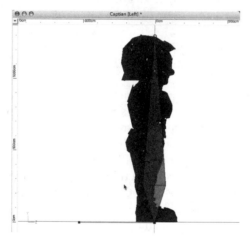

FIGURE 7.15   The root bone.

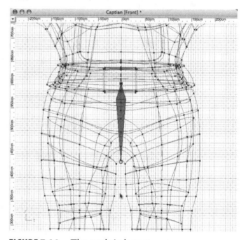

FIGURE 7.16   The pelvis bone.

Once this bone has been added, rename it in the PWS (select the name of the bone in the PWS and press F2 to edit its name) to pelvis. Make certain that it is a child of the root bone (see figure 7.17). If it is not, drag and drop it onto the root in the PWS.

Legs are direct children of the pelvis bone. In real anatomy, ball-and-socket joints attach them, but in A:M, hierarchy does that job. Starting with the right leg, select the pelvis bone and draw a chain of four bones down the center of the leg, representing the thigh, calf, heel, and toe bones in order. The toe becomes the end of the kinematic chain you have drawn.

The positions of the bones themselves are very important. The thighbone must begin at the end of the hips and extend to the knee. The calf extends from knee to ankle, the heel from ankle to the ball of the foot, and the toes from the

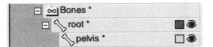

FIGURE 7.17 Check your hierarchy on bones often.

ball to the tip of the foot. In few places will the roll handles be as important as they are here. For the thigh and the calf, the roll handles should point forward; for the heel and toe bones, they should point down. These are, to a certain extent, arbitrary directions, and as long as you keep them consistent, you should have no problems. If you plan on using actions on multiple characters, then it is also important that they remain consistent from character to character. Once the bones are placed in the mesh, double-check that they are under the pelvis in the hierarchy and then name each bone in the PWS as appropriate (see Figure 7.18).

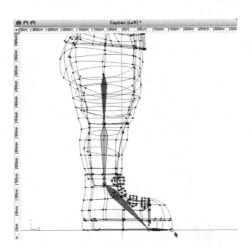

FIGURE 7.18 The leg bones.

Because the second leg is identical to the first, you can save some time drawing bones by duplicating this set of bones. Drag the pelvis in the PWS while holding down the Option/Alt key, and drop it on the pelvis. The result will be an exact duplicate of the entire pelvis and leg hierarchy with the number 2 appended to it. You want this hierarchy on the left side of the body. Flip it first. Select the Pelvis 2 bone that was just created in the PWS. Now click the title bar of the Model window to make it active (if you do not do this, the PWS will be active and the S key will do nothing). Bring up the Scale Manipulator, either with the toolbar button or the S keyboard shortcut. In the x scale field of the manipulator's properties, type –100. This value will flip the orientation of the entire hierarchy.

Note that the entire hierarchy of bones is affected when using the manipulators. This makes it simple to scale, rotate, or translate entire skeletons. Now rename your bones to indicate which side of the model they are on and to remove the extraneous 2 from the duplicated set of bones.

Up from the pelvis, a spinal column needs to be established. This can vary from model to model, depending on the number of cross sections the torso has. Each section up from the torso needs its own spine bone. Draw these in as a chain at the same level in the hierarchy as the pelvis: children of the root. The Captain, as modeled in Chapter 5, "Character Modeling for Animation," will need five spine bones. After you draw in the bones, go back and double-check that each is attached to the parent and that its roll handle is pointing backward. Also, note that most spines will have an arch at the upper section of the torso, starting about where the arms are and curving up into the neck. Rename these bones Spine1 through Spine5 (see Figure 7.19).

From the spine, the hierarchy breaks off into three directions: the head, the right arm, and the left arm.

The neck and head are extensions of the spine, so it makes sense to tackle them next. Select the last spine bone and draw three more bones up from the top of the spine: two for the neck and one for the head. The neck you modeled had a ring in the middle of it for flexibility, and the two neck bones should meet at this spline ring. The head starts at the base of the jaw and extends up to the top of the head. Name these bones Neck 1, Neck 2, and cranium, respectively (see Figure 7.20). You name the head bone cranium to free up the name "head" for the control bone.

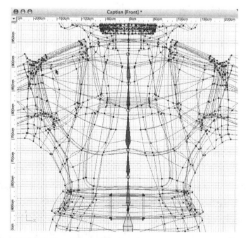

FIGURE 7.19 The spinal column.

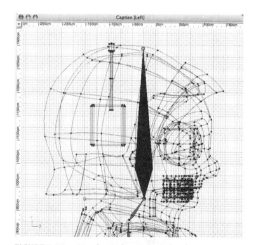

FIGURE 7.20 Neck and cranium bones.

Again, make sure that each of these bones is attached to the parent and that the roll handles are pointing straight back. This is critical, as the Orient Like constraints you use to control these bones later will assume that the roll handles are all pointing the same direction. Note that you *could* point all the roll handles forward, so long as you maintain consistency and are aware of it when you build the control structure.

The arms are mirrored, so you can use the same technique you did on the legs to get them in place, starting with one-half of the body and bringing the bones across when you are finished. Start with the clavicle bone and draw a four-bone chain down the length of the arm in the center of the related geometry. One of the spine bones should serve as a parent to this chain; in the case of the Captain, Spine 4 served this purpose. The clavicle extends from the spine up to the shoulder, the bicep extends down to the elbow, the forearm extends to the wrist, and the hand extends to the tip of the fingers (see Figure 7.21).

Rename these bones, and ensure that they are attached to the parent (with the exception of the clavicle, which cannot be attached to the spine bone). The roll handles on the arms can point either forward or back but should all face the same direction. Once you have that done, duplicate the chain as you did for the legs. But this time scale the chain –100 in the z-axis, then instead of translating the arm, bring up the Rotate Manipulator and rotate it 180 degrees in the y-axis. This should line the chain up precisely with the opposite arm, but the roll handles are reversed, so go through the chain and point them in the same direction as the other arm. Now rename your bones to indicate the side of the character they are on and remove the extraneous 2 at the end of the names of the duplicated chain.

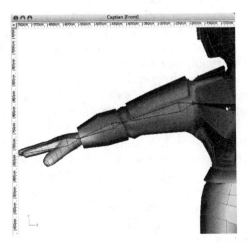

FIGURE 7.21   The arm bones.

This is the simplest control rig that you could have in this character. Assign control points, lock the bones in animation, and you have a workable forward kinematics (FK) animation setup. However, any amount of animation with the rig would likely leave you frustrated at the lack of control. You will build in more features, but first you need to assign CPs to the bones. To get started, use the Auto Assign Bones feature by bringing up the contextual menu in the Model window and selecting Auto Assign Bones. This will roughly assign the CPs in your model for you.

Once the computer has roughed in the CP assignments, it is time to put that action window to use. In the action window, choose a limb—the left leg, for example—and lock all the bones on it. Give each a little rotation to see how the auto assigned has done with the points. At this point, look for any major problem areas, but don't try to solve all the creasing and potential nastiness that may occur. You will be using fan bones and SmartSkin to deal with those problems later.

A common problem may be the pelvis not having control over enough CPs, causing unsightly shearing in the hips. In the Model window, reassign any CPs. You need to have a roughly functional model for that limb. For the legs and arms, you can then just duplicate the CP assignments on the opposite limb.

To make it easier to assign control points to the limb you are working on, in the Model window switch to Modeling mode (press F5), and select just the CPs for the limb you are adjusting the assignments on and then lock the model. When you return to Bones mode, those will be the only points that you can assign to bones, making mistakes (such as selecting the points on the mirrored limb or in the main body of the character) impossible to make. Getting the control point assignments right for any given character is more art than science, and there are numerous ways that you could assign one limb's CPs that would all be acceptable. Look at the Captain_v12.mdl file on the CD-ROM to get an idea of one possible solution.

ON THE CD

Once you have one limb assigned satisfactorily, go back to Modeling mode (press F5) and unlock the CPs, then assign the CPs identically on the opposite limb. Lock all the CPs but the current working limb, if it makes things easier for you. Proceed this way one limb at a time until all the CPs in the model are under control of roughly the appropriate bone.

Your next step in getting this character ready for animation is to add the fingers, eyelids, jaw, and eye bones. These will be the last of your pure geometry bones before you start adding fan bones and working with constraints. These are applied separately to as they can be complex.

While still in Modeling mode in the PWS, Shift-click each of the four named groups that you made for the eyelids; this will multiselect those groups in the PWS. Bring up the contextual menu in the PWS for the selected groups, and choose New Group from selected. Once A:M makes the new group and selects all the CPs in it, click the Hide button to hide the rest of the model. The eyelids will need one bone for the top and one for the bottom for each side. You want to work with the CPs for each eyelid independent of the others; so click-select one of the groups and lock the rest, so that you can easily assign the CPs to it later.

Change the Modeling window back to Bones mode and select the cranium bone. Since the eyelids are attached to the head, the bones you add for them need to be children of the cranium. Draw the bones for the eyelids starting at the pivot for the eye and pointing out to the front of the eye; assign the appropriate CPs to the bone you added. In the action window, rotate the new bone to check the pivot. If it doesn't pivot around the center of the lid—opening straight and smooth—adjust the bone in the Model window until it does. Do the same for each of the four eyelids (see Figure 7.22).

Once the eyelids have bones assigned, name the bones upper eyelid and lower eyelid, remembering to add left or right to the front of the name.

Switch back to Modeling mode (press F5), and unhide and unlock the model. Multiselect the two named groups for the whole eyes that you made when modeling and hide the rest of the model. Switch to Bones mode again (press F6.) This time add two bones, again children of the cranium, one for each eye starting at the dead center of the eyeball and extending out to the edge of the cornea. From a front view, it is an easy matter to assign the control points to each bone. Now rename the bones right eye and left eye, respectively.

Go back to Modeling mode (press F5), unhide the model, and select the head group and lock the mesh. Back in Bones mode, select the cranium bone and add a new bone, roughly in position as the jaw of the character. Assign the points for the jaw lower lip and the bottom set of teeth to this bone, and name it jaw (see Figure 7.23).

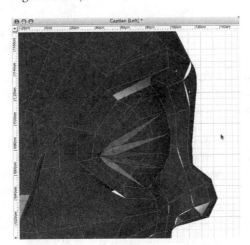

FIGURE 7.22   The eyelid bones.

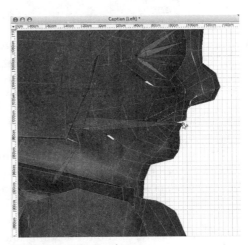

FIGURE 7.23   The jaw bone.

One more trip to Modeling mode to unlock the control points and you are ready to move on to the hands.

The hand bone will be the parent for all the fingers. Each finger will take three bones except the thumb, which takes two. The bones are placed into the fingers running down the centers, with the roll handles pointing opposite the direction that the fingers bend. This means that the thumbs will have the roll handle pointing at an angle.

The base of the first finger bone starts at the knuckle and moves to the first joint of the finger, and the second goes to the second joint with the third going to the tip, as might logically be expected. As the hands were modeled, each bone gets two rings assigned to it. While lying the bones down, be certain to check a front or back view to get the bones properly aligned (see Figure 7.24).

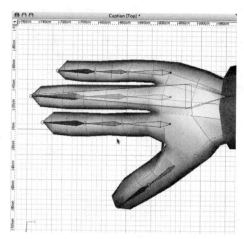

FIGURE 7.24   The finger bones.

Once one set of digits is complete, use the same technique that duplicated the arm rig to transfer the finger bones to the opposite side of the model. Use the hand bone to duplicate, move, and scale all the fingers into position as a group, then move the fingers from under the duplicate hand to the one you originally placed. Delete the duplicate hand and name your finger bones something logical. The example model uses this naming convention: Right/Left_DigitName_Base/Mid/Tip.

Test out the bones one final time in the action window. Pay attention to the jaw: Does it distort the face too much when it moves? If so, perhaps you have too many, or the wrong, control points assigned to it. Adjust it in the model until it looks right. Look at the fingers: Do the finger bones control points on the wrong digit? If so, go back to the Model window and reassign them to the appropriate bone. While you give the mesh a quick shakedown, also look for places that kink, pinch, stretch oddly, or could use some smoothing. You will deal with these trouble spots next.

FAN BONES AND CP WEIGHTING

After going as far as possible with bones on their own, there will remain areas in the mesh that will present animation problems. It is possible to repair these problem spots (distorted mesh, creasing, and shearing) with muscle motion on a frame-by-frame basis, but that would be a labor-intensive solution in the best of circumstances. A more elegant solution involves the use of CP weighting and a common constraint-based blending method called fan bones.

CP weighting, as discussed in Chapter 3, is great for simple characters such as the flour sack, but for complex characters it must be applied more selectively. Certain areas of the character are ideal for weighting; in this character's case, the spine in particular is ideal. Starting with the Spine 1 bone and working up to the Spine 4 bone, adjust the falloff so that the envelope for the bone covers the width of the torso from the front view. In the example model, this is about 24 cm of falloff. Once the falloff is set, bring up each bone's contextual menu starting with Bone 1 and choose Compute CP Weights. This will compute the weighting for only that particular bone instead of the character as a whole.

The greater control that this affords will let the spine bend smoothly without affecting the arms, legs, or head of the character. You could attempt to use CP weighting on the knees and elbows as well, but the amount of falloff that would be required in those areas would likely bleed the control over into parts of the character that you did not want to affect. Instead, these joints are blended with the aid of constraints using fan bone rigs.

In order to build this rig and have it save with the character, you need to create a pose. A pose is a type of relationship that you will explore in detail in Chapter 8, but for now it may help to think of it as a switch that can be used to turn things on. The things it controls are defined in the Pose window.

Create a new pose by bringing up the contextual menu for the model and selecting ON/Off under pose from the new heading. This opens a *Relationship window*. A Relationship window is a special kind of action window that is used to link elements into a relationship. You will be building your fan bones here.

A fan bone is the term that A:M users have given to a bone or bones that use multiple Orient Like constraints to average the effects of two or more bones on a model. The simplest example of this can be applied to joints such as the character's knee.

In the Relationship window, lock the bones for one leg. In the Model window, hide all of the mesh except the pant leg for the leg you locked, and then go into Bones mode.

In the simplest terms, this leg is a tube with five cross sections, three of which make up the knee joint of the character. With no CP weighting, the two bones that control this joint allow no smooth transition between their enforcement. To achieve a smooth bend along this joint, a secondary bone must be created that will use Orient Like constraints to average the mesh as the leg bends.

In the Model window, select the thighbone for the leg you are working with and draw a short bone across the center cross section of the knee. It is important that this bone has its roll handle facing the same direction as the thigh and calf bones. Assign the center ring of the knee to this new bone and rename it Knee1, remembering to add the right or left as appropriate.

In the Relationship window, bring up the contextual menu for the Knee1 bone. You can do this by directly control-clicking (Mac) or right-clicking (PC) on the bone in the workspace or the *shortcut* to the bone in the PWS under the relationship action, or, if the bone is currently selected in the Relationship window, the Properties panel.

From the contextual menu, select New Constraint; then from the Rotation submenu, select Orient Like. The cursor will become an eyedropper when placed inside the Relationship window. Use it to select the calf bone. If you miss the bone or the eyedropper does not appear, look to the properties for the constraint, which should be active in the Properties panel and choose the appropriate calf bone from the Target Properties pop-up menu.

If the constraint is not currently active in the Properties panel, select it by bringing up the contextual menu for the Knee1 bone, and from the Select heading, choose the Orient Like constraint from the Constraints subheading. Once the bone has been constrained to orient like the calf, it will follow all the calf's rotations, which merely changes the bone that controls the knee ring.

In order to get the knee to blend between the two bones, you must average the rotation of the Knee1 bone with the thigh and the calf bones. This can be done in a couple of ways: a second Orient Like constraint could be added to the Knee1 bone to orient it like the thigh. The problem with this technique is that it is more effort than is needed.

Recall the discussion of bones and character setup in Chapter 3, where it was stated that hierarchy is king and that a bone will inherit its rotation and roll properties from its parent unless explicitly told otherwise. In this case, the Orient Like constraint is telling the bone to ignore its parent, the thigh, and to take its rotational cues from the calf bone.

However, you can change how much it takes from the calf by reducing the enforcement of the constraint, rather than adding a second constraint. Give the Orient Like constraint a 50% enforcement value, and it will blend equally between its parent and the constraint target.

In the Relationship window, move the thigh and calf bones to see how the knee bone averages between the two bones to help smooth the curve of the knee. In most of its range of motion this will give good results, but when the calf is bent back more than 90 degrees, the two rings above and below the smoothed knee crease and have issues with mesh penetration.

These problems can easily be solved with two more fan bones. Add one for each of the two remaining knee rings, both as children of the thigh. Name these bones Knee2 and Knee3, remembering to add right or left as appropriate. The upper ring should orient like the calf 25% and the lower ring should orient like the calf 75%. This will make the mesh smoothly bend at the knee. The mesh may not bend exactly where you would like it to because the rotation is pivoting around the base of the bone. Adjusting the base of the bone in the model can change the effect the fan bone has on the rotation as a whole.

There are countless positions that would work for each bone. It may take several adjustments to find one that works for you (see Figure 7.25). Once you have a good working fan setup on one knee, simply duplicate it on the opposite knee.

The same principle is applied to other joints on the character. The density of the mesh around the joint determines how many fan bones a particular area may need. The elbow, for instance, likely needs three fan bones, much like the knee, while the wrist requires only two.

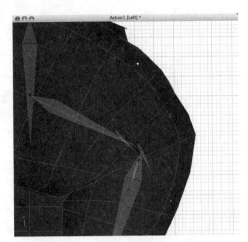

FIGURE 7.25   Once the fan bone is set up, the joints will bend smoothly.

The wrist bones will need additional constraints to blend the roll-based rotations of the hand into the mesh of the forearm. Start by putting the fan bones into the model. Draw two bones as children of the forearm bone with their bases roughly aligned with the last cross section of the arm and the first of the hand. These two bones will blend the rotations of the hand into the arm with Orient Like constraints targeted to the hand bone.

The exact enforcements can be arrived at with some experimentation. For the example model, the bone closer to the hand was enforced 55% and the bone closer to the forearm was enforced 30%. While these were ideal for smoothing the wrist as it bent, for rolling the wrist they caused shearing because they were not enforced enough to smooth the roll of the hand into the forearm.

Add an additional roll-like constraint to each bone. The bone closer to the hand should be enforced 90% and the one closer to the forearm 80%. This allows the hand rotation to move naturally up the forearm and maintains smooth bending as well (see Figure 7.26). Again, once the rig for one-half of the character has been worked out, it is replicated on the second half, changing the right or left names as needed.

After the relationship has all the fans and smoothing bones applied to it, remove any keyframes that are not specifically constraints. Set the keyframe filters to filter every key except constraints and the whole model. This ensures that you won't affect the constraints. Click the Delete Keyframe button. The only keyframes that are active in the character now are those for the constraints.

To test the relationship, create a new action. In the Pose Sliders window you should see a pose labeled Pose1. Turn it on, move the character around, and the constraints you built should be in place. However, the character is still a bit hard to manipulate; some simplified animation controls would be nice.

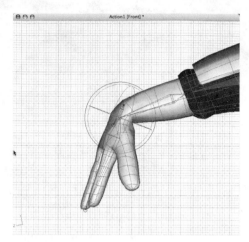

FIGURE 7.26   The wrist needs to blend its roll as well as rotation.

Legs

The first control structure that we cover is the legs. Legs are easy to get working right and demonstrate most of the concepts that character rigging involves, so we tackle them first. Before you can rig, you need to know what you want to accomplish. For legs, the list is pretty short: you want the feet to stick to the ground; the pelvis and the feet to move independently of one another yet share control of the knees, which should always bend forward; and to be able to control the toe and heel independent of the foot, yet fall under the foot's control by default. That's not that much, but without knowing what you wanted the controls to do, you would have serious problems coming up with an effective rig.

You already did a lot of the work for the rig when you set up the geometry bones for the character. Remember: hierarchy is king. All you have to do is find the places where the hierarchy doesn't do what you want and add control for it.

The first thing that you need to take care of is the feet. You will be doing all the rigging for the character in an on/off pose relationship just as you did for the fan bones. Use a new relationship for each section of the rig, if you like. We will cover how to combine them all under one slider later. For now, open a new pose for the character and get started.

Leave the Model window open and in Bones mode because you will be moving back and forth between them a lot as you build this rig. The foot needs a control bone. This will make animation simpler in a number of ways and will be the first step to solving the problem of both keeping the feet in place and removing them from the effect of the pelvis. In the Model window, draw a bone as a child of the root bone in the character's hierarchy that starts at the heel of the foot and extends forward past the toes. Extend it far enough that it will be easy to select later. As with most bones in this setup you will be selecting them a lot. To save time finding the bones in the PWS or the various veiwports use the A:M Timeline window to hold the bones you need by screwing them down while they are still selected.

All by itself the foot control bone won't do much; its main purpose is to act as a handle. Add a second layer of bones to get it to actually control anything. These are termed targets, as they will be the targets of constraints later. The first is the ankle target. This bone will do two things: it will put the foot under the control of the control bone and it will isolate the foot from the hips. It will do this with a combination of hierarchy and constraints. The hierarchy comes from making the bone a child of the foot control you already added. This will make the target move based on the translation and rotation of the control bone. Draw the ankle target with its base at the joint of the calf and heel bones (see Figure 7.27).

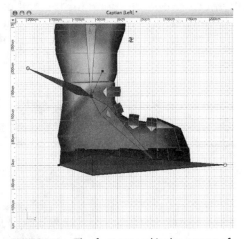

FIGURE 7.27   The foot control is the parent of the ankle target. Together they isolate the foot from the pelvis.

You apply the constraint in the Relationship window. The goal of the constraint is to force the calf bone to follow the movements of the foot control and, at the same time, to keep the calf and foot from moving when the hips and upper body move. Do this by selecting the calf bone and applying a kinematic constraint with the ankle target bone as the target, turning on the support limits and damping property, to ensure that the target is reached regardless of what the Aim At constraint on the thigh may do with the IK chain.

Now any time you move the foot control bone, the calf will do its best to stay pointed at the ankle, and any time you move the upper body down the foot will remain attached to the control, instead of punching though the floor. This solves one problem but creates another. This makes the knee bend each time the foot is moved, but if the foot is in the wrong position, it can allow the knee to bend backward. To solve this problem you need another target.

The primary knee target bone is also a child of the foot control. You will add a secondary knee target later to help average the control of the knee between the foot and hip bones. It is placed in front of the knee where it will indicate to the thigh that this is the front of the body and that the knee should go this direction when it bends. You indicate this with a constraint. In the Relationship window, add a constraint to the thighbone to aim at the primary knee target bone. Now the thigh will always point forward.

The next step is to ensure that the foot rotates with the control bone, which requires more bones and more constraints. The foot rotates from the ankle out, and you could use an Orient Like constraint on the heel and toes to rotate the foot like the control bone, but this is too limiting for a control. Instead, use targets to accomplish the same rotation and give further control over the foot. You will specifically need two targets: one for the ball of the foot and one for the toe. In the Model window, you add two bones as children of the foot controller: one, the FootBallTarget, with its base at the joint of the ball and toe, and one, the ToeTarget, with its base at the tip of the toe (see Figure 7.28).

FIGURE 7.28 The complete foot control structure.

In the Relationship window, each bone will be a target for the foot bones. Add a Kinematic constraint to the toe's geometry bone with the ToeTarget as its target. Turn on the Supports Limits and Damping property, ensuring that the Aim At cannot pull the toe away from the target. This will not only point the toe in the direction that the control bone is pointing, but will also give you a control over just the toe later on. To the heel bone, add an Aim At Like constraint with the FootBall bone as the target. This will enforce the direction that the toe can bend.

You may notice that this mirrors the constraints that you used on the leg earlier. This series of constraints is one of the most commonly used ways to control chains of bones, especially for hinge-style joints like the knees.

This set of bones gives you your primary control system for the legs and feet. Some refinements that can be made are discussed in the next chapter, but for general control, this is all that is needed. The opposite leg is duplicated from this rig, and then you are ready to move on to the torso.

Hips and Spine

The hips are the center of movement, as you learned in Chapter 4. Since this area is so important, you need to access the control for it easily from any view—the perfect job for a null. Bring up the model's contextual menu and choose null from the New heading. Position the null at the base of the spine and make it large enough to be easily seen and selected (see Figure 7.29). When it is in place, drag and drop it in the PWS to make it a child of the root bone.

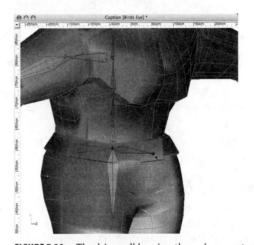

FIGURE 7.29   The hip null begins the spine controls.

This control has no effect until you tie the spine and pelvis bones to it. You don't want them to orient like the null or base any other portion of their movement on this null. Create a new on/off pose, and in the Relationship window, apply a Translate To constraint to the Spine1 and pelvis bones with both targeting the hip control null that you just added. Now when the control moves, the position of the rest of the body shifts to compensate.

When you made the leg rig earlier, you made a primary knee control bone that allowed you to position the knee based on the rotation of the foot. This is good, but in a realistic range of motion, the knee only partially follows the foot. You can blend the Aim At constraints on the thighs with a set of targets that are children of the pelvis null to give this control. Position the secondary knee target at the same position in the model as the first. In the example, the new bone has been angled up to differentiate the two visibly, but this is not required (see Figure 7.30). Remember that the Aim At constraint that you will apply aims at the base of the bone.

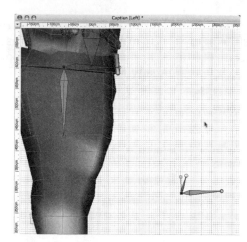

FIGURE 7.30   The secondary knee target.

In the Relationship window, add a constraint to the thighbone to aim at the secondary knee target. If you leave the enforcement of the constraint at 100%, when it is applied with the primary knee target the two will average the location of the knee exactly between them; to make the knee favor the foot slightly instead lower the enforcement to 80%.

The spine is difficult to control as it exists primarily because there are so many bones in it, and the neck bones are very small and difficult to select. You want a more easily selected and reliable control for the spine. This needs to include at least two controls, so that you can arch the back as needed and a third to control the head. All these controls need to follow the hips. The spine controls need to function in such a way that the main spine bone controls the entire spine, and the bone you add for arching the back can be used in addition to or to counter the main spine (see Figure 7.31).

Making the main spine a child of the hip control and then adding the secondary spine as a child of that will do the job, but the secondary spine bone needs to start at the point where the back should arch. The head control will need to stick to the spine where the top of it arches; so it should be a child of the secondary spine bone, but it should not be attached to parent. Attaching it to the parent would make it part of a kinematic chain, which is, to a certain extent, what you are countering with this portion of the setup.

In the Relationship window, you need to make the various spine bones arch gradually from the hips to the head. You do this with a series of blended Orient Like constraints. The spine of the character needs to arch more the farther from the pelvis it gets, and the top portion of it needs to be tied closely to the secondary spine control to allow arching of the back. This means that the enforcement of the spine to the control bones needs to increase as it moves up the chain, and at some point, control needs to transfer to the secondary spine control.

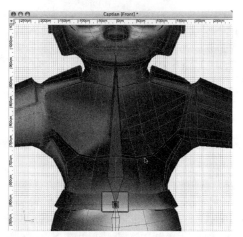

FIGURE 7.31   The main spine controls will simplify the movement of the upper body.

Starting with Spine1, apply the following constraints:

Spine1: orients like the spine control bone 5%

Spine2: orients like the spine control bone 20%

Spine3: orients like the spine control bone 35% and like the secondary spine control bone 20%

Spine4: orients like the spine control bone only 10% (this is where you hand off control to the secondary bone to allow the back to arch properly) and the secondary spine control bone 60%

Spine5: orients like the secondary spine control bone a full 100%

The neck bones need to transition the arch of the spine up into the head. You accomplish this again with blended Orient Like constraints, this time starting at the base of the neck: Neck1 needs to orient like the secondary spine control 80% and like the head control 20%. Neck2 only needs an Orient Like constraint to the head control. Because it takes its cues from Neck1, an enforcement of 50% will provide the needed amount of blending. The cranium bone, of course, needs to orient like the head 100%.

While you are dealing with the head, you should also take care of the eyes. As a child of the head control bone, create a new bone in the model and name it eye target. In the relationship window, apply an Aim At constraint to each eye bone. Now when you move the eye target, the eyes will follow. Simply place the target where you want the gaze to rest when animating.

Test this setup in an action window, and you should have very decent control of the spine and head with just these three bones. Also, turn on the fan bones and the leg setup and test that they all function. You should have almost full control of the character, with the exception of the arms. If the legs and spine are working correctly though, go to the model and hide the geometry bones and targets to leave just the control bones exposed. This way the geometry bones will not get in your way when selected. You may also want to select each of the control bones and screw it down in the Timeline. A screwed item remains persistent in the Timeline throughout the interface, and its screwed state will be saved with the file. This will make it easy to find just the needed bones when animating later.

This type of blended constraint chain is also used to reduce the number of controls in tentacles, tails, ropes, and other long IK chains. If this chain were longer, you might build layers of progressively simpler controls.

Arms

All that remains is to make some decisions regarding to the control of the arms. Arms, unlike the rest of the body, are often animated in two different ways. The first uses FK in which the bones at the end of the chain have no effect over the bones at the base of the chain. You must position the arm starting from the shoulder; this is used very frequently, unless the character must interact with sets or environments. Pressing down on a table, for example, would be difficult with FK arms.

The second method, IK, behaves like the legs you have already rigged where the hand controls the arm but the body has no effect on the hand's position. If a character is to be doing push-ups, for example, IK is much easier and preferred. The optimal solution is to build a system that allows the animator to switch between these two setups on the fly, a very complex challenge for rigging. We will cover the setup for each type of arm here and explain the basics of starting a switching mechanism.

The FK arm is the simplest and more or less duplicates the geometry structure. The main difference is that an FK setup has none of the bones parented to one another. We duplicate the structure rather than change the properties of the geometry bones, because they need to remain in an IK chain in order for the IK arm setup to function.

In the Model window, as a child of the secondary spine control, draw three bones that duplicate the position and roll handle orientation of the bicep, forearm, and hand bones. Name the bones BicepFK, ForearmFK, and HandFK, respectively, adding right and left as appropriate. Draw the bones as a chain and then turn the Attached to Parent property on each off.

Create a *percent pose*. A percent pose is like the on/off pose, except that it can have a variable state from 0 to 100. Rather than acting as a simple switch, it behaves like a slider. This is discussed further in Chapter 8.

In the Pose window, orient the bicep like the BicepFK bone, orient the forearm like the ForearmFK bone, and the hand like the HandFK bone. This is the extent of the FK setup. Not a whole lot to it, but it does allow for easy arm positioning and posing in animation.

IK arms require more work. They are much like the leg rig, in that they need a way to move independently of the body and a target to force the elbow to bend the proper direction. However, unlike the leg, the position of the elbow is not very dependent on the rotation of the hand. This will then require two different control structures. The hand control is added at the top of the hierarchy positioned exactly where the geometry hand is, but extended out beyond the hand far enough to make it easy to grasp during animation. The roll handle for this bone also needs to face the same direction as the hand's roll handle. Name this bone HandIK.

The second control structure is for the elbow. Make a new bone as a child of the secondary spine control at the shoulder and pointing just behind the elbow. Name this bone WingBone. This marks the point where you want the elbow to aim, but because the Aim constraint only points to the base of a bone, you need to add a child to the wing bone that will act as the target. Name this bone IkelbowTarget (see Figure 7.32).

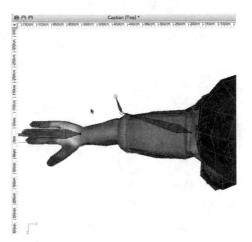

FIGURE 7.32   The IK arm controls.

In a new percent pose, you need to apply the constraints that will make this arm behave as an IK chain. The hand needs to orient like the HandIK bone. You create the IK chain by kinematically constraining the forearm bone to the HandIK bone. Applying an Aim At constraint to target the bicep to the IkelbowTarget bone completes the IK rig.

Test each of these rigs in an action independently of each other and in conjunction with the remainder of the rig. All the major functions of the rig should now be in place. Hands will be covered in Chapter 8 because they are the perfect place to use A:M's relationships to establish simplified control.

Why are there are no limits applied to the model to keep the parts in line? Primarily because sometimes in order to get a pose to read correctly, a natural range of motion is too restrictive and disjointing a character is necessary. Besides which, most animators find working with models that have limits applied to be restrictive to the process. Rather than rely on limits, use your own judgment as to what is correct.

There are many refinements and additions that can be made to this rig if you are so inclined, and you are encouraged to explore and experiment.

SUMMARY

Learning how to build constraint rigs for characters is challenging, to say the least, but the challenge of rigging is nothing compared to what you will face trying to animate a poorly rigged character.

You should have a fully constrained character by this point, ready for the last stages of refinement that relationships can offer you (before you go to animate it). You should also have a clear idea of the kinds of things that can be controlled with constraints.

8

RELATIONSHIPS

In This Chapter

- SmartSkin
- Poses and User-Defined Properties
- Transformation Relationships
- Surface Properties and Relationships
- Nested Relationships and other Advanced Applications
- Building "Smart" Characters

I n this chapter, we look into what a relationship is and how to create and edit one, beginning with the wizard-generated relationships (SmartSkin and poses) and moving on to user-defined properties and organization of pose sliders. Each type of user-defined relationship will be examined, and examples of their use will be given.

Finally, we discuss applying relationships to your character from Chapter 5, "Character Modeling for Animation." You will need to have already applied and understood the constraint rig from Chapter 7, "Constraints."

By the end of this chapter, you should have a ready understanding of what a relationship is and how it can help your animation, and have added relationships to the character that you modeled to make it smarter.

Before we can tackle relationships in a practical application, it makes sense that you would need to understand what they are and how they are intended to work in A:M. Relationships can be defined as an animate-able attribute, whose value drives other animateable attributes. This very vague definition hides the power that this tool provides. When you consider that almost every attribute in a character, from surface properties to control points to bones, are animateable, the broad range of possibilities starts to become clear. Not all properties can drive relationships; however, those that can will have a new relationship item available in their contextual menu.

A relationship consists of a driver and the attributes and properties that it controls. Each relationship can have any number of properties beneath it, and each driver can have any number of relationships associated with it.

Two types of relationships are so common that they have been given specific names: SmartSkin and Pose Sliders. These names are from previous versions of A:M for features that behaved similarly, but it is important to make the distinction for the longtime user that the relationship-based versions of these features are much more powerful than their predecessors.

SmartSkin

In its most basic aspect, SmartSkin is a bone-rotation-based relationship. It is not limited to any particular axis, and will drive any animateable attribute based on the arbitrary rotation of the bone. The traditional use for this feature is to manipulate control points based on bone rotation. This allowed for adjusting the model as the bone was manipulated or for muscle motion and joint smoothing. Because SmartSkin is often used to smooth joints, the question arises: Why do we use fan bones for smoothing? The simple answer is that fan bones are easier to set up and control. The reason behind this is the way that A:M interpolates control point, or muscle, animation.

Most simple joints are based on rotation, such as the knee that you set up with fan bones in Chapter 7, but individual control points when animated always *translate* between keyframes without a defined pivot. This means that for Smart-Skin to smoothly control the joint, you would have to have multiple frames of SmartSkin that simulate a rotation by translating control points in small increments. This could be as easy as one extra SmartSkin key or could require dozens of them to hit all the various angles of rotation. For this reason, SmartSkin-driven CPs are better used to fix minor imperfections after the majority of the mesh has been taken care of with fan bones and other bone-driven solutions.

In addition, CP manipulation generates a lot of data in the model. This not only makes the model file larger on the disk, it also requires RAM and time to calculate when rendering—not much, but every clock cycle counts.

In fact, there is a strong case to be made for using bones exclusively to control all aspects of a mesh. The traditional problem with this has been that as the geometry bone structure became more complicated, equally complicated constraint rigs had to be implemented to reduce the control structure to a reasonable amount of bones. With relationships, you can reduce the level of complexity required at the constraint level by creating relationships that simulate new types of constraints.

ON THE CD

For instance, open the Bicep_flex.prj project from the projects folder on the CD-ROM. This is a simple bicep, defined enough that you would expect to see the muscle flex as the forearm comes up (see Figure 8.1). You could use control-point manipulation driven by SmartSkin to achieve the desired results, but this would require several SmartSkin keys to get realistic muscle motion, and you would need to be cautious of improper translations in CPs. However, you can assign a bone, or series of bones, to the bicep muscle portion of the mesh to be driven with SmartSkin instead. At the same time, you can create bones to drive the triceps. All of these bones can be driven by the rotation of the forearm.

Starting with the bicep, the basic bones for the arm are already in place, as well as a series of fan bones for the elbow. Add a bone to control the bicep. In the model, you can see the spline ring that defines the bicep. Only the top of the arm should move so you can place a bone, with its base sitting at about the middle of the bicep muscle (see Figure 8.2).

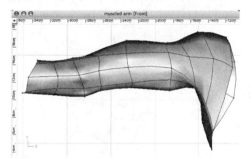

FIGURE 8.1   A complex arm might require some muscle movement.

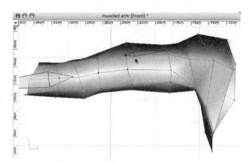

FIGURE 8.2   Adding this bone to the arm will give us a control for the bicep.

Now all we need to do is to tie the movement of this bone to the rotation of the forearm. Bring up the contextual menu for the forearm bone and choose new SmartSkin. A relationship-editing window will open and the forearm bone will be rotated 90 degrees in the *y*-axis. The relationship-editing window is a temporary action window and has all the properties of the action windows that you learned from Chapter 4.

Note that the Define Relationship button on the Manipulators toolbar is down. This indicates that any changes you make will be recorded as a key in the SmartSkin relationship that you are defining. The first thing you need to do is get the forearm bone into the proper position. You could do this by dragging the bone by its tip but, to make changes in the future easier, typing in exact rotation amounts is recommended.

Type 0 into the *y*-rotation field to return the forearm bone to its default position, then determine which direction and how far you want to move the forearm to set up the keys. In your example, –90 degrees in the *x*-axis will provide a good starting point. Type –90 into the *x*-rotation field; as you do this, note that the rotation numbers in the PWS, Timeline, and Properties panel are all highlighted red, indicating the property that is driving the relationship, in this case, the rotation properties of the forearm bone.

Once the driver has been set to the position that you need, simply adjust the properties that you want it to drive, in this case the bicep muscle bone. To simulate the way a real bicep contracts and pulls the forearm up, translate the bicep muscle bone toward the deltoid and away from the center of the arm. This may make an undesirable transition between the rest of the arm and the bicep muscle. In this case, rotate the bicep muscle bone until the transition feels natural to you.

Untoggle the Define Relationship button and close the SmartSkin window. In a new action, take your new bicep for a spin. Note how every time the forearm comes up, the bicep reacts as you would expect. The tricep is done in the same fashion, and it can even be enclosed in the same SmartSkin. It is a good idea, however, to use one SmartSkin for each muscle group that you wish to control in this fashion. So make a second bone for the tricep, the muscle on the bottom of the arm that works counter to the bicep (see Figure 8.3).

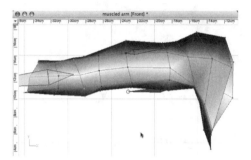

FIGURE 8.3   The tricep control bone is placed under the arm, counter to the bicep.

Make a second SmartSkin on the forearm bone and follow the same procedure to create the motion for the tricep, this time decreasing the bulge that is modeled into the arm. A third bone might be needed to smooth the transition from the tricep to the elbow. This can be in the same SmartSkin group.

Depending on how extreme you set the motion for the bone in the SmartSkin window, you may be completely satisfied with the way that your arm muscles are functioning at this stage. If you are not completely happy, you have a few options as to how you can handle the situation. The best course of action depends on the problems that you are having. The most common issues you might encounter are a sudden popping in the motion of the driven properties; overshoot might make the keys you set appear too extreme at certain rotations; you may feel that the driven properties are not extreme enough.

If you are encountering popping in the SmartSkin, you likely need to adjust the radius factor of the SmartSkin in question. This, like most of the attributes and properties of relationships, are hidden by default, unavailable until you enable the Show Advanced Properties option located on the Global tab of the Options panel (see Figure 8.4).

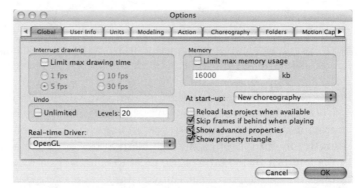

FIGURE 8.4   Enabling the Show Advanced Properties option allows you to see more information in the PWS.

Open the Options panel by choosing Options from the Tools menu. Click the Global tab, and select the Show Advanced Properties option. This reveals a number of properties in the PWS that were not previously available. Unless you are editing relationships or doing specialized character rigging tasks, you will not often need to access them. Hiding these properties when not in use helps keep the clutter in the PWS to a minimum.

Now you need to find the SmartSkin in the PWS. It is found deep in the hierarchy under relationships, bones, forearm, transform relationships, and rotate relationships. Once selected in the properties for the SmartSkin, you will see three properties: enforcement, radius factor, and lag.

For the problem of popping, the radius factor is what interests you here. As animation, there are channels that indicate how each key generated when creating a SmartSkin transitions in and out of each other. Unlike animation, Smart-Skin is not a simple 2D graph based on time and value; rather it is a complex 3D set of data that interpolates in all directions at once, depending on the proximity of the keyframes that surround it. This interpolation radius is calculated internally and is modified by the radius factor property.

A setting of 100% leaves the falloff between keyframes at the default internal calculations. The settings from there behave roughly the same as magnitude does when shaping splines. A setting of 200% would produce a curve roughly twice as soft between individual keys; a setting of 0% would be similar to peaked control points in a channel.

Care must be taken with this setting, as the falloff is set based on the two physically closest keys in the SmartSkin and applied to all keys based on those calculations. If you change the radius factor and then add more keys to the SmartSkin, the results could be difficult to predict. Leave this adjustment until you are certain that you are not going to be adding to the SmartSkin.

A larger setting should help with popping of SmartSkin. If a property is simply too extreme or not extreme enough, adjusting the enforcement percentage can give you a bit more or less of the SmartSkin. This is why it is a good idea to do individual muscle groups as separate SmartSkins: This setting affects all keys in the SmartSkin. If you have only one key that you feel needs adjustment, you will need to open the SmartSkin and make your adjustments on that key in relationship mode.

These same techniques can be used to change *any* property based on the rotation of a bone. You can use it to adjust the control points in the model based on bone rotation, too, but to limit it to that is missing the power of this tool.

For joints that rotate on more than one axis, like the shoulders or hips of a character, it is often difficult to get fan bones to control the mesh easily. They may smooth the joint through most of its rotation, but at some point the enforcement of the fan may be too little or too great to effectively smooth the joint. At this point, SmartSkin can supplement the constraint solution. Open the hip_smartskin.prj from the projects folder on the CD-ROM and look at Action1.

ON THE CD

Step through this simple 12-frame action, and notice that the fans in the hip joint smooth out most motion adequately but motion forward and to the left causes creasing as the range of the fans control is overreached. To the right, the joint up to the hip is actually too smooth; the fans work against what we need here.

Your first step is to adjust the enforcement of the relationship that holds the constraints for the hip. Again, leave the brute manipulation of control points until all other options have been explored. Be certain that the new SmartSkin will have the pose with the hip fans in it applied. If the pose isn't active, the Smart-Skin will actually toggle the on/off state of the pose. Select the model in the PWS, and under user properties, change the default state of the pose to on. Any new actions, relationships, or choreographies that use a shortcut to this model will now open with this pose applied.

Create a new SmartSkin for the thigh. The new window will open with the bone rotated 90 degrees in the *y*-axis; as before, type 0 into the *y*-rotation property field to place the bone at its starting point. Now any point to which you rotate the bone has the potential to be a key in the SmartSkin. Moving the bone to random locations and making adjustments can quickly become confusing and can lead to irregularities when animating later. It is better to work in a methodical fashion. Pick an axis of rotation for the thigh and rotate it to the most extreme position in the axis that you feel it will hit when animated, then rotate it an additional 5 degrees to give the SmartSkin some headroom. Figure 8.5 shows the thighbone rotated –65 degrees in the *y*-axis.

When you have the bone in the extreme position, find the property you wish to change. In this case, you want to adjust the enforcement property of the hip fan pose relationship. If you look at the PWS, there are two possible places to select this property: under the model in the objects section of the PWS, or under the shortcut to the model under the relationship in the action section. This is an important distinction. You want to create an animation channel inside of the relationship.

You do not want to alter the default 100% enforcement of the pose. If you look at the properties for each pose in the PWS, you may notice that the values of the properties under the relationship are gray, while the values at the model level are black. A:M imparts important information based on these colors in the properties. Specifically, a black property is the default value for that property.

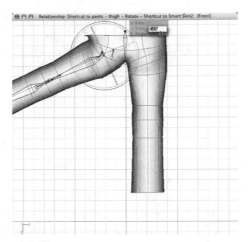

FIGURE 8.5   The thigh has been rotated –65 degrees for the first adjustment.

A gray value indicates a shortcut that has not yet been altered or is still using the default value for its property. For what you are doing, this means that you need to make your adjustments at the shortcut to model level. Select the shortcut to the relationship from under the shortcut to the model, and change the enforcement percentage until the fan bones smooth out the joint more effectively. Note that after you change the value of the enforcement that its value is colored blue, indicating a keyframe value. The level of enforcement you will need to use depends on the direction and amount you rotated the thigh.

Do this again for the other axes of rotation.

This may still not be perfect, but it should be much closer than before. The final portions of the hips can be smoothed with a second SmartSkin. In the second SmartSkin, rotate the thigh as you did for the first, but when you have it in the extreme position, switch the mode to muscle and sculpt the control points to smooth the last portions of the joints.

The example leg is a simple model. With a more complex model, you could also adjust gamma and magnitude to create complex folds to simulate a cloth surface, or, as you did for the bicep and tricep muscles, you could drive the flexing of the leg muscles. Even this barely scratches the surface of what SmartSkin can do for you. Experiment with it on your own to see how you can incorporate it into your own models.

POSES AND USER-DEFINED PROPERTIES

You have already briefly encountered user-defined properties in the form of poses. Up to now, you have used them almost exclusively for holding constraint data, but like SmartSkin, they can control almost any animateable attribute in a model.

Other than being a place from which to build and apply constraints, poses are also commonly used to define muscle poses for characters. This can be used to build phonemes for lip synch or to raise an eyebrow. Poses are ideal for this as they are tied to a control in the Pose Slider window that makes animating multiple states of a character easy. Pose relationships can drive relationships or can themselves be driven by relationships. This nesting of relationships allows for powerful interactions among all aspects of a character.

Creating a pose is the same, regardless of what attributes you want it to contain. Simply bring up the model's contextual menu and choose the type of pose that you wish to create from the New heading.

On/off poses store two states, either of which can affect a portion of the model. It is normal to use only one state for an on/off pose, but data can be stored in both states. For example, two sets of constraints for a character can be stored in a single on/off pose. This assumes that you will always want one or the other constraint system applied to a character, and that you do not need or want a smooth transition between the two.

Due to the rigid nature of on/off poses, they are typically used for things that do not need to be changed very often. For properties that need to change frequently or blend into one another, percent-based poses are more commonly used. If you have created a pose and then later decide that you need that pose to be percent-based, you can change the type of the pose by bringing up the contextual menu for the pose property and choosing Switch Type to percentage. If you do this, the current On state of the pose will be set to 100% on the new percent range, and the current Off state will be set to the 0% position.

Percent poses are created with a default range of values from 0% to 100%, with 0 being the initial value. This range and other properties of the relationship can be changed, as we will discuss. Percent poses are used to slowly transition from one state to another or through a series of states. This is useful for creating shapes for facial animation or for creating constraint systems that can change from one set of enforcements to another.

Building facial animation poses is a large part of preparing a character for animation, so let's look at that first. The concept behind creating poses for animation with sliders is one of the most important concepts of animation in A:M. The focus is not on creating large blocks of animation, but rather creating small portions of animation that can be used in a number of ways, or blended with other small portions of animation to create a more complex whole. When applied in an action, the effects of multiple poses are blended with one another; a slider that tilts the mouth can be combined with one that makes it smile, letting you build a crooked grin without having to create a specific action for that.

ON THE CD

Open facial_poses.prj from the project folder on the CD-ROM and do just that. Here is a simple head just waiting for you to give it some life (see Figure 8.6).

You want to create poses that allow you to make this face smile and tilt its mouth. You could build a pose that had all of this built in, but it becomes more useful if you break the motion down to its discrete elements and create a pose for each. For the mouth, this leaves you with a choice of how to proceed. You can

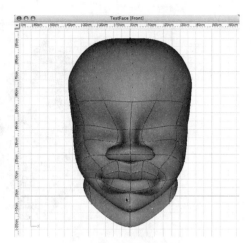

FIGURE 8.6   A head awaiting a life.

either build small elements out of muscle motion, or you can look to bones to drive your face. You will have a preference, but the trend is toward using bones in A:M for the reasons already discussed: arced motion and defined pivots for control points.

In order to move the mouth, decide what kind of control you need and how fine you want to make that control. In order to get the most out of it, you need to be able to discretely control and blend the controls for each cross section of the mouth. This requires a fair number of bones and a large number of poses (one for each direction of motion you want to push the cross section in), but it will reward you with flexibility when it is time to animate. With that in mind, start small and build very fine controls now and look at ways to simplify those controls later.

Each cross section on the mouth can move in one of three ways: In-Out, Left-Right, and Up-Down. This means you need to supply each cross section with at least three bones. Each cross section is set up in an identical fashion; only one is discussed in depth now.

Start by adding a new bone to the character under the head bone. This bone in and of itself will not do anything; it is simply in place to hold the other bones in the system and prevent clutter in the PWS. Draw this bone, as in Figure 8.7, starting at the center of the mouth and moving straight out and past the mouth.

The second bone for our system will be the In-Out bone for the first cross section of the mouth. This will move from the center of the mouth (establishing a pivot for the motion of the mouth) and point out to the pivot of the group it will eventually control. The easy way to ensure that the pivot is accurately targeted is to select the points in Muscle mode and take note of the group's pivot as noted in the Manipulator Properties window, then simply type the exact same numbers into the bone's end position property. Name this bone something that both indicates its position on the mouth and its function, UppperLip_In_Out, for instance. When it is in place, duplicate the bone twice by simply pressing Ctrl (PC) or

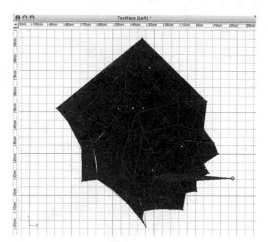

FIGURE 8.7   The first bone will act as a
container for the system.

Option (Mac) and dragging it onto the Container bone. This will create two duplicate bones. Drop the first duplicate onto the original In_Out bone, and drop the
second on the first copy. This will give you a hierarchy, as in Figure 8.8.

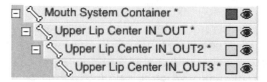

FIGURE 8.8   The initial hierarchy for the bones that
will manipulate the lips.

Rename the new bones for their function UpperLip_Up_Down and Upper-
Lip_Left_Right, for instance. You want to limit the rotation that these bones can
make so as to prevent them from providing bad data in a pose. You can do this by
adding constraints to each bone limiting its rotation, but it is easier to simply set
the Manipulator options. Manipulator options are an advanced property of a
bone. Enable them by checking the Advanced Properties box on the Global Options panel. Set the Manipulator options of the Up_Down bone to Rotate Only,
enable the Limit Manipulators property, and in the property group, turn off the
y- and z-rotations for the Up_Down bone. For the Left_Right bone, turn off the
z- and x-rotations. Now when you are in an action, Choreography, or Relationship window, the bone will draw just one ring of the rotation manipulator by default. This ring will be how you manipulate the bone.

Now you need to set up the poses for each of these bones. The poses are actually very simple, and you can probably guess by the name of each bone what to do with it. Start with the IN_Out Bone. Create a new percentage pose. The pose slider that you are creating will be visible in a number of places: the Timeline, the Pose Slider window, under the shortcut to the model in the action section of the PWS, and in the shortcut to the Models properties.

Note that it is highlighted red, indicating the property that is driving the current relationship. It should be set to 100, indicating that the changes you make in the relationship-editing window will be applied gradually from 0 to 100 as the pose slider is moved. You want this slider to hold two extreme positions for this bone, an IN position and an OUT position, and you want the default position of the mouth to be as it was modeled. For this, you need to change the range that the slider will allow. Bring up the contextual menu for the slider and choose Settings. The Settings menu allows you to change various aspects of the pose slider and how it will function in the interface. As you can see, it defaults to a range of 0 to 100, and the default value is 0. Change the range so that it goes from –100 to 100 with 0 remaining the default, as in Figure 8.9.

FIGURE 8.9   Change the settings of the new pose to match these.

The process at this point is very simple: With the pose at position 100, translate the bone straight forward. This is not perfect along the bone's *z*-axis though; so when you bring up the Translate manipulator, it will not be in the correct orientation. Simply click the Show Manipulator in World Space button to alleviate this issue. With the Manipulator in World Space, translate the bone in the *z*-axis forward into an out position. This will likely look odd to you, and it should because you have just moved one ring of control points without affecting their neighbors. Remember, however, that this is a building block rather than a final shape. Drive the pose fairly extreme. It is easy enough to use less than the full 100%, but adding more to the pose later will be a fair amount of work. Once you have the 100 position set, move the slider to −100 and translate the bone in the negative z-axis. It may collide into the teeth or push inside the head. Don't worry about that. Remember, this is not a final pose. Close the Pose window and rename the pose to something useful such as Upper_Center_IN—-OUT.

If you take this slider for a spin in an action, you should see it drive the segment you assigned to the child bone in and out along the z-axis.

For the Left_Right bone, you create a similar pose with a similar range, and simply rotate the bone left at −100 and right at 100. Likewise, the UP_Down bone gets its own pose slider. Go through this entire process for each ring of the mouth. When you are done, you have a set of pose sliders that allow discrete deformation of every aspect of the mouth. You can then use these sliders to drive larger motions, blending each up/down/left/right pose to shape various aspects of the mouth.

Create a new pose and adjust the pose sliders for one-half of the mouth to form a smile. When you make the smile, make it a little more extreme than you think you will normally need. This gives you room to push the shape later (see Figure 8.10).

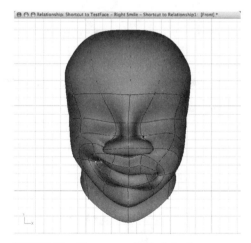

FIGURE 8.10   Shape one-half of the face to create a portion of a smile.

You want to make a second pose to control the opposite side of the face as well as this one, and you want them to be mirrored. A:M has tools to make this easy. Without closing the first Pose window, create a new percentage pose. Create a mirrored keyframe from the one you have already set up in the first Pose window. To do this, copy the animation data from the first Pose window. Bring the first pose to the front and then copy, either by using the keyboard shortcut, the button on the standard toolbar, or Copy from the Edit menu.

Bring the second Pose window forward. If you paste the data into this window, you only duplicate the previous pose; to make this pose to the opposite side of the face, A:M provides a tool called Paste Mirrored. Select Paste Mirrored from the Edit menu. If the model you are using is constructed properly, then the bone data will apply itself to those that lie exactly opposite the ones that were copied. This is the primary reason that you use the Left/Right naming convention for bones.

Now you have two poses. Each makes one corner of the mouth come up into a smile position. Close both Pose windows, and create a new action. If it isn't already, open the Pose Sliders window. If you move the sliders, you should see the mouth curl up into a smile.

Next, consider frowning. It is not very likely that you will want to pull a corner of the mouth up and push it down at the same time. Given separate controls for each of these actions you might even mistakenly pull them both, causing problems when animating. To prevent this and to help simplify the controls of a character, place the frown portion of the mouth movement in the same pose relationship as the smile.

To add the new frown motion to the pose, bring up the contextual menu for the pose and choose Edit Relationship. When the new relationship editing window opens, the red highlighted slider should be at the default not set value; drag it to the left until it is at −100, then sculpt the mouth poses to a frown. Now if you scrub through the pose, you should see a range of motion from the frown to the smile.

Open a new action and give the sliders a whirl. As you can see, even with just these two sliders, you have created a wide range of possible expressions for the mouth. Use this same technique to create a set of lip-synch controls and other facial animation features.

Other than percent and on/off values, there is one other option for user-defined properties: the folder. Just as folders can help you organize the PWS, you can create folders to group your poses. The two sliders you just created, for example, could be the start of a facial controls group.

To create a folder, bring up the contextual menu for the users properties property under the model and choose Folder from the New Property heading; the other two properties available are the same that are available from the model's New Pose heading. The folder will appear just like any other user-defined property. To place the other properties into the folder, simply drag and drop them in the PWS or Properties panel.

Opening the model in an action window and looking at the Pose Slider window will reveal that at the top of the window there is a new tab labeled with the name of the folder you created. Clicking the tab will show just the sliders in that folder. Using tabs, you can take a large number of poses and break them down into logical groups available at the click of a mouse (see Figure 8.11).

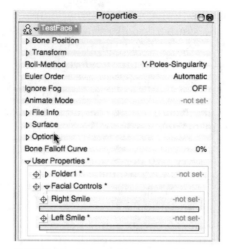

FIGURE 8.11 Using folders to separate poses gives greater control over that information you need.

TRANSFORMATION RELATIONSHIPS

In 3D terms, a transform is any rotation, translation, or scale change to an object. All 3D motion is based on at least one of these concepts, and quite often all of them together. Since these are easily measurable quantities, they are perfect drivers for relationships.

SmartSkins, which have already been discussed, are nothing more than rotation-based relationships. For items that are not bones, such as nulls, there is no SmartSkin option in the object's contextual menu. There is no real difference between a rotation-driven relationship and a SmartSkin, so you can think of them as the same.

Translation and scale relationships are functionally the same as SmartSkins and are created in much the same way. A driver is selected. In this case you must select it from the properties of the object you wish to be the driver. Select the type of transformation you wish to be a driver and select new relationship from the contextual menu for that transformation. A new relationship-editing window will become active, and you create the relationship in the same manner discussed for SmartSkins: Change the driving property to the desired end point of its triggering, and then adjust the properties that you wish it to control.

You can also create a relationship for a single axis of transformation in the same manner. This allows you to have a very strictly controlled relationship. Simply bring up the contextual menu for the translation or scale axis that you wish to drive the relationship, and choose New Relationship. Once the New Relationship window opens, the process is the same: adjust the driving property to set the key and then change any attribute in the model. Then as you animate the driver in an action or choreography, the values of all driven properties will change based on the keys that you have set. This lets us use nulls and other object types in the model as triggers or controls for relationship driven action.

SURFACE PROPERTIES AND RELATIONSHIPS

One of the most powerful and easily overlooked aspects of relationships is that they can drive things that are not explicitly part of the mesh or bones of the model, even though that is all you have dealt with up to this point. We said at the beginning of this chapter that a relationship could drive *any* animateable property, and this is true. The single limitation to this is that the properties to be driven must be contained in the model file. One model, for example, cannot drive the actions of another. There are ways to work around this limitation that will be discussed in Chapter 14, "Rendering and Compositing."

Nevertheless, even with this limitation in place, relationships are a powerful system. Surface properties come to mind as a simple example of a powerful way that you can use relationships to automate things that would otherwise be exceptionally complex.

ON THE CD

Open the Teapot_relationship.prj project from the CD-ROM, and look at the teapot model. This model has some surfacing applied to it for the benefit of this exercise, with both decaled images and procedural textures. You will learn all about both types of surfacing in Chapter 11, but for the purposes of this exercise, you do not need to know the details of how the surfacing is created or applied to the model. This one teapot can become a shelf of teapots with different colors and patterns, all driven by where the pot is located on a shelf.

The driving property for this relationship will be the translation of the *location* bone. In the teapot model, there will be a range of colors for the teapot, from black to white across the entire spectrum, and one of 15 patterns will be placed on the surface of the model. Knowing what you want to accomplish before you start creating a relationship is one of the most important steps in using this feature.

Select the bone in the PWS, and in the Properties panel find the Translation property under the transform disclosure triangle. Bring up the contextual menu for the Translation property and choose New Relationship. A new relationship-editing window will open with your teapot in it. Looking at the properties for the location bone, you see that the translation properties are all highlighted red, indicating that they will all drive the relationship.

You will be creating the relationship based on six translation coordinates roughly describing a box inside of which the values you are driving will change. Change to a top view, and zoom out a good distance. Right now, the bone is sitting almost on the origin of the window. It was moved to the side slightly when you created the new relationship to indicate that this was a translation relationship. Move it to any arbitrary dimension to mark the first corner of your cube. Select the shortcut to the model from the PWS, and expand the disclosure triangles in the Properties panel until it shows the surface properties.

You are making this a simple color change, but you could change any of the available surface properties. Change the color to a vibrant red color. Before you move the bone, also change the decal's property. Under the shortcut to the model, find the Teapot_01 image under Decal 1 and select it. In the properties for the image, find the frame setting. This setting allows you to specify the image in a sequence that the decal image map will display on the model. This particular sequence has 20 images in it, so set the frame value to 20.

Move the teapot again, and this time change the color to a bright blue and set the decal to frame 0. Repeat this process four more times, changing the decal frame and color of the teapot at each point. When you are finished, close the Relationship window.

Open the shelf of pots choreography and choose the camera view by using the keyboard shortcut (1) or the contextual menu for the viewport, and do a progressive render. You will have something similar to Figure 8.12.

FIGURE 8.12   Each teapot comes from the same model. The colors and patterns on their sides have been changed by a relationship.

If you look under the choreography item in the PWS, you will see that each teapot is simply an instance of the one original. All differences and variations in the colors and patterns on the sides of the models were changed based on the physical location of the teapot, based on the relationship you just defined.

This is a contrived example, but it shows you a little more about what relationships are capable of. Instead of a pattern on the side of a teapot, an image sequence could simulate cloth based on the rotation of a character's arm. A character could turn red with anger by simply dragging a slider marked Angry. The possibilities are limitless, and we look into a few examples that are more practical before we finish our discussion of relationships.

NESTED RELATIONSHIPS AND OTHER ADVANCED APPLICATIONS

Another very powerful feature of relationships is their ability to drive other relationships. This allows you to build smaller, easy-to-conceptualize building blocks that can be joined together into larger, more complex relationships. You have already looked at this concept a little bit when you made the smile/frown pose sliders. By dividing the motion of the mouth to cover only one side at a time, you created two small relationships that can be used together to form a larger whole mouth movement.

To more fully explore this ability, you will be working with a pair of eyes and eyelids. You will be creating relationships to keep the eyelids in the proper position on the eye itself. You will also be creating relationships that will override this behavior to allow for blinks and winks and to open the eyes wide. Finally, you will simplify this down to two control sliders. Open the eyelids project and let's get started.

The eyes and lids model has been created to be very simplistic, but a more complex set of eyes could be rigged in the same fashion.

Each eyelid can be driven based on the rotation of the eye bone. This makes the job ideal for a SmartSkin. Bring up the contextual menu for the right eye bone and choose New SmartSkin. When the relationship-editing window opens, the right eye bone will be rotated 90 degrees on the y-axis. You will be adding SmartSkin on this axis later, but for now type 0 into the y-rotation field and switch to a side view. The eyelids normally move in conjunction with the eye, with the top lid resting just on the top of the pupil and the bottom lid sitting on the edge of the iris. Since the pupil is an unknown factor, based on muscle movement you will have to approximate where the eyelid needs to be. You can use your control sliders to fine-tune this relationship later. Rotate the eye bone up about 80 degrees on the x-axis. This is more than you are likely to need during animation and gives your SmartSkin enough headroom to do its job.

While the bone is rotated, rotate the upper and lower eyelid bones to reveal the eye. Position the upper eyelid bone about halfway from the pupil to the edge of the iris. This will let you use a slider to hit it accurately with the pupil later. While the bone is still in this position, rotate the lower eyelid bone so that the lid rests just on the edge of the iris. This takes care of the up position. Now do the same for the down position. Rotate the eye to −80 degrees in the x-axis, and adjust the eyelids as needed. As you rotate the eye bone through its range of motion, you should see the lids respond in a realistic manner. All that remains is to shape the lid for side-to-side motion.

Return the eye to the 0 position and rotate it 90 degrees in the y-axis. This position will already have a little shaping from the earlier SmartSkin, but to accent this position you can rotate the eyelids in the z-axis to open in the direction of the look. On a more realistic eye, this would not be necessary or at least not to this degree, but for these simple cartoony eyes it adds emphasis to the direction the character is looking. Rotate the eye to –90 degrees and repeat the action. Untoggle the Relationship mode, and rotate the eye bone. You should see the eyelids remain open and track the eyes throughout the range of motion. This same process is simply repeated on the left eye.

To make controlling the eyes easy, they need to be aimed at the eye target. Create a new on/off pose, and constrain each eye to aim at the target. With the line of sight for each eye established, the SmartSkin will maintain the positions of the eyelids. You will notice, however, that the eyes never close; you need to create a way to do this.

Since each eye can close independently, or in some cases open wider than the default we have established, you need to create a way to control each eyelid separately in two directions. This is a good place to use a percent-based relationship. On the user-defined properties container on the model, bring up the contextual menu, and choose Percentage from the New Property heading.

A new property will appear under the pose you created for the eye constraints. Before you create a relationship for this property, you need to change its settings. The control of the eyelids needs to both open and close the eye that it is adjusting, so bring up the contextual menu for the percent property that you just created and choose the Settings heading.

In the settings for this property, change the minimum value to –100%. This gives you a slider with a range from –100 to 100. When you are done, create a new relationship for the percentage property by binging up the contextual menu and choosing New Relationship.

In the relationship-editing window with the percentage set to 100, change the enforcement on the SmartSkin relationship for the right eye to 200 percent. This will make the eye open wider than what you have set up in the SmartSkin. Then change the slider's value to –100% and set the SmartSkin's enforcement to 0%, which, since there are no keys driving the eyelids, will bring them closed. When you are done, close the relationship-editing window. Repeat the process for the left eye. Name each slider something you will be able to recognize in the Pose Slider window, such as "right eye close –|- open wide" and "left eye close –|- open wide".

Open a new action, and move the eye aim target around. Watch as the lids stick to the eyes. Then adjust the sliders to watch the eyes open and close. Controlling the size of the pupil can also be done with a simple percent slider that drives muscle motion for the pupil control points.

BUILDING "SMART" CHARACTERS

Using these concepts, you can continue with the rigging work on your character. Much of what Captain needs happens to be almost identical to the exercises you completed in the previous section; so you can simply duplicate that rig here. So, what other areas of the character could benefit from relationships? How about the hands? At this point, each finger on the character's hands has three control bones. This can be greatly simplified without the need for complex constraints.

Ideally, you can reduce each finger to a single control bone. You might be tempted (and it would be technically possible) to reduce that to just one control for the entire hand, but it is important to maintain individual control of the fingers. There are a number of methods for controlling fingers, and with some experimentation, you may find one that you prefer over the one discussed here.

There are three types of motion in a finger: move side-to-side, lift up/point down, and curl under. We cover the first two with a simple hierarchical control; curling we will build relationships to control. Since the finger is an IK chain, any rotation to the parent of that chain will transfer down the length of the chain. This means you can use the base to control the side-to-side, up-and-down motion of the entire finger. However, the base of the finger is difficult to select and control, and you still need to have a control that ties those two rotations in with the curling of the finger.

Keeping this in mind, you can create a single control bone for each finger that starts at the base of the finger and extends out past the hand (see Figure 8.13). These control bones should be children of the hand, at the same hierarchy as the fingers.

FIGURE 8.13   An additional bone will drive the relationship and make the fingers easy to control.

Now you need to tie the movement of the fingers to their new controls. Create a new on/off pose for the finger constraints, and for each finger base, constrain it to orient like the finger control bone. As you apply the constraints, turn the store roll property for each constraint to off. This will keep stray movements of the control bone's roll handle from rotating the fingers. Since fingers don't, in general, rotate, this saves you from having to be extra careful with the controls.

Once the constraints have been defined, all that remains is to define the relationship that will drive the curl of the fingers.

By isolating the finger bones from the control's roll-based rotation, you have not only made correctly animating the fingers easy, you have also provided a way to simply drive the rotation of the fingers. By creating one simple SmartSkin, you can use the roll of the finger controls to drive the curl motion of the finger. Bring up the contextual menu for each control bone and select New SmartSkin.

When the relationship-editing window opens, type 0 into the *y*-rotate field to bring the finger back to its center position. Now type −90 into the *z*-rotate field, curl the bones of the finger down and under to the position that the finger would be in if the hand were making a fist. Then type 90 into the *z*-rotate field and curl the finger bones back just a little (see Figure 8.14).

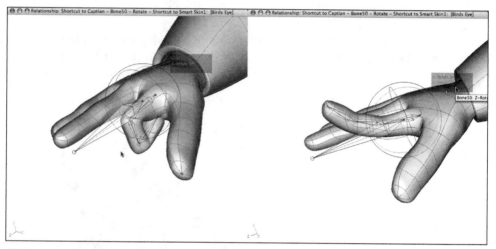

FIGURE 8.14 These two keys for the control bone's SmartSkin will allow you to control the curl of each finger based on the roll of the control bones.

While you have the SmartSkin window open, you might also want to do a little Muscle mode adjustments to keep the finger smooth throughout its range of motion. When you are satisfied, close the window. Open an action window and try out your new fingers. You should be able to move the bone to point the finger and then roll it to control the curl amount. With two simple relationships, you have reduced the bones to control each finger from three to one.

By considering the character's hierarchy and the controls that you will need when animating, you can reduce the entire set of controls in this fashion, making your characters smarter to animate.

Another spot in the mesh that is likely to cause trouble are the areas that might trap and cause issues with the cloth simulations that you will apply later. You want to ensure that even at the most drastic of rotations, the armpit and crotch of the character will not penetrate into each other. (If you had a character without cloth simulation you might be OK with an arm that just penetrated the torso in the armpit because we would never see it. But your requirements are driven by the tools you plan to implement.) The basics of how you will handle this were learned in the bicep that you looked at earlier. The only major difference is one of hierarchy. In order for the arm to come down and the shirt to behave as you expect, you need to control more of the mesh than just the shoulder or the sleeve. You can isolate the potential trouble areas by adding single bones to the mesh.

The bones in each of these areas will be used to primarily translate the control points into a new shape as needed. The only concern you need to have when adding them to the mesh is getting them parented under the proper part of the existing hierarchy.

The bones immediately around the shoulder area should be children of the clavicle; this will tie them into the movement of the shoulder control for shrugs and slouches. The other bones, starting at the armpit, should be children of the spine geometry bone whose control points they are taking over. Figure 8.15 indicates good positions for each bone and the parent to which it should be assigned. Once the bones are in place, simply assign the control points for the side of the shirt to each bone.

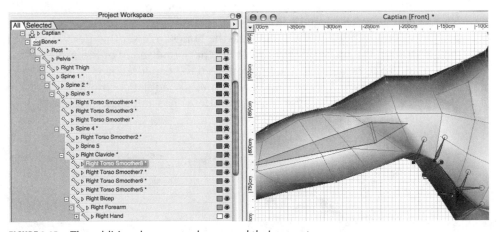

FIGURE 8.15   The additional geometry bones and their parents.

The other set of control points that you need to drive through SmartSkin are the two rings for the sleeves. Make two bones children of the bicep, starting from the base of the bicep and extending to the ring that they will be controlling (see Figure 8.16). Assign the control points of the arm to these bones, taking care not to catch any of the costume's control points in the process.

Once the bones are in place creating your shoulder, control becomes a simple matter of adding a SmartSkin to the bicep bone. Bring up its contextual menu, choose New SmartSkin, and move the bones to deform the mesh more appropriately. For this SmartSkin, it is important that you go through the entire range of motion for the arm and well beyond what you expect to need. It's better to have

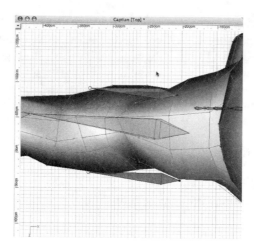

FIGURE 8.16   These two bones will give you more
discrete control over the shape of the arm.

overanticipated your motion than to find out later that you have not gone far
enough. Again, it is better to take this methodically and be able to come back and
edit your keys simply. Start with the arm down, for instance. Once the arm is in position, translate, rotate, and scale the bones to offset the mesh and stop it from pene-
trating the body (see Figure 8.17). The actual shape of the mesh isn't too important
as the costume covers it, but you need to keep it relatively close to its original shape.

Once the arms are in order, carefully adjust each of the bones on the sides of
the body. Move these bones as little as possible. The arm should look similar to
Figure 8.18 when you are done.

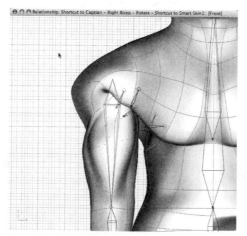

FIGURE 8.17   Start by adjusting the arm to not
penetrate the torso.

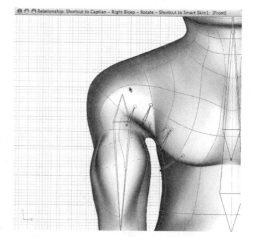

FIGURE 8.18   After adjusting all the bones for
the down position, the arm will look something
like this.

Now move the arm straight up and into the character's head. You may never need the amount of rotation you put onto the driver bone in actual animation, but putting it there gives you headroom. The problems that you need to counteract in this extreme are the creasing at the top of the shoulder; while you are here, you might want to look at any of the armor plates and ensure that they fall correctly on the arm (as they will not be dynamically placed this is very important to handle here) (see Figure 8.19).

Again, start with the arm bones, rotating them until the deltoid is in the proper shape. Then carefully adjust each of the side bones to make the torso shape move in and up a bit (see Figure 8.20).

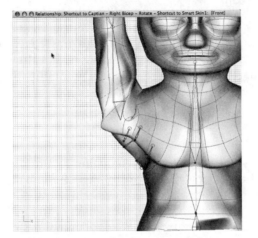

FIGURE 8.19   When the arm goes up, the problems are even more apparent.

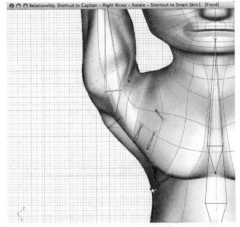

FIGURE 8.20   After you move the bones the shape is much more convincing.

Do the same thing for the arm's front-to-back rotations. Even though the arm does not typically rotate backward, you want to cover that range. It's better to have too great a range covered with SmartSkin than not enough. It may help to hide everything except the torso and to work in a top view. Once you have adjusted each range of motion, close the SmartSkin window and open a new action.

When you are finished with a rig, the last step is to put it through a shakedown. In your new action window, apply the leg constraints, the FK arm constraints, and the general body constraints. Once the controls are active, move the character through as much motion as you can. Look for trouble spots in the mesh, paying special attention to the areas that you have just changed.

Does the SmartSkin behave throughout the arm's full range of motion? If not, you may need to add additional keys, or change the radius factor or enforcement percentage for the SmartSkin.

Do the finger controls work the way you expected? How about the thumb? If not, you may need to adjust them. How about the eyes?

One of the most complex areas of a character and one of the areas most in need of smartening up is the face. You looked at some basic facial poses earlier, but you will want to tie these poses into a cohesive and complete system that makes it easy to animate any expression the character might need.

It starts by setting up the base-level poses. You can go about this systematically, thinking about what the core areas of motion for a character might be and how fine your controls will need to be. It helps to break the face down into areas and address the needs of each area one at a time. The mouth is a good choice, and it requires a high level of flexibility

In short, every aspect of the character you have built controls for in the last two chapters needs to be put through as much torture as you can manage. Any aspect of the character that doesn't hold up should be adjusted here, before animation begins. A good test is making the character run through a series of exercise poses: touching toes, jumping jacks, side stretches, sit-ups, the whole gamut. Even if you never animate any of these actions, the poses that they require are generally at the limits of a character's flexibility and will point out any portions of the model that need to be fixed.

Summary

Relationships are simple on the surface but can be combined to form powerful and complex operations in your models, from controlling the movement of bones and control points to surface attributes to the movement of eyes. Almost every aspect of a character that you might manipulate individually can be driven with a relationship, reducing the number of controls needed to animate. The things covered here are by no means the outer limits of what you can do with relationships. However, they should give you a firm footing when exploring their uses in your own character.

The thing to remember is that they are designed to make your job easier when animating. If you find that a simple IK bone chain is easier for you to set up and control than a complicated 600-bone rig with 30 relationships per bone, then that is the best solution for the job. There is a tendency to get overly complicated where simplicity will suffice. Remember the old axiom: K.I.S.S. (Keep it simple, Silly.)

EXPRESSIONS

In This Chapter

- Syntax
- Squetching the Captain
- Practical Procedural Animation

In this chapter, we look into expressions, one of the most complex parts of A:M. You might consider most of this optional. Expressions are sometimes hard to grasp and even harder to apply, but the hope is to show you some simple and direct applications that you can use in all your animation.

When we talk about expressions we are talking about defining behaviors in raw mathematical terms. The types of behaviors we can define are ruled by the limits of A:M's expression syntax and fall into two broad categories: procedural animation and property control. We will go over both after a quick look at A:M's expression syntax and a brief introduction to the most basic concepts of expressions. Then we apply this knowledge to Captain Splines and Polygozmo, adding some sophisticated squash and stretch control to the Captain and automated animation to Polygozmo.

Syntax

Understanding syntax for expressions is a daunting task, but in order to fully use this powerful tool, learn we must. If you have a foundation in math, especially algebra and trigonometry, most of this will come to you fairly quickly. If you do not, then you may find some of these concepts a bit challenging. We will explore the mathematical aspects of expressions as visually as possible, and every effort has been made to put things into layman's terms.

Start by looking at a hypothetical property called "Property." For your needs, this property needs to meet some basic requirements. It needs to be animateable, and it needs to take numerical values (i.e., just about everything will work). It could be the color of an object (three values r, g, and b) or the rotation of a bone in a single (or multiple) axis. When you are driving the value of Property with an expression (equation), you are saying that this property is equal to the final answer to the equation. You can link one property to another with a simple expression like this:

$$Property = Property2.$$

Think of this like a constraint where one thing equals another. With this you can apply constraints to properties that are not on bones. You can also use basic math such as addition(+), subtraction(–), multiplication(*), and division(/) to make one property a constant offset of another. For example:

$$Property = Property2/2.$$

This would make Property constantly one-half of Property2. This is the way in which all expressions are evaluated. Given this, can you figure out what this expression will do?

$$Property = Property2–(Property3*12).$$

Take a moment and just read it left to right. Property is equal to Property2 minus the result of Property3 times 12.

So if you want to see this in action, look at three pose sliders.

- Property1 is a pose slider with a range of –100 through 100.
- Property2 is a pose slider with a range of 0 through 100.
- Property3 is a pose slider with a range of –20 through 20.

You are setting the value of Property1 with the given expression. So if you set your sliders for Property2 and Property3, as in Figure 9.1, then the value of Property1 is automatically set by your expression.

In addition to basic math, you have access to functions that allow you to increase the complexity and usefulness of expressions. A function is an encapsulated way to invoke a more complex concept in an expression; identified by the parenthesis that follows it, this parenthesis is where any arguments that the function takes will be listed. Some functions don't take any arguments at all. Pi(), for instance simply returns the value of pi. The parentheses are still, however, required. The functions that A:M has built in are outlined in the following section.

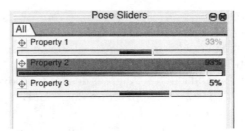

FIGURE 9.1   Property2 is set to 93%, and Property3 is set to 5%, giving Property1 its final value.

Value Functions

This group of functions will provide a value within a range or of a given value. Use them to both control your expressions and to access common mathematical constants (such as pi.)

Abs(n): Absolute Value, returns the absolute value of any value (be that a property or the result of other operations) meaning that it will remove the positive or negative sign of the value and use the result (effectively making all results either positive or zero). For example, Abs(6–12) would return a value of 6 (6 minus 12 is –6), and so would Abs(3+3). This is useful when you need to ensure a positive response from an expression. If, for instance, you were setting the value of a color property or a slider with no negative value, then Abs() would preserve the result but keep the value in an acceptable range.

Floor(n): Floor takes any value and rounds it down to the nearest whole number. This avoids decimal numbers as results for your expressions. This can be important if you use a logical test as part of your expression or if you need a value to provide an On/Off Yes/No response. This means that if the value (n) is 2.3 then the result will be 2. If the result is –2.3, then the result will be –3. Note that the value will round to the next lowest value, regardless of the closeness to the lower value.

Ceiling(n): Ceiling takes any value and rounds it up to the next highest whole number. This is exactly like the Floor function but reversed. A value of 2.3 will become 2 and a value of –2.3 will become –2. Any decimal amount is enough to move the value higher.

Mod(n, n2): Mod returns the Modulus or remainder for a division operation, where n is divided by n2. This means that n2 can never be 0 (division by zero is not possible). If n2 is ever 0, your expression will have a syntax error. If, for example, you have the expression Mod(6, 4), the result will be 2. 6/4=1r2.

Pi(): Pi returns the value of pi for use in other functions. The return is more accurate than 3.14 and results in more accurate functions.

Sqrt(n): Sqrt returns the square root of the value n. This requires n to be greater than 0. If your value is ever 0 or negative, this function will result in a syntax error. Because of this, n is sometimes encapsulated in an Abs function like so: Sqrt(Abs(Property1)). This nesting of functions is common and is where a great deal of the power in expressions comes from.

Round(n, n2): This function does not simply round a number up or down; instead, it allows you to specify the amount by which a value will be "stepped." For instance, if you have the following: Round(n, 3.0), you are telling A:M that you want to round the value of n to the nearest value that is a factor of 3. So, for instance, 22.4 will be rounded down to 21, while 23.6 will be rounded up to 24 (both factors of 3). You can also specify a decimal step, so for example, if you use Round(n, 0.5), 22.3 or more would be rounded to 22.5, while 22.2 would be rounded to 22.0. Due to the way the Round function operates, the n2 value must be positive or A:M will give a syntax error.

Trunc(n): A:M's final rounding function simply removes the decimal portion of any number without regard to the decimal value, so that both 22.1 and 22.9 will result in a value of 22.

Return Property Value Functions

There are times when you will need to get a fixed or at least predictable piece of information from A:M, knowing what direction a bone is pointing from the world origin or what frame you are on, or perhaps a randomly generated number. To this end, you have a set of useful functions in A:M that simply provide you with values.

ChorTime(): This returns the current frame of the choreography as a decimal number. It is based on the FPS of the project so that frame 1 at 24 fps and 30 fps will give you different values (.04 and .03, respectively). This is a predictable and steady set of values and is used often to provide data for other functions. This function uses the global time of the choreography, regardless of where the expression is contained.

GetTime(): Almost identical to ChorTime(), GetTime gives the frame value of the action in which the expression exists. For instance, if you had an action that contained some procedural animation driven by the GetTime() function, the rate of that animation would be tied to the rate of the action, meaning that if the action took half as many frames to complete in the chor as it did in the action window, then the Procedural animation would move twice as fast. If ChorTime() had been used, then the change in the action's length would have no effect on the procedural animation's rate.

GetWorldPos(3D Vector): This function takes a 3D vector, specifically the vector defined by the translation of a bone in all three axes. (A vector is a mathematical term; in this case it refers to a point in 3D space defined by three numbers, the X, Y, and Z translation of a bone. Instead of giving each axis separately, you can simply provide the parent Translate as a vector that contains all three numbers.) It then returns a vector containing the actual position of the bone taken from the 0 point of the current window. This can be useful since the positions of bones are normally only given from their own default origin points.

GetWorldDir(3D Vector): This function takes a 3D vector, specifically the vector defined by the rotation of a bone in all three axes. It then returns a vector that describes the rotation of the bone in reference to the world space. This is similar to the GetWorldPos() function in its application and usefulness.

Sign(n): If all you need to know is if a value is greater than, equal to, or less than 0, you can place the value in question inside the Sign function. The results tell you where the value sits. If the valule is a positive number, the result will be 1; if negative, the result will be –1; if the value is exactly 0, the result will be 0. This can be used to turn on or off a pose or to test values in an If() function.

Rand(): Returns a randomly generated number and keeps doing so for each frame of an animation. The range of numbers will be between 0 and 1 meaning a decimal number. You can set the range by simply multiplying the function by the highest value you want returned, so for instance, Rand()*10 would return values from 0 to 10.

Trigonometric Functions

In mathematics, these are functions of angles and are used extensively when studying triangles. For your purposes, their ability to model periodic data is much more useful. To understand what periodic data is and how you can make use of it, look specifically at the function Sin().

Sin(n): Sine is one of the six trigonometric functions available to you in A:M and one of the more useful of them. But as you will see, the results of all of the trigonometric functions follow a basic pattern. Without giving you a full course on trigonometry we can graph the output of the Sin() function and you will probably recognize it (see Figure 9.2) as what we call a sine wave.

The output of a Sin() function will always have a value of between –1 and 1, depending on the value you place inside the parentheses. If you were to provide it with a value that changed at a steady, predictable rate (the current frame of time in an action or chor, for instance) any parameter that was driven by the expression's output would simply oscillate between –1 and 1. This is a perfect example of periodic data. You will look at this a more closely in a little bit, and see some practical uses.

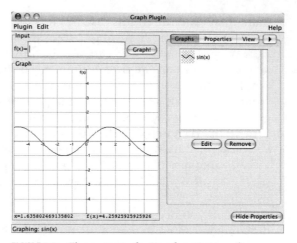

FIGURE 9.2   The output of a Sine function can be graphed in a recognizable pattern.

 It helps to be able to see the output of your expressions before you work on them in A:M. Download a free graphing calculator off the Internet to assist you, such as the one here: http://gcalc.net/.

Cos(n): Cosine, as its name implies, is closely related to the Sine function. In fact, the graph it produces (see Figure 9.3) looks identical to the one for Sine, running in a wave-like pattern from –1 to 1; but if you overlay them (see Figure 9.4) the difference becomes immediately apparent: The cycle of the waves is offset by exactly one-quarter of a cycle. Again, how this can be useful and some practical uses are explored shortly.

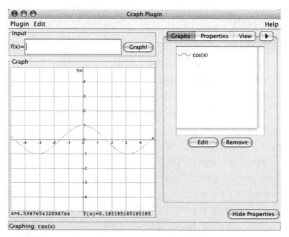

FIGURE 9.3   The graph of a Cos() function looks very similar to that of Sin().

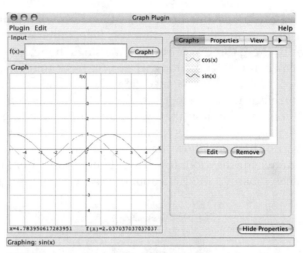

FIGURE 9.4　Overlaying the graphs for Sin and Cos shows the difference lies in the position of the cycles.

Tan(n): Tangent is capable of generating periodic data, but the data it generates is very different than that of Sin or Cos. It doesn't cycle smoothly, but rather jumps from end to beginning of each cycle without oscillation (see Figure 9.5). This lack of oscillation makes the data provided by Tan more useful for rotations and other data where the end and beginning align. Even then though, the data provided is not as smooth in its range as Sin or Cos.

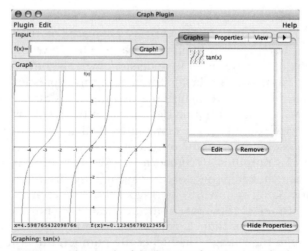

FIGURE 9.5　The graph of the Tangent function is cyclical but lacks oscillation.

Before you move on to the other four trigonometric functions, which can vary quite a bit from the core three, take a moment to look at some implementations of these three expressions on a single bone.

Open the Trigfunctions.prj project from the CD-ROM and look at the open choreography. You have a single sphere sitting on the ground; not exactly Pixar, but for your needs it's perfect. There are already some expressions in place here, and you can see how they work by simply stepping through the frames of the choreography. The sphere is moving in a perfect circle in the choreography. If you look into the translation channels you will notice, however, that there are no set keyframes for the motion you are seeing. How, then, is the motion being created? You can look into the PWS and find two expressions, as shown in Figure 9.6.

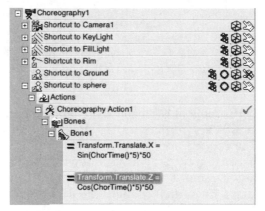

FIGURE 9.6   The expressions that are moving the sphere are located in the choreography action.

The two expressions you have are placed on the *x*- and *z*-axis of translation for the sphere. Look at them one at a time to see what is going on in each axis, and then put them together to understand what is going on with the sphere as a whole. Your *x* translation is being driven with this expression Sin(ChorTime()*5)*50. You can immediately recognize the two functions already discussed, Sin() and Chor-Time(), but might not be clear on what the result of this expression is. If you put this expression into your graphing calculator as sin((x)*5)*50, however, you can get a useful graph of the output of the expression (see Figure 9.7).

This output is, of course, a Sine wave, but in this instance you have adjusted the rate and amplitude of the wave to make its output more useful for your translation. Look at how this works exactly. Your expression has two basic parts. First, ChorTime()*5 is the rate of the Sine wave. By multiplying the ChorTime() by any number greater than 1, you have increased the rate at which the waves will run through their range; the higher the number, the faster they will move. If, on the other hand, you want to slow the rate down, you would divide instead. Second,

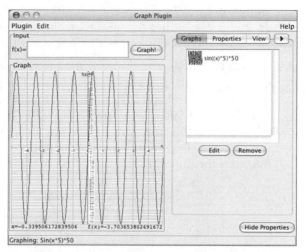

FIGURE 9.7   Putting the expression (or a close equivalent) into a graphing calculator can show you what the output of the expression is.

you have the amplitude of the expression Sin()*50. By multiplying the output of the Sin() function, you increase its range from –1 to 1 up to –50 to 50, or in your case, you have told the sphere to translate from –50 to 50 cm in the *x*-axis.

The second expression is very similar, except that it uses the Cos() function rather than the Sin() function. We did this so that the waves for the axes would be offset. In this way, when the sphere is translated as far as it will go in the *x*-axis (either positive or negative), it will be only half as far as it will go in the *z*-axis. This is where you get the circular movement of the sphere.

Try this: Change the expression of the *z*-axis (simply click on it in the PWS, and it will become an edit box that you can type into) so that it is a Sin function just like the *x*-axis, and then step through the frames.

Notice that now the sphere only moves in a diagonal line because the waves for x and z are now synchronized.

You can affect the path of the sphere as it moves in other ways. No matter how much you increase the rate or the distance of these expressions, the results will end in a spherical (or ovoid) path for the ball. If, for instance, you want to tighten the magnitude of the sphere so that the ball moves in more of a square path, you could modify the output of the Sin with other functions, such as Tan().

Go ahead and change the expressions so that they are inside a Tan() function: Translate.X = Tan(Sin(ChorTime()*5))*50 (notice the 50 is outside the Tan; if it is inside you will get unpredictable results), Translate.Z = Tan(Cos(ChorTime()5))*50. Now step through the frames again, notice how the path the sphere follows is more linear. If you want it to be perfectly linear, there are other functions you can use (which you will look at shortly) to do that.

The thing to look at here is how functions can be layered with other functions to provide useful data either for motion, as in this case, or for other aspects in a model. Go ahead and experiment with a few variations on these functions.

ASin(n0...1): Takes a range of numbers from 0 to 1 (meaning fractional numbers less than 1 and greater than 0.) and returns a range of values between pi/2 and –pi/2. This will produce a finite graphed area similar to one slope of a Sine wave (see Figure 9.8). There is no oscillation or periodic value to this function, which may make you wonder where you can use it, especially when you spent so much time showing practical animation uses for the other trigonometric functions.

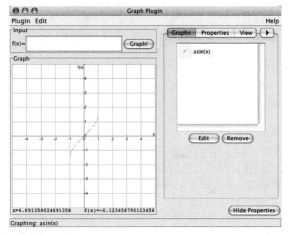

FIGURE 9.8   The graph of the Asin() functions shows no periodic data.

The primary utility of this function lies in its ability to modify the Sin function in a very useful way. When you give the results of a Sin() function and pass it though the filtering function of ASin(), the result is what we call a triangle wave. The expression looks like this ASin(Sin(X)) and returns a graph similar to Figure 9.9. You can use this much like you did the Sine wave earlier, but this will provide linear movement. Combined with your next function, you could make an object translate in a perfect square.

ACos(n0....1): Takes a range of numbers from 0 to 1 (meaning fractional numbers less than 1 and greater than 0) and returns a range of values between pi and –pi. This is to Cos what ASin is to Sin.

Atan(n): This is almost identical to the Tangent function but its graph will be rotated 90 degrees (see Figure 9.10), and it does not give periodic data. Instead, it gives a range of data from pi/2 to –pi/2. You can use it as you did Tan to modify the output of Sin and Cos functions, but instead of lowering the magnitude of the arcs, as discussed with the Tan() function, it increases the magnitude to make the circle rounder.

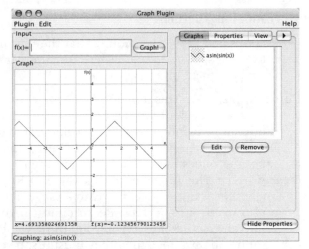

FIGURE 9.9   Filtering a Sin through an ASin produces the classic triangle wave form.

Atan2(n, n1): This variant of the Arc Tangent function above takes two values (Y and X) and gives the angle required to hit the values on a 2D plane in Radians. This function is useful in taking an arbitrary point say, for example, the location of a bone, and generating an angle from it, which can then be either further modified or fed into any property that takes an angle, such as bone rotation. You will look at this more in depth shortly.

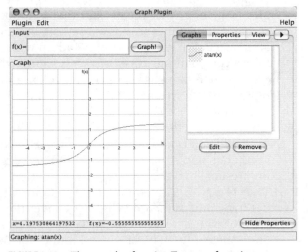

FIGURE 9.10   The graph of an Arc Tangent function.

Property Formatting Functions

Many functions and properties require that the information that they are given be presented in a specific format. These functions take numbers (or groups of numbers) and put them into a specific format.

Color(N, N2, N3): This function takes three values (expressed as percents) and creates a color based off of their values. This is equivilent to the standard Mac convention of defining colors based on the 0% to 100% blending of the three base colors: Red, Green, and Blue. The Color function takes the values in order to represent their respective RGB counterparts.

Degrees(Nr): This function takes a value of Radians (a way to express an angle similar to a degree, but with a range of 0 to 1 rather than 0 to 360) and converts it to degrees. Because most trigonometric functions return their values as Radians, if you want those values to be useful as degrees of rotation, for example, then they must first be converted.

Radians(Nd): This function takes a value of Degrees and converts it to Radians. Radians are useful in many trigonometric functions, and if you needed to feed something like a rotational axis into a trigonometric function, you would first need to convert it from the standard Degrees to Radians via this function.

Quat(X, Y, Z, W): Quaternion rotations are what A:M uses for most bone rotations. This is a more robust way to describe rotations than simple vector rotations and avoids many of the problems associated with vector rotations. What the four numbers actually represent is fairly complicated but can be thought of as two separate, but related, pieces of information. X, Y, and Z indicate a 3D vector. This is a single point, and you might be tempted to think of it as a simple indication of rotation as in "this bone rotates to point at this vector" but that is fundamentally wrong. The XYZ component describes an axis of rotation, and the W value describes the rotation around that axis. So you wind up with something like Figure 9.11. Where you point the *axis of rotation* is identified by the XYZ vector. The object you are rotating is kept perpendicular to this axis at all times and then rotated around this axis. W indicates this rotation by a range of values from −100 to 100. The actual value of W is equal to Cos(angle/2)*100, so you won't see a direct correlation to the actual angle of rotation and the W value, but you can easily derive the value by knowing that 100 is equal to no rotation and −100 is equal to a full 360 degrees of rotation. Thus, you can presume that 0 is 180 degrees of rotation and 50 is 90, and so on.

RGB(N1, N2, N3): This is similar to the Color() function with the exception that it uses the standard Windows convention of representing each color channel with a value between 0 and 255 instead of a straight percent. The results of RGB(128,128,128) and Color(0.5, 0.5, 0.5) are exactly the same.

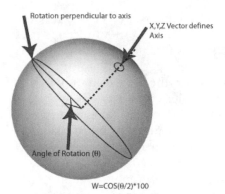

FIGURE 9.11 Quaternion rotations can be difficult to visualize until you understand the elements that comprise them.

Vector(N, N2, N3): This function takes three values and places them into a single "vector." Being that it is the basis for almost all aspects of 3D animation in general it is pretty much impossible to overstate the importance of understanding what a vector is and how it works. Many of our more advanced expressions will make use of the Vector function, as you will see.

Euler(X, Y, Z): This function takes three values and formats them as a Euler. This is typically used to format the output of expressions for Bone rotations, but can also be used to compare a bone rotation to a given point in logical expressions.

Algebraic, Vector, and Matrix Math Functions

Ln(N): This function takes a number greater than 0 and returns the natural logarithm of that number. Natural logarithms are highly useful and can be used to describe spirals, decay, or intensities.

Log(N, B): This function takes a number (N) greater than 0 and returns the logarithm of that number to the base (B) specified. This allows us to generate series of complex numbers to any base you might need for an expression.

LogTen(N): The other common base for logarithms is base 10 (which is the base of our numbering system). It has much the same use as the natural and specified logarithms.

Cross(V1, V2): The Cross Product function takes two vectors and returns a vector perpendicular to the plane they describe. This can be a very useful function, and much of 3D is based upon it. The normals of a surface, for example, are generated from the Cross Product of the vectors that define the plane of the surface that it lies on.

Dot(V1, V2): The Dot Product function takes two vectors and returns a floating point number that results from the multiplication and addition of the elements of the vectors. It is useful for extracting any member of a vector for use in other functions (as you will see in a moment).

Exp(N): This function raises *e* (which is the base of a natural logarithm) by the power specified. It can be useful for creating Specified Logarithms that follow the same output patterns of a natural logarithm at a greater or lesser scale.

Fact(N): This function takes a number greater than 1 and returns the factorial of that number. A factorial is the process of multiplying a series of numbers from 1 up to the value of N, so if you have Fact(5), your result is 1*2*3*4*5=120.

Norm(V1): The Normal function returns the length of the specified vector. This is then commonly used to produce a Normalized Vector, which is a vector scaled to a length of 1, allowing you to work with just the direction of the vector without regard to its length. You make good use of this when working with vectors.

Vectors, for all their being the fundamental core of 3D, can be hard to visualize and encapsulate into useful expressions. Bob Croucher at Hash, Inc. provided the following example found in the DotCross.prj in the projects folder on the CD-ROM). Given that Bob wrote the code, look at his example and see what you can pull from it.

ON THE CD

If you look at Figure 9.12, you see the choreography of a very simple scene. You have a shape sitting on a plane and a shadow cast out behind it, but more careful observation of the shadow reveals that it is actually a disk of patches trailing out behind the object.

FIGURE 9.12   This simple-looking project actually conceals some very complex expressions.

To see the expressions at work, select the light in the chor window and drag it around. You should notice that as you do, the position and length of the shadow move as well. This is not because the light is casting a shadow, but rather because the shadow is scaling and rotating itself based on what it knows of the position of the light in the choreography.

This behavior is driven by two expressions on two bones that control the points of the shadow. Look at the expressions now, and then dissect them to understand what they are doing. Expression 9.1 shows the equation that drives the scale of the shadow, while Expression 9.2 shows the equation that drives the rotation.

Expression 9.1

```
bone1.scale.z = Sqrt(1-Dot((..|..|..|..|..|..|Shortcut to Rim.Transform.
Translate-..|..|..|..|..|..|Shortcut to Model1.Transform.Translate)/
Norm(..|..|..|..|..|..|Shortcut to Rim.Transform.Translate-..|..|..|..|..|..|
Shortcut to Model1.Transform.Translate),Vector(0,1,0))
*Dot((..|..|..|..|..|..|Shortcut to Rim.Transform.Translate-
..|..|..|..|..|..|Shortcut to Model1.Transform.Translate)/
Norm(..|..|..|..|..|..|Shortcut to Rim.Transform.Translate-
..|..|..|..|..|..|Shortcut to Model1.Transform.Translate),
Vector(0,1,0)))/Dot((..|..|..|..|..|..|Shortcut to Rim.Transform.
Translate-..|..|..|..|..|..|Shortcut to Model1.Transform.Translate)/
Norm(..|..|..|..|..|..|Shortcut to Rim.Transform.Translate-
..|..|..|..|..|..|Shortcut to Model1.Transform.Translate),Vector(0,1,0))
```

Expression 9.2

```
bone2.rotate.y = Degrees(Atan2(Dot(Cross((..|..|..|..|..|..|Shortcut to
Rim.Transform.Translate-..|..|..|..|..|..|Shortcut to Model1.Transform.
Translate),Vector(0,1,0)),Vector(1,0,0)),Dot(Cross((..|..|..|..|..|..|
Shortcut to Rim.Transform.Translate-..|..|..|..|..|..|Shortcut to Model1.
Transform.Translate),Vector(0,1,0)),Vector(0,0,1))))-90
```

If your eyes glazed over at the sight of Expression 9.1 don't feel bad, it's a very daunting-looking expression, quite a step up from your previous experience. But if you pull it apart and analyze it, all will soon become clear.

Expression 9.1 drives the bone scale that gives the shadow length. This expression relies heavily on the Dot function. Simplify some of the paths in the expression first. This will make them easier to read. There two vectors that are used quite heavily, specifically: ..|..|..|..|..|..|Shortcut to Rim.Transform and ..|..|..|..|..|..|Shortcut to Model1.Transform.Translate. You know these are Vectors because they refer to the Translate channel rather than any individual axis of it. To make these vectors easier to read, simplify them as V1 and V2, respectively. This reduces your expression to this:

bone1.scale.z = Sqrt(1- Dot((V1-V2) /Norm(V1-V2), Vector(0,1,0)) * Dot((V1-V2) /Norm(V1-V2), Vector(0,1,0))) / Dot((V1-V2) /Norm(V1-V2), Vector(0,1,0)) Dot((V1-V2) /Norm(V1-V2), Vector(0,1,0)),

which is far more manageable. It also brings something to light: The Dot functions are all basically the same—Dot((V1-V2)/Norm(V1-V2), Vector(0,1,0)).

We are replacing the paths and other elements of the expressions here just for clarity. In your expression editor inside A:M, the full paths and all other portions of the expression must remain intact or you will be given a syntax error.

This Dot function is used three times in all, so that you can further simplify things if you use D to represent it throughout the expression:

$$bone1.scale.z = Sqrt(1-D*D)/D,$$

which is suddenly not that bad at all. Take this and examine what you are asking A:M to do.

Say your model is located exactly at the origin of the choreography (0,0,0) and the light is put into an arbitrary position (1,4,–5). Replace V1 with (1,4,–5) and V2 with (0,0,0) so that your Dot Product looks like this:

$$D=(\ ((1,4,-5)-(0,0,0))\ /\ Norm((1,4,-5)-(0,0,0)),\ Vector(0,1,0)\ ).$$

You can then work out the vector math subtractions $(x,y,z)-(a,b,c) = (x-a, y-b, z-c)$ to arrive at this:

$$D=Dot(\ (1,4,-5)\ /\ Norm(1,4,-5),\ Vector(0,1,0)\ ).$$

A:M will then calculate the length of the Vector(1,4,–5), which will return a value of 6.4807 or:

$$D=\ Dot(\ (1,4,-5)/6.4807,\ Vector(0,1,0)\ ).$$

You can then work out the division of the vector by its length. This gives you the "normalized" vector, which is a vector in the same direction as (1,4,–5) but with a length of 1. This division $(x,y,x)/n = (x/n, y/n, z/n)$ gives you this:

$$D=Dot(\ (0.154,\ 0.617,\ -0.772),\ Vector(0,1,0)\ ).$$

All that remains is to find the Dot Product of the two vectors. This is done by first multiplying each of the vector elements in turn and then by adding them all together: $Dot((x,y,z),\ (a,b,c)) = x*a + y*b + z*c$ which simply leaves us with

$$D=\ .617.$$

Plug this into your original expression like so:

$$Sqrt(1-(.617*.617))/.617=1.2754.$$

The value 1.2755 is then applied to the scale value of Z on Bone 1 to give it a Z scale of 127.55%.

A:M stores percentages internally as decimal numbers so that 50% is the same as .5. As a result, there is no need to multiply a number by 100 in order to represent a percent, as you might suspect from the values as they are represented in the PWS.

This scales the shadow portion of the model correctly depending on the angle of the light in regard to the object. All that remains is to rotate the shadow to fall opposite to the light source. To that end, look to Expression 9.2, which while nowhere near as long as Expression 9.1 is still a lot to look at. Simplify this one as you did before by replacing paths in your notation with simplified variables. Start by replacing the Paths in the expression with the same V1 and V2 variables, as these are the same two vectors you had in the previous expression:

bone2.rotate.y = Degrees(Atan2(Dot(Cross((V1–V2),Vector(0,1,0)), Vector(1,0,0)), Dot(Cross((V1–V2),Vector(0,1,0)),Vector(0,0,1))))–90

You can immediately break this down into two Dot Products, but these are different Dot Products. Look at them and see what makes them different:

X = Dot(Cross(V1–V2), Vector(0,1,0)), Vector(1,0,0))
Z = Dot(Cross(V1–V2), Vector(0,1,0)), Vector(0,0,1))

Notice that the last vector on each dot product is different. The first has the 1 in the X position, and the second has it in the Z. But you can still simplify them both by looking at the Cross product they contain, which is identical for both, and will return a vector you can refer to as V3, thus:

X = Dot(V3, Vector(1,0,0))
Z = Dot(V3, Vector(0,0,1))

If you want to use this to simplify the main expression further you can represent the values you will get from the Dot products with X and Z like so:

Bone2.rotate.y=Degrees(Atan2(X,Z))–2,

which is, again, much easier to read. Run through the math on this so you can come to an understanding of what you are asking A:M to do. Use the same translates as before: (0,0,0) and (1,4,–5). The innermost simplification then is:

V3=Cross(((1,4,–5)–(0,0,0)), Vector(0,1,0)) or
V3 = Cross((1,4,–5), Vector(0,1,0)).

Notice that you are not normalizing the vector this time though. This is because in order for the Atan2 function to give you a useful angle you need the exact coordinates of the light in relation to the base of your object. The math on the Cross product is done like so:

V3.x = (V1.y * Vector.z) – (V1.z * Vector.y),
V3.y = (V1.z * Vector.x) – (V1.x * Vector.z),
V3.z = (V1.x * Vector.y) – (V1.y * Vector.x),

which you can equate to this:

V3.x = (4 * 0) – (–5 * 1) = 5,
V3.y = (-5 * 0) – (1 * 0) = 0,
V3.z = (1 * 1) – (4 * 0) = 1,

V3 = (5,0,1).

Then place the value of V3 into the Dot product equations for X and Z, and solve as before:

$$X = Dot((5,0,1), Vector(1,0,0)) = 5+0+0=5,$$
$$Z = Dot((5,0,1), Vector(0,0,1)) =0+0+1=1.$$

These two values give you a point in space that indicates two things about your light: how far to the Left/Right is this light from the object (X), and how far to the front/back is this light from the object (Y).

This, through the Atan2() function, tells you the angle of the object in relation to the direction the light travels to it. You can then place the value of X and Z into the base expression to arrive at this:

$$Degrees(Atan2(5,1))-90.$$

Atan2(5,1) returns an angle of incidence of 1.3737 Radians, which you then convert to degrees to make it easier to conceptualize and deal with, which gives you your angle of incidence as 78.6901 degrees. What you want is the angle exactly perpendicular to this, which is simply your angle minus 90 degrees: 11.30 degrees (see Figure 9.13).

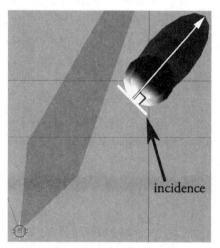

FIGURE 9.13 The angle of the shadow is perpendicular to the angle of incidence between the light and the object.

In this way, you see the use of vectors in A:M expressions. They allow you to get precise relationships between objects in 3D space and drive properties based on those relationships, even relationships between multiple models.

Logic and Control Functions

These functions allow you to direct your expressions with logical choices based on values. They consist of a comparison and a result based on the true or false return of that comparison. You have the option of using either specific predetermined comparisons or building your own set of tests and results. When you create your own comparisons, you have the use of traditional logical comparitors: >, <, =, <=, >=, !=, And, Or, and Not. We look at how these work as we explore expressions throughout this chapter.

If(Comparison, TrueValue, FalseValue): If is the most powerful of your logical functions. It encapsulates complex comparison operations and allows you to branch your expression based on data you have collected. It requires two arguments. First, it must make a comparison, and that comparison must be something that can be resolved to be true or false. This comparison is the equivalent of asking a simple question: Is X greater than or equal to Y? A:M will look at the two arguments and answer the question yes or no. You then reply with the second argument to the function: If it is, then we want to use Value Y. The third argument, False-Value, is optional, and if it is not present and the answer to your comparison is "no" then the function returns nothing. So, for example, if your expression was If(1 > 0, 1, 0) you would be saying: If one is greater than 0 then return 1: if not, return 0. In this case, of course 1 will always be greater than 0, and so you would always get a result of 1. It is more common then to compare things when you don't know the values they might have: If(Property1 > Property2, 1, 2). If property 1 is greater than property 2, then return 1, otherwise return 2. The result of this expression would be completely dependent on the value of the two properties.

This concept can, just as easily be expanded beyond a simple two-value comparison. With the addition of And and Or, you can link and compare as many properties as you like: If(A > B AND B > C AND C > D OR C < E, 1, 0) If A is greater than B and B is greater than C and C is either Greater than D or Less than E, then return 1 otherwise 0. If you say AND, then the comparisons on *both* sides of it must be true in order for the True Value to apply. If you say OR, then at least one of the values must be true, but not necessarily both.

In addition, you can nest If statements into the TrueValue and False-Value: If(A > B, If(B > C, 1, 2) , If(B < C, 1, 3)). If A is greater than B, then see if B is greater than C. If it is, then return 1, if not return 2. If, however, B is Greater than A, then check to see if B is less than C, if it is, then return 1, if not, return 3.

In this way you can specify the exact conditions in which any property gets a particular value.

Max(n, n2): Max takes two values and simply returns the larger of the two. It is in a simple way to say: If n is greater than n2, then the result is n, else the desired result is n2.

Min(n, n2): Min takes two values and simply returns the smaller of the two. This is the reverse of the Max function, in effect saying: If n is less than n2, then the desired result is n, else the result is n2.

While you will no doubt find more applications for some of these functions they all have their uses, and there are moments when they are indispensable. We have looked at some examples already as a way to explore functions and give a practical reference for some of the more esoteric values; now look at applying these functions in some real-world applications.

SQUETCHING THE CAPTAIN

One of the most practical applications of expressions comes in the time-honored principal of animation called Squash and Stretch, or more modernly Squetch. The idea is that as a character moves, the masses of the character shift to give weight and expressiveness to its motion. Think of a bouncing ball: It can fall and bounce a few times, as shown in Figure 9.14, but it looks rather stiff doing it.

By simply squashing the ball down when it hits the ground and then stretching it out as it flies up and again before it hits the ground, you get a much more lively bounce (see Figure9.15).

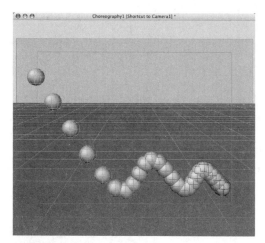

FIGURE 9.14 The bounce of this ball seems unnaturally stiff.

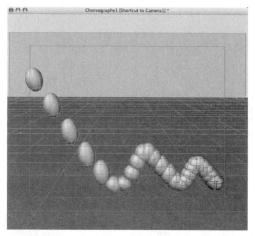

FIGURE 9.15 Adding squash and stretch to the bounce gives it both life and weight.

These same ideas apply to almost every aspect of your character, even areas that would be realistically rigid can benefit from Squetch.

There are two basic aspects to any useable Squetch system: isolation and conservation of mass.

Isolation, simply put, means that the Squetch of a given bone (the bicep), for instance, will not Squetch any children. To show why this is, look at Figure 9.16. Here you have an arm bent at an angle. Nothing has been squetched (which in the simplest terms is just bone scale), and everything looks fine

If you apply any scaling to the bicep, however, you can see that while the bicep itself looks fine, the forearm and hand become distorted (see Figure 9.17).

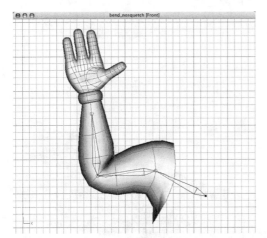

FIGURE 9.16   A normal, unsquetched arm bent.

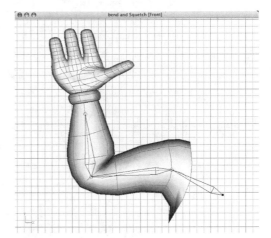

FIGURE 9.17   Upon squetching the bicep, distortion becomes immediately apparent in the children.

This is because you have a group of bones that are all part of a chain (as you must, in order for your character control rig to function), and the scale of the parent affects the entire chain, but not as you might want. You might think that scaling a parent 110% on the z-axis would also scale its child 110% along the child's z-axis. The reality, however, is that the bone scales along the parent's axes, so that if the rotations happen to be aligned, or if all three axes of the parent are scaled the same amount, then everything looks fine. Since most of our characters have a need to bend their arms at one point or another, this is not feasible. Instead, you need to build in isolation. You could remove the children from the control of the parent, but this would then require that you install secondary sets of bones and add constraints: You would have to complicate your bone setup more than is really worth it. With expressions, on the other hand, you can quite easily counter all scale operations from propagating down a chain of bones. Open up the captain and do this for the right arm.

The first step to countering anything is to determine where it is coming from and how it moves into the chain. For transformations such as scale, this is fairly straightforward, but it still helps to consider this from the broader perspective. In the case of bone scale, the scale comes from the parent, and it moves into the chain by distorting the local axes of the chain. So, for instance, instead of rotating around a sphere, bones rotate inside an ovoid. In order to counter this, you need to insert a bone into your chain that scales in exact opposition to the given bone, in effect undistorting the local axes for the children. This additional bone needs to be a child of the scaling parent and a parent of all other bones further down the chain. So to start, add a bone to your arm called Bicep Squetch Counter, as shown in Figure 9.18

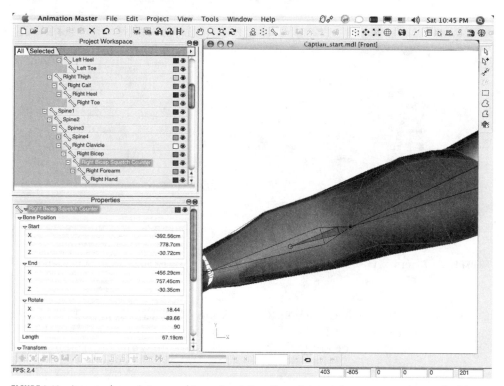

FIGURE 9.18   Insert a bone into your hierarchy at the elbow joint at the same rotation as the bicep.

This counter bone offsets the scaling of the arm with the use of a relatively simple expression. The expression needs to have a container and a convenient way to switch its effects on and off. To this end, create a new On/Off pose for the model. This will contain all of the Squetch-related expressions.

Before you start building the expressions for this model, you need to set up your interface to allow you to work easily. First, you need to enable some of the preferences for the PWS. Open the Options panel (Tools > Options) and bring the Global tab to the front. On this tab, enable the last two options: Show Advanced Properties and Show Property Triangle (see Figure 9.19). The first will reveal previously hidden properties in the project, some of which you will need as you work with expressions; the second will reveal a disclosure triangle in the PWS that will give access to all the properties that you would normally access in the Properties panel.

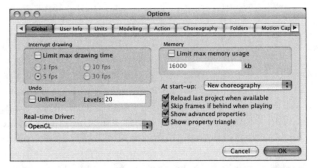

FIGURE 9.19   Enable the last two properties on the Global Properties tab.

You will also need to have the Properties panel open. You won't be accessing properties in it specifically; rather, you will use it as the area where you edit your expressions, while the PWS will allow you to access the properties you need at the same time. When you have your interface set up, select the Right Bicep Squetch Counter bone in the Relationship window. When it is selected, the properties for this bone will be presented in the Properties panel. The one property you are interested in is the Scale property, which is what you want to counter from the Bicep. As you did before, bring up the contextual menu for the property you are working on, and choose Edit Expression. This will do two things, as you learned earlier: create a new expression object (this time in the relationship container in the model rather than in a choreography action) and bring forward the Expression Editor dialog. This time, though, you are not just inputting mathematical equations and functions into the expression; you will be feeding data from other properties into your expression, and for this you need to work from the editor in the Properties panel. Click Cancel to dismiss the dialog and focus your attention to the properties. You should see something like Figure 9.20.

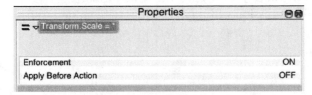

FIGURE 9.20   The properties for the expression.

The area immediately under the Transform.Scale= heading is a clickable edit box. If you click in it, you can type in your expression just as you would in the dialog. What you want from the expression is to take the scale of the Bicep in all three axes (which is a vector) and counter it on all three axes (which is the inverse of that vector). To find the inverse of a vector, you simply divide 1 by the vector so: iV = 1/V.

You can easily type in 1/ to do the 1 divided by portion of the expression, but how do you put in the vector of the bicep's scale?

Click in the edit area on the Properties panel, and type in the beginning of your expression: 1/ and without clicking anything else or pressing the Enter key, go to the PWS. While the Edit window is open in the Properties panel, you can navigate the PWS without closing it, and any property you click on will be placed into the expression with the correct syntax. You want to add the scale of the Right Bicep bone to your expression, but where do you find the correct placement of that property? If you look to the model and find the bone, you can expand the properties triangle and indeed find a Transform.Scale property. The problem with this property is that it is the cache value for the bicep's scale and will never change during the course of an animation. What you need is the property relative to the shortcut to the model, either in action or choreography, where any scaling will actually happen.

You can find this property under the shortcut to the model in the temporary action that holds your pose. But it will not be immediately visible to you. The reason for this is that by default A:M hides a lot of the properties of a model in actions and choreographies, revealing them only when you animate them, creating a driver. If you want or need to see the entire tree of properties for an object, tell A:M to show you more than just the drivers. To this end, there is a toggle in the PWS that does just that (see Figure 9.21).

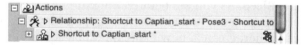

FIGURE 9.21   The circled toggle after the shortcut to an object in the PWS will reveal more than the drivers for that shortcut.

Clicking the toggle will reveal the full range of folders and properties for any object. Now that it has been revealed, drill down in under the Bones folder to find the Right Bicep bone. Expand its properties to reveal the Transform properties. When you can see it, click the scale property (see Figure 9.22). As soon as you do, your expression will have the following added to it: ..|..|..|Right Bicep.Transform. Scale.

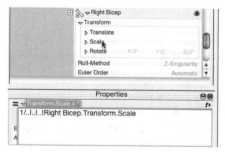

FIGURE 9.22   Simply clicking on the desired property will add it to your expression.

This format is the relative path to the given property based on the PWS tree. It moves up with each ..| one level. In this case, it rises from the level of a driver under the Right Bicep Squetch Counter bone up three levels to the Bones folder of the shortcut. From there it goes directly to the Right Bicep bone. Each level of property on any object is indicated by the dot symbol (.). So when we say Right Bicep.Transform.Scale, we are indicating the Scale property of the Right Bicep. If you wanted, for instance, to indicate just one axis of scale, Z, you would append that with a dot like so: Right Bicep.Transform.Scale.Z. It is more likely that you would have simply clicked on the Z scale property in the first place, though. It is almost always more direct to simply click the property you need rather than typing it in.

Once the property is in the expression, you are done with the Edit window and you can simply press the Enter key to commit the expression. If you have done our job correctly, nothing will happen. If you have made a mistake somewhere, A:M will likely present an alert telling you there is a syntax error in your expression. If this happens, read your expression and try to decipher where it is. You should now have an expression that looks exactly like this: 1/..|..|..|Right Bicep.Transform.Scale.

That simple expression will now counter all scale from the Bicep from moving, distorting the rest of the arm chain, and if your hierarchy is correct, you will not have caused any conflicts in the animation rig already installed.

Now that you have countered the effect of this bone on the hierarchy, you can tackle the second part of the Squetch: Conservation of Volume. This is a very well-documented expression, documented in the Technical Reference online help and various demo videos available from Hash, Inc. The base concept is that Volume is maintained when the scale of all three axes can be multiplied to arrive at 1 (or 100%) so that if one axis is scaled up the others are scaled down to compensate. This requires two expressions on the axes that you will not be scaling, which for the bicep (like is most often the case) will be the *z*-axis.

You want to create a new on/off pose to hold this, and all future, volume maintenance expressions. In the Pose window, select the Bicep bone. Find the properties that you want to apply the expression to, which in this case will be the X and Y scale properties. Start with the X scale, select it, bring up the contextual menu, and select Edit Expression. This time you can enter the expression directly into the dialog, not because it doesn't use a property to drive its value, but because the path to the property is known and very simple. Since you are at Transform.Scale.X and you want to get to Transform.Scale.Z you only need to move up one level or ..| and then back down to the Z property: ..|Z.

The expression you need here is based on the knowledge of what you want as a result: $X*Y*Z=1$, which can be equated to $(X*Y)=1/Z$. You also know that in this particular instance X and Y will be scaled the same amount, which can then be $X*X = 1/Z$, and by algebraic reduction $Sqrt(X*X) = Sqrt(1/Z)$, or more simply $X=Sqrt(1/..|Z)$. Knowing this, simply type $Sqrt(1/..|Z)$ into the expression editing dialog and click OK.

The exact same expression added to the Y scale will complete the volume conservation expressions for the Bicep. You don't have to change anything or worry about your scale countering expression. Because it counters all three axes of scale, it will automatically compensate for all your scale operations.

That is all you need to do to get the bicep to scale, but what you lack at this point is a simple way to control the Squetch during animation. You could simply unhide the geometry bones and scale them, but this is clumsy and less than ideal. What would make this easier is a set of direct controls. This has already been discussed to a certain extent in Chapter 7, "Constraints," and Chapter 8, "Relationships." Placing controls is more than half the challenge of a good rig. You can drop controls into a rig anyplace you like or even just leave all the control of the rig contained in pose sliders, and while it would function, it makes it less intuitive and more work to use. What you need is an interface for squashing and stretching your character, and you need to have a way to enable and disable the interface. But like the facial animation controls you installed earlier, it all starts with the pose that drives the bones. In this case, you want a pose to drive the scale of the bicep bone. Create a new percentage pose. This pose needs to have a range from −100 to 100, which you can set on the Settings panel of the pose. When the Relationship window opens, simply scale the bicep bone up 200% in the z-axis. (Remember: your expression will take care of the volume.) Then move the pose slider to −100, and set the scale of the bone to 20% (if you think you might use more of a range, feel free to scale more).

With this pose in place, you have the squash and stretch functionality. You can put the interface into the model in any way that makes sense to you. For this example, follow the standard set with the facial controls, Set up a nonrendering spline box directly above the bicep similar to Figure 9.23. This box will indicate the area you will move your direct control in. Line it up with the bicep so that its use is clear. Use the Font Wizard to make the words Squash and Stretch as simple spline outlines with no faces, bevels, or sides, as shown in Figure 9.24.

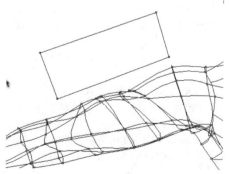

FIGURE 9.23 Start the interface with a nonrendering spline box.

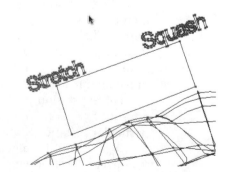

FIGURE 9.24 Labels for the control box are made with the Font Wizard.

You want these interface elements to remain with the bicep even as it rotates. The easiest way to do this is to simply add a bone as a child of the clavicle drawn exactly over the bicep. This will be the Bicep Squetch holder. You will only use it to keep the control and interface in place. Assign the points in the interface to the container.

Create a new null and make it a child of the Bicep Squetch holder (see Figure 9.25) and positioned in the center of the control box.

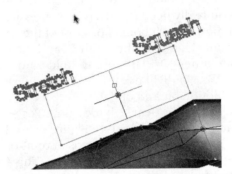

FIGURE 9.25   Add a null as a child of the squetch holder bone. This will be your direct control.

Now you just need to tie the value of the squetch slider to the null's translation inside the box so that as it approaches the end labled Stretch, the bicep is scaled up, and as it is scaled down when the null moves toward the end with the Squash label. If your null is aligned with the box correctly, this should simply be a relationship of the null's X translation.

Create a new relationship for the X translation, move the null to the stretch end of the box and set the pose slider to 100. Then simply move the null to the squash end and set the pose to −100.

In order for your interface to move with the bicep, you need to add a simple Orient Like constraint from the holder to the Bicep Bone. This way, any time the arm moves (rergardless of IK or FK motion), the interface will move with it.

The interface is great when you are working on the squetch of a character, but it can be in the way if you are working on other aspects of animation. You can create a simple hiding pose that will hide this and all other portions of the interface. Create a new on/off pose, and when the Relationship window is open scale the holder bone down into the arm by scaling the x- (or y- if your roll handle is pointing any way but back) axis of the bone down to 1%. This will move all aspects of the interface inside the arm, effectively hiding it from view when you are animating. Close the relationship and name it, and your bicep squetch is complete. You can now proceed to each part of the character and set up a similar set of expressions and poses for each segment that you want to squash and stretch.

PRACTICAL PROCEDURAL ANIMATION

You have already looked at some procedural animation techniques, but they were more examples than practical application. In order to give you a more grounded view on the process, look at using what you have learned to drive some of Polygozmo's mechanical aspects. The gears in the character's chest provide a perfect place to drive motion with procedural expressions. It's something you *could* animate by hand, but why would you want to?

ON THE CD

You will find a rigged Polygozmo on the CD-ROM in the models folder called Gozmo_rigged_v3.mdl. Go ahead and load this model into A:M.

All you really need for this is an expression on each of the gear bones to drive the *z*-rotation of each bone. For most of the gears, you won't have to worry about the rate, but Gear_2 meshes with Gear_1, so set up its rotation to match.

Create a new On/Off pose to hold your expressions and name it Procedural Gear Motion. You will use this as a container for the gears and as a simple way to turn the motion on and off later.

First, select the Gear_1 bone in the Pose window. You should see its properties in the Properties panel (see Figure 9.26). Expand the properties to reveal the Rotation properties. Click the *z*-axis of rotation and bring up its contextual menu. From the menu choose Edit Expression. This will bring up the Expression Editing dialog, and for this simple expression we can enter it directly here. You want this cog to rotate continuously throughout the animation at a steady rate. To get this, you need to have a value that you can call on that will be constant and steady throughout the animation: ChorTime() will give the bone the current frame number in the project, which is steady and predictable, so this is a perfect time to use it. Your Expression could be as simple as ChorTime(), but that would make for pretty slow rotation. A more useful value might come from multiplying this value by a larger number so that the motion is perceptible. ChorTime()*200 will likely suit, but you can change the multiplication with any value you like. (You could even use a pose slider to set this value, so that you could quickly change the speed of the Gear's rotation during an animation.)

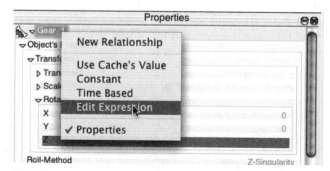

FIGURE 9.26   In the Properties for Gear 1, select the *z*-rotation, as this is what you want the expression to drive.

Once your main gear is rotating, use this rotation to drive all the other gears in the chest.

Moving to Gear_2, you have to be certain that this gear is rotating so that the teeth mesh with those on Gear_1. Since both gears have the same number of teeth, this is simply a matter of having Gear_2 rotate at the same rate, but in the opposite direction as Gear_1.

This is done very easily by multiplying the value of Gear_1's z-rotation by −1: ..|..|..|..|Gear_1.Transform.Rotate.Z*-1.

The other two gears are not related to Gear_1 directly, so you can either use the ChorTime() function to get a different rate of rotation or you can alter the existing rotations from Gear_1. The easiest method is to simply give each gear its own Chor-Time() expression. When you are done, close the Relationship window and put Polygozmo into a choreography. As you step through the frames of the chor, you will see that the gears in the chest rotate on their own without any intervention by you.

SUMMARY

Expressions are complex because they let you get into the raw guts of the numbers that make 3D animation happen. They allow you to change the way things behave on a fundamental level. But with more user-friendly tools they can make things possible that would otherwise be impossible (or at least very difficult).

While they can be complex to understand, they can also be very simple to use, and the more you understand the syntax and mathematics involved, the more powerful they become.

ANIMATION

In This Chapter

- When Action, When Choreography
- Cycles
- The Camera (Lock it Down!)
- Acting versus Action
- Setting Your Keys (Blocking)
- Channels
- Lip Synch: Muscle Shapes and Phonemes

In this chapter, we expand on the basics covered in Chapter 4, "Action Basics," explaining the fundamentals and theory behind animation and presenting the choreography as an animation tool. We discuss using cycled action by taking the hop you animated in Chapter 4 and applying it to a path in the choreography.

Moving on to concepts like staging and acting, we explore what makes animation memorable. Finally, we explore some action with your more complex character that you set up and modeled in the previous chapters, moving through the process of methodical animation focusing on timing and pose and looking to incorporate the principals of animation into your work. By then end of the chapter, you will have animated a shot for a short film.

WHEN ACTION, WHEN CHOREOGRAPHY

In Animation:Master, there are two options when animating: action and choreography. You used the action window in your flour sack example. The way you animate in either window is the same, but in the choreography window you can be certain of what the camera will see.

A lot of power in A:M comes from its nonlinear animation tools. Nonlinear animation is the buzzword in the animation industry for doing what actions in A:M have done for over a decade: layering small portions of animation over each other to produce a final performance. This allows you to concentrate on one element at a time, and it lets actions be used more than once. A wave hello, for instance, could be applied to a character as many times as needed and only needs to be animated in one action. With nonlinear animation, each wave could even be slightly different (for example, by scaling the time over which the action plays back or blending a second action with the first). Consider the actions as instruments in an orchestra. Each has its part and its own characteristics. Taken alone, a part is not very interesting and doesn't convey the full intent of the composer, but when all are played at the same time under the guidance of the conductor, the result is a symphony.

Another benefit of nonlinear animation is the ability to use actions on more than one character. It becomes just as easy to make a dozen characters wave as a single character, reducing the time it takes to animate groups. The only requirement is that you name the bones the same in all characters that will be using the action.

Given all the benefits that actions afford you, you might be tempted to use them for everything, but there are benefits to working directly in the choreography. The largest plus to animating directly in the choreography is that you can tailor poses and animation to the camera, saving time by not animating things that are not in the camera's frame. There is also a level of spontaneity that animating directly in the choreography lends. Interaction with an environment can be difficult in an action but is simple in a choreography. Using action objects can help to a certain extent in actions, but it is not practical to use action objects for every element of a set.

However, choreography actions are not readily transportable between multiple characters, and their reuse on even a single character outside of the original choreography is not very feasible.

Thankfully, it is not an either-or proposition in A:M: Actions can be layered over other actions, and they can be blended with choreography animation. The ability to have more than one choreography action on a model also brings the nonlinear benefits of actions to animation created in the chor.

Generally speaking, it is desirable to use actions over choreography animation any time you are creating a loop or cycle or a small motion that needs to be used more than once or by more than one character. Lip synch is also a perfect candidate for the Action window. In the final analysis, you should use what you feel more comfortable with. You will explore both in this chapter and learn how they can work together to create more compelling animations.

CYCLES

Almost everything you need to know about animation can be learned in the creation of *cycles*. In animation, a cycle is any action that repeats itself over time. Perfect examples are walks, runs, and other forms of locomotion.

Cycled animation is in many ways very difficult to do correctly. The challenge is not necessarily in creating a cycle but in creating one that does not *look* like a cycle. You have already animated a cycle of your flour sack character hopping. But you have so far only seen it in the Action window, one hop at a time. You need to be able to look at a cycle repeated several times before you can identify whether or not it is executed well. To see the full cycle, you need to place it in a choreography.

A cycle is typically intended to go someplace. When a character walks, hops, or runs it is generally in motion (unless you are using a lack of motion for story purposes, like Wile E. Coyote running in air waiting to realize he is about to fall). In A:M, the easiest way to make an object move from one place to another in the choreography is to place that object on a path. To see how this works, put your flour sack on a path.

Before you do anything at all, change the FPS for the project from 30 to 24. All the timings and frames in this chapter assume a frames-per-second rate of 24. If you are working with an FPS of 30, you may have difficulty following along.

Create a new choreography. In a top view, you want to create a new path along which you want your character to move. Click the Add Path button and draw a simple two-point spline. You want to draw it where the camera will be able to see it, so make sure to put it in front of the camera cone. This will get the object from one side to another, but it won't be at all interesting. Give it some variance. Notice that when you created the path, the mode changed to Modeling mode and that a subset of the basic modeling tools became available. This is because a path is the same thing as a spline in a character. The only difference is that you will be using this path as a way to guide motion rather than building shapes with it. Use the Add tool (A key) to add control points to the spline. Do this by clicking on the spline where you wish to add a control point. Add two points to the path and position them in a flat *S* shape (see Figure 10.1).

Once you are satisfied with your path, click anywhere in the choreography window to exit Modeling mode. Import the flour sack you modeled earlier into the choreography by bringing up the contextual menu for the choreography item and choosing Other from the Import Model subheading. A dialog box will open and ask you to locate a model. Find the flour sack, and it will be imported into the project and into the choreography. You should see the sack at the origin of the choreography waiting for you to tell it what to do.

You want the sack to follow the path and move across the screen. How long it should take to do that and what it should do along the way, you will decide later. To get the object to follow the path, you need to add a constraint to the object. Bring up the contextual menu for the shortcut to the flour sack and choose Path from the Other Constraints subheading. Select the path you just created as the target; the flour sack should jump to the start of the path (see Figure 10.2).

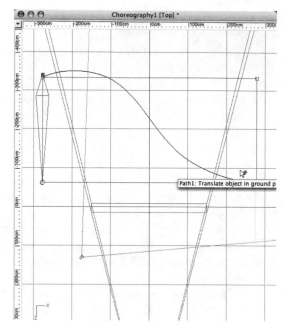

FIGURE 10.1 Add points and position the path so that the object will move where you want.

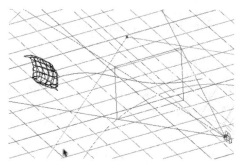

FIGURE 10.2 The path constraint moves the flour sack to the start of the path.

Switch to the Camera view and step through the frames, either with the plus key on the numeric keypad or by clicking the Next Frame button on the Frame toolbar. The sack moves along the path and arrives at its end at the end of the choreography. The length of a choreography defaults to 1 second, so this results in the sack flying across the screen in a mere 24 frames. If it were running for its life this would be fine, but if you want the hop to work as a form of walk you need to slow this movement down.

There are several ways to control the length of time that it will take the sack to get from one end of the path to the other:

1. Make the choreography longer.
2. Make the path shorter.
3. Change the speed of the object's movement.

A longer choreography will force the object to move slower along the path, arriving at path's end at the new end time. Making the path shorter is obvious: If the object has less distance to travel, it will be able to move slower to get there in the 1 second you have. Both methods work, but you sacrifice a certain amount of control with them. The third method—animating the Ease property on the path constraint—lets you easily change the speed the object moves along the path. The Ease property determines what point the object is on the path with a simple percentage—at 0% the object is at the beginning of the path, and at 100% the object is at the end of the path. So give your flour sack 5 seconds to get across the screen.

At frame 0, go to a top view and adjust the Ease percentage until the sack sits just outside the camera cone. This will avoid any dead time waiting for its entrance. Then advance the time to 5 seconds by typing 500 into the field of the frame counter. This assumes that you have left the counter in the default SMPTE time code format. If you have changed it to frame number or cel format, the actual frame number will be 120. This advances you 5 seconds in time. Notice that the sack has not moved. This is because you have overridden the default behavior of the path constraint by setting a key for the Ease channel. Adjust the Ease on the path constraint until the sack is just outside of the camera cone.

Now if you step through the frames from 0 to 5 seconds, you will see the flour sack move across the screen at a much slower pace. However, Flour Sack still is just sliding along; you need to give him something to do.

Import the hop action that you made in Chapter 4 (it needs to have been saved externally to the project) by bringing up the contextual menu for Shortcut to Flour Sack and choosing Action from the Import heading. Note that if you already have actions in your project, you will see a list of them after the Action subheading; if the hop action is not in your project, you will need to select Other from this list. In the dialog that follows, navigate to the hop action on your hard drive. You should immediately see the sack's position change to reflect the action.

If you step through the 5 seconds of your animation now, you will see that the sack moves through the action in the first second of time and stays held for the rest of the action, sliding along as before. To change this, tell A:M how many times you want that action to cycle. Select the shortcut to the hop action and look at its properties. When you animated this cycle, you took a total of 1 second, which, even though it was animated at 30 fps and your current project is at 24, remains the same. Animation:Master scales action based on time rather than the specific frame settings, so multiple animators can work to whatever frame rate they are comfortable with and be assured that the actions will work later.

With the knowledge that the action was designed to take 1 second, simply change the repeat property to 5, giving you five hops each placed a second apart. This gives you a rather languid set of hops across the screen. The sack has somewhere to get to but isn't rushed. What if you wanted it to go faster? Say you had animated a run cycle and had used 1 second in the action window to do it. Chances are that it would read incorrectly in the choreography, once applied to a path in this manner. Luckily, the frames in an action are very malleable. Using the action's properties, you can specify the length of time one cycle of an action should take in a choreography.

The cycle length property does just this. It defaults to the same value as the action's original animated length, but can be shortened to speed up the action or lengthened to slow it down. Change the cycle length from 1 second to 12 frames. If you step through it at this point, you will notice that the sack only hops from frame 0 to 2 seconds 12 frames. This is because you still have the repeat set to 5. For the new action length to cover the full 5 seconds, change the repeat to 10. Now if you step through the frames, you can see that the sack is taking shorter, quicker hops.

This works fine for hopping, but for walks and other actions where foot slippage becomes very noticeable, you need to ensure that things hold together.

The same methods work for practically any action. It is always better to have planned the original action to work at the proper frame rate than to rely on tricks to stretch the time out, but the tools to do that are there when you need them.

Now that you understand how to put characters on paths and apply actions as cycles, you can really dig in and get to what makes A:M great: its character animation tools.

After the bouncing ball or hopping sack of flour, the most common exercise for students of animation is the walk cycle because every single aspect of what makes animation work is exhibited there. An average walk cycle merely takes a character from Point A to Point B with little or no fuss. A good walk cycle will do the same but will also exhibit some personality. A *great* walk cycle will tell you the life history of the character. You don't need to worry about being great today—that is a lifelong journey. However, you will be looking at the processes that go into making a walk great and how to use A:M's tools to achieve them.

First, look at the anatomy of a basic walk.

Figure 10.3 shows your new friend: Super Ordinary Walk Cycle Guy. All Guy does is walk; he walks the most plain, ordinary walk there is. You are going to watch him as he walks to see the various parts of a walk and how they work together. Open the SOWCG.prj file on the CD-ROM in the projects folder, create a new action, and follow along.

Starting with the feet, Guy starts and stops all his cycles from what is called a heel strike pose (see Figure 10.4). The heel strike is the point where the heel first touches the ground, but before any weight is placed on the foot. There are at least three of these in every cycle. The first one is identical to the last one, so that when the cycle starts over there is no pop in the animation. The third heel strike is reversed with the opposite foot forward. Once you pose the character on the first frame, creating the other two heel strike poses is simple. Copy the frame after you

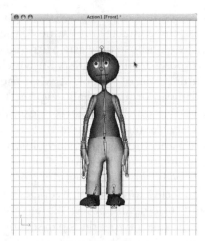

FIGURE 10.3 Super Ordinary Walk
Cycle Guy.

have built the pose, and then advance to the end of the cycle, typically a second for a single stride. At the end of the action the pose needs to be identical to the first frame, so paste the keyframe; this sets an identical set of keys at the last frame.

You will probably want to do this again at the end of the process to make sure that these two frames remain identical. Now move to the middle of the action—exactly 12 frames if you are making a 1-second stride. From the Edit menu, choose Paste Mirrored. This pastes the data on the model exactly opposite based on the names of the bones. Any keys on a bone that starts with right will be pasted inverted on the left of the model, which makes this heel strike exactly mirrored to the one you created on Frame 1.

About halfway between each heel strike pose, Guy does what is called a *crossing pose* (see Figure 10.5). This is where the foot that is carrying the weight is straight up and down. It is acting as the fulcrum, levering the weight of Guy's body forward. There are at least two of these in every cycle, the second a mirror opposite of

FIGURE 10.4 The heel strike pose starts and finishes each cycle.

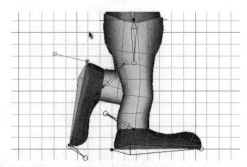

FIGURE 10.5 The crossing pose happens between each heel strike.

the first. On 24 fps, it is easy to place these poses; they go at Frames 6 and 18, respectively. Pose the character on Frame 6, then using the same technique as the heel strike, copy it and use the Paste Mirrored command to set up Frame 18.

These two poses form the pillars on which a walk is built. The character of a walk is determined here, so look at what the upper body is doing during these two poses during an ordinary walk. Figures 10.6 and 10.7 show Guy at his ordinary best. Note that on the heel strike pose, the torso leans forward, pushing his weight to the front where the forward foot is catching it. The hips on the leading foot side are up and the shoulders are down. The arms run counter to the legs, and the entire upper body is lower. On the crossing pose, the torso straightens and the entire body moves up slightly. Note also that in both poses, the head is straight up and facing forward. On average, Guy has about six frames between his heel strike and his crossing poses. His second opposing heel strike falls at about Frame 12. So, he takes two strides per second of animation. If an animator were timing Guy out at 30 fps, he would have his first crossing pose somewhere between Frames 7 and 8 and his second heel strike at Frame 15 or so. In general, Guy prefers to move the crossing pose to Frame 7 when he's walking at 30 fps.

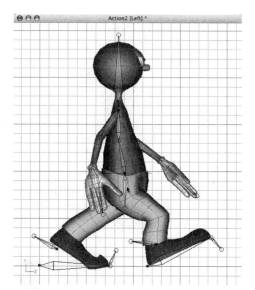

FIGURE 10.6   The full body in the heel strike pose.

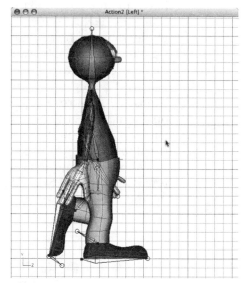

FIGURE 10.7   The full body in the crossing pose.

Obviously, it takes more than these two poses to make a walk; these are just the extreme positions that the rest of the cycle is based on. There are two more parts of a walk that are important. In animation terms, these poses are called breakdowns. They help establish the arcs of the motion and ensure that the in-between frames that the computer generates are what you want.

Look at a walk that is left up to the computer first so you can understand what you are countering. Figure 10.8 shows the first 12 frames of a walk cycle layered on top of each other, letting you see all the frames at the same time. The only two keys that are set for this walk are the heel strike and the crossing pose. Pay close attention to the heel as the foot moves from the strike position to flat for the crossing position. It pushes through the floor and doesn't get flat until it hits the crossing pose. Similarly, the trailing foot drags through the floor and up into the crossing position linearly. To avoid these problems and to give a little weight to the walk, take another look at Guy.

Before Guy pulls his back foot off the ground, he likes to get his weight situated firmly on his front foot. Therefore, he flattens his front foot out in about two or three frames, pushing his mass further down, and at the same time leaves his back toe just touching the ground. This is your first breakdown, and like the crossing pose, it has a mirror opposite on the second stride of the cycle. The arms spread even wider to help Guy maintain his balance while he shifts his weight forward and to build energy for his push up into the crossing pose (see Figure 10.9). This movement down and forward helps establish the weight of the character.

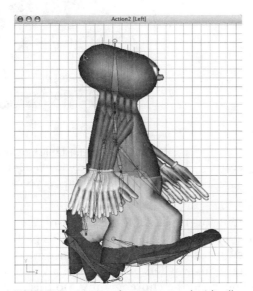

FIGURE 10.8   Letting the computer decide all the in-between frames without any guidance is generally a bad idea.

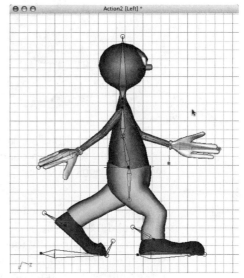

FIGURE 10.9   The first breakdown establishes the character's weight and hits the bottom of the arc.

The second breakdown pose comes three or four frames after the crossing pose (see Figure 10.10), and this time Guy is pushing his body up and off the crossing pose, moving his torso forward, preparing to catch his weight on the next heel strike. This is the highest portion of his stride, filling out the arc of his movement in a smooth fashion.

Now, if you let the computer do the in-betweens (see Figure 10.11), you get a much better result. You can see that the foot flattens out and stays on the ground without pushing through. The rear foot also picks up and arcs into the crossing position rather than moving linearly. Notice the outline of the head's movement. It makes a very nice arc, with a slight dip at the beginning. This slight dip will read as the bottom of the previous arc when the cycle loops. There are refinements that you can make to this walk, but these four poses are the basic building block of the walk cycle.

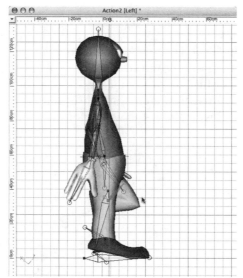

FIGURE 10.10 The second breakdown establishes the top of the arc and prepares for the following heel strike.

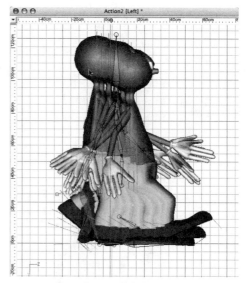

FIGURE 10.11 After establishing the breakdowns, the computer does a much better job with the in-betweens.

When building cyclical actions for use in A:M, there are some considerations to be made. Since the action is typically used on a character on a path, you do not want to move the body forward. Instead, keep the walk in place and have the feet slide under the character. Doing it this way lets you establish a walk that you can be certain will not have foot slippage in the choreography. Do this using a special tool that A:M has for just this purpose: stride length. In order to get A:M to use this calculation, you must enable the Has Stride Length property for the action (see Figure 10.12). Any cyclical action can have stride length, which will force A:M to calculate how many times an action will need to repeat to move along the path without having any sliding or slipping in the feet.

For actions that move at a steady rate, such as a walk, this means that the cycle must be constructed with the character in place. For actions where one portion of the cycle lingers longer than another, such as a sneak or a hop, the character is animated in the Action window, moving forward, and during the portion of the

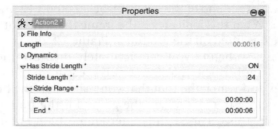

FIGURE 10.12   Activating the Stride Length property
tells A:M that this action is a cycle.

action that it needs to remain stationary, it is slid back to the starting point. This
might sound confusing, but when you see it in practice, it will make more sense.

Another thing to consider is that you can build your action in parts, or layers.
Perhaps one action will just move the legs and hips (maybe it will include some
tilt to the torso), another might have the arm motion, a third could have the head
motion. Every element that you can break down into its own action gives you the
ability to not only reuse actions easier, but the freedom to establish different timings on different portions of the body.

When you activate Stride Length, a ruler and a grid appear in the Action window. The grid is a simulation of the ground plane that the character will walk on.
As you step through the frames the grid will move; watching it tells you if the feet
will slip when the action cycles along a path.

The ruler is used to measure the character's stride and how you tell A:M how
far the character will move in one stride. Start at Frame 0, the heel strike, and find
the end of the ruler that is marked "00:00:00." This indicates where the foot first
makes contact with the ground (this is why you start with the heel strike position
when creating a walk cycle). Drag the ruler so that it sits directly under some recognizable mark, such as the base of the foot control bone (see Figure 10.13).

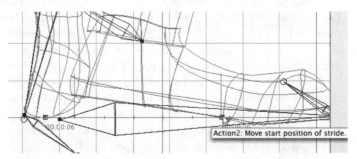

FIGURE 10.13   The zero end of the ruler indicates the first contact the
foot has with the ground.

The other end of the ruler is labeled 00:00:12, by default half the length of the action. What this indicates is the frame that the foot that you started measuring at Frame 0 is lifted off the ground at Frame 12, the end of the stride. This may not be the case; so before you can accurately measure the stride, you need to tell the stride length ruler what frame it is measuring to in the action. Step through the frames and watch the foot that you planted in the heel strike. The frame immediately before the foot leaves the ground is the frame you want. In the case of the example, this occurs slightly after Frame 12 at Frame 15.

In the action's properties, find the Stride Range properties under the Stride Length group. Change the end value to the frame that the foot is last in contact with the ground, or, in this case, 15. This tells A:M how much time in the action the stride takes. Now you just need to tell it how long it is. On Frame 15, move the end of the ruler under the same marker that you used at Frame 0 (using a guideline can help get the measurement more accurate), as shown in Figure 10.14.

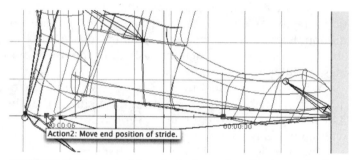

FIGURE 10.14 The end of the ruler indicates how far the marker has traveled in the stride.

If you switch to a bird's-eye view of the action and step through, the feet should move accurately along with the grid.

Now, test your action out as a cycle. Just as you did for the flour sack, create a chor and add the character to a path, but after the action has been applied, you only need to change the length of the chor, or the path to change how fast the character will walk. The stride length will determine how many times the action repeats and ensure that no matter what you do the feet remain planted on the ground.

Give at least 5 seconds to make sure that any irregularity in the cycle becomes apparent. With a cycle, any tiny bump or hiccup in the action will be magnified a thousandfold once it is in the choreography. The longer the cycle has to repeat the more apparent it will be. If you want to make the cycle even less apparent simply animate two more steps. In fact, the longer the action with the walk in it is, the less likely it is to read as a cycle.

From this basic walk, you can add variation and refinement by changing the actions you have just created, by creating new actions to layer over them; or you can simply animate the character in the choreography on top of the cycled motion. This concept is called *action overloading* and has been an integral part of how

A:M works since its inception. Each action that you add to a choreography by default replaces underlying action, meaning any action that is closer to the base of the hierarchy. However, you can specify other methods for A:M to use to blend the top action with those that lie underneath it. Other than strict replacement of an action, you can choose to let the action add its motion to the underlying motion or to blend into and out of the top action.

Additive motion is designed to augment an underlying action. This would allow you to increase the amount an arm swings by creating a new action with just a slight amount of arm swing in it, for example. The additive motion is applied to the underlying motion as an offset, simply indicating that you want to alter a motion by a certain amount, which can increase or decrease an action. Additive actions are difficult to use with actions created separately and overlaid, but work very well when used by a choreography action.

Blend lets you mix two actions based on a percent of control. So if an action that you have built arbitrarily, such as a wave, needs to be laid over the arm motion of your walk cycle, and the motion of the walk would be counteractive to the wave, you can use blend to slowly switch the control from the walk to the wave and back again.

Open a new action for your character and animate a simple wave for one arm. The principals here are the same as for the arm motion cycle. Start with the extreme poses, in this case the arm down, and the arm up, and then the arm back down again. If you act out the motion, you might find that an average wave takes about 3 seconds, perhaps a little less, with the arm up longer than it is down. If this was the case, you might space your extreme frames starting at 0 with the arm to the side. At Frame 8, the arm is up in the wave position and it might hold there for 2 seconds, then take eight frames to drop down to the character's side. Given those timings you would need four keyframes: the first and last being the same, and the two in the middle being the same or slight variations. Once you have those, simply move on to the breakdowns, concentrating on adding overlapping motion to the arm as it comes up and goes back down. In the 2-second space you wave the arm back and forth, again paying attention to overlap. Check out the Wave.act file in the actions folder on the CD-ROM to see an example of a finished wave.

ON THE CD

In the choreography, add the wave motion to the character and set the choreography range so that it occurs while the character is in the camera frame. If you step through the motion, you will see the action applies itself and overrides the arm motion that you originally created. This, obviously, is not what you intended. In order to get the action to blend with the arms in the walk, change its properties from Replace to Blend. Once you have, the Blend Percentage property becomes available. The blend percentage moves the control of the motion from one action to another. In this case, you want to set the blend to start at 0%. This is done in the choreography by selecting the shortcut to the action and setting the blend percentage to 0 at Frame 0. Then advance the frames until you want the character to start his wave, say 2 seconds or so into the animation, and then set another keyframe with the blend at 0%. To do this, type 0 into the Blend Percentage box.

You do this so that the blend will only start rising above 0% after the 2-second mark. If you simply move to 3 seconds and turn the blend percentage to 100 instead of the transition starting from 2 seconds, it would start a slow transition from Frame 0.

This is an important concept to understand. If you set a keyframe at 0 to have the character in a pose, and you want the character to hold that pose for a number of frames, say 12; and then start transitioning into a new pose, you need to add an extra keyframe with the character in the *same* pose it has at Frame 0. This is called a hold in animation terms, and 3D animation has a specific variation of this called a moving hold. The moving hold is crucial to 3D character animation; it is covered further later in this chapter.

Set the value of the blend to 0% at the 2-second mark, and advance the number of frames you want the character to transition an arm into the new motion. Try 12 frames for now. Once you are where the character should be fully into the new action set the blend to 100%. Since you only animated one arm in the action, all the other motion from the previous actions should be unaffected. In the same fashion that you held the 0% value, you want to hold the 100% value until you are ready to move out of this action and back into the standard arm swing, and then give it 6 or 12 frames to transition to 0% blend. This should create a nice smooth transition between the two actions. However, if the action for the wave starts at the wrong portion of the action, you might not like the way the action reads. Control this by animating the Ease property of the action.

The ease of the action allows you to specify how the action plays back in the choreography. Ease is a percent-based progression from the start to the end of the action. This allows you to control the speed at which an action plays in the choreography, or in cases like your wave, you can control when the action starts without having to adjust the position of the action in the Timeline. You can, for example, move to the same frame that you start the transition and set the ease of the action to 0% and then advance to the frame after you have blended back to 0% and set the Ease to 100%. This forces the action to play back only during the time that you have it contributing to the action in the choreography.

ON THE CD

Now if you step through the choreography you should have an animation of the character walking into the shot, waving, and walking on, similar to the Wave_Walk.mov file on the CD-ROM. Notice in the example render how the transition from walking to waving is transparent. All this was done without setting up any keys to move from one action to the other. This is the power of non-linear animating.

If you want to add some subtleties to this motion, you can create a new choreography action by bringing up the shortcut to the model's contextual menu and having it add to the underlying action. Animating in this fashion lets you build complex actions by simply layering small portions over one another.

Using these same principles with some modifications for stride length, you can create an action for a nonsteady form of locomotion such as the classic cartoon sneak. The cartoon sneak is actually very close to the walk, but there are three key poses rather than the two of the walk. Open a new action for Guy, and teach him a new trick.

The first pose that the sneak needs is similar to the heel strike from the walk cycle: The weight is on the back foot, with the forward foot coming to catch the body as it moves forward. When you animate a sneak, the heel strike leads with the toe rather than the heel; the character is actually testing the place he will be stepping to avoid making noise or hitting a loose board (see Figure 10.15).

This pasted and mirrored just as you did with the walk cycle, but since a sneak is slower than a walk, you will most likely want to use a 36-frame (one-and-a-half-second) action placing the strikes on Frames 0, 18, and 36. After the character has tested the ground, he moves his entire weight forward and down onto the front foot. This falls at about Frame 6.

In the example, Guy is pretty extreme in his motion. You can use a less extreme pose if you need to. This pose is the bottom of the arc, and by pushing the mass of the character so far down onto the foot, you get the feeling of squash (see Figure 10.16). Paste the mirror of this pose onto Frame 24 for the other half of the cycle.

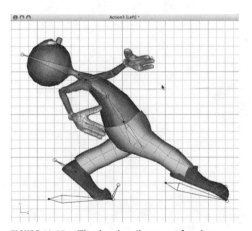

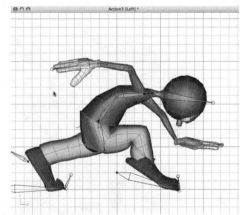

FIGURE 10.15   The heel strike pose for the sneak.

FIGURE 10.16   The bottom of the sneak pushes the mass down and forward.

At Frame 12, you have the crossing pose. Unlike the walk where the feet move back and the hips remain stationary, shift the hips forward over the ball of the leading foot. This is to let you rest on this foot before the character goes into another heel strike. The main difference with this crossing pose and the one from the walk is that the character remains on the ball of his foot, and his opposite leg comes up with the knee high (see Figure 10.17). This pose is mirrored on Frame 30.

The crossing pose falls into the heel strike that follows on Frames 18 and 36. This is the basic blocking of the sneak action, and with just a few breakdowns you have a good action. In order to smooth out the arcs of the motion, put a single breakdown between each of these key poses. Figures 10.18 through 10.20 show some possible breakdown poses. These generally fall exactly in between poses so at Frame 3 for the first breakdown, 9 for the second, 15 for the third, and so on. They are, of course, mirrored on the opposite half of the cycle.

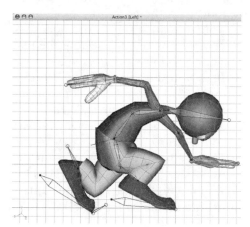

FIGURE 10.17   The crossing pose for the sneak.

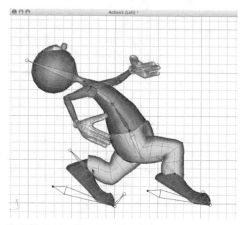

FIGURE 10.18   The first breakdown eases the arc into the down position key.

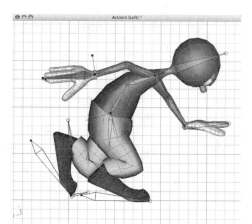

FIGURE 10.19   The second breakdown centers the mass over the leading foot. Note that the hips are forward here.

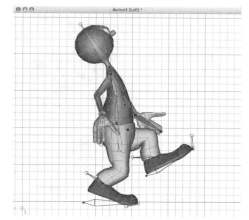

FIGURE 10.20   Much like the walk cycle, the breakdown after the crossing pose pushes the arc higher, and the forward foot makes the fall into the following heel strike snappier.

With the breakdowns in place, the cycle works well, and all that remains is to set up the stride length. Since the body remains in one place for such a long time, the result of placing this action on a character on a path would be a lot of sliding when you want him to remain still. You could play with the stride length to minimize this, but it would not solve the problem entirely. Luckily, body is pulled forward instead of sliding the feet under the hips when you animated this action.

If you step through the action, you see that the body moves forward and then slides back in the Action window. If you hadn't animated it this way, you would need to change the positions of your poses. The strike positions become the back pose, and the character moves forward into the crossing position, his feet sliding back on the ground into the next strike pose. Now when you set up the stride length watching the grid under the character will show that the character remains in place on the sliding ground as he moves back. To see this in action, look at the sneak_stride.mov file in the render output folder on the CD-ROM.

Before you move on to animating in choreography, you should cover one more thing in the Action window. To demonstrate this, use Guy again. You are going to have him pick up an object from a table. This seemingly simple action requires the use of three new tools in an action for you: action objects, constraints in an action, and Compensate mode. Open up a new action with Guy in it, and get started.

Guy is in this Action window all by himself, and you want him to interact with a second object. If you couldn't see the glass in the Action window, this would be a very difficult task. To solve that problem A:M has action objects. In the SOWCG.prj file, you will find two models—table and glass. You want Guy to be aware of both these objects as you animate him. To place them into the action, simply drag and drop the models from the PWS onto the action or into the Action window. You may also drag and drop models out of the library or import them from your hard drive with the action's contextual menu. Once they are in the action, you may need to adjust the scale of each object to match each other (see Figure 10.21).

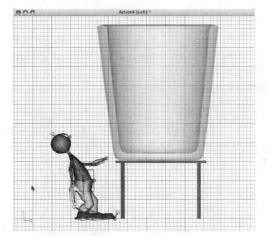

FIGURE 10.21   It's not very likely that Guy could pick up that glass.

You can scale the object in the action, but the better option is to change the model in its Model window. Large-scale adjustments can have a detrimental effect on render times and quality. Once both the table and the glass arc in the action, position them so that they are in front of Guy and the glass is well within his reach. Pose Guy with his arms down at Frame 0. You should have something like Figure 10.22.

Now take 12 frames or so to bring Guy's hand up to the glass; a breakdown at Frame 6 can be used to keep his hand from passing through the table. Place the hand exactly where it contacts the glass (see Figure 10.23). At this frame, transfer the control of the glass to Guy's hand, forcing it to follow all translations and rotations of the hand bone. However, if you simply constrain the glass to translate and orient like the hand, it will jump unless the bone in the glass is placed exactly in line with the hand. Since that would be difficult, if not impossible, to accomplish, you can use offsets on the constraints instead.

FIGURE 10.22 Action objects in the Action window allow you to animate interactions outside a choreography.

FIGURE 10.23 You want the glass to start following the hand at this frame.

Select Bone1 under the glass object. From the contextual menu for this bone, create a new translate to constraint. The cursor will turn into an eyedropper so that you can choose the bone that you want the glass to translate to. Don't select a target bone yet. Before you translate the glass to Guy's hand, tell A:M that you want the glass to have offsets for its current location generated; this keeps the bone from jumping to the base of the hand. Click the Compensate Mode button, which does exactly that. Once you are in Compensate mode, select the right hand bone either by clicking or by selecting it from the target pull-down on the Translate to Constraint's properties. The glass will now follow Guy's hand no matter where it moves. However, it will maintain its own rotation. To tie the glass more fully to the hand, add a second constraint to orient the bone like the right hand, again using Compensate mode to generate offsets. Once the glass has been constrained to the hand, Guy can pick it up and take a drink (see Figure 10.24). When he is ready to put the glass down, turn the enforcement of the constraints to 0%. This same technique can be used in the choreography to make objects interact.

FIGURE 10.24   Thanks to compensated constraints,
Guy can have a drink.

When you want to achieve an overall performance rather than simply moving the character from Point A to Point B, the methods that working with overlaying actions require can be inhibiting. For a more immediate response and an idea of what will happen in all parts of the action at once, the preferred method is to animate directly in the choreography. This topic is covered in stages in the next few sections of this chapter. More of the theory behind how you work than the mechanics of moving the character will be discussed, but the techniques you learned with Guy remain applicable.

When a new process is needed, we will break from the discussion to cover the tools in A:M. Covering them as they are discovered in the process will give you the context needed to understand them.

THE CAMERA (LOCK IT DOWN!)

Before you can convincingly animate a character, you need to establish where the camera is and what it can see. One of the principals of character animation is staging. This refers to both the pose of the character in the camera frame and the position and movement of the camera itself. You need to establish a convincing composition in the camera frame to best present the action to the viewer. You do this by applying rules that traditional artists have used in their compositions for centuries, and the techniques that cinematographers use in films. Remember: Even though you are working with 3D models, your final output will be a 2D image. If you don't compose your shots with this in mind, your animation will suffer. There is not enough space to cover everything there is to know about composition and framing here, but you can look at least at the basics.

The rule of thirds is a common compositional tool used to build interest into your images. Basically put, it means that if you divide the camera frame into thirds both horizontally and vertically, framing your shot so that the center of interest is at or close to one of the intersections or running along one of the thirds, creates a more visually compelling image. Look at Figure 10.25 and compare it with Figure 10.26. Notice how static the first is compared to the shot composed on thirds.

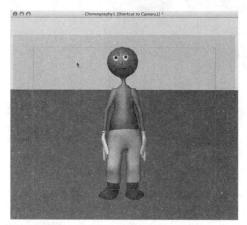

FIGURE 10.25   This shot has the character framed in the center of the image.

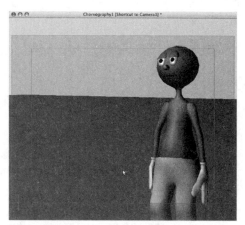

FIGURE 10.26   This shot is more interesting due to the off-center composition.

Staging your shots to use the 3D nature of your elements is also important. For example, Figures 10.27 and 10.28 are composed of the same elements but framed slightly differently. Notice how much more depth seems to be in Figure 10.28 because of the framing of elements so that they overlap and break out of the image area.

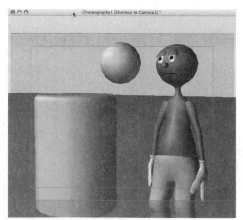

FIGURE 10.27   The depth in this image is weakened by the framing.

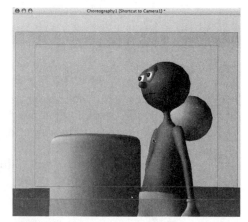

FIGURE 10.28   This composition has the same elements, in the same locations, but framed differently by the camera.

If none of your objects overlaps, it is difficult for the viewer to understand the depth of the image. Keeping this in mind, it is important to avoid tangencies as well. A tangency is when two edges barely touch one another in an image, as seen in Figure 10.29. The result is that the two elements appear to be touching, so it is important to ensure that the edges overlap more. This also applies to the edges of the frame.

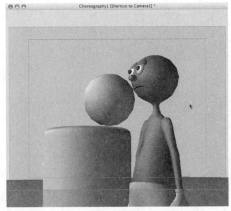

FIGURE 10.29   Tangent edges can make two objects appear to be touching even if they are far apart. This is generally bad.

2D framing is just one part of the equation; you can also move the camera to frame shots at different sizes. There are established shots used in film that you can use as a basic vocabulary, each of which describes how much of a frame the subject will occupy:

Long or wide shot: Shows the entire subject in frame, sometimes from a very great distance (see Figure 10.30).

Medium shot: Shows the subject from about the waist up (see Figure 10.31).

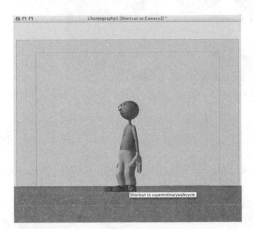

FIGURE 10.30   Long shot.

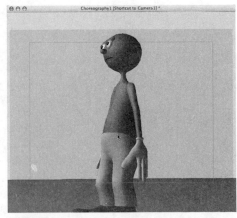

FIGURE 10.31   Medium shot.

Medium close-up: Shows the subject from about the shoulders up (see Figure 10.32).

Close-up: The subject's head fills most of the frame (see Figure 10.33).

Extreme close-up: Typically focuses on a single feature of the subject, an eye for example (see Figure 10.34).

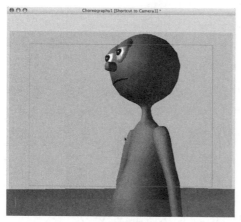

FIGURE 10.32   Medium close-up.

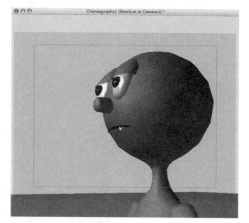

FIGURE 10.33   Close-up.

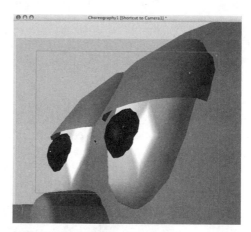

FIGURE 10.34   Extreme close-up.

These are how shots are typically called out in a script and are to be used as a guideline.

Camera angles add interest to a shot, and they can be used to convey a sense of emotion to a scene. There are two basic angles for a shot: high and low.

A high-angle shot is one that has the camera positioned above the subject and pointing down. A low-angle shot is one where the camera is placed underneath the subject and points up. When a character is framed by a high-angle shot, it looks smaller, vulnerable, distant, or weak. A low-angle shot, on the other hand, can make a subject appear to be looming, powerful, or menacing. You can use these angles to augment the story in a script.

Alfred Hitchcock was considered one of the masters of camera angles. He knew that the angle at which the audience sees the action has a profound effect on how they interpret the scene. Another good reference for the use of angle to augment story is comic books. A good comic artist will draw the hero from a low angle to make him appear larger; the same angle on a villain can make him appear menacing (see Figure 10.35).

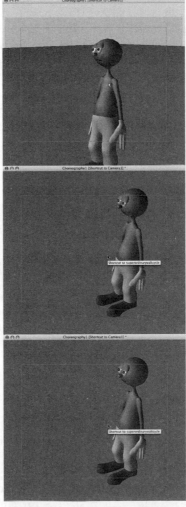

FIGURE 10.35 Using different camera angles can give different effects.

When more than one character is in the shot, the camera angle can give subtle clues about what is going on. For instance, in Figure 10.36 you have two figures, the low camera angle makes the standing figure appear to be looming over the character on the ground. This is a trick of perception: The figure that is higher in the frame appears to be more powerful. If two characters are fighting, for instance, placing one character slightly higher in the frame makes it seem like that character is winning.

Focal length also plays a role in how your shots are staged. The perspective of the shot can be flattened out or increased to comic proportions by adjusting the focal length. A high focal length simulates the effects of a telephoto lens on the camera, while a short focal length makes it seem more like a wide-angle or fisheye lens (see Figure 10.37). This is useful if you are trying to simulate a certain kind of lens; television shows, for example, tend to use shorter angle lenses, which flatten out their shots. If you are trying to mix live action and computer-generated (CG) elements, then matching the perspective of your shot to the perspective from the live-action shot makes adjusting the focal length properly very critical.

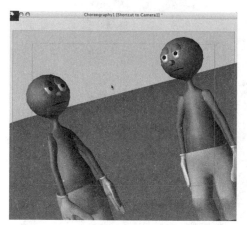

FIGURE 10.36 Placing one character slightly higher in the frame can increase that character's presence over the other.

FIGURE 10.37 The focal length can change the perspective of a shot.

Focus, oddly enough, doesn't have anything to do with focal length in 3D. 3D images are perfectly in focus at all times, unless you tell them not to be. This is one of the things that is commonly overlooked in 3D imagery. People are used to seeing images from still cameras and the artifacts that they add to images. A film camera exhibits what is known as depth of field (DOF), where a portion of the image is in perfect focus, and anything closer to the camera or farther away from the camera than this focal range is blurred. The depth of the focal range varies with the settings and lens used, but all cameras display DOF to some extent. You can use DOF effects to help stage your character and bring it out of the background elements. You can also use it to shift interest between two elements in a shot. This is called rack focus. In order to have DOF on a shot, you must turn it on for the camera (in the Render Options group of the camera's properties). Once it is turned on, the camera will have a set of handles on the camera cone in the choreography that allows you to adjust the various aspects of the focus.

Finally, look at moving the camera. Since the camera in 3D is virtual and not restricted by the limitations of real-world cameras, you can do almost anything you can imagine with it. You could zoom from deep space to an extreme close-up on a character's eye in 20 frames or move the camera constantly from frame to frame without stopping. However, just because you can do something does not mean that it is necessarily a good idea. Of all aspects of 3D, the camera is the one where the most restraint is needed. There are established conventions for camera moves that audiences are used to after years of seeing them in live-action films, and you should think before just tossing them aside. Typically, a camera is restricted to the following moves:

Truck or dolly: Refers to simple translation movements of the camera. Dollying is generally moving in and out of the shot, while trucking is typically a left-to-right or up-and-down motion.

Panning: The camera stays in one place, but is rotated (up-down or left-right). Animation sometimes uses what is called a *zip pan*, which moves the camera extremely fast, often blurring everything in the frame.

Roll: Tends to make shots appear skewed and can be used to convey that something is not right about a scene. It was used heavily to show the villains in the old *Batman* television series.

Zoom: Means to change the focal length to move in or out of a shot.

Rack Focus: Describes two effects: a shift in the focus of the camera and a simultaneous truck-out and zoom-in of the camera. This keeps the subject exactly the same size in the frame but changes the perspective of the background. It is used often in horror pictures or to imply a separation of the character from events or the set.

Knowing all this, you need to have some idea of what you want out of a shot before you can correctly frame it. You also need to know whether or not the shot will require camera animation.

 The camera must be animated first, or at the very least at the staging portion off the character's animation. If you don't know what the camera will be looking at, you won't have a clear idea of how you should animate your characters.

Your first guide is the script for the shot. All shots, regardless of their complexity, should have been scripted out before animation begins. The script tells you how the character is to be framed (that is, close-up, medium shot, and so on) as well as telling you if the camera needs to move. Beyond that, it is up to you to establish the shot in an interesting manner. For this chapter's exercises, you will be using this script:

```
Fade in
Exterior Sky, Day
Clouds roll across by serenly
Title: David Rogers Presents
Title: Captain Spline in
CAPTAIN SPLINE flies into the camera from behind a cloud, his jet pack
    streams smoke out behind him. He banks sharply and exits camera
    right.
Title: Gimble Lock
Cut To
Exterior Curvopolis, Day
A quiet city street lined with apartment buildings. CAPTAIN SPLINE flies
    around the corner of a building and turns back toward the camera.
PAN to tracking shot of the CAPTAIN as the buildings blur by
Captain flies out of frame to camera left
End Tracking
PAN to follow the captain as he flies up a hill toward a deserted-look-
    ing warehouse.
CUT TO
Interior Secret warehouse base, Day
MEDIUM SHOT
POLYGOZMO stands before a huge switch labled "throw switch to begin
    world domination."
POLYGOZMO reaches up toward the switch.
CAPTAIN SPLINE crashes through a skylight and flies into POLYGOZMO just
    before he can pull the switch.
CUT TO LONG SHOT
The two combatants fall apart to opposite sides of the warehouse and get
    up to face each other. They hesitate a moment and then charge. Just
    as they are about to collide…
CUT TO BLACK
TITLE: To Be Continued
CREDITS
```

Notice how this script calls for more cuts than movements. In many ways, cuts are more comfortable for the audience to watch than constant camera moves. The framing is only called out twice; the rest of the shots have been left up to your discretion.

In a typical production, this script would then be turned into storyboards, in which the director and layout artists would make the decisions on how to frame the shots; in an independent production, *you* are the director and layout artist. There is no set format for a storyboard, but on the most fundamental level, it is simply a sketch of the shot with a simple description of the scene, and indicators of camera movements.

One possible set of boards for this shot is shown in Figure 10.38. You can use these to build your shots, or draw up your own. Even stick figures will help you flesh out the ideas for the shot before you move on. Alternatively, you can experiment in 3D and use simple renders to make a 3D storyboard. Use the method that works best for you.

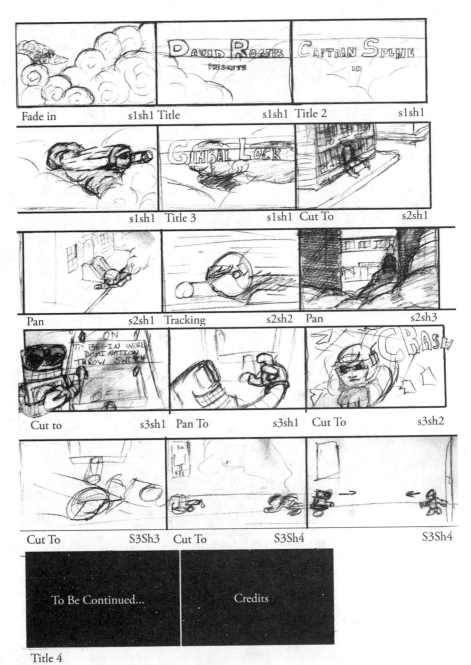

FIGURE 10.38 These storyboards describe the script.

After the storyboards are set up, you typically establish the timing for each shot with an *animatic*. An animatic is a simple preview of each shot typically no more than simply cutting together the still images of the storyboard and holding them in place for as long as a given shot is to last. You can use any video-editing application to create one. or you can use A:M to do the job with a camera roto-scope or layers. The animatic is used to get a feel for how long each shot will need in screen time. If you have a dialog or soundtrack it should also be incorporated into the animatic. An animatic using this script can be found on the CD-ROM.

ON THE CD

Once you hammer out all these details, where to place the camera and how to make it move is a simple process. Open the street set that you modeled in Chapter 6, "Inorganic Modeling," or open the Camera_blocking.prj on the CD-ROM, and get the second shot set up. The first shot in the storyboard is a straight shot of the street, as shown in the first panel of your storyboard. If you haven't yet done so, open the choreography and move the camera into position. Be certain that you are on Frame 0 when you do this. If you are not, the camera will be animated into position rather than starting there. You can roughly approximate its location by moving it by the control bone in the side, top, and front views of the choreography until the camera cone aims roughly where you want it.

ON THE CD

Once you have it roughly in place, make the fine adjustments from the camera view. When you look through the camera there are ways that you can change the framing of the shot without changing views, which allows you to more quickly line up the shot that you need. Use the Move, Turn, and Zoom tools with modifier keys to manipulate the camera while in the camera view.

The Move tool (keyboard shortcut M) can truck or dolly the camera. Activate the Move tool and hold down the Shift key while clicking and dragging in the camera view, and the camera will dolly in and out of the shot. Holding down the Command key on the Mac or the Ctrl key on the PC will truck the camera left to right or up and down.

The Turn tool (keyboard shortcut T) can be used to pan or roll the camera. Activate the Turn tool and hold down the Shift key while clicking and dragging in the camera view to pan the shot. Holding down the Command key on the Mac or the Ctrl key on the PC will roll the camera.

The Zoom tool (keyboard shortcut Z) can be used to change the focal length of the camera. Activate the Zoom tool, and hold down the Shift key while clicking and dragging in the camera view to change the focal length. If you are on a PC and have a wheel mouse, the wheel performs the same function.

At Frame 0, position the camera so that the street and the corner in particular are in clear view, allowing enough room for the captain's entrance later on in the shot. You might have something similar to Figure 10.39.

Reference your animatic frequently while you work. You could open a window and have it running in a separate application, but it is just as easy to have it available in the camera view at all times. Import the animation file into A:M, and drag and drop it onto the camera. This creates a camera rotoscope, which you will look at as a way to combine live action and CG. You want this rotoscope to sit in the camera view as a picture in a picture to remind you what you had decided

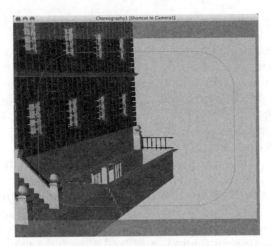

FIGURE 10.39   The blocking of the first shot.

when you roughed out your timing (see Figure 10.40). To make sure that it is always visible, select the rotoscope under the camera in the PWS and on its properties change the on-top property to on. This works exactly like the rotoscope in the Model window. Move and scale the movie down until it is out of the way. Now advance to 30 seconds in the Timeline and change the frame property of the camera rotoscope to 900 (30 seconds at 30 FPS, which is what the file was saved at). Now as you step through the choreography, you have a clear view of the animatic at all times. Turn off the pickable status of the rotoscope to make working easier.

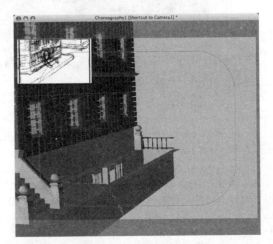

FIGURE 10.40   The camera rotoscope can show you your animatic or a test render at the same time that you are working.

At Frame 0, position the camera so that the bus stop sign is clearly visible and framed like the first panel in the storyboard. Then advance a few seconds into the choreography (four based on your animatic) and key the camera in its current position by clicking the Set Keyframe button while the camera is selected. This keyframe will eliminate any unwanted drift in the camera before this point. This is the time where the character would fly into frame. Wait until the character is just about to fly out of frame and then set another key. This is based initially off of the timing established in the animatic, but after the character is in place you might want to make some adjustments.

Advance one more second, and translate and pan the camera to match the shot in the animatic that describes the camera pan. This frames the character against the building and is the start of your tracking shot. When a camera moves in real life, it speeds up from a stop gradually and then cushions in to the final position. In animation, this is called ease in and ease out. From a standstill, you ease in to your motion. A:M by default has some ease built into the motion you animate (see Figure 10.41), but you can and often will tweak this motion to a more pleasing curve by editing the channel.

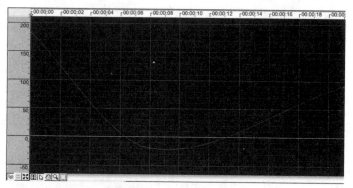

FIGURE 10.41   The channels of motion that A:M creates already exhibit some ease.

Open the Timeline and switch to channel view. If you have the camera selected, you will see the chanels for the motion you have set for the camera. This motion defaults to what is called spline interpolation. If you want the arc of the camera's motion to be smoother you might select the last two frames' worth of keys (in all the keyed channels) and set the interpolation to 0-Slope. This is briefly discussed this in Chapter 4, but take a moment to look at it closer now.

As previously discussed, you can set the interpolation (as well as pre- and post-extrapolation methods) in the PWS for any given channel by using the channel type indicator/drop-down menu item. You can also change any single point along a spline directly in the Timeline window. There are a few ways to do this, and we explore them now. If you drag a selection around points in the Timeline window, either by clicking and dragging starting from empty space or by using the Group tool located on the Timeline's mini toolbar, the points you select will have a yellow bounding box surrounding them. This is exactly like the bounding box you get by selecting a group of control points in a Model window, and like that box you can right-click (control-click on the Mac) and bring up a contextual menu, as shown in Figure 10.42.

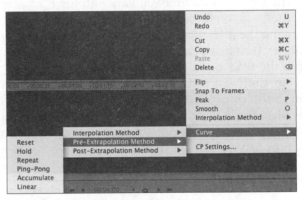

FIGURE 10.42   The contextual menu for a Timeline group has some helpful items.

Most of the items in the menu should be fairly familiar to you by now. Undo and Redo, Cut, Copy, Paste, and Delete are as you would expect them. Flip has a submenu that allows you to flip the selected keyframes either in time (*x*-axis) or in value (*y*-axis) allowing you to change a positive number for a negative or to flip the position of two keyframes along a spline. Snap-to frames will force all keyframes in the selection to line up to whole frame numbers

It is very possible to place a keyframe on decimal portions of a frame. These "subframe" actions can be very useful when working with multipass render effects such as motion blur or depth of field. You will look at a couple specific uses for these in Chapter 14, "Rendering and Compositing."

Peak and Smooth function just as they do for splines in a model, In fact, the easiest way to get linear in and out interpolation for a keyframe is to simply peak that point in the Timeline.

The interpolation method submenu lists all the types of interpolation that you can assign to a channel plus a default interpolation type.

- Default will make the key have the same interpolation as the entire channel curve (as set in the PWS).
- Hold will give the selected point (or points) hold (or stepped) interpolation, without affecting the rest of the channel.
- Linear will effectively "peak" the channel(s) as it moves through the selected point(s).

- Spline is the default curved interpolation for most channels.
- Zero-Slope will flatten the curve out as it approaches the point. It is best used for the highest peaks and valleys of a curve and gives a curve more "ease."

This is the easiest way to change any given point to a different type of interpolation.

The Curve submenu is similar, with the exeption that it allows you to change the interpolation for all the points along all the selected curves. This is the same as changing the interpolation in the PWS (or pre- and post-extrapolation as the case may be), but for most things, it will be easier than tracking down the correct driver in the PWS or Properties panels.

For the most minute control of the keys you have in the Timeline, the last item in the contextual menu will open the CP Settings dialog (see Figure 10.43). This dialog will allow you to set the frame or value either absolutely or as an offset of the current value of the CP; and set the interpolation method, peak the point, or numerically set the bias for the spline as it enters and exits. This level of precision is good for mechanical motion, but is not used very often for character animation.

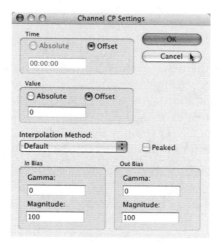

FIGURE 10.43   The Channel CP Settings dialog

Which method you use is largely a matter of personal preference and dictated by the needs of the moment. Select the last CPs of your camera move and, by any of the methods discussed, set them to 0-Slope interpolation. Note how the channels change to reflect this; they should move more gradually into and out of the motion.

This is all the camera movement required for this shot. You will set up a cut to a different chor for the tracking shot, one that allows you to set up a set of simplified backgrounds to rush past your character in a blur. Each shot in your sequence needs to move to a different choreography. This is how you keep track of each shot. Think of it like this: Each project is a sequence that can contain any number of shots. Each choreography in that project is a shot. A single shot could be one steady take of a camera view, or it could be the same scene rendered from three cameras to allow for editing as in dialog. The easiest way to determine when a shot needs to change is the set. Anytime you need to change the set pieces you should start a new shot and a new choreography.

Render out a small test animation by clicking the Render to File button and saving this as a QuickTime movie (see Chapter 12, "Surfacing," for more on rendering). Watch it a few times and analyze the camera motion. Is it fast enough? Do the transitions from moving to still feel too abrupt? If, for example, you felt that it just took a little too long to pan, you might select the end keys for the camera and move them back in the Timeline a few frames to make the motion of the camera faster. Watch the overall timing and make any adjustments you feel are needed. Then look at the framing of the shot. Does it feel right to you? Does it reveal portions of the set it shouldn't? If so, find the frames that are causing the trouble and adjust the camera's framing.

When you are happy with the motion and framing, then the camera is what is called *locked down*, meaning that no further changes are made to it. Locking down the camera is a vital part of the process and needs to be done before character animation begins. In order to present the best performance, a real actor needs to know where the camera is. For the same reason, in order for you to animate the best performance possible, you need to know what the camera sees. To ensure that the camera isn't moved by accident, make it unpickable in the PWS.

ACTING VERSUS ACTION

This leads to an important point. Before you move on to animating your character, learn the difference between acting and action.

Action is easy: You move an object from point to point. You might make the motion pleasant, or you might make it jarring, but no matter how well it might move, it's still only moving.

Acting is an expressive art, and in animation it is the line that separates great from average. Acting creates empathy for a character and gives the impression that the character is thinking on some level. Bringing acting to your character is not easy. It takes time, effort, and practice. The mechanics of it are the same as action, but it is the intelligent application of the mechanics and a basic understanding of live-action acting techniques that help you create a performance.

There is no simple formula, no three-step process to follow that gives a character personality and depth, but there are some basic concepts that you can look at and work toward applying. Knowing your tools is vital. Well enough that you do not get hung up in the mechanics of them while you are trying to create a performance. Make certain your character rig goes through a complete shakedown to ferret out any problems with rigging or modeling before they interrupt your flow.

If your character is going to act, then it needs a thought. It needs to be thinking something at all times, and it needs to be 100% committed to that thought. The thought needs to register not only on the character's face, but also in its body language. Every aspect of the character needs to be dedicated to the thought. Even if the character is torn between two thoughts, it needs to shift back and forth 100% from one thought to the other.

Your character should always be doing something. If it is standing on a street corner, it should be there for a reason, doing something, going somewhere, or even deciding where it wants to go and what it wants to do.

The best guide for acting is to watch people around you every day. Pay attention to the way they stand and the way they move. When you are animating a shot, act it out yourself. You might feel silly at first, but it's the best way to get a feel for the action. If you can, videotape yourself acting; if not, using a full-length mirror can be invaluable.

Watch great animation frame by frame, and decide what you like about it. What makes the animation work? Films like *Iron Giant* or *Pinocchio* can help you learn what works.

Finally, get critiques on your work. An honest, open criticism can open your eyes to problems that you were not aware of and is a vital part of the learning process. Find someone who isn't related to you, though. Friends and family tend to be supportive more than critical, and when your work is being reviewed, don't get defensive. It's okay to disagree, but take everything that is said about your work into consideration.

Getting a performance out of a character is a distinct challenge and one of the most rewarding aspects of animation, and working out the process of animating is the first step to getting there. You will be looking at a method that many professional animators use to quickly block in animation and get to a finished product. This is not the only way it can be done. If you find a method that suits you better, then go with what makes you comfortable.

SETTING YOUR KEYS (BLOCKING)

You have already looked at the concept of extreme poses in an action, and that is the foundation for the first pass of your animation. Unlike the way you worked in the Action window, however, you will want to isolate the keys so that you can simply focus on the timing of them. Do this by setting the interpolation of the channels to hold. In this pass of animation, you aren't trying to get anything perfect, but you are establishing the basics of the performance. So dropping the Captain in the scene you have blocked the camera in, go ahead and look at how to block a shot in A:M.

At the start of the animation (Frame 0), the Captain needs to be out of the shot. Place him behind the foreground building and pose him in a flying pose similar to the one in the storyboards. Take a look at the shot at the end of the camera move and get a feel for where the character needs to be. Then at Frame 0 drop the character into the choreography either in the PWS or into the workspace window, and position it just outside the frame of the camera. Check back at the end of the camera move to be certain that the character remains out of frame. If it is in the frame, go back to Frame 0 and adjust the character there. If you move the character on a later frame it will create animated keyframes, which is most of the time not what you will want it to do.

Now you have everything set up and ready to animate. You could animate the character in actions and apply the Captain to a path in the chor, just as you did for the flour sack earlier. However, to understand how these tools work on their own, let's animate this straight in the choreography. The principles are the same, but you are going to be focusing on the performance of the entire shot rather than the mechanics of a single action.

In film terms, a shot is any length of time where the action is framed without a cut. Based on your animatic, this will be the first shot, up to the cut where the character notices the flyer on the ground or roughly 10 seconds, according to your animatic. Break down the motion in the shot based on the performance you want to give, and then your first task is to block in the motion.

Blocking means that you establish the key poses, the extremes, and get a feel for the timing without being concerned with the in-between motion. You just want to establish the poses that *have* to be there, the ones that define the action. This is similar to the way that you handled the extreme poses in your walk cycle, but you need to be conscious of the camera and how the poses read. Your first step is to review the animatic; specifically, you need to have a general idea of when each segment of the shot happens. The character flies on-screen at the 4-second mark. Then you have about 2 seconds to move the character to the edge of the frame before your second shot begins. You don't have to be locked to this as an absolute scale, but try to come as close as you can.

The character flys in, probably looking sternly forward watching where he is going, possibly looking at the street or the building, perhaps behind him. As he approaches the edge of the frame, he glances up and forward. This tells the audience where he intends to go, which gives his flight a purpose. As he reaches the pole, he will definitely look to see if the bus is coming. Once he sees that it is not, he leans against the pole and prepares to wait.

Rather than provide a series of exact poses and the frames to place them on, finding a good set of poses is left up to you. Figures 10.44 through 10.46 show some of the more important poses. More important to the discussion here are the mechanics of the animation in the choreography and the techniques to get the blocking in place. So, break the action up into its parts and look at the process in the choreography.

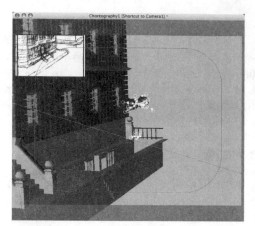

FIGURE 10.44 Captain appears around the corner.

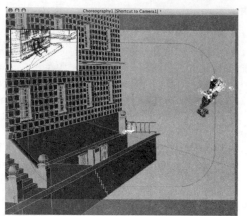

FIGURE 10.45 Glancing back.

FIGURE 10.46 The captain focuses his attention off camera in anticipation.

The action starts by flying onto the screen. Select the character and enter skeletal animation mode by clicking the button or pressing the F8 keyboard shortcut. Start this animation with the extreme poses of the flight across the screen: the point where Captain enters the shot, the point where he changes direction, and the point just before he exits the frame. Pose the character in a basic flight pose at Frame 0. This pose will remain held until the point where the character enters the frame. If the Timeline is not showing, make it visible by selecting it from the View menu. When a bone is selected for animating, it is shown in the Timeline until it is deselected. Pin the timeline view in place.

As you animate, the channels for the bone you are animating are shown in real time as you work in the Timeline. It looks confusing at first, and for simple adjustments of time, it is more than you will want to look at; so toggle the Channel view to Timeline view mode at the bottom of the Timeline window. Now you will see simple blocks indicating keyframes.

You work with the key filters on the Frame toolbar extensively in this process. While you are dealing with the bones in the character, your primary keyframes will be rotation and translation; so enable the filters for those and disable the rest. For the scope of the key filter, you will want to work with the entire model for the most part; so make sure that is enabled. Copy this frame and paste it about 3 seconds into the animation, and you will see that in the Timeline you have a key for each control at both the first frame and the new one we pasted (see Figure 10.47). Having the keys laid out in this fashion makes adjusting the timings easier.

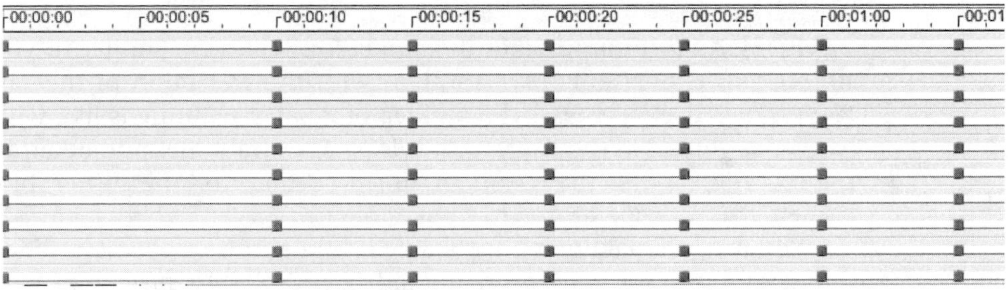

FIGURE 10.47   Keeping the Timeline organized helps when you need to adjust your timing.

Each time you create a pose, you want to force all the control bones to set keys. This ensures that each pose remains intact when you move keyframes to adjust the timing. At each pose you set, click the Make Keyframe button. This creates a key for each control bone on each pose. If after a test render you feel that the action is rushed or moving too slowly, it's a simple matter to select the keys for each pose and adjust the timing. For example, the entire flight might take up 2 seconds of screen time, but after playing it back this might seem too fast. You might want 3 seconds. Simply move the keys forward 1 second until the timing feels right. If you have to lengthen or shorten the scene, you can do that. The animatic is not a straitjacket, only a guide.

The goal of the blocking pass is to focus in timing. Once you have your key poses in place, this can become hard to judge. The interpolation between the poses by the computer can confuse the issue. The slow, lazy nature of curves can make poses seem too far apart. To make the timing more obvious, change the interpolation of the channels to show only the poses and the space between them.

It is a simple matter to show the channels: Switch the Timeline window to Channel view and select the Bones folder for the shortcut to Captain under the choreography. Once the channels are displayed, drag a bounding box around all the keys in the channels, and from the contextual menu's Interpolation heading, choose to hold the channels. They should look like stairsteps or a city skyline (see Figure 10.48). This means that each keyframe is held until a new key is encountered when the character will pop to the next pose.

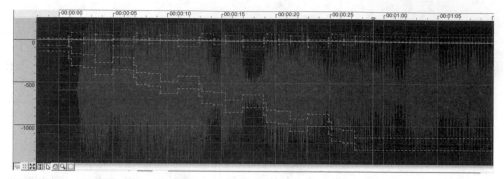

FIGURE 10.48 Held keyframes have no interpolation between them.

Rendering this out makes the animation look very similar to your animatic, still images shown one after another, with the exception of the camera move. Playing this back will give you an idea of what the timing is like without the in-betweens getting in the way. View this pass several times and determine if it feels right to you. Does he have enough time to get around the corner, or does he feel rushed? Does he look forward soon enough?

You are not looking for any subtle acting at this stage; instead, focus on your timing and poses. If you feel that a different timing or spacing of the keys would work better, then it is just a simple matter of selecting all the keys for the pose you want to move and sliding them in the Timeline. Since you keyed the entire character on each pose, the entire pose moves easily in this manner. Another quick render lets you preview your timing changes.

Once you have the timing for your extreme poses down and are happy with the overall pacing of the blocking, move into the first pass of real animation and start establishing your breakdown poses.

Breakdowns

The concept of breakdowns for your flight with the captain is the same as it was for the walk. You have established your extreme poses at the start of the flight, the base of the arc, and offscreen, but the time in between these poses is, currently, entirely left to the computer. What you need to do is to step through the animation and find those poses and transitions between poses that look weak, or unclear, and add a brerakdown to strengthen the pose. The most likely use for breakdowns in your flight are for timing and anticipation.

To set up your new poses, follow the same procedures that you did for establishing the extreme poses: Position the character to anticipate the next extreme pose, and with the key filters set to key bone rotation and translation for the whole model, set a key for all existing channels. To begin, add the anticipation poses four or five frames before the pose you are anticipating. This might not be correct for every pose, but will give you a good place to start. Render out the animation and check the timing of your anticipation poses. Make as many adjustments to the spacing of these frames as you need to make the action read correctly. This is a good point to start looking for a critique. You can often overlook things in your own animation that other people will notice.

Once anticipation is established and you are happy with the timing, move forward with getting the animation to work in standard interpolation.

Go back to the channels, and change the interpolation back to spline. If you render this out now, you will see that the action becomes mushy; the pleasant snappiness of the hold interpolation is, for the most part, lost. Some of your anticipation poses might still be snappy, but the rest of your in-betweens are likely to be less than desirable. To make the transitions snappier, add additional keyframes, especially in the areas of the shot where the character has long gaps between poses. There are a number of ways to add snap to the motion, but the easiest of them is to simply create a moving hold that quickly transitions into the next pose. A fast transition between held poses will read better than slow transitions to poses that occupy very little screen time.

Moving the new set of keyframes forward, closer to the next pose, shortens the length of time between the two poses, giving snap to the motion. It is almost always better to move very quickly, into a new pose than to not. Most of the time a transition of six frames or less will be perfect. Go through each of the poses in the animation and add snap to the transitions in this manner.

Getting the Arcs

Once the timing is established and the anticipation, breakdowns, and snap are added it is time to refine your in-betweens so that the motion is smooth and natural looking. If there is one thing that can give a natural look to motion, it is the application of arcs. Take a head turn as a quick arc example.

Figure 10.49 shows three frames of a head turning without an arc. The head simply rotates from left to right. When played back, this not only looks mechanical, but the motion is boring. Watch the line of the nose and notice how it remains straight: There is no arc here. A much more interesting and natural motion comes when the head moves in an arc, as in Figure 10.50. The slight dip of the head as it comes around makes all the difference in the world.

You can apply this principal to almost every aspect of your animation, but it is most evident in the head. Consider a walk cycle, for instance. The head moving up and down is what establishes the arcs for the walk, giving it its character. This motion is driven by the hips, but you notice the head first. Watch your animation again, and this time look for any motion that does not follow an arced path. Pay particular attention to the head and the hips, but also to the path Captain takes as he turns the corner. How much arc can you push into it? His velocity is bound to push him pretty far out, and you will need to arc into the turn very hard. The flight onto and off the screen should follow a wide arc as well.

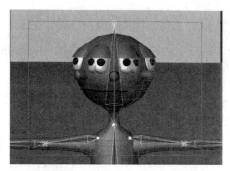

FIGURE 10.49 The lack of arcs as this head turns makes the motion look stiff and mechanical.

FIGURE 10.50 Adding a slight dip to the middle of the turn makes the motion much more natural.

Once the arcs are in place and the timing feels right, it is time to offset the keyframes of the motion to take that last aspect of mechanical motion out of the action. This will add the overshoot and overlapping motion to your animation. Do this in the same way you did for the walk cycle: Select the keys in the Timeline, and offset the trailing or leading parts of the character by a frame or two. Wait to do this until after you are certain that your timing is correct, because it will destroy the neat rows of keys that you had in your Timeline, which makes adjusting a single pose much more complicated (see Figure 10.51).

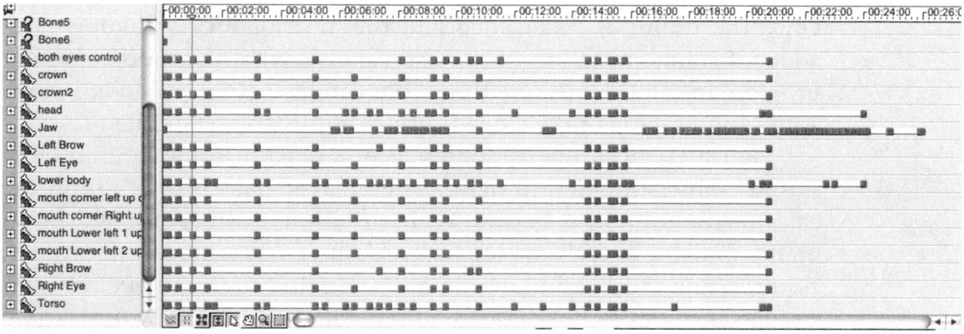

FIGURE 10.51 After you offset the motion the Timeline is less organized.

Polishing Pass

At this point, your animation looks pretty good and could even be called finished if you ware rushed for time, but by taking a little extra effort you can add the small touches that can make the motion shine.

Secondary motion can mean many things, but it generally refers to the small offsets and overlaps of motion in things like fingers, hair, clothes, and facial animation. The Captain's design involves dynamic elements for his hair and clothes, which give us a lot of secondary animation for free, but for things like the eyes, hands, and even so much as the legs and arms, you can give a set of motion that can add life to the character.

The facials are controlled with a set of pose sliders that affect individual aspects of the face. For your animation, the facial expressions can be very subtle: a slight change in the direction of the glance, a blink as he turns the corner, and a deeper set to the brow as if determination was strengthening for the captain. You can paint most of these expressions on broadly, and indeed if you are too subtle, you might find that the performance seems lifeless. The most obvious and important aspects that make the character livelier are the eyes.

As a general rule of thumb, every time the character shifts its gaze or turns its head, it needs to blink. The mechanics off a blink are very important and require more than simply closing the eyes and opening them again. In a standard blink, the character's eyes close and open again in four frames, but rather than closing halfway and then all the way, then opening halfway, and then opening all the way, you offset the opening and closing of the eyes so that they snap closed and then snap back open.

On the first frame of the blink, key the eyes open all the way. If you don't, you get a very slow transition from the last frame you keyed the blink slider on. Advance one frame and close the eyes about one-quarter of the way. Advance one more frame and close the eyes all the way. This is the snap shut. Moving forward one more frame, open the eyes one-quarter of the way. Again, advance a single frame and open the eyes all the way.

By placing a blink before each change of expression or at the bottom of each anticipation you lend thought to the character's actions. Making the audience believe that the character is a thinking, living being is the entire goal of animation.

Go through the animation and add the facial expressions to the character. Apply the same principles and techniques here that you did to the animation of the rest of the character. Run through the animation and block in the facials, then add anticipation. Finally, add snap and offset the keys for the facial poses. When you offset the keys, remember that the eyes should lead the face: a blink comes before the change of expression or a change in the direction of the character's gaze.

The final touch is the squash and stretch that give weight to the character, even though he is flying thorugh the air. As the captain comes into the turn he will compress down into the corner of the arc and then stretch back out as he flies off-screen. You installed a set of squash and stretch controls into the captain in Chapter 9, "Expressions," and now is the time to turn on the poses that hold the expressions that drive the Squetch and also those that reveal the control nulls. Proceed with the Squetch just as you did with the animation. Squetch the character in each pose as seems necessary proceeding to the extremes first and then hitting the breakdown and offset poses. You might find it easy enough to just hit the squash in the main part of the turn, but if you explore it you will find that some subtle squetch can be applied to most of the action in this shot.

CHANNELS

You have already explored channels to some extent, but before wraping up discussion here, we need to dig into them a little more in depth. Each animated property has an associated function curve called a channel, which determines how the value that it represents changes on the way from one keyframe to the next. You have already done some basic channel manipulation by changing the interpolation of keyframes during the blocking phase of animation. This is just the most basic way in which you can alter the channels of animation.

Each curve is a spline, with each keyframe indicated as a control point along that spline. Like splines in models, you can peak, smooth, or adjust the bias it passes through a point or a group of points. These bias adjustments are limited to magnitude and gamma since channels are strictly 2D representations of your animation. They can be difficult to understand completely, but learning to adjust the bias in a channel lets you fine-tune the motion you have created. Typically, channels are the last thing that you deal with after offsetting keys and adding secondary motion, because adding keys to channels that have major bias adjustments on them can create anomalies in the playback of the animation.

To understand how channels work, look at something simple before you dive into the animation of a full character. Look at Figure 10.52. Here is a simple channel that represents a foot that holds on the ground for three frames and then lifts up in the *y*-axis over three frames.

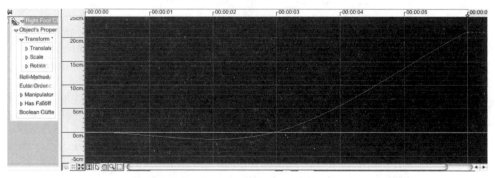

FIGURE 10.52   This basic channel represents the translation of a foot in the *y*-axis.

When you set these three keys in the action or choreography, you would probably expect the foot to remain firmly planted from the first key to the second; but looking in the channels reveals that the foot pushes down between those two keys, even though they are the same. Why? Because, like splines in a model, the curvature of a channel is affected by any neighboring points along the spline of that channel. The third keyframe that pulls the foot up also affects the spline between the first two keys. This is referred to as *key drift*. Since this is not what you want to happen, you need to counter it. Once you know where the problem is, fixing it is easy. Selecting any control point with the bias handles showing allows you to simply move the bias handle to flatten out the offending portion of the spline (see Figure 10.53). This is identical to the way that you flatten out portions of a model for beveling when working with objects. You can also simply make the second point interpolate as 0-slope. This makes the bias of that point run parallel to the *y*-axis of the channel (which flattens it in and out of the point).

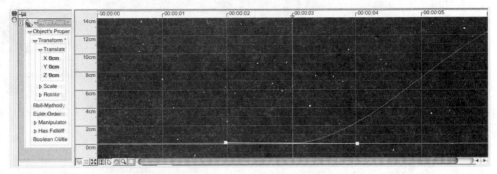

FIGURE 10.53   Tweaking the bias for the channel is a simple fix for key drift.

You can even ease in and out of each key by adjusting the bias rather than using extra keyframes (see Figure 10.54), although extra keys are generally easier to deal with for complex motions.

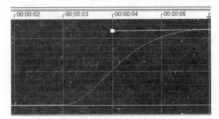

FIGURE 10.54   Adjusting the bias for each control point can also be used to ease in and out of keys.

This doesn't seem difficult, and when you take it one channel at a time it isn't, but animating with spaghetti gets difficult when you have hundreds of channels at a time to deal with (see Figure 10.55).

For the majority of motion, though, editing the channels is not needed; it should only be used to fine-tune motion. For cycles, it comes in handy to make sure that the motion doesn't pop at the end. Changing the interpolation method for all channels of a cycle on the first and last keys to 0-slope will smooth it out quickly.

Once you get the hang of it, you can even get a feel for what channels like those in Figure 10.55 represent.

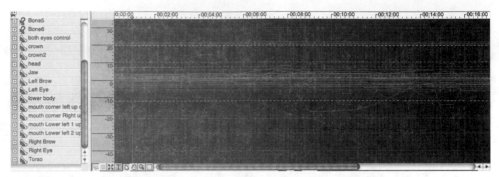

FIGURE 10.55   Looking at all the channels for an action can be very intimidating.

LIP SYNCH: MUSCLE SHAPES AND PHONEMES

One of the biggest mistakes in lip-synching animation is the tendency to use a standard set of phoneme shapes, and reading traditional animation books would seem to suggest that this is the proper course. For traditional animation as well as CG, there are no hard-and-fast rules, but the danger of creating such a rule in CG when none should exist is far too easy. The basic shapes of phonemes are as follows:

- M, B, P
- C, D, J, R, S, X, Z
- F, V
- TH
- N, L
- E, K, hard C, short U
- Long A, Ah
- Long O
- OO, long U

There are schools of thought that have even more. The problem with this list is that in 3D the tendency is to make a single shape, a pose for each of them, and to hit them every time the appropriate phoneme appears in dialog. This is contrary to what works for most animation unless the character is singing. In traditional animation, the drawings don't just hit the phoneme, but also take into consideration the shape that comes before it. Often a traditional animator will skip over whole phoneme shapes entirely, simply hitting the accents and the closed-mouth shapes.

The shape of the mouth needs to be different for each phoneme depending on several factors: the speed of the speech, accents in dialogue, the sound that comes before, and the sound that comes after. In traditional animation, since each line of dialog is drawn rather than traced from a stack of predetermined shapes, these considerations are made on some level for each frame of animation.

Look into a mirror and say, *"What's the scoop, Betty Boop."* It may sound silly but it will illustrate the point. Say it naturally and at full speed, and watch your mouth. The word "the" can hardly be noticed, most often phrased with the same lip shape as the end of the word "what's." If you hit every syllable of every single word, you would pull the mouth open to accent the "e" shape in "the." This is not how people talk naturally. In other instances, a particular phoneme shape will differ based on the sounds that surround it, particularly when saying "Boop."

Technically the *B* and the *P* are the same phoneme, but if you say it normally, you will notice that the *B* shape is wider and the *P* shape is more drawn in or pursed. This is because of the positions of those phoneme shapes in relation to other sound shapes. A *P*, *B*, or *M* following an "oo" sound will be pursed.

So just make a new shape? No, that would only cover one instance of the sound when there are dozens of other possible combinations that may alter the way your phonemes will turn out.

So, do you ignore phoneme shapes? No. Phonemes are a useful tool and a good starting point for animating dialogue, so much so that A:M has a set of lip-synch tools based on their use. As is often the case the solution lies in finding the middle of the road. You use a base set of phonemes to get started and to quickly block in animation by using pose sliders for each phoneme that in turn drives additional poser sliders. We can use this base and then make adjustments to the finer, underlying controls.

This does not mean that a slider needs, to be created for each of the over 40 muscles in a human face, or that they need to be anatomically correct. Simplification of the basic facial movements is more than often enough.

For the majority of lip-synch needs there are typically only eight poses needed, on four sliders, for the mouth motion. This can be increased to split the motion for each side of the face, but strictly speaking, this is not always necessary.

The basic poses are as follows:

- Close mouth —|— Open Jaw
- Ooooo —|— Uhhh
- Smile — |— Frown
- F/V —-|—- Pout

Given these four sliders in combination most lip shapes can be achieved. Normally, two or more poses at 100% will look bad, but lower numbers can generate some great facial animation.

Apply this to the captain. Figures 10.56 through 10.59 show each of these poses in its extreme. You build these controls with the sliders you created in Chapter 7 when you set up the facial deformation controls. By using the underlying bone rotations, you can ensure that the mouth and other parts of the face follow clean arcs as they animate into new shapes.

 You can, of course, build interface elements for these controls as you did in Chapter 9 for the Squetch controls. It makes it easier to animate the face if you do so.

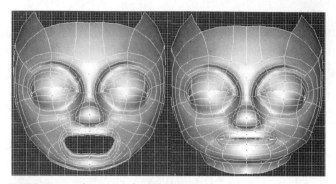

FIGURE 10.56   Close mouth and open jaw.

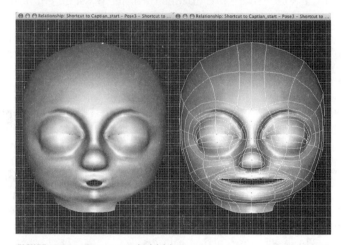

FIGURE 10.57   Ooooo and uhhhh.

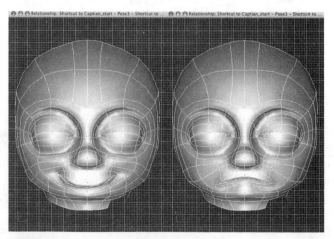

FIGURE 10.58   Smile and frown.

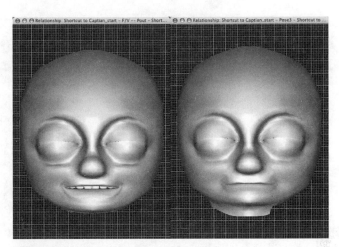

FIGURE 10.59   F/V and pout

With these sliders, you can build your set of simple phoneme shapes. You want each phoneme to be a separate percentage-based pose slider. The reason for this becomes apparent when you get into using A:M's built-in lip-synch tools. You will need to build at least nine phoneme shapes for A:M, and what you name those shapes is very important.

- A I
- E
- O
- U
- M B P
- F V
- W Q
- C D G K N R S TH Y Z
- L

These default phonemes are based on the set illustrated by Preston Blair in his book *Cartoon Animation*, and A:M's documentation refers to them as the Preston set. There are additional phoneme shapes that you can create, but you will be using your underlying fine-tuning sliders to change this set rather than going to the work of creating the additional 40-plus shapes that A:M recognizes. Figures 10.60 through 10.68 show each phoneme on the captain and indicate the slider values used to achieve them.

Once you have the poses in place it is necessary to have a sound file to examine and animate to. One is provided on the CD-ROM. Open Scoop.wav on the CD-ROM in A:M by double-clicking the sound folder in the PWS and browsing to the file location.

ON THE CD

A:M will only load in audio files in the .WAV format, specifically uncompressed PCM WAV files.

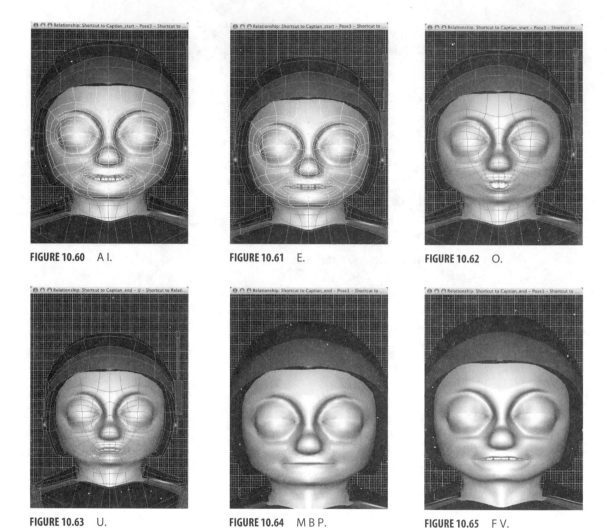

FIGURE 10.60   A I.

FIGURE 10.61   E.

FIGURE 10.62   O.

FIGURE 10.63   U.

FIGURE 10.64   M B P.

FIGURE 10.65   F V.

The breakdown of audio in A:M is made easier by the use of the Dope Sheet tool. In traditional animation, a sound technician carefully listens to the sound that is to be animated and breaks down each word into its base phonemes, indicating the frame that each would fall on during the animation on a sheet of paper that is called the dope sheet. It uses a dictionary of known words to break down lines of text into words and phonemes. You can then position each word or phoneme in the Timeline to match with your sound file. The dope sheet then applies each phoneme pose based on these positions. This is why it is important to name each phoneme properly (see Figure 10.69).

Get the captain to say your line of dialogue. Create a new action for the captain and if the Scoop.Wav file is not already in your project, load it in now. Drag and drop the sound file from the PWS into the Action window. You should see

FIGURE 10.66 W Q.

FIGURE 10.67 C D G K N R S T H Y Z.

FIGURE 10.68 L.

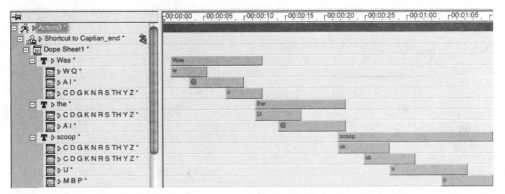

FIGURE 10.69 The Dope Sheet tool breaks down a line of dialogue into phonemes.

the sound waves in the Timeline. Now that you have your sound and your character together, you need to create a dope sheet and break down the dialogue.

Bring up the action's contextual menu and choose Dope Sheet from the New heading. A dialog will prompt you to enter a sentence or phrase. Enter "Was the scoop Betty Boop." Notice the misspelling of "what's" as "was." This is because the word what's is not in the dictionary file. If you get a dialog asking you to locate the Dictionary.dic file, then you will need to get the dictionary before you can continue with the dope sheet. This file should be installed in the same directory as A:M, but if yours is not you can find a copy online at *ftp://ftp.hash.com/pub/misc/Dictionary.dic*. This file contains the words that A:M knows and how they are broken down. When the dictionary is in place the words that it recognizes are broken down automatically, and the poses for the phonemes are added.

Each word in your sentence is positioned in the Timeline with an editable region, which allows you to position it at the appropriate spot to match the sound of the dialogue. For some words, "Boop" for example, there will be no entry in the dictionary and you have to create the phoneme shapes one at a time. Do this by bringing up the contextual menu for the word. In this case, choose the Add Single Phoneme option from the menu. A list of all the poses in the model is presented. Select the one that matches the phoneme you need. For example, Boop would start with the "M B P" shape. Do this for each phoneme in the word, M B P, then U, and a final M B P in this case.

Now if you play through the animation, you should see the lips perform something like a synch. It will likely not be perfect, but you can adjust the timing and spacing of each phoneme to match the dialogue. In the PWS, select the Dopesheet object in the action. It and all its children are available in the Timeline. Go ahead and tack the Timeline, so you can work on this without worrying about accidentally deselecting it. Each word is presented as a bar that you can drag and scale in the Timeline to line up with the dialog. Click and drag the WAS word. Note that as you do so, A:M plays the audio for the portion of time that the word covers in the Timeline. Position and scale the word "was" until you can only hear the sound for the word "what's" in the audio track. If you expand the word, you will then have access to the individual phonemes that comprise that word. These phonemes work exactly the same as the word, and you work with them in the same manner. Drag and scale each until you can hear only the sound associated with that phoneme.

Since you created your phoneme poses by using your shape sliders, you can use these same sliders to make refinements to the animation. Deemphasizing certain aspects of the dialogue, toning down hard accents, or pursing the lips on the last P shape, the work that you laid down with the dope sheet becomes a guide to work against rather than a final animation. Since the phoneme pose directly drives the shape sliders, the adjustments are easy to make and have no problems with additive slider data.

SUMMARY

Animation:Master has some of the most sophisticated character animation tools available, and while the pursuit of creating great animation is a lifelong process, the methods and tools used to animate should not get in the way of that act. We have spent a lot of time covering theory for animation and mixed the meat of the tools in throughout, because it is impossible to discuss the tools without the context of how they are used.

When the process is moving smoothly, the tools should be invisible. If the tools make themselves too prominent, then the task loses its artistry and we become technicians. To work best, we need to understand the tools well enough that we can forget about them.

The exercises in this chapter took you through the first scene in a two-scene short animation. It is left up to you to finish the second scene. If you pursue it, we would love to see your progress. Swing by the Hash forums and show off!

LIGHTING

In This Chapter

- Preparation for Lighting
- Light Types
- Three-Point Lighting
- Set Lighting
- Radiosity
- Other Light Properties
- Hierarchical Lights

In this chapter, we look at lighting, introducing the tools for it and explaining its importance. The basic three-point lighting and secondary set lighting will be discussed, looking toward building compelling compositions. Qualities of light and shadow and how to achieve specific effects in A:M will be discussed, and finally, A:M's radiosity solution is explored.

By the end of this chapter, the scene you animated in Chapter 10, "Animation," should be lit and ready to texture and render to file.

PREPARATION FOR LIGHTING

Lighting is one of the most crucial and overlooked aspects of creating compelling 3D imagery. In theory, it seems simple enough: You identify the sources of light in your scene and use one of A:M's light types to simulate it. In reality, as much time, effort, and thought needs to go into placing lights into your shots as in placing splines in your models. The most important thing to remember about lighting 3D scenes is that when it is all rendered out and viewed, the final result will be 2D. This makes the function of the lights in the shot even more important: They become the cues to the viewer that the image is actually 3D.

Lighting is done in the choreography after modeling and animation are completed. The animation is typically done first so that the lights can be intelligently placed in the scene to accentuate the character and bring any important details into clearer focus. At the same time lighting is being done materials and textures are also finalized. The colors on the surfaces and how they interact with the lights are related topics covered in separate chapters in this book for clarity.

When a new choreography is created in A:M, by default it uses a basic three-point lighting rig and a ground plane. This is great for previewing models and for rough illumination for the animator, but when you are lighting a 3D scene control, it is the key to success. Any light in the shot that you do not deliberately place is counterproductive. So the first step is to delete all lights in the choreography. If you find yourself doing this often, you can create a new default choreography with no lights in it, or anything you may want. Simply create a choreography the way you would like to have it as the default and save it externally with the name Default Chor.cho. This file will replace the file of the same name in the directory that A:M resides in. You will probably want to keep a backup of the original default so that you can restore it later if you need to.

Once you have removed all the lights from the scene, do a progressive render of the shot from the camera view. It should look like Figure 11.1.

FIGURE 11.1 A solid black render should be the first thing you see.

Don't adjust your monitor. It is intended to be solid black. If you can see any of your models with no lights in a scene, then you have ambience turned on one or more of the model's surface attributes. In most cases, ambience is undesirable.

Rather than cheat a little light into your scene it will flatten out your shadow areas and kill details in your models. As a general rule, unless your model is self-illuminating, a lightbulb for instance, it should have an ambience setting of 0.

 While ambience in a very general sense is a bad thing, a little can do wonders for smoothing out small surface irregularities on your models. If you have problems with lumpy surfaces, you can ease a little of the pain of straightening them out with a surface ambience of 10 or so. Be aware of the trade-off involved, however.

With a completely dark choreography, you can be certain that all the light in a shot is placed there deliberately.

LIGHT TYPES

Lights in Animation:Master come in three varieties: bulb, klieg, and sun.

A bulb light starts at an infinitely small point and spreads light rays out in all directions. The intensity of the light starts at the center and proceeds at full intensity until it reaches the falloff distance. Once it reaches the falloff distance, it begins to give less and less illumination to objects based upon the attenuation property of the light.

Klieg lights simulate real-world spotlights. The light starts from an infinitely small point and travels out in a conical pattern at full intensity up to a distance equal to the falloff of the light. Beyond that point, the light's attenuation determines how much light continues on into the scene. Intensity of the light also varies from the center of the cone to the edges, based on the width softness property of the light. A softness of 100% makes the intensity of the light lower from the center to the edge of the light, while 0% will not show any difference at all across the entire light area.

Sun lights simulate distant lights such as the sun, whose rays are parallel once they reach their destination. The light starts as if from an infinite plane, and travels parallel, in a single direction, evenly illuminating all objects in its path. The light is an equal intensity and travels an effectively infinite distance across an entire choreography.

The properties for all lights are basically the same even though there is some variation across light types; for example, width softness only works on klieg-type lights, suns have no attenuation, and so on. All the properties for a light can, as with all objects, be found in the Properties panel when the light is selected (see Figure 11.2).

The properties that are common to all light types start with Bone Position and Transform properties, which are used to set the default length of the light's control bone and initial position in the chor. Unless you are using hierarchical lights,

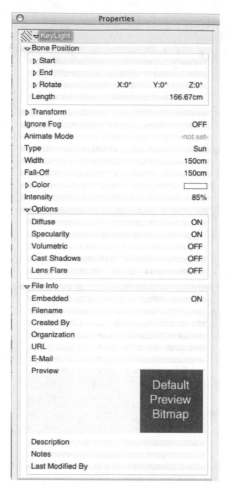

FIGURE 11.2   The properties for a light
control the quality of that light.

you will not need these settings very often. The rest of the properties are used
much more frequently:

Ignore Fog: This property is an object property that does nothing for lights.
Ignore it.

Animate Mode: This is the same as the Animate mode on the Mode toolbar
but it applies only to the light object. When this is turned on, any changes
you make to the light will not animate as keyframes. This allows you to
change the properties of a light on any frame without having those
changes change over time. When you are working on lighting, it is often
necessary to adjust lights to work, based on the position of a character or
the angle of the camera. But you don't want those changes to interpolate
across time most of the time.

Type: This is where you set the basic light type. New lights are created as bulbs. Using this property, you can make them klieg or sun-type lights. Changing this property will show and hide the properties specific to each specific type of light (more on that shortly).

Width: Indicates the physical size of the light source. This does not change the fact that light emanates from a point, but does allow the software to compute area shadows when using multiray ray-traced shadows, or penumbra shadows in the case of z-buffer shadows on klieg lights. For all soft shadow types, this setting will control the degree of softness a shadow can have. The higher the number the softer the shadow.

Fall-Off: Indicates the distance from the initial point that the light will travel at full intensity. All light after this point will begin to decay. This applies to both bulb and klieg lights. Sun lights have an effectively infinite falloff.

Color: Indicates the RGB color of the light. The use of color for lights is discussed in detail later in this chapter.

Intensity: Indicates the maximum brightness of a light. For most things a range of 100% to 120% is sufficient for the main light in a scene. A lower intensity makes the light darker, a higher intensity makes it brighter, and intensity with a negative value removes light from an area.

Options group: Contains various toggles to control what aspects of a light are rendered. We cover each of these settings in depth as we continue.

File Info: Allows you to save the light externally from the project for reuse in later projects, as well as showing the information on who created the file and offering space for notes.

In addition to these properties, bulb and klieg lights have unique properties that do not apply to sun lights, and klieg has properties (and options) that are not available to any other light type.

Attenuation is found on both bulb and klieg lights and determines the method that A:M uses to decrease the light's intensity as it moves past the falloff line. By default, the property is 100%, which produces what is called "quadratic" falloff. This means that the light reduces in intensity 75% every time the distance past the falloff doubles. This is a very accurate light model, but there are other useful types of falloff. If you set the attenuation to 50%, A:M calculates the falloff linearly, meaning that the light reduces in intensity an even amount as it moves past the falloff distance. Setting the attenuation to 0% gives the light constant radiance with no falloff at all. You can, of course, use values between these to achieve variations on these common attenuations.

Width Softness is unique to klieg lights and as discussed will make the light fade from maximum intensity to lower intensity from the center of the light cone to the edge. A 100% softness gives the light a linear falloff from center to edge, and a 0% value will remove all softness.

Cone Angle is unique to klieg lights and simply indicates the degree of the light cone's angle. It can range anywhere from 0 to 180. The wider the cone angle, the more area in the chor will be affected by the light.

There are also properties in the Options group that are unique to klieg lights. Those are explored when you look at shadows.

THREE-POINT LIGHTING

One of the most basic concepts of lighting characters in animation comes to us from photography and film: three-point lighting. It is not a count of the number of lights in a shot or on a particular character. Rather, it is the number of functions a light can play on a character. These functions are key lighting, fill lighting, and backlighting.

Key lighting indicates the strongest source of light that is applied to a character. Normally there is only one key light in a shot. Multiple key lights can cause confusion for the viewer as to the origin of the main source of light in a shot. As you might guess, anything that causes confusion is undesirable.

Fill lights indicate ambient room light, fill in shadow areas, and *model the forms* of your model more fully in 3D.

Backlights are not needed in all circumstances. They are used to clearly define trailing edges of objects to bring them out of a background. Often you will find that the contrast in color and saturation will do a good enough job pulling the foreground into focus.

When all three points are positioned and set properly, you should be able to see the fully modeled 3D forms of your subject (see Figure 11.3).

FIGURE 11.3   A properly lit subject has full clear 3D forms despite the 2D output.

ON THE CD

Take the captain into a choreography and see how this works in practice. Open the three_point_start.prj project from the CD-ROM and look in the choreography. Change to camera view and do a quick render. Notice that there is no light in the shot, meaning you are ready to begin. You will only need to light the first frame of this shot, so you have a lot more leeway with your lights. In an animation, you would have to be more aware of what the lights are doing throughout the shot.

Three-point lighting starts with the key light. In the setting that the captain is in right now, you have a lot of freedom as to where to place the key in this shot, but in an environment the key is generally positioned coming from the same direction as the most powerful motivated light source. A motivated light source is one where you can immediately tell what is causing the light. In most outdoor shots this would be the sun. It is important that the brightest motivated light source is the key light on the subject, unless style or script indicates otherwise; if it isn't, the subject will seem out of place with its environment.

For sourceless lighting, such as your exercise, there are still some conventions and guidelines as to where a key light should and should not be placed. Unless you are trying to make the subject look frightening or in terror for its life, it should be key lit from above. The light should be a good distance to one side or the other of the camera; lighting that is too close to the centerline of the camera will flatten out your subject. Keeping these guidelines in mind, create a new light by bringing up the choreography's contextual menu and selecting Light from the New heading.

The new light will be a bulb located at the origin of the Choreography window. Move the light into position and make some decisions about what properties it needs to have. Move the light above and in front of the character and to the left of the camera. A quick render of this shot might look like Figure 11.4.

This light is fairly harsh and can be made to look a lot better. First, unless you specifically need a different type of light to simulate a lightbulb in a lamp, for instance, klieg lights are the most flexible and the easiest types to control. For this tutorial, all lights will be kliegs. Change the Light type to klieg. Since they are directional, you will then need to point the light's controlling bone at the character. An easy way to do this is to apply an Aim At constraint on the light targeting the character's pelvis. To make this light less harsh than the bulb light was, adjust its width softness. For glamour lighting, such as you are working on here, full 100% width softness produces the nicest results. Do another quick render to see how things are shaping up, You should have something similar to Figure 11.5.

FIGURE 11.4   The key light adds the brightest illumination to your shot.

FIGURE 11.5   Full width softness on the key light makes the edges less harsh.

Get used to doing quick renders in your camera view to gauge your progress. While this is better than the first render, the shadow areas are still very harsh. Use A:M's soft shadow features to make them less so. There are two types of soft shadows available, which are discussed more thoroughly later. In the properties for the light, go to the Options section and find the shadow's disclosure triangle. This light is already casting shadows or you would have to turn them on here. Right now, the shadows on this light are set to be ray traced with one ray cast. This tells A:M that you want these shadows to be hard-edged. If you wanted the shadows to be soft, increase the number of rays that the light casts, or change the shadow type to z-buffered and scale the light up. For this image, go with z-buffers because z-buffer soft shadows render much faster than their ray-traced counter-parts. The trade-off is in accuracy: If you want truly accurate shadows you will want to use ray-traced soft shadows.

Change the shadow type to z-buffer. Change the softness of the shadows to 50% or so and do a quick render of the scene, not a progressive render because z-buffered shadows do not render in Progressive Render mode. You might have something like Figure 11.6. The shadows are soft and overall very nice but there are some issues with banding and blocky artifacts. These are two possible side effects of z-buffer shadows; to get rid of these artifacts, increase the quality of the shadows.

The quality of z-buffered shadows is most directly controlled by the Map Resolution property. This is due to the way that the shadows in a z-buffer light are calculated. Two versions of the image are rendered: one from the camera view and one from the light, and the two are compared to see which point in a scene is closer. If the point from the light view is closer, then the camera renders it as a shadow area. The render from the light's angle is termed a z-buffer and is stored in an image map, the resolution of which is determined on the Properties panel. The larger the map, the more accurately the shadow areas render, and the longer they take to render. Raise the setting for map size one at a time until the artifacts disappear. In the example, a setting of 768 × 768 did the job. Render this one more time, and you should have something similar to Figure 11.7

FIGURE 11.6 The softer shadows look good, but the z-buffered artifacts are distracting.

FIGURE 11.7 The resolution of the z-buffer map is increased to eliminate artifacts in the shadows.

If you look at the character standing on the ground and want accurate softness at the feet, you would not get it. Think of how in real life shadows are more crisp as the object casting them and the ground grow closer together. This sharpness at the feet (for instance) falls off as the shadow moves away from the casting object. Z-buffers cannot do this on their own. It is inherent in ray tracing, though. To combat this limitation, A:M has a property for shadows called Penumbra. This property takes a sampling of nine *z*-buffer shadow maps and averages them together to get accurate soft shadowing of almost ray-traced quality. Since you aren't in need of that much accuracy in your character's shadow, you can ignore this property for now.

This establishes your key light, but the shadow areas of the scene are too dark. You cannot make out any details. Time to add the fill light. Fill light, typically not as bright as the key light, simulates bounced light and general room ambiance. Since it plays a supportive role to the key light, positioning the fill is a straightforward process. The fill light is placed on the opposite side of the camera as the key and at an opposite angle, so if the key is high, the fill is placed low and vice versa.

Create a new light, and position it roughly the same distance from the character on the opposite side of the camera as the key light and about as high as the character's waist. Like the key light, you want to make this a klieg light, but while you are changing things on the light's properties, turn off the shadows for the fill. Most of the time you only want your key light to add shadow areas to the scene. And you need to reduce the intensity of the light so that it does not overpower the key.

How low you want to set the intensity of the fill has a lot to do with what kind of style you go for in your lighting. We discuss the feels that you can achieve later in this chapter. For the most part, an intensity of 45% on a key light will do a good job of filling out the forms without being overpowering. Do a quick render of the scene, and you should have something similar to Figure 11.8.

FIGURE 11.8   Adding the fill light lets the details in the shadow areas show through.

This already looks really good, and you could probably get by without adding a backlight to the character. But adding one allows you to pull out some of the interior details on the shadowed side of the face a little better. The backlight has many names: rim light, hair light, and edge light are just a few. Regardless of what it is called, the function is the same: to pull the edges of the subject out from the background. In 3D, you can use a nonshadowing light to pull even more details out of a character than a real-world cinematographer can. The goal of the rim light is to paint every shadow edge on a character with just a hint of light to make it more distinct.

Because this light is also a nonshadowing klieg light, you can use a second instance of the fill light you added earlier and animate some of its properties to get the effect you want. Drag and drop the light from the PWS into the Choreography window, and position it behind the character and pointing forward. Pull out the details on the bottom edges of the shadow side of the character, such as the chin and the eyes, so you can position it similar to the fill light; but rather than in front of the character, place it behind. You want the backlight to be bright enough to overpower the fill light in the shadow areas; so you will need to adjust its intensity, but since you used an instance of the fill light as the backlight, adjusting the intensity at the light object in the PWS would increase both. Instead, select the shortcut to the light under the choreography and adjust the intensity there. This allows a single light object in the PWS to perform multiple functions in a scene. An intensity of anywhere from 100% to 200% can be used for the backlight depending on how intensely you want to make your edges stand out. For this example, an intensity of 100% is used.

A quick render might give results similar to Figure 11.9. The difference between this and the previous version is subtle but important: The details of the chin, nose, and eyes are just slightly more visible, and the shapes of the character have just a little more dimension. These subtleties are what can make a piece stand out.

FIGURE 11.9   The finished three-point lighting.

If you are having difficulties placing your lights to achieve similar results, look at the three_point_finish.prj project on the CD-ROM and consult Figure 11.10, which shows a front and top view of the choreography with each light indicated. Remember, this is a creative process and there is no wrong way to do it. Any method that arrives at the desired result is a good one.

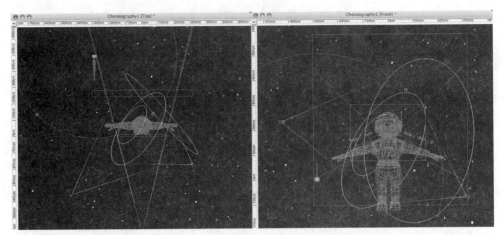

FIGURE 11.10   Use this as a guideline to placing your own lights.

SET LIGHTING

The fourth purpose a light can serve in a scene is to illuminate a part of the set. Often, three-point lighting will do a good enough job establishing lighting, not only for the subject, but also for the entire scene; but it is difficult to focus lights on a single subject and still illuminate the majority of the shot.

Lighting sets generally means that you will be establishing the key light in your shot from a motivated light source, such as the sun or a streetlamp, and most of the time this light will take care of the primary illumination on the subject and the set. Both set and subject might also share at least one major fill light, but more often than not, you will want to fill and backlight your subjects separately from the scene.

In many cases, you will also want to establish light on the subject that is generated from the scene and needs to light the character only, such as light bounced off a wall or the sidewalk. In these cases, it is very important that you remain in control of the lighting. It is far too easy to get lost when adding lights. Focus on one light at a time, and consider the effects of each light before you place it in the shot.

To effectively light both scene and subject, sometimes it is necessary to separate the lights for both. To get separation of lights, use light lists. A light list is a way to isolate the effect of a light to specific models. For example, in Figure 11.11 you have a vase sitting on the table. It has a very powerful rim light on it that floods the table as well as backlighting the vase, and because it is not casting any shadows, its light travels unimpeded into the rest of the shot. However, all you really want it to do is light the vase.

To isolate the backlight on the vase, simply drag and drop the light's shortcut onto the shortcut of the vase in the PWS. A dialog will ask you if you want to create this light list with just the selected light or with all the lights currently in the choreography. It will also give you the option of excluding the light from models

FIGURE 11.11   The backlight on this vase floods out the table.

without light lists. You can toggle this in the options group in the light's properties, with the Light All Models property.

Once a light list is created on a model, only the lights in the list will affect the model. If any light has its Light All Models property turned off, any model that does not have that light in its light list will not be shaded by it. For this reason, it is generally best to create light lists after you know that the lighting on the object is complete.

To take this in context, open the street shot that you animated in Chapter 10. You know from the script that this shot takes place in the daytime, which makes your life easier since night-time shots are more difficult. This also tells you the source of your key light: the sun. All you have to do is decide where to place it, and what type of light to use for it.

Again, before you start anything, do a progressive render of the window and make sure that the shot is 100% black. A sun-type light seems the obvious choice, and for establishing even light across the entire set, it is. So, create a new light and change its type to sun. Where you position the sun isn't absolutely critical, but you will want to ensure that it gives adequate lighting to your character; so placing it on the side of the shot that would not be in shadow from the building is probably the logical choice. A relatively high-noonish angle will also help establish shadows on the ground for your character without making them drape oddly across the set. Advance to the frame where the character enters the shot, and do a progressive render of the shot from the camera view. Much like animation, good lighting plays to the camera. Whether or not it looks bad from a different angle matters very little. The camera is the most important thing. You might have something like Figure 11.12.

The primary fill light for this shot will come from the sky. A sun-type light makes a good choice. A very wide klieg light could also do the job and would give you more options, as far as softening the effect of the light. A third option is to use

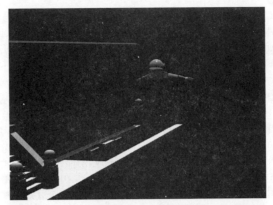

FIGURE 11.12   After establishing the key light for the shot.

a sky light, an array of lights that simulate the full light of a sky dome. It is sometimes called global illumination, but this is an inaccurate description.

Sky lights have the effect of making the details in models more prevalent by darkening the valleys with multiple overlapping shadows and lightening the rest of the surface with soft, even light. You can create sky lights by placing lights by hand or by using one of the available utilities for building them. The results of a good sky light can be fantastic, but each light increases the time it takes to render your frames. Often, acceptable results can be achieved with one fill light or by several very large bulb lights casting three rays. Rigs that are even more complex can be used that have hundreds of lights in them (see Figure 11.13).

FIGURE 11.13   This image was lit using 100 bulb lights arrayed in a tight spiral.

For animation, sky lights are normally too render-intensive, so use a simple sun or klieg as a fill. For very large scenes, more than one fill might be required; use your judgment.

For your shot, a single klieg light will suffice. Add a new light to the shot, but before you do any thing else to it, turn off the Animate property to let you make your changes while the character is in frame. Change its type to klieg, and position it to fill in the shadow side of the character. In this case, you will probably want the fill on a relatively high angle. Turning its intensity down to 45% or 50% will make the shot feel more evenly lit. Since this is a fill light, also disable shadow casting. You also want to give it a very wide cone angle, and ensure that its attenuation is constant by setting the attenuation property to 0. After placing your fill, your scene may look something like Figure 11.14

FIGURE 11.14   After adding the fill light the scene starts to take shape.

The lighting on the set pieces is in good shape, but the light on the character will probably need some work.

When light strikes a surface in real life it doesn't stop; rather, a portion of the light's energy is reflected off the surface. This is what your eyes are seeing: the light that wasn't absorbed by the surface. The light bouncing back into the environment is one of the primary things that fill lights are there to simulate. In order for the character to look convincingly integrated into a scene, it needs to be hit with lights representing some of the more dominant fills in the shot.

One of the most effective—and often overlooked—is a fill up from the sidewalk that illuminates the underside of the character. Lights that provide this particular type of fill are called bounce lights. The color and intensity of a bounce light are very important. The color needs to match the surface that is bouncing it, and the intensity will vary depending on the color. A red surface, for instance, bounces more perceptible light into an environment than a blue one.

In your scene, the sidewalk likely produces enough bounce light to be seen, especially with the level of shadow that is currently in the shot. Placing a sun light directly under the scene and pointing straight up will add bounce light to the character, but it might also add unwanted light to the rest of the scene. Add a new sun light to the scene, and disable its shadows. Again, turn the Animate Mode property off. This light should be less bright than the fill, so lower the intensity at the shortcut to 20%, and your shot may look something like Figure 11.15.

FIGURE 11.15   After adding bounce lights, the character is better integrated into the shot.

This is okay, but light is bleeding into areas of the set that should not be lit. You can easily fix this by creating a light list for the character from the bounce light and turning off its Light All Models property.

This lighting would probably do the job just fine. You may want a backlight on the character later, but that is easier to determine once the textures on the character are in place.

Once the lights are in place, consider the *quality* of the lighting. When we say quality, we are not making a general good/bad consideration. Instead, we are looking at the properties that give the light its characteristics: shadows, color, and intensity.

Shadows

We have already talked a little about shadows, focusing on z-buffers in the three-point lighting discussion, and in a way, the major aspects of the qualities that shadows can give a scene have already been covered. Go back to your vase on the table, but this time render it without shadows (see Figure 11.16).

Even this simple render shows how much shadows contribute to a shot, most especially when they are not there. This is the first quality that shadows give to light—simply being there ties elements together and creates interest. While some

FIGURE 11.16   Without the shadows, this simple render is missing something.

shots could be rendered without shadows—and there are tricks that you can use to simulate shadows—more often than not a shot will suffer without them in place.

Shadows themselves have more than a little bit of control over how light is perceived in a scene. The size, position, intensity, and softness of a light are all indicated by the shadows. Position and intensity are simple factors of light placement, but size and softness are directly related to the softness of the shadow.

While the attenuation of a light can make it look soft, if the shadows are hard-edged, the light source is perceived to be harsh, like a bare unfrosted bulb. Also, the softer the shadows are, the larger you perceive the light source to be.

In 3D, shadows are often shut off on all but the key lights in a scene to save on render times; but in real life, all sources of light contribute shadowing, even bounced light. The reason you can get away with only one real shadow-casting source so often is that most of the time the source of the light is so large that the shadows it contributes are imperceptible due to their softness.

There are two types of soft shadows in A:M: z-buffer and ray-traced. You have already looked at the basics of z-buffers and how to add them to your shot; remember that they are only available to klieg-type lights, so if you use a sun or bulb you will have to use the ray-trace option. Since z-buffer soft shadows are created by simply blurring a shadow map, the softness of the shadow is defined by the amount of blur applied to the shadow map. This is changed by the softness property, which is a percent to indicate how much blur should be applied to the map. The higher the value, the softer the shadows and the longer it will take to calculate them. Ray-traced shadows, however, are softened based on two factors: the number of rays that the renderer will use to calculate the shadows, and the physical size of the light. The number of rays cast must be greater than one in order to get any type of soft shadowing, but even as low as two will soften shadows. Beyond that, the number of rays cast increases the quality of the shadows, and not inconsequentially, the time it takes to render, not the softness. The amount of softening in ray-traced shadows is determined instead by the size attribute of the light. The larger the light, the softer your shadows will be. Ray-traced shadows generally take longer to render than z-buffers, but the trade-off is in the level of accuracy.

Ray-traced shadows are realistic and accurate down to the level of the shadow's bias property (only available when you have Show Advanced Properties on), which indicates the size of the smallest object that will cast a shadow. Shadows that are ray traced inherently start out crisp at the base of the object and get gradually softer as they get farther away from the object. They are not subject to self-shadowing and other *z*-buffer artifacts, and they are always accurately attached to the base of the casting object. However, ray-traced shadows can, and do, look grainy if the number of rays that the light uses to calculate them is too low. The more rays used, the smoother the shadows will be, and the longer the image will require to render.

Z-buffer soft shadows, on the other hand, are softened an equal amount along the entire length of the shadow and can creep away from the casting object if the light source is large. This requires the adjustment of the shadow bias (which is not the same as the ray-traced property of the same name, but is likewise an advanced property) to bring the shadow in line with the object that is casting it. Larger map sizes can also fix this problem, but larger maps take longer to render. Whether to use *z*-buffer or ray-traced shadows is a decision that must be made by weighing the realism of the shadows against the time it takes to render them, and with ray-traced soft shadows, the number of photons cast.

Other than softness, *z*-buffered shadows can be tinted. Tinting changes the color of the shadow that is cast by the light—an effective tool if you are working on a stylized piece. Used more subtly, it can be used to blend CG shadows with live-action plates or video.

You can also change the level of darkness that a shadow casts. This is great for integrating CG into live action where shadows are rarely, if ever, completely black, as well as having shadows "feel" right on objects with ambience intensity to their surfaces.

Other than merely existing, or being soft, shadows can also tell you a lot about the environment. Look at Figure 11.17. You have the same two shots rendered with the same lights in place, but the shadows in the second image tell you about the part of the shot that you *can't* see. You can immediately tell that somewhere off-screen there is a tree. This not only gives great detail to your scene, but it saves you the need to model and render a real tree to imply that one is there. Instead, the tree shadow is created with a simple black-and-white image used as a cookie-cut map on a single patch. (We look into cookie-cut and other mapping techniques in Chapter 12, "Surfacing.")

In film terms, this patch is called a *gobo,* which means go-between. If a shadow pattern is needed, say the pattern of Venetian blinds in a hard-boiled detective story, a gobo could be placed to create the needed throw pattern. In 3D, you can do the same thing to add interest to your scenes. The same effect can be accomplished with a black-and-white image applied to a light as a rotoscope. Light rotoscopes give over the intensity and color of the light to an image added to the light. To add one, simply drag and drop any image from the Images folder in the PWS (or from the library) and drop it onto a light.

FIGURE 11.17   The shadow pattern indicates things that might be off the screen.

Color and Intensity

The color and intensity of a light also tell you about the environment. We haven't the room to go deeply into the theory of color, but we can look at how color affects your scenes.

So far, all the lights in your scenes have been the default white color, but light is almost never actually white. In 3D, you tend to look at two things to determine how you should use color in your lights: temperature and style.

First, consider the temperature that you are trying to establish, and by this we don't, necessarily, follow the actual color of light temperatures. For example, the light that you see on a sunny day, is actually blue, but if you were to use a scientifically accurate blue light in a 3D environment it would be perceived by the audience as cold rather than portraying a warm, sunny day. Similarly, cooler light sources are, in strictly accurate terms, more toward the yellow/red end of the spectrum, but these colors are perceived as being warm. In the case of color, it is usually better to consider the expectations of the audience.

Secondly, consider stylistic choices in your lights. You can use very realistic colors for all your lights, but if you are rendering something that is cartoony, a more saturated key light with a contrasting fill can provide wonderful effects. Color can also be used to trigger emotional responses. A red light in the right place can indicate danger.

The intensity of a light depends a great deal on what purpose you want a given light to take in a shot, as you have examined. However, the relative intensities of key and fill lights have a great effect, not only on how a scene looks, but also on how it is perceived by the viewer. The higher the fill light's intensity in a shot, the flatter and fuller the lighting in the scene looks; the lower the fill, the higher the contrast. High-contrast lighting is, in general, more edgy and can make a shot feel dangerous or mysterious. Conversely, low-contrast lighting, where the fill is closer to the key, feels more open and welcoming. Most situation comedies on television, for instance, use low-contrast lighting.

The intensity of the key light, of course, has a great effect on how high- or low-contrast lighting is perceived. If the lighting is high key, meaning bright, with low contrast, you get the traditional sitcom lighting; but if the lighting is low key and low contrast, the mood takes on a horror movie feel. Care must be taken with low-key, low-contrast lighting, as it tends to become very dark, and details tend to get lost.

With low-key, high-contrast lighting you can achieve effects similar to those found in dramas and other serious genres of film. High-key, high-contrast lighting is most obviously used in film noir and to great effect. What combination of key and contrast you use is dictated, to a certain extent, by the subject you are lighting.

In your scene, you can use these principles to good effect. Changing the key light to a light, creamy, yellow-orange, and the fill lights to light blue-violet makes the day feel warmer and adds a sense of realism to the shot. The key light is high intensity, but you can raise it to 120% or so and then drop your fill lights to 40% or so to make the mood of the shot more intense, which would match the script better for this shot.

The next scene in this script, where Captain is fighting Polygozmo inside the warehouse, can feel more intense and anxious by simply decreasing the key and using high-contrast fill lights. The tension of the situation can also be indicated with the use of more saturated colors on the lights. Manipulating the lights in this way can increase the punch of your animation and storytelling.

Before you commit to a final lighting setup for your shot, you need to start texturing the models. The colors you use on your lights and the textures you use on your models will need to work together. Texturing is covered in depth in Chapter 12, and you should be considering the lights that you have established here as you make your textures and change any aspects of your lights that you need to make them work to accentuate your models and textures.

RADIOSITY

Radiosity in A:M is based on photon mapping techniques, where a single light source can give illumination to an entire scene through the calculation of the physical properties of light photons. You can achieve highly realistic lighting with radiosity with built-in fill and bounce light from every surface in a scene. Some of the properties for radiosity are only available when advanced properties are shown via the Global Properties panel.

The largest problem with radiosity is the time that it takes to calculate. Since it is such a processor-intensive effect, its use for animation is less than ideal, and most of what it does can be simulated with clever use of bounce lights. That being said, radiosity is a property of a choreography. By enabling it on the Properties panel, you tell A:M to make an additional set of calculations for each frame to calculate the bounce of a light from one surface to another, transferring light and color based on the surface attributes of each object. You also reveal the properties and settings that will affect how A:M handles the calculations. Finding the optimal settings for your scene can be a fair amount of trial and error.

Photons Cast indicates how many photons you want stored into the map of the scene. This may be more than the actual number of photons in a shot, as each photon is likely to be stored more than once as it bounces around a scene.

Sample Area determines the size of the area that is used to determine the radiance of each photon. Photon mapping uses techniques that involve the averaging of energy from neighboring photons. If photons from widely disparate areas are considered, the reliability of this averaging is much lower. You then restrict the area that the averaging can have by the sample area property, which is stated in values of .001 of a centimeter. For some applications (such as tight caustics) this many need to be lowered, but for the most part the 100 (or 1 cm) default works fairly well.

Photon Samples is related to the sample area property and indicates the maximum number of photons that are included in the range of the sample area. If more photons than this hit the area they are not added to the map for this area.

Intensity can be used to increase or decrease the effect of radiosity in a scene, but is primarily used only with caustics. If a scene is rendered over bright or over dark, it is more useful to adjust the lights in a scene than the intensity. Caustics, on the other hand, are not as easily tweaked with the lights in a scene and may need some additional adjustment.

Max Bounces is when a photon hits a surface in a scene it stores that hit into the photon map of the scene and then bounces off the surface back into the scene to look for more surfaces. It continues this process until it reaches the number of max bounces specified by this property. This keeps a photon from bouncing around a scene forever and helps reduce the amount of time needed to calculate radiosity.

Caustics is a toggle that turns off indirect illumination and turns on Caustics in a scene. A caustic is the refraction pattern formed by highly transparent objects such as gemstones (see Figure 11.18) or the reflective light pattern formed by mirror-like surfaces (see Figure 11.19).

Final Gathering is basically the averaging where each pixel is given a number of samples from the photon map to determine the overall illumination of that pixel. Without this turned on, the photon map will be used directly with no averaging or seeking out other information, but this is dangerous as the map is only a rough picture of the true illumination of the scene. When this is on, two other properties become available.

Sampling indicates the number of samples collected for each pixel. In general, the default 150 is more than enough, but you might need more or less depending on your scene.

Jittering introduces an amount of noise to the sampling that is performed in the Final Gathering stage. Without Jittering, the sampling will follow a regular pattern and can, in some cases, be seen in the final render.

Precompute Irradiance If Final Gathering is on (and it should almost always be on), then so should this property, as its most noticeable effect is to reduce the render time involved when you use Final Gathering.

FIGURE 11.18   Caustics from transparency.

FIGURE 11.19   Caustics from reflectivity.

The way you place your lights in a scene for radiosity you follow different rules and guidelines, from the type of lights used to how they are placed in the scene. While you can use all three types of lights with radiosity, the most efficient type of light (and the one that gives you the most control) is the klieg light, and for the most part you will want to use them exclusively when lighting for radiosity. Bulbs send photons out in all directions and may send out photons that are lost or contribute nothing of value to the scene. Lost photons are important to keep to a minimum as the time to cast them and check for bounces is also lost. Sun lights are more in line with klieg lights, except they do not behave as you would expect them to from normal rendering behaviors. In a normal render, the sun light casts light out from an infinite plain hitting all surfaces equally. In radiosity rendering, phtons are emitted only from the area of the square defined by the light. The photons that are emitted are strictly parallel to one another, which, unlike the distributed pattern of the Klieg, exhibits no power falloff, so photon power is strictly a property of the intensity and falloff properties of the light.

Which brings us to an important point of discussion: light properties and their effect on radiosity.

Width indicates the area from which photons are emitted. Tthis is more than a trick to determine shadow softness, as with ray-traced lights, but is rather an accurate area light. With bulb lights, this indicates a sphere, the surface of which emits the photons into the scene. With klieg and sun lights, this is the width of a flat disk that emits photons.

Falloff is perhaps the most important of the light properties. When you light a scene with ray-traced or *z*-buffered lights, you tend to include the entire scene inside the falloff range of the light,to ensure that your shots are not too dark. With radiosity, however, this results in extremely overlit scenes.

Look at Figure 11.20. On the left is a shot lit for regular illumination, which looks pretty good. The light is evenly distributed, and there are no real problems. Without changing any of the light positions or settings, and simply turning on Radiosity, the scene becomes extremely overlit.

FIGURE 11.20   The same scene with the same settings renders very differently when using radiosity.

In order to get the lighting to work for radiosity, the ideal situation is to have the light point into the scene, but to have its falloff set so that none of the objects in the scene fall within the falloff area of the light. The result will be a much more evenly lit, if somewhat dim, version of the shot (see Figure 11.21).

Once the falloff is set, the intensity of the light is adjusted to give the correct level of illumination to a scene. This will vary depending on the number of lights in a shot, and does not follow the same general guides set forth earlier for basic lighting. You will need to experiment to get the lighting just right for your shots (see Figure 11.22).

FIGURE 11.21   Reducing the falloff of the lights results in more even, but dimmer, illumination.

FIGURE 11.22   The light level in the scene is then simply adjusted by the intensity of the lights themselves.

The color of a light also comes into play. Darker-colored lights inherently have less energy than lights with brighter colors. This is a good way to control the amount of illumination that fill lights add to a scene, if you use fill lights at all.

Before wrapping up here, we need to discuss caustics a little bit. Although they are more related to the surface properties of a model, they also cross over into the realm of radiosity lighting. Caustics were touched on briefly earlier, but it might help to see exactly what a caustic is. Look at Figure 11.23, a render that shows both types of caustics. The sphere casts a reflective caustic, while the cube is transparent and shows refractive caustics. These caustics come from the surface properties of the objects and are only calculated with radiosity only when the Caustics property is toggled on. As mentioned before, when calculating caustics, the indirect illumination aspects of radiosity are not used. This means that caustics are used in conjunction with traditional lighting techniques rather than as a replacement for them.

FIGURE 11.23   Caustics from radiosity.

In addition to a change in the way you set up lights and the surface properties of your models, radiosity also requires that you consider what is going on in the scene when you build your sets. When discussing set building earlier, the point was made to not model or place anything that is not seen by the camera. This works well for traditional lighting techniques but is not as ideal for radiosity situations. First and foremost, make an effort to completely enclose your scenes. This means, at the very least, a dome for the sky and a plain for the ground that holds everything in the shot inside it. This will keep photons from bouncing out and being lost (remember a lost photon is lost time). If a photon is lost, it must be replaced, which adds to the render time. You also need to determine the general size of the area you are lighting as this will have a direct impact on what you need as far as how you set up the sample size and photon sample properties of your scene. Yves Poissant has made a very helpful spreadsheet available that can allow you to calculate ideal settings based on what you know of the scene. You can find it here: *http://www.ypoart.com/tutorials/Downloads/PhotonsSetup.xls*.

OTHER LIGHT PROPERTIES

Beyond controlling the color and intensity of a light, the Options group on the light's properties lets you toggle various effects and aspects of the light. You have already looked at shadows, the most common of these, so let's look at the other options and how you can use them.

You can toggle the diffuse and specular aspect of a light on a surface, which is commonly done for fill lights because multiple specular highlights can look odd. If you just wanted the specular aspect of a light (on a character's eyes, for instance), you could turn off the diffuse element.

Volumetrics is the term used to describe dust, smoke, or other particles in the air that often make rays of light visible. Toggling the Volumetric setting of a light tells A:M to simulate this effect for the selected light. This, of course, takes longer to render. Once you have turned Volumetrics on, the specific settings available for controlling it become active.

There are three settings:

Quality: Settings, obviously, affect the quality of the shot. A setting that is too low will make the volumetric not visible or will display visible banding in the effect when rendering. Adjust this setting carefully because it will take longer to render higher-quality settings.

Brightness: Indicates how much brighter than the light the brightest area of the volumetric effect will be.

Contrast: Indicates how much difference there is between the light and dark areas in the light.

Volumetrics on a light have no variance over the spread of the light. To make the effect resemble random particles of dust or realistic smoke, we must add turbulence to the light. This is done by choosing the type of turbulence that you wish to add from the Add Turbulence heading in the light's contextual menu. Turbulence and the settings are discussed in Chapter 12.

Lens flares are an artifact of real cameras, seen when a bright light or specular highlight hits a camera lens at an appropriate angle. This option is best used sparingly, if at all. Live-action cinematographers go out of their way to avoid lens flares, and so should you for the most part.

That being said, there are a few instances where lens flares are needed: Sequins on a showgirl's dress, for example, can literally sparkle with the use of lens flares. A:M has one of the most comprehensive and powerful sets of tools available for the creation and control of lens flares. Once you enable the lens flare option, the settings and properties for the flare on the light become available to you. We haven't the space to cover them all in depth here. It is recommended that you begin with one of the many preset flares and work with the settings it until you get the particular effect you are looking for.

There are three components to each flare—glows, beams, and reflections—which can be turned off or adjusted as needed. Glows are the flare itself, the bright center that indicates where the light source is. Beams are the arms that extend out in a starburst pattern around the glow. Reflections are the small reproductions of the glow that appear to come forward in the image. Each component can use different presets or be adjusted to custom settings. By default, they all use the 50mm prime default setting.

The best way to get a feel for the Lens Flare tools in A:M is to experiment, so place a single bulb in an empty choreography and get to work.

HIERARCHICAL LIGHTS

Lights can exist on their own, as you have done so far, but they can also be part of a model. This is useful in things such as cars, or flashlights, as it allows you to attach a light by simply dragging and dropping it into the model's bone hierarchy, or choosing Light from the New heading on the model's contextual menu. Lights can be at the end of any bone chain but cannot hold children.

Other than headlights and flashlights or other physical light sources, you can use hierarchical lights to your advantage with characters. An old film used in film noir and most notably in the original *Dracula*, used to emphasize the eyes and create nice prominent specular hits, was called an eye light. This was simply a light that was aimed into the actor's eyes. In a well-lit situation, the effect is hardly noticeable and brightens the highlights in the eyes, but in lower lighting, the effect can be very dramatic. You can do the same thing with your characters but to a more controlled degree. Doing so is a great way to help your characters appear more alive.

By adding two hierarchical klieg lights as children of the head bone in a model you can focus light directly into the character's eyes without affecting any other portion of the model or scene (see Figure 11.24).

FIGURE 11.24   The highlights and brightness of the character's eyes, even in this dimly lit scene, make them appear more alive.

SUMMARY

Lighting an image properly not only allows you to see the various elements in the shot, it adds to the composition and structure of the image as a whole. Good lighting can make an average scene look great, and bad lighting can make an otherwise stellar scene seem somewhat lackluster. Using the principles discussed here, you will be able to take your renderings to the next level.

12

SURFACING

In This Chapter

In this chapter, we focus on the tools and techniques used to add surface textures to your models. We examine decals and procedurals in turn, and talk a little about their pros and cons. Then we discuss practical applications to begin texturing your character and preparing it for rendering.

SURFACING BASICS

Before discussing the specifics of how to apply surfaces to your characters, you must first know a little about surfacing and how it works in 3D. Various attributes are combined to produce the visible surface properties of any object, the most prominent being the diffuse color and specularity of the surface. In real life, these properties are intrinsic in the materials that make up an object, but in 3D you have the ability to control each aspect of a surface individually. Before you can effectively surface an object, you must understand what each attribute is and what it contributes to a surface.

The diffuse surface of an object describes the base attributes that determine how light bouncing of its surface will react. This is not to be confused with reflectivity, which is covered later. It is represented by three attributes in A:M:

Diffuse color. This is the distinct base color of an object. It is the most prominent attribute of a surface. The default is white.

Diffuse falloff. The surface color of an object gets darker as it falls away from a light source, until it is completely in shadow. The diffuse falloff setting indicates how quickly the surface transitions into shadow (see Figure 12.1). The higher the falloff, the softer the transition.

FIGURE 12.1   The falloff controls the transition from the shadow side of an object to the lit side.

Ambience color. This attribute allows you to specify a color to use for the shadow side of a model when ambince is enbled on a surface. This can be used to simulate a colored fill light or to build contrast into shading.

Ambience. This attribute indicates the amount of ambient light that the shadow side of an object receives. Except for self-illuminating surfaces, this attribute should be used sparingly, if at all, as it tends to flatten out an object.

Specularity on an object is best shown by a shiny plastic or wet surface. The white highlight on a surface (actually a reflection of the light source) is called a specular highlight. In 3D, three attributes control the specularity of an object:

Specular color. Indicates the color the specular highlight on an object will be. For most objects, the default white color is correct. Some surfaces such as metals will have a different color for their specular hit.

Specular size. In real life, the size of the specular hit on a surface is determined by the size of a light source and the material that makes up the object. However, specularity in 3D is not a genuine reflection. Instead, it is a simulation of one. This attribute is used to vary the size of the specular hit on an object.

Specular intensity. The brighter the specular hit on an object, the shinier that object appears. You control the maximum value of the specularity with the intensity percentage. Note that the values for all these attributes in the A:M interface are represented as percentages, but they can all be set to a much higher value.

Every surface in 3D is smooth by default, but you can change this by applying bumps to the surface. This can be done through the application of bump map decals, BumpMat materials, or through simple roughness. All these solutions have no true effect on the underlying geometry, as you will learn later, but do affect diffuse and specular attributes of a surface.

At the base level, you have roughness, which is controlled by two attributes:

Roughness. This simply indicates the intensity to which the surface will be bumped. A high value produces high contrast areas on the surface; a low value produces a more subtle effect.

Roughness scale. Indicates how large the pattern of noise is in relation to the surface. A high value indicates that the values that shift from the high points to the low points are farther apart.

Some surfaces, such as glass, allow light to pass through, altering the waveform of the light based on the diffuse properties of the surface and the density of the material. In 3D, this is controlled by four attributes:

Transparency. Indicates to what degree a surface will allow light to pass through. A more transparent surface stops less light.

Density. Indicates how far into the surface the light can travel before the impurities and nontransparent particles stop the light from continuing. This gives a sense of depth to the surface.

Index of refraction. Indicates how the light bends as it enters and exits the transparent surface. This can make objects behind the transparent surface appear distorted. There are specific values for different materials, as is discussed later.

Translucency. Some surfaces, such as paper, only allow light to pass through them in a highly diffused manner and produce shadowing for objects between a light source and themselves. This is termed translucence.

Two surface properties indicate the amount of an environment that an object will reflect in its surface:

Reflectivity. An entirely reflective surface will not exhibit any diffuse color characteristics of its own, but will instead show only the environment around it. Lesser amounts of reflection blend the reflection of the environment with the diffuse properties of the object.

Reflection filter. This property allows you to specify how much of an underlying surface's color is factored into a reflective surface. Setting this to

100% on a 100% reflective surface keeps the full reflection of the scene, but tints it to match the underlying surface. This would normally be imposible, as 100% reflective surfaces take on all the colors and other aspects of a rendered scene. This is important when you are working with metallic surfaces such as gold.

Reflective blend. This property allows you to override the default additive nature of reflective surfaces and use a more realistic blend method instead. Additive reflections add the reflection into the base color of the surface, not completely obscuring it until the reflectivity is set to 100%. Blended reflections, on the other hand, reduce the diffuse color as the reflectivity increases. The visible difference can be difficult to notice, but primarily you will see it in the brightness of reflected items in the scene. Reflective surfaces tend to brighten as they increase in rerflectivity. With blending added, they retain their brightness as you would expect.

Reflectivity falloff. The surface of most objects is not perfectly smooth, and for reflective surfaces, the small subsurface roughness will break up the reflections that you can see. The greater the roughness of the surface, the less distinct the reflections will be. This phenomenon is more noticeable the farther an object is from the reflective surface. The falloff indicates how far away an object can be and still reflect clearly in a surface.

Radiance. When calculating radiosity, all surfaces are considered reflective. This is how photons travel around the scene. But some—not all—surfaces reflect light in the same way. This property allows you to adjust the intensity that photons are reflected, either contributing less or more to the illumination of a scene.

Glow. This property enables a glowing "halo" effect around an object. It is often used to give sources of illumination (such as lightbulbs) the appearance of brightness. The color of the glow is determined by the diffuse color of the object. The intensity is controlled by the ambience of the object, and the glow radius is controlled by the Choreography property of the same name.

Toon lines. This property group holds the settings used when the Toon render is enabled on the camera. You can set the thickness, color, and other attributes of the lines here.

Toon shading. This property group holds the settings used for surface coloring and falloff when the Toon render is enabled on the camera. You can change the type of falloff and set up custom gradients to handle shading.

Diffuse Render Shader. This allows you to choose a plug-in render shader to change the way A:M handles diffuse surface shading. If you select one of the installed plug-ins from the drop-down menu, the properties for that shader become available here as well. We discuss shaders more in Chapter 14, "Rendering and Compositing."

Specular Render Shader. Similar to Diffuse Render Shader, this presents a drop-down menu from which you can select any of the installed specular render shaders you may have. This gives you the ability to override the default way A:M handles specular highlights in a render.

Ambience Render Shader. As you may guess, this property allows you to select any installed ambience render shader plug-ins that you may have. In the exact same manner that diffuse and specular shaders work this allows you to override the default way in which A:M handles ambient render calculations.

There are also specialized rendering attributes and surface properties that you can achieve with complex materials, but all surfaces exhibit most or all of these basic properties. These properties can be applied to a model as decal images or procedural materials.

A:M has two basic ways to apply attributes to a surface, and there are pros and cons to each technique. The most significant factor you should consider in determining which method you use is you. Every artist will have his or her own preference, and neither method is superior to the other. Most of the time, you will use a mix of the two techniques.

DECAL IMAGES

Decal is the term given to a bitmap image applied to a model to create surface attributes. They are generated in a program outside of Animation:Master, such as Adobe® Photoshop®. Decals can be taken from photographs, scanned objects, or custom-painted images. Many software packages can create and edit bitmap images, and almost any of them will do the job for you. The only requirements are that your program be capable of exporting to a format that A:M can read (PNG, TGA, EXR, JPG, and so on) and capable of producing an alpha channel.

Once you create an image, import it onto A:M in the same manner that you brought in the rotoscopes for modeling. In fact, there is no practical difference between images used for rotoscopes and those used for decals. You can use any image for either, or both, in A:M.

ON THE CD

The intended use of a decal is the greatest dictator of what it should look like and how you should create it. The surface properties that a decal sets are based on the type of property of the image. Open the DecalBasics.prj project from the CD-ROM. You have a simple sphere with a map decaled on to it. Under the decal folder find the example_decal image and select it. The properties for this image let you indicate what type of decal this is and what attributes it will apply to your surface. By default, it is used as a color image, which simply maps the colors from each pixel of the image to the surface of the object.

Once a decal has been applied, it remains stuck to the surface of the model. You can see this by moving control points in the model and doing a quick render (or watching in real-time shaded mode with decals visible) to see that the decal moves with the surface as you would expect. There is a way to change how a decal sits on a surface called UV editing that is discussed later.

The default color type can be changed to make the decal affect other aspects of a model's surface properties.

Clicking on the property will bring up a pop-up menu that lists all the possible types:

- Color
- Transparency
- Bump
- Specular size
- Specular intensity
- Diffuse
- Reflectivity
- Ambiance Intensity
- Cookie-cut
- Displacement
- Fractal
- Next Map Factor
- Other…
- Normal

Color changes the diffuse color of the model based on the color of the pixels in the image map. There are ways to limit which pixels on a map are applied to a model, giving you the ability to map something other than a rectangle on a surface. If an image is 24-bit, meaning that it contains only three channels of data, one for each of the colors red, green, and blue, then you can specify that an RGB color be ignored. This is similar to the color keying process that films use to place actors in virtual sets, or that your local weather reporter uses to stand in front of the changing map. If an image is saved in a 32-bit format, indicating that it has an additional channel of data, this channel does not display a color, but rather indicates the opacity of each pixel. This is called an *alpha channel*. The alpha channel lets you gradually fade out a decal or mask complex shapes easily without having to worry about an edge artifact from key colors. If you need to mask a decal, do it with an alpha channel. Figure 12.2 shows an example of a color image type.

Transparency varies the transparency of a surface from transparent to opaque based on the luminance values or alpha channel of the decal. The easiest way to think of this is with a simple black-and-white image. All the areas in the image that are white will be opaque, and all the areas that are black will be transparent. This will not change the index of refraction for a surface, only the amount of transparency. If the black-and-white information is stored in an alpha channel, it works in exactly the same way, with the white areas of the alpha channel being opaque and the black areas being transparent. Using an alpha channel allows you to embed the transparency information into the same decal that you use to do color mapping. Figure 12.3 shows an example of transparency mapping.

Bump mapping simulates irregularities on the surface of the model, allowing you to create the appearance of a much more complex surface without the need

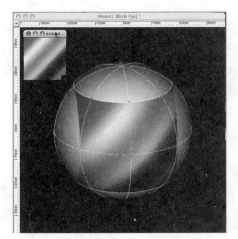

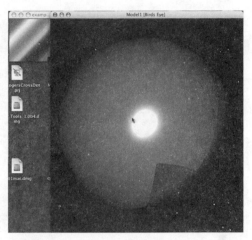

FIGURE 12.2   This map was decaled with the default type color.

FIGURE 12.3   A decal applied as a transparency map.

to model explicit detail. This creates shadow and highlight areas on the model, but does not alter the profile or geometry of the surface, making it good for small details, but large perturbations need to be either modeled or created with displacement mapping. Bump maps use grayscale images to indicate the way light should react to the surface: A light value indicates that the surface is higher, and a dark value indicates the surface is lower. A 50% gray value indicates no change. Rather than using an alpha channel or a key color, you can control the effect of a bump map by controlling the gray values in the image. Figure 12.4 shows an example of a bump map.

Specular Size maps change the size of the specular hit based on grayscale values. A white area will have a larger specular size than a dark area. This can be useful for changing how light reacts on a surface. It definitely is useful for areas like faces on characters where the nose and lips might have a tight specular highlight, and the cheeks might have a broad highlight. Figure 12.5 shows an example of a specular size map.

Specular Intensity works in much the same way as Specular Size, but instead changes the *intensity* of the specular hit. These are often used in conjunction with specular size maps. Figure 12.6 shows an example of a specular intensity map.

Diffuse maps change the diffuse falloff for an area based on grayscale values. This often makes the underlying surface look darker where the map is most intense. But the only real darkening is because the light is falling to shadow faster; the actual color of the surface is unaffected. Diffuse maps are often used to add dirt or grime to a surface, or to vary the look of a surface with a repeating decal to make patterns from repetition less visible. Figure 12.7 shows an example of a diffuse map.

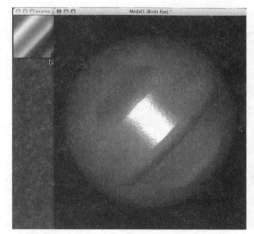

FIGURE 12.4   A decal applied as a bump map.

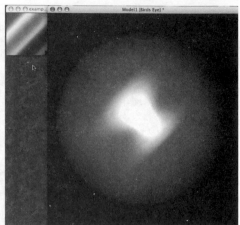

FIGURE 12.5   A decal applied as a specular size map.

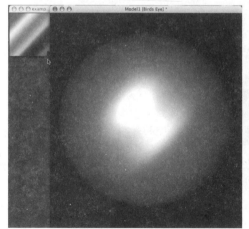

FIGURE 12.6   A decal applied as a specular intensity map.

FIGURE 12.7   A decal applied as a diffuse map.

Reflectivity maps change the reflectivity of a surface based on grayscale values. A completely white value will be 100% reflective, where a black value will be nonreflective, with the gray values being somewhere in between. This is used to make specific areas of a model reflective or to vary the reflectivity across a surface. Figure 12.8 shows an example of a reflectivity map.

Ambiance Intensity maps, sometimes called luminosity maps, increase the level of ambience based on grayscale values. White areas in the map are 100% ambient, while black areas exhibit no ambience. This is useful for controlling how ambience is applied to surfaces such as lightbulbs, which might be self-illuminating at the top but not at the base. Figure 12.9 shows an example of an ambience map.

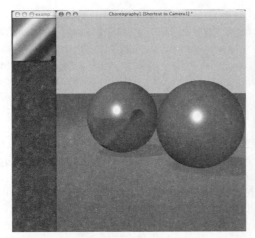

FIGURE 12.8   A decal applied as a reflectivity map.

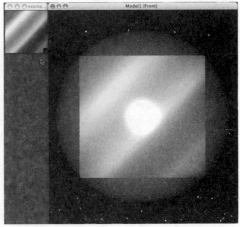

FIGURE 12.9   A decal applied as an ambience map.

Cookie-cut maps use the alpha or key color on an image to cut away portions of geometry. A classic example is a leaf: Rather than model all the edges and surfaces of a leaf, you can apply a cookie-cut map to a single patch and create a reasonable approximation of a leaf. For complex trees, this is a very effective way to create leaves without overburdening the geometry. Figure 12.10 shows an example of a cookie-cut map.

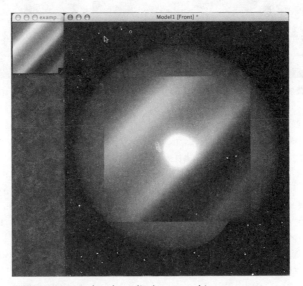

FIGURE12.10   A decal applied as a cookie-cut map.

Displacement maps work exactly like bump maps, with the exception that they displace the actual geometry, so that the profile and cast shadows of a model actually show the deformations. Displacement mapping is useful for creating detail that must be seen in profile or in the shadows of an object. A:M uses a technology called pixel displacement to deform a mesh. This technology differs from most displacecment techniques in that it does not require a dense mesh to produce detailed deformations; rather, the detail of the deformation is based upon the resolution of the map applied to the model. A one-patch surface and a 50-patch surface will render the same regardless, given the same displacecmcnt map. This works very well with A:M's traditionally lightweight geometry. Figure 12.11 shows an example of a displacement map.

Fractal maps are identical to displacement maps, with the exception that they shade the surface with facets rather than smoothly. Figure 12.12 shows an example of a fractal map.

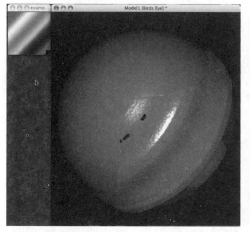

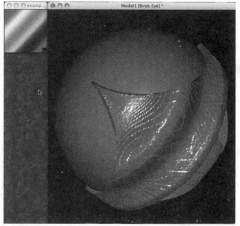

FIGURE 12.11   A decal applied as a displacement map.

FIGURE 12.12   An example of a fractal map.

Next Map Factor mapping uses grayscale maps to adjust the effect of the next map in the decal container. Areas that are white are used as is; areas that are black are not used at all. This can be useful when you wish to use a map for multiple areas on a model that precludes the inclusion of an alpha channel.

Other... gives you the ability to drive other types of properties with a map, most notably hair properties. We go into greater depth on this and the types or properties that can be modified in Chapter 13, "F/X."

Normal mapping can be thought of simply as a higher-resolution bump map. Where you can indicate that a surface moves up or down with a bump map, a normal map allows you to adjust the direction a normal faces at any point on a surface. This allows you to build in a great amount of detail in areas with less dense geometry. Painting normal maps by hand is, however, less straightforward than a bump map, as each color channel has a different effect. There are, how-ever, ways to convert simple bump maps to make them normal maps. Figure 12.13 shows an example of a normal map.

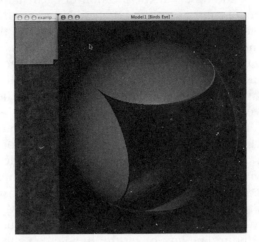

FIGURE 12.13   An example of a normal map.

Combining these image types lets you create almost any surface attribute you might want. While looking at the properties of the image, note that the image it-self is a property group. This allows you to select any image that is in the project to use in the decal, letting you change the image with a new one, without having to reposition and stamp the decal. You can also specify if the decal repeats or not. Expanding the disclosure triangle for the image property reveals the repeat group and the seamless property. The repeat group allows you to specify how many times the decal repeats in the *x*- and *y*- axis of the image, not to be confused with the axis of the model window. The seamless property will flip the image as it re-peats, so that the edges align. This makes the edges seamless, but makes patterns in the images more easily recognizable. The better option is to create a seamlessly tileable image in your graphics-editing program before importing it into A:M.

The percentage property on the image allows you to adjust how much the image affects the model. This varies depending on the type of decal that the image is. For color decals, for example, a value of less than 100% allows the underlying properties of the model to show through, while a higher value oversaturates the colors. This is an animateable property and can be driven by relationships.

Map Export Method is an advanced property used to determine the default method for handling image maps when exporting a model to a polygonal format, such as OBJ. Reference original maps will have the new exported file look to the original image for texturing, while the Include in Patch maps option will generate a new map that will hold texture data for each patch in it.

A number of methods are used to applying a decal to a mesh, but the basic procedure is the same. First, add the decal to the model, then position the decal in the workspace window. When you are satisfied with the decal's position, apply it. The application of the decal creates a stamp. Each decal can hold any number of stamps, and each decal can hold numerous images. All the images in a decal are applied to the model at the location of each stamp. This allows you to position and stamp a color image, and then add bump or diffuse images to the same decal and be certain that they are aligned exactly with the color map. This is especially useful for bump features that match color details.

The easiest way to add a decal to a model is to have the image that you want to use in the project already. Bring any image into the current project by double-clicking the images folder in the PWS. An Open File dialog will let you import any image you like. Once the image is in the project, adding it to a model is a simple matter of dragging and dropping the image from the PWS into the Model work-space window. When A:M asks if the image is a rotoscope or a decal, choose Decal and click OK. A semitransparent version of the decal should appear in the work-space window, allowing you to position it anywhere on your model you like.

The image that appears and the level of transparency are set in the applica-tion method group of properties for the decal. Move and scale the image in the Model window, the same as you did for rotoscopes, by clicking and dragging in-side the bounding box or by the handles on the bounding box. You may also move and turn the model view to apply the decal from any angle you like, even a bird's-eye view. If the image is not oriented the direction you want, flip it hori-zontally or vertically by selecting the appropriate direction from the Flip heading in the contextual menu for the decal.

When it is where you want it, bring up the contextual menu for the image and choose Apply. If this is the last stamp you want to make, click outside the bounding box to deselect the decal. If you accidentally deselect the image before you have applied it, or wish to create more stamps later, simply bring up the decal item's contextual menu in the PWS and choose Position. You may also recall the position used to create any stamp by selecting Recall/View position from the stamp's contextual menu. This is useful for adjusting the position of a decal that is only slightly off.

There are three ways that an image can be applied to a model's surface:

- Planar
- Spherical mapping
- Cylindrical mapping

You can set the application method on the decal's properties, or you can bring up the contextual menu of the image in the workspace window and choose from the Application Method heading.

By default, a decal is applied with the planar application method, meaning that the pixels are mapped straight down onto the surface from the location you applied it to the model. This works fine for most images, but for some surfaces you might need a different type of application. Spheres, for instance, will exhibit distortion at the edges of the map as the surface curves away.

The other two application methods are designed to eliminate these artifacts. Spherical mapping applies the image to the surface of the model from all directions, very similar to a globe. Cylindrical mapping wraps the decal around the object; it can pinch on the tops and bottoms of the model. Figure 12.14 shows the same image mapped to a cube with each of these methods.

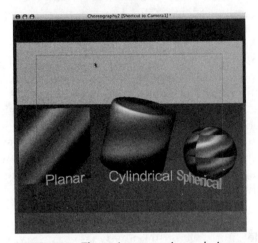

FIGURE 12.14 The various mapping techniques.

When you are creating decals for application on your models, your biggest concern is the resolution of the map. If, in an animation, the camera gets close to the surface, the decal needs to be larger. As a rule of thumb, the decal needs to be at least twice the pixel size of the intended final render. If it is applied to an exceptionally large model, it also needs to be larger. Decals also require a lot of disk space. An ambitious project can have hundreds of megabytes (MB) in decal images.

The other type of surfacing in A:M avoids both these problems, but introduces some limitations of its own.

PROCEDURAL MATERIALS

A procedural material is a texture that is generated by the computer at the time a model is rendered. It places patterns of attributes on the surface of the model based on an algorithm. These allow you to control every aspect of a model's surface without an image map.

In A:M, procedural textures come in two flavors: materials and patch colors. The difference between the two is a matter of degree only, as the same attributes used to define a patch color are used to define the nodes in a combiner.

Patch colors, are also known as base or group colors in A:M, and are applied directly to the model or to groups of patches within a model. When you are just starting to lay out the textures on a model, patch colors can help break down and separate surfaces, as well as tell you what you haven't done. Every model has at least one patch color already applied to it; this is defined by the Surface properties group for the model. We have already discussed what each of these parameters represent, and the fastest way to understand what they do is to adjust them and do test renders on a model.

Each named group in a model also has a set of surface properties that can be adjusted independently. These surface properties are confined to the patches that make up a particular group and are applied to the model in a hierarchical fashion. This means that if two groups contain the same patches, the group farther down the list of groups will override the attributes of all groups underneath it.

This is an important concept to understand about Animation:Master's approach to procedural textures. As you will see, all textures are hierarchical in this manner. Even when you apply multiple materials onto a group or model with simple color attributes this results in a complete change, but combiners can be constructed so that attributes from lower in the stack can still be seen.

Materials can be simple attributes or they can consist of combiners and others. You create new materials by double-clicking the Materials folder in the PWS. When you make a new material the Material window opens with a sphere showing the current state of your surface. This can be useful for getting started with a material, but more often than not, until you see the material applied to an individual model, it is difficult to know what changes you need to make to the material.

A new material is created with a single attribute node. This node contains the same surface attributes that patch colors do, but you can change this base attribute into any number of combiners. Do this by bringing up the node's contextual menu and choosing the desired material type from the Change Type To heading. There are three subgroups of node types: combiners, particle systems, and plug-ins. Most of what you do will be accomplished with the first and third group. Particle systems is covered in Chapter 13.

There are four types of combiners. Each will mix two attribute nodes to make one surface. The methods used to mix these attributes vary based on the type of combiner.

Checker combiners break 3D space into a series of stacked cubes. Each attribute node under the checker combiner is applied to alternating cubes in the pattern (see Figure 12.15).

The size and 3D position of the cubes are changed with the Translate and Size properties of the checker combiner. The Blur property softens the transition between the two attribute nodes by blurring them into one another. If you want the texture to be slabs instead of cubes, changing the size of an axis to 0 will make the texture infinite in that axis. For horizontal slabs, a size of 0 in the x- and z-axes produces layers of attributes (see Figure 12.16).

Spherical combiners break the 3D space of the material up into a series of concentric spheres. When you create a spherical combiner, the Preview window will look like nothing has happened. This is because the shape used to preview the material is a sphere. Changing the Translate properties of the spherical combiner will make the attribute nodes visible (see Figure 12.17).

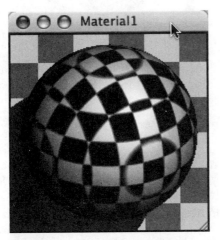

FIGURE 12.15   The checker combiner.

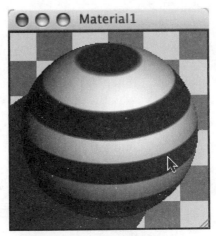

FIGURE 12.16   Changing the size of two axes to 0 makes infinite slabs instead of checkered cubes.

The Blur, Translate, and Size properties for the spherical combiner work in the same way as the Checker properties of the same names. Additionally, you can change the thickness of each ring with the Ring 1 size and Ring 2 size properties. One of the most common uses for the spherical combiner is to simulate wood grain. By changing the y size to 0% you get concentric cylinders instead of spheres, which simulates wood rings inside a tree, making a perfect starting point for wood grain (see Figure 12.18).

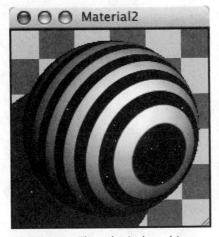

FIGURE 12.17   The spherical combiner.

FIGURE 12.18   Changing the y size to 0% gives you a starting point for realistic wood textures.

Gradient combiners make a smooth transition from one attribute node to the next. There are two ways you can specify for it to blend: from the edges of the shape to a specific center spot, or linearly from one 3D location to another. The first method is controlled by the Edge Threshold property for the gradient combiner. Setting the start or end location to anything other than 0,0,0 changes the way the gradient falls off to the edges of the object. If you change the start or end location of the gradient without specifying an edge threshold, the gradient holds the first attribute until the start location, and then smoothly transitions to the second attribute up to the end position and holds that attribute (see Figure 12.19).

Edge threshold gradients are used to give a surface an anisotropic, or varied (depending on the angle of view), quality; we discuss this concept later in this chapter.

Turbulence, the fourth combiner category, is a group of seven combiners that mix two attributes in semirandom noise patterns. We say semirandom because getting different results with a turbulence combiner with the same numbers in it would be frustrating, and no two frames ever render the same way. Instead, turbulence materials generate a texture that appears random but look identical with the same set of inputs every time it is rendered. The differences between types of turbulences are largely aesthetic ones, and those same aesthetics are generally what recommends one turbulence over another.

Three types of turbulence—cellturb, grid turb, and extended grid turb—deviate from this basic pattern, so let's look at them first.

Cellturb is a turbulence material designed to look like organic cellular structures (see Figure 12.20).

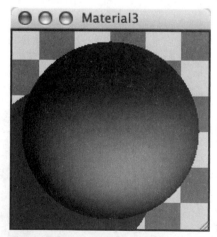

FIGURE 12.19   A gradient combiner.

FIGURE 12.20   Cellturb can generate organic-looking cell patterns.

The translate and scale attributes work the same here as they do for the other combiners. The amplitude and octaves properties are common to all turbulence combiners. Without getting too technical, amplitude will weight the value of the two attribute nodes of the combiner. The lower the amplitude, the more weight the second attribute will exhibit; the greater the amplitude, the more the first attribute will add to the overall material. This is not a linear transition. Amplitude of 0 will, for instance, be completely composed of the second attribute, while amplitude of 6000 will still exhibit some of both attributes. Octaves are the level of complexity the boundaries between each attribute will exhibit.

The other attributes are specific to cellturb. Cellular noise determines the type of pattern that the turbulence will exhibit. Each can be considered a different turbulence combiner and has a unique look. Threshold changes the way the second attribute falls off from the center of the cell to the cell's edge. A higher threshold will create a sharper distinction at the cell boarders. Point density indicates how many cells the turbulence will put into a given area. Euclidean distance is a toggle to change the way that the material computes the falloff from one attribute to the other (see Figure 12.21). With these attributes, you can achieve many different effects with cellturb, but it is one of the more computationally expensive procedural textures available.

Gridturb creates a regular pattern of gridlines, rather than a random or organic turbulence (see Figure 12.22).

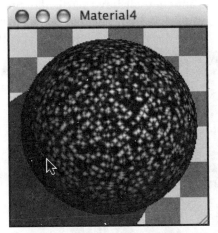

FIGURE 12.21   The Euclidean distance changes the falloff of the cells.

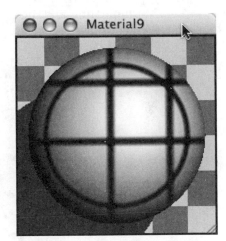

FIGURE 12.22   A grid turbulence texture.

Translate, size and amplitude behave the same as the properties of the same names from cellturb. Grid type changes the orientation and application logic of the grid. The default type X + Y + Z produces a 3D grid that produces the same basic pattern of cubes as a checker combiner. X + Y produces a 2D grid projected along the z-axis infinitely. Sphere map applies the grid in the same manner a spherical map of a grid would be. Consider it as if it were the longitude and latitude lines marked on a globe. Cylindrical map applies the texture in the same manner a cylindrical image map would be.

Octaves, in the case of grid turbulence, change the scale of the tiles in the grid pattern; a higher value makes the squares smaller. Grid size changes the thickness of the gridlines.

Extended Grid Turb takes the same basic concept of the Grid Turb and exposes more control, allowing you to drive more options. It starts with the same basic regular grid pattern and has the same basic Traslate, Size, and Amplitude properties.

Grid Type begins the deviations from the form, where the types of grid are based on the same projection methods as decals: cubic, spherical and cylindrical. Each of these methods is used in different situations, most often to match a particular type of geometry.

Following the grid type, you can toggle the inclusion of each of the axes of grid lines, turning them off or on as you need them. Contained within each axes property group there are three subproperties. Size scales the entire grid up, making the spacing and thinckness of the lines greater. Ratio increases the amount of space used for grid line as opposed to the filling space between. It is visually seen as an expansion of the thickness of the grid line. Blur, as you might suspect, softens the edge of the grid line; A higher number can give a very soft effect to the grid.

The other types of turbulence are based on the same set of properties, but applied to different algorithms. With names like fBm and fractal sum, they can seem intimidating and incomprehensible, but they all have particular properties that might suit a given texture. Start by examining them side by side (see Figure 12.23).

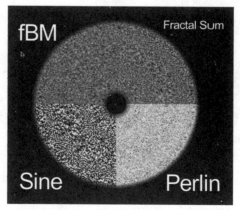

FIGURE 12.23   Each type of turbulence has its own look.

As you can see, each turbulence has a distinct look all its own. The sine turbulence, for instance, has a high-contrast splotchy look that, scaled up large enough, can make great cloud textures. fBm turbulence has a soft, layered look that works well for tree bark. Fractal sum is a softer variation of the Sine turbulence material. It can be useful for subtle organic textures like skin. Perlin is a vivid, high-contrast turbulence that resembles a plate of worms or pasta. At large scales it makes an excellent base for marble textures.

How and where you use each of these textures is a very subjective issue, and as you grow used to the properties of each texture, you will find more uses for them than you had imagined possible. These combiners are all very simple in their use. All four have the same properties that perform the same functions in each. Translate and scale behave the same as the properties discussed with checker and spherical combiners. Amplitude and octaves are the same as associated with cellturb.

Turbulence can be used as a material combiner, or it can be applied to any other combiner. For instance, if you have a checker combiner and you wanted to break up the regularity of the edges, or make them imperceptible as checkers, you can bring up the checker combiner's contextual menu, and choose a type of turbulence from the Add Turbulence heading (see Figure 12.24). Varying levels of added turbulence can create very subtle and realistic texture effects.

The real power of procedural textures comes into play when you start to nest combiners inside of combiners. A checker material, for instance, is created by changing a single attribute node into a checker combiner, which in turn has two attribute nodes, each of which is capable of becoming a combiner. You can layer combiner upon combiner upon combiner in this fashion until you have the complexity that you will need (see Figure 12.25).

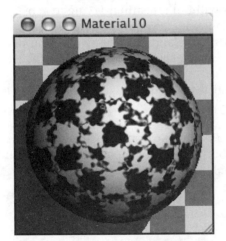

FIGURE 12.24   The regular pattern of this combiner was broken up with the addition of fBm turbulence.

FIGURE 12.25   This wood combiner uses nested spherical and turbulence combiners to great effect.

You can also layer materials onto a model by leaving one or more attributes untouched. When dealing with combiners, an untouched, or "virgin," attribute is one whose properties are listed as "not set." Any property that is not set will allow underlying properties of the same type to show through. If you have a red diffuse color on a group and apply a material with a checker combiner that sets one attribute to blue and the second attribute is left not set, the result will be a red and blue checker pattern on the model. This works for all attribute properties.

Other than combiners, you have a set of plug-in material types available with A:M. These plug-ins provide easy ways to get effects that would be difficult or impossible to achieve with standard combiners alone. There is a brief look at all the plug-ins that ship with A:M at the end of this chapter.

WHEN TO MAP, WHEN TO MAT

With these options at hand, which method should you use to texture your models? Procedurals and texture maps have pros and cons to their usage, but the most important consideration is what you are most comfortable using. In general, you can look at the strengths of each method and show some examples of what each type of texturing does best.

Decals are the best choice for specific detail, such as signs, letters, and bumps on skin. The data in them is easy to control and manipulate; placing a spot at a very specific place is a simple task. Trying to do something so specific with procedural materials, while not impossible, is more labor intensive.

Procedural textures are the best choice for organic surfaces, such as wood, stone, and skin tones. They do well with this because they are made from fractal patterns and can cover large areas without repeating. Trying to achieve similar effects with decals requires tiling images or exceptionally large files. Procedurals are also capable of altering surface attributes and creating effects that decals cannot, anisotropic surfaces, for instance, which have different attributes when viewed flat than when viewed edge-on.

Beyond these areas, they tend to be equally well suited to most tasks, and how you prefer to work should be your guide. In most cases, though, we use both types in our texturing.

For an example, look at Captain and start surfacing him. Most surfacing begins with base colors, separating out portions of the model visually and laying in the basic attributes you might need.

TUTORIAL CHARACTER TEXTURING

Open up the captain you modeled and rigged earlier, or simply open the Captian_Start.mdl model from the models folder on the CD-ROM.

ON THE CD

When laying in the base colors for a model, start the process by creating named groups that have similar, or the same, texture applied to them. Most of the time, these groups are connected in a single mesh. In Modeling mode, start with the obvious groups like the Pants. Select one point on the Pants and press the / (backslash) key to select all connected control points. While they are selected, change the name of the new "untitled" group in the PWS to Pants or something memorable like that.

To rename a group (or any item in the PWS), select it and press the F2 key. This changes the name to an editable text area.

Once it has been named, invert the selection and lock or hide the control points. This keeps the group you just created from being selected and makes singling out other portions of the mesh easier. Proceed the same way, grouping the helmet, skin areas, and the various portions of the shoes. Once you are done, your PWS might look something like Figure 12.26.

FIGURE 12.26   Named groups give you the foundation to create full texturing.

Note that these groups could have been established during modeling, and you might find that easier.

Once the groups are established, assign simple patch colors to them to get started: green on the cloth portions of the uniform, black for the boot soles, and so on. You will be replacing most of these with finalized textures later, but this roughs things in for you so that you see what you have to work with. A common technique is to put very bright placeholder colors on these groups, so that you know what you have done and what you have not.

The base skin color is a good place for a procedural material, so start there. Create a new material, and drag it onto the group you created for the skin tones on the character. It is recommended that you close the material preview window and work with progressive renders on the model for most materials. This speeds up changes to the material; you do not have to wait for the Material window to refresh. Texturing a surface requires at least some basic lighting be in place, and preferably a rough approximation of the lighting that will be used in the final render. Until you see how a texture looks under lit conditions, you are really just shooting in the dark. The Model window has lighting of a sort, but it is light from the same angle that you are viewing the model. This is insufficient and does not show the true effects of specularity, bump mapping, or a number of other surfacing techniques. Even if you use the default choreography, you have a better idea of what your textures are doing.

So, put the captain into a choreography, but keep the Model window open, as you will be moving between these two windows frequently as you work. Hide the entire model, except the points that are flesh, and get to work on the base material.

Skin tones on humans exhibit a lot of really complex shading that is difficult to achieve in 3D. New algorithms to simulate subsurface light scattering are just now being developed, but you can use the tools that are already at your disposal to simulate many of the intricacies in skin. Start with an edge threshold gradient material. Remember, an edge threshold changes the attributes of a surface dependent on the angle of viewing. With this, you can change the surface of the model to be slightly different at the edges than it is facing you. This is great for simulating the way light plays on skin tones.

Start by making the attributes of the gradient simple colors that leave no doubt what part of the surface they are shading. A very bright green and a very bright red work well. You won't be keeping these colors, but they will help you adjust the attenuation of the gradient material. The edge threshold on a gradient material starts at 0%, so move it up to 50% or so and do a progressive render in the choreography. What you are looking for is the surface to be predominately one attribute with a slight halo of the second attribute at the edges.

You may need to increase or decrease the edge threshold slightly to get the effect on your model. In the example, a little experimentation arrived at 35% being a good amount. It is important to say here that you are not working with absolutes. The numbers and values of these textures are all based on personal tastes and preferences; to a certain extent, the types of combiners and attributes used are subjective.

With the attenuation set, adjust the properties of the material. Start with the main attribute. A solid color on the skin makes the character look very cartoony and might now be what you want here, so use a turbulence combiner to create the variations in the flesh tones. Cellturb tends to work really well for this type of surface. With a little work, you can achieve anything from freckles to rotting zombie skin. Go ahead and change the first attribute to a cellturb combiner.

We are going for a slightly freckled, but subtle, skin color. Start with two bright marker colors. Use these colors to tell you what the changes you are making are doing to the surface. If you start with the subtle colors you intend to use at the end of this process, it is harder to see your changes. After some experimentation with the cellturb parameters, you might find that the following settings generate what you are looking for:

- Setting an amplitude of 10% pushes the coloration of the combiner to a more subtle blended level. This will be even more so when the final colors are in place.
- Changing the cellular noise pattern to ridged gives a nice pattern with distinct edges that remain irregular enough to simulate freckles.
- Raising the threshold to 80% pushes the freckles far enough apart to look more natural.
- Increasing the octaves to 2 gives more edge detail on the freckles. An octave of 1 would probably do just as well, but that is a matter of personal preference.
- Leaving the point density at 100.
- Turning off the Euclidean distance setting will give you freckles that are more distinct.

These settings were all arrived at with experimentation based on an understanding of how the cellturb combiner functions. You might find a set of attributes that works better, or you might prefer a different combiner altogether.

ON THE CD

Once the texture places the placeholder colors where you want them, change them to more accurate flesh tones. The small spots should be a reddish-brown color, and the main shade should be a pale pinkish/orange. Look at the finished Captain_v19.mdl model on the CD-ROM to get an idea of some working attributes.

Now you can turn your attention to the second attribute on the gradient combiner. Its purpose is to soften the material as it goes around the edges of the character, simulating the natural translucency of skin. The limited amount you see this texture doesn't justify the use of the cellturb combiner, so a simple surface color will probably do the job. The red color that you assigned as a placeholder actually has a nice warmth to it, but is far too pronounced. Simply back the intensity of this color off to get some fairly decent rersults. Clicking the color chip brings up your system color picker. Use it to lighten the color and lower the saturation until you are happy with the difference between the old and new colors.

A progressive render of the character at this point should reveal a decent skin tone. If you wanted to, you could break down the solid masses in the cellturb by changing the attribute to a turbulence combiner. The surface could be broken down in this manner indefinitely. For this character though, this is a good skin tone.

Once the skin tone is right, turn your attention to the next group that makes sense. The next largest group seems to be the cloth, so work on that next.

Again, start with creating a simple material and dropping it onto all the groups that should be cloth (such as the pants and shirt). Cloth is another place where an edge threshold gradient can give extra dimension to a surface. The parts that fall off from the camera on real cloth tend to have loose fibers that while not distinctly visible on their own catch light and give a soft, almost glowing edge to many types of cloth. Start by changing the initial attribute to a gradient as you did for the skin, and set the Edge Threshold property to 50%.

After giving the attributes placeholder colors, do a test render. It's fairly likely that 50% is too much of a threshold. Back it down and test render it until you are happy with the look. This example goes as far as 10%. Now anaylize the type of surface you are trying to make and decide what attributes it needs. Is this to be a rough cloth or something like silk? Knowing the captain's love for rough-and-tumble combat, it's not very likely he'd opt for silk or velour. It's far more likely he'd go for a nice, sturdy cotton, or the nearest high-tech equivalent. It's also pretty likely that his jumpsuit is not out-of-the-package clean. Take that into account as you work. Start by changing the first attribute of your gradient to a fractal sum noise to get large color variation across the surface. Set the attributes of the turbulence to be placeholders, and do a test render. You should have something similar to Figure 12.27.

FIGURE 12.27   The placeholders on your turbulence give you a good idea of what the material is doing.

It's pretty noisy, not really what you want, but you can make some adjustments to the turbulence: Set the amplitude to 40 to tone down the contrast between the two nodes. They will still be a bit noisy, though. Scaling the material up to 600% can change this, and you should have a more subltle pattern. Not great, but when we set the final colors there will be less contrast to draw attention to the noise. Go ahead and set the colors you want to use for the captain's jumpsuit. We've gone with a daring little red number, but you can use anything you like. The trick is to keep the values of both the nodes fairly close to one another, which gives just a little sublte variation on the surface color without standing out as noise.

Once you have the main color of the jumpsuit set, it is time to deal with the other node of the edge threshold gradient. You want this to simulate the light that catches on the edge of cloth as it falls off, and it can also serve as a way to break the character out from any background. The best route is generally to go with a contrasting color (green in this case) and set it to a very light value.

With the color aspects of the cloth set up, you can focus on the other aspects of it. You want the other aspects of the cloth to apply equally, without regard for the edge threshold. You could set up a second material to do this, but it is just as easy—and simpler when it comes time to keep track of your material—to do it inside the same material as the color aspects.

Right-click on the material in the PWS and choose New Atrribute from the contextual menu. You find that A:M adds a new attribute node to your material (see Figure 12.28)

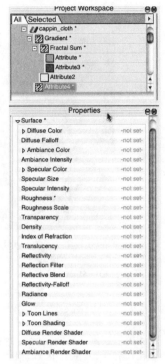

FIGURE 12.28   You can add a new attribute to store other aspects of the surface.

This attibute contains the elements of the surface that do not relate directly to its color. Start with the diffuse falloff. Cloth, like all rough surfaces, has a smoother grade from light to shadow. This is due to self-shadowing from the roughness of the surface so we can raise the falloff to 150% to start giving this material a cloth feel.

The surface should also have specularity, you don't have to set the color since the default (white) is what you want in this case, but the size and intensity are important. A high intensity and small size make the surface seem glossy, which for rough cloth is not at all what you want. You want exactly the opposite: a wide specular size and a low intensity that contribute to the rough feeling of the surface. Set the specular size to around 500% and the intensity to about 10%. Do a test render. If it feels too shiny, increase the size and lower the intensity some more.

The final step is to introduce roughness to the surface. This makes sense as you have discussed how cloth is a rough surface already. But be careful when you set this attribute: Roughness that is too small can, and will, shimmer when it is animated. With a little exprimentation you might find that a roughness of 5% and a scale of 85% provide enough breakup to the highlight without introducing noise (see Figure 12.29). As far as the actual cloth bump, that is addressed when you start decaling the character.

FIGURE 12.29   After you add roughness to the cloth, the specular highlights are more subtle.

Now you proceed from a soft, rough material to a hard, smooth material, specifically the plastic that makes up the surface of Captain's helmet. These surfaces are highly polished space-age plastics that can take—and likely have taken—a lot of punishment. Focus on just getting the shiny space-age part now, and adress the punishment later when you start working on the decals. Create a new material, and apply it to the groups that will have the plastic surface, just as you did for the previous two groups.

This material is much simplier than the ones you have already made, as plastic is one of the surfaces that 3D rendering does exceedingly well. Use a simple attribute to provide the surface. First, assign a base color. You can use any color you like but it is generally best to avoid pure white, pure black, or any other 100% saturated hue. That being said, a slight off-white color is the standard for space-age armor, so go with that here. Set the specular size to 10% to ensure that you have a tight specular highlight for this glossy surface, then set the specular inensity to 150%. A quick render shows a nice, tight highlight, as shown in Figure 12.30 (the diffuse color is changed to black to show the highlight more clearly).

You can lend even more gloss to this surface by adding just a touch of reflectivity; even as little as 20% brings the gloss factor up. But it also causes the surface of the armor to "lighten" as the colors reflected into it are added to the already light white. If a white object happens to be reflected, it will practically glow. The

Reflective blend property will blend the reflections into the surface to look more realistic. Set it to 100% (see Figure 12.31; note diffuse color is still black to show the effect more clearly).

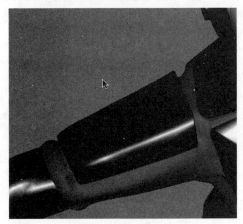

FIGURE 12.30 Setting tight specular highlights helps give a surface a more glossy appearance.

FIGURE 12.31 The reflectivity gives the surface a nice glossy sheen.

Next up is the boots. Start with the soles. These should be a rough rubber material, which requires a few things. First, get the surface color. Like most things, this needs to be a mix of colors rather than a single, solid color. Look to your turbulence combiners again to give you a start. Create a new material, close the preview, and drag it onto the group you made for the boot soles. Now change the attribute to a turbulance combiner. The one you use is largely a matter of prerference. For this example, Perlin is used to get the high contrasting areas of color. We didn't adjust any of the properties for the combiner itself; rather. default noise values are left as they were. The attributes of the combiner don't need marker colors because you aren't changing the combiner settings, so you can get right to work. For this example, one attribute is set to a warm gray and one to a cool gray to vary the specular intensity for each attribute (20% on the first, 30% on the second). This slight variation in attributes will give just a little interest to the surface when rendered. But you need to set a couple values across the entire material as well. Create a new attribute as you did before and set the diffuse falloff to something high (to give the surface a little roughness). A setting of 180 gives good results in the example. Finally, set the specular size to very broad (which coupled with the low intensities earlier will make for a dull surface) value. A setting of 550% is used in the example.

While you are on the boots, the remainder of the boots are covered with leather, worn in places and shiny in others. Most of these attributes need to be placed with decals, as getting them exact with procedurals is more work than you would typically want to deal with. The base color can be set with a procedural as you did for the rest of the character, but because so much needs to be addressed with decals later, a simple patch color will do for now. Set the color for each of the groups that make up the laces, toe, and uppers to black.

The belt is the next accessory you want to deal with. The belt itself is a variation on the rubber for the soles—a perlin combiner with a warm and darker cool gray as the attributes. You want this combiner to be a bit larger and the contrast between the colors to be reduced. A scale of 500% on all axes brings the pattern of the nose up, and an amplitude of 50 will ease the contrast. Add a new attribute just as before to deal with the overall attributes. What you are looking for is a worn, yet smooth leather surface. This means that the falloff will be slightly lower (a value of 70 to 80 should do), and the specularity should be fairly tight and fairly bright, but not to either extreme used thus far (a size of 30 and an intensity of 50 will do nicely). You also want some roughness on this surface, but not the tight noisy type you built into the cloth. Rather, you want a broader wave of rougness, enough to break up the specular highlights, but not so much that you notice it on the surface. A roughness of 5 and a roughness scale of 120, and you should have something similar to figure 12.32.

FIGURE 12.32   The belt's texture.

With the belt textured, your attention will likely move to the buckle. The buckle is a good place for a metallic texture. Metals are deceptive. They look simple—a color and reflectivity—but are actually very difficult to get to look right in 3D rendering. Create a new material, and drop it onto the buckle group. All of your settings will only require the use of one attribute. Start with the color of the surface. Determine what you are trying to make. Is the buckle silver? Brass? Gold? Decide on a material, and make the color match what you would expect. Now set the specular attributes. Unlike most surfaces, metals (not chrome) have a tint to the specular highlight on the surface. Click the specular color and set the highlight color to a very light version of the buckle's diffuse color.

Metals are also very smooth, so the specular size should be relatively small—around 10% should suffice—and have a high intensity. Try 100% and adjust from there to your taste. Reflectivity should be very high for the surface, as high as 100% for a highly polished metal. The difficulty being that a reflectivity of 100% completely obscures the color of the surface, making the object look like chrome, regardless of any underlying metallic shade. You can offset this by increasing the Refelctivity Filter property. A Reflectivity Filter of 100% and a Reflectivity of 100% will give the surface a good polished look and retain the underlying tint.

As we said, metals are typically very smooth, and as discussed earlier smooth surfaces have a low diffuse falloff to them. Lowering the diffuse falloff to 10% or so brightens up the surface greatly and gives it a more glossy metallic sheen. If this makes the surface look too bright or chrome-like, you will need to darken the diffuse color to compensate.

A quick render will look similar to Figure 12.33.

FIGURE 12.33   The surfacing of the character is taking shape.

All that remains now are the detail portions of the helmet, most of which can actually use matrials already created, either as is or with just a few tweaks. The antenna, for instance, can use the same rubber that you used on the boots. The base of the radio unit is the same material as the armor (and helmet shell itself).

For the visor, you can drop the same material we had for the buckle and make some tweaks just on this group to alter it. When you drop a material onto a group in the PWS it creates what is known as a shortcut to the original material, meaning that it references the original material but you can change any of the animateable properties of the material directly in the shortcut. By simply changing the color of the material *only* on the visor group to a different hue than the one on the buckle, you can differentiate the materials and also lower the Reflectivity Filter property to make it look more like chrome and less metallic. Any changes you make to the shortcut are not shown on the original material, and any other groups or objects that reference that material will not be changed. With this you can alter any material to fit any group or model exactly without losing the original material!

Your character now looks pretty much done (see Figure 12.34), but there are finer details that will go further to adding depth to the raw materials you have used thus far. You will be applying those with decals in the next section of this chapter.

FIGURE 12.34   The materials you applied are a good base for the character.

FLATTENING AND APPLYING DECALS

The easiest way to apply a decal and be certain where the image will lay on a surface is to use planar mapping. However, as discussed, planar mapping can lead to stretching of the image where the surface falls away. This is common in places like a character's head. The problem then with mapping faces and heads with mapping types other than planar lies in getting the proper details in the proper places. To make this process easier, you need to flatten the mesh.

Flattening a mesh is a process where you take a round shape, such as a head, and move the points on its surface so that they lie flat, or close to it, along one plane. This process is so common that A:M has a tool, conveniently called Flatten, to get you started. Flattening is normally done in an action, or a pose is created to make the flattened shape easy to get back to without needing to keep track of the action. It is not done in the model, as it is a temporary change to the shape of the model. Start by hiding the parts of the model that you don't need. This includes the back of the head and the inside of the mouth. All you want to be looking at is the face mask. Once you have the extraneous bits of the model hidden, select the face mask and bring up the rotate manipulator. In a basic sense, the Flatten command works by using the pivot point of the selected group and applying scale commands. This means that if you want to control its behavior, you need to adjust the pivot. The first thing the pivot tells the Flatten command is what plane to flatten the mesh along, so from a side view pull the pivot back behind the head (see Figure 12.35).

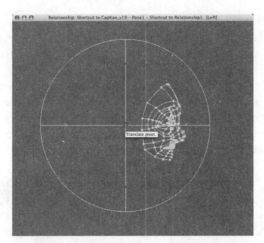

FIGURE 12.35   Position the pivot behind the face mask.

The Flatten command flattens the model on the *y*-axis, rotate the pivot to put the axis parallel with the face. Do this by rotating the *x*-axis of the pivot 90 degrees, but the direction you rotate it is important. Again, from a side view rotate the *x*-pivot back *away* from the face mask 90 degrees. The handle for the *x*-axis pivot should be pointing straight back. Now, without deselecting anything, bring up the contextual menu inside the group and choose Flatten. If your pivot is in the right place you should have something like Figure 12.36. If it looks like Figure 12.37, you have rotated the pivot the wrong direction. Undo it, reset the pivot, and try again.

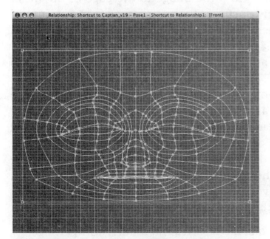

FIGURE 12.36   The face mask after the Flatten command.

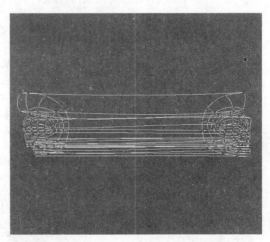

FIGURE 12.37   This face had the pivot rotated the wrong direction.

After the Flatten command does its job, you will still need to adjust the mesh. Move the CPs so that no portion of the model overlaps another. If two parts of the model are overlapping when you apply decals to the model, some areas of the model will not accept the decals.

Once the mesh is flattened and prepared for a decal, you must paint the image that you will use. There is a fine art to the creation of these maps, and it takes time and patience to master the techniques behind them. Look at various maps on the captain but all of them start with the basic process of breaking down the model into groups that need a particular map, flattening them and preparing the points for decaling.

When a group of points is ready for a decal, the first step is to get a screen capture of the mesh and load it into your paint program. For the tutorials in this chapter, you will be using Adobe Photoshop, although almost any program could be used to the same end. You will not be going into the full range of features in Photoshop, but you should take time to familiarize yourself with your paint program of choice, as you will use it extensively when creating decals for models.

PAINTING BUMP MAPS FOR FACES

Fill the screen with as much of the mesh as possible; it will serve as your guidelines when placing wrinkles, pores, and lips. The more resolution you get, the easier it will be to sort out the mesh when painting. Separate objects can be shifted around to empty spots during flattening, making use of dead space in the image map.

Take a screenshot and load it into Photoshop by pressing Alt+Print Screen on a PC, or Command+Shift+3 on a Mac. On the PC, paste this image into Photoshop; on the Mac open the resulting PDF image (normally found on your Desktop) as you would any other (see Figure 12.38). Crop the image to the edge of the mesh and immediately save a copy of the new document as your image map you intend to use, such as FaceBump.tga. Save the original as Facebump.psd. Keep the layers intact. It is important to name your images so large projects don't get confusing.

Go back into Animation:Master, and load in your newly saved image map (FaceBump.tga) into the images folder. Dragging and dropping the image into the Pose window will only allow the creation of a rotoscopes. In order to get the image into the window for positioning, add it as a decal to the model. Bring up the contextual menu for the model and choose Decal from the New setting. Select the decal from the contextual menu, and it will apprear in the Pose window floating above the model semitransparently. Move and scale the image with the yellow bounding box handles until the wireframe in the decal aligns with the wirerframe of the model. Apply the decal to your mesh by double-clicking the decal. When rendering (see Figure 12.39), it should look as if the surface is simpy a copy of the wireframe.

 If you apply a color image to a surface that has a procedural texture, always remember that the color attributes of a decal will always appear on top. If you want the surface color to show through, you must lower the value of the decal, but in most cases you will simply use the decal for some other type, as we are about to.

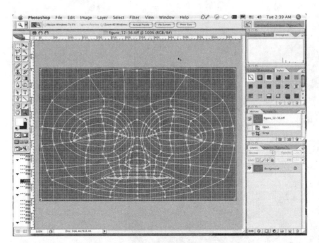

FIGURE 12.38   The image file after it has been applied as a decal.

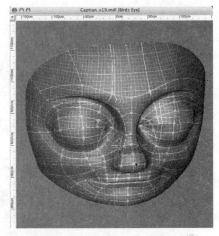

FIGURE 12.39   If you have positioned the decal correctly, it will look exactly like a wireframe of the model.

Change the type of texture from color to bump. Values between 100 and 300 work well, depending on how subtle the bumps are. Different lighting conditions may wash out the bump maps, so start larger and make your way down.

You no longer need to do anything else in Animation:Master except render the scene or window when you want to see the bump map working.

Faces are among some of the hardest objects to model and shade in 3D. This is partially due to the toolset and partially due to the task at hand. You see faces every day. Their nuances and movements, surface blemishes, and translucency are so common you tend to overlook these small features so prevalent in the figure and the face in general when you work on your own creations.

Truly realistic CG characters require surface detail with such minute distortions and features, that to model everything would be greatly impossible—and forget about animating should you succeed! This is where bump maps and displacement maps help speed up the process.

Bump maps in Animation:Master mimic the appearance of actual geometric distortion by altering the implied position of the surface in question, one pixel at a time, during rendering (see Figure 12.40). In other words: a bump map lies. It makes a surface look textured and complex when, geometrically, it isn't.

Since faces require so much important detail, it only makes sense to learn how to properly alter the bump maps in question to make the wrinkles look old, the lips look puckered, and the dimples merry. The list of techniques is short, but will provide enough power to create virtually any other textures you may require in your digital world.

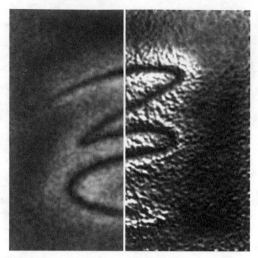

FIGURE 12.40   A black-and-white image and the bumpy texture after rendering.

SETTING UP THE PHOTOSHOP DOCUMENT

Open FaceBump.psd, and make sure it is in a new layer. Also, make sure that you have enough resolution to paint in detail. A good pixel resolution for bump maps should be somewhere close to 1024 × 1024 pixels or higher. The more pixels you have, the more detail you can paint in. If you don't have enough pixels, the rendering may look very washy. If your image is too small, increase the image size in the Edit File menu. Do this before you do any painting.

The current wireframe layer will serve as your guide for lining up the wrinkles on the right geometry. Sometimes it helps to fill in parts of the image (that is, eye sockets and lip edges, nostrils, and hair transitions) with different colors or shades to define a boundary line (see Figure 12.41). It will be easier to identify where one texture will transition to another when painting. Set this layer anywhere from 5% to 10% transparent—just enough to see the guide, but not be distracting. Once the wrinkles are roughed in, you can hide this layer and concentrate more on the shape and placement of the bumps and wrinkles.

Create two more layers in your document: Background, Dark and Light. Fill the background layer with gray.

Bumps vary in depth and height across a face. They can go deep in some areas and shallow in others. Sometimes you may find that you cannot push a valley any lower or a hill any higher when painting bump maps. You should treat the creation of this map the same as a sculptor would a relief. Think of making the bump map like a slab of clay. You can add some clay to make a hill, and you can carve out some clay to make valleys and trenches. You can paint both by starting from a middle ground, a gray area that can go darker or lighter depending on the

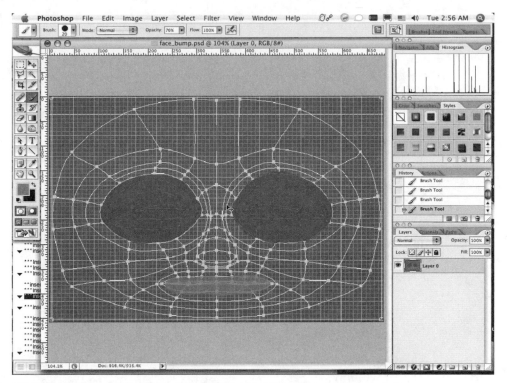

FIGURE 12.41   Color-coded, flattened screenshot in Photoshop, ready for painting.

surface you want to paint. This is a much easier approach when it comes to editing the bump maps later on.

In the layer window, add two layers below our geometry reference layer and name them light and dark. These layers will hold the light and dark values that define your bump map (see Figure 12.42). Set the light layer's blend mode to overlay, which will only lighten values—adding clay, so to speak. Leave the dark layer's blend mode on normal.

Use darker colors on this layer to carve into the map. The idea behind this technique is nondestructive editing of the texture. Light and dark brushstrokes in different layers will be faster to fix than by straight painting both on a single layer. By creating the textures this way, you can control the amount and depth of wrinkles and bumps around any area of the skin without reselecting a gray color and painting out the mistakes.

Remember, any time you need to check up on your texture-mapping work, select Save a Copy as from the File menu, and overwrite your FaceBump.tga file. Go into A:M and render a view in the Model window or choreography to see the new textures take shape. Make sure to deactivate the Geometry Reference layer in Photoshop before you Save a Copy As; otherwise, it will show up on the geometry

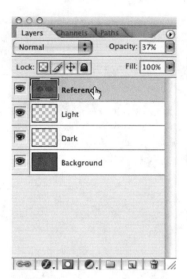

FIGURE 12.42 Adding and naming the layers for painting the bump map.

looking like stitch marks. Just click on the eyeball icon in the proper layer in the Layer window.

PAINTING THE TRENCHES AND HILLS

The first step in painting the bump map is to paint the dark areas first, then bring up the light areas. Lighter shades of gray will make quite a difference to the depth of a wrinkle on a face or a knuckle. It may also help determine what kind of material, and how thick it is.

Different areas of the face have different textures, and approaching each may require several different techniques. As a general start, alter your brush sizes so you can move from small brushes to large ones quickly during painting. You can do this by double-clicking the brush to bring up the properties for that brush. Set your Airbrush tool to a light pressure, such as 15% or 30%; it's easier to add more dark and light than to take it away. Get in a habit of using shortcut commands, too. Left and right bracket keys ([ ]) select different brush sizes for you. Ctrl+ and Ctrl"-" for PC and Command"+" and Command"−" on a Mac will zoom in and out from your canvas.

Here are a few basic textures you can layer together when you are painting:

Pores on the nose and around the cheeks and chin much resemble a strawberry type of texture, minus the tiny seeds in the center (see Figure 12.43). Pores can be made by painting small blotches in clusters. However, painting small blotches on a 1024-×-1024-pixel-image map may take quite some time.

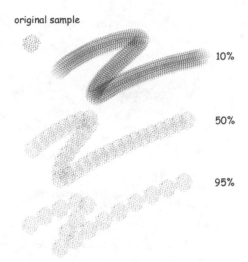

original sample

10%

50%

95%

FIGURE 12.43   Defined brush for nose texture and the spacing percentages while painting.

Luckily, you can make a stamp out of any selection and use that to paint. To start, open a new document and paint several dark, small dots on a white background. Select them with a rectangular or circular marquee. You can define that selection as a brush by using the marking menu in the Brushes palette. By setting the spacing of the brush to a high percentage, like 80 or 90 in the brush options, you can lay down many dots in a single brushstroke. Use lighter pressure as you get farther away from the center of the nose area.

The lips are composed mostly of horizontal and vertical lines, warped around in a donut shape. That is, the lines fan out as you get farther away from the center of the mouth (see Figure 12.44).

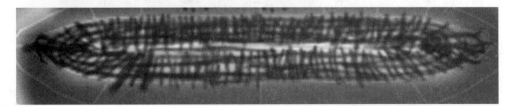

FIGURE 12.44   The bump map for the lips is made up of concentric rings and wrinkles.

Lay in vertical wrinkles that look like lightning bolts, varying the pressure and width of a small, soft brush. Start with heavy pressure and lighten up as you get farther away from the center of the mouth. Go back overpainting the same style of lightning-like brushstrokes, but horizontally. Use shorter strokes to connect and bridge the vertical lines. Afterward, in your light painting layer, bring up the centers of this grid with a wide brush and little pressure.

By varying this technique, you can simulate everything from elephant skin to tree bark (see Figure 12.45).

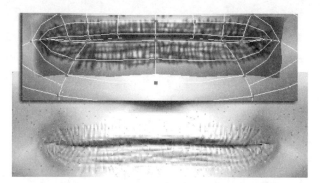

FIGURE 12.45 Lip texture applied as a color map and rendered as a bump map.

When you are painting in the lighter parts, remember to favor the radial direction; that is, the horizontal lines are drawn with less pressure. To make the lips look dry, old, or weathered, use a small light brush to run around the edges of the dark cracks (see Figure 12.46).

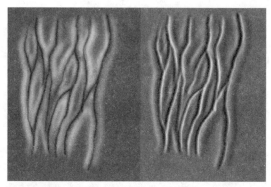

FIGURE 12.46 The effects of painting white around the edges of a wrinkle.

Cheek wrinkles consist of dark lines drawn in a general direction, mostly where a part of skin folds quite often. The more wrinkles in each area, the more weather-worn and older your character might start to look. Start with a small brush and draw the area around using a lightning-style shape, while varying the pressure of the brush (see Figure 12.47).

Select a large, soft brush and retrace your wrinkle using little pressure. In the white layer, use a large, soft brush, and paint between the wrinkles to round out the texture (see Figure 12.48). Thin, delicate wrinkles like laugh lines, and thin skin can be made by painting lighter areas on just the bottom of each wrinkle.

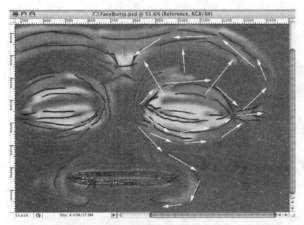

FIGURE 12.47   Arrows show direction of the paintbrush for the wrinkles.

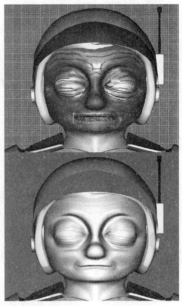

FIGURE 12.48   Wrinkles applied to the model as a color map and as a bump map.

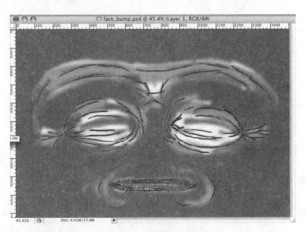

FIGURE 12.49   Round out the wrinkles in the white layer.

Muscle movements and general mannerisms help create wrinkles for the face. Skin on every section of the body is constantly fighting gravity, fat, or clothing. Skin on a lean character may be more wrinkled than muscled characters. Pores and hair follicles on the skin will look stretched and distorted, depending on what area of the face it is in. Learning where to properly place these types of textures will greatly affect the realism and caricature of your character (see Figure

12.50). Practice, observation, and resourcefulness will improve your skills when approaching these types of challenges.

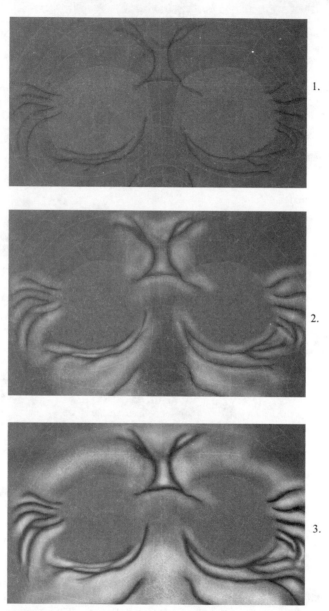

1.

2.

3.

FIGURE 12.50   Wrinkles painted on the right parts may define the character of the model.

ADJUSTING LAYERS

After the general areas have been painted in and detailed, it is important to stand back and search for large-scale adjustments. Just as working from a gray background helps get the proportion of a wrinkle more accurately, so does seeing each wrinkle and bump in comparison to each other (see Figure 12.51). The depth of the pores on the nose and the wrinkles on the eyelids are not equal, even though you may have painted them that way.

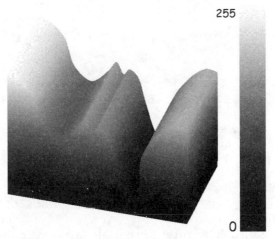

FIGURE 12.51   Varying levels of grayscale determining the shape of the bump.

Create a new layer above your painting layer and label it Equalize (see Figure 12.52). This will be used to adjust the depths of the bump textures as a whole. Leave the Blend mode at normal. Using a fairly large brush, paint a neutral gray (128,128,128) value over areas that need wrinkles to be shallower. This brush needs to be large enough to cover a lot of area in one stroke, such as the whole bridge of the nose, an entire eyelid, or a complete mouth. Remember to use light pressure to add the strokes.

For added control, especially if the wrinkles are too deep or too high, adjust the corresponding layer's transparency, or while inside A:M, adjust the bump map value up or down in the decal's property panel.

To further enhance natural bumps and break up any unnaturally smooth areas, add a neutral gray layer with the Noise filter and Despeckle applied from the Filters menu (see Figure 12.53). Set this layer's Blend mode to Overlay. This layer will enhance the realism of your texture by adding a slight variation in the bump heights, making them look more natural. This effect only needs to be slight, so opacity values from 10% to 30% work well for breaking up the surface.

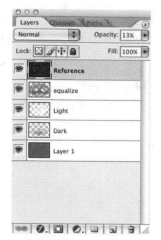

FIGURE 12.52   A neutral gray layer controlling the depth of the bump map in different areas.

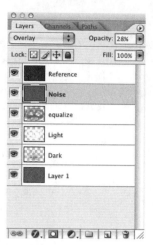

FIGURE 12.53   Neutral noise layer applied for a more natural bump map.

By copying the corresponding layer onto a new layer above it you can amplify its effect; two layers set to multiply will darken the grays twice as much. If you paint out areas on one layer, you can selectively steepen the wrinkles. Adding tileable textures to separate layers with different blend modes will save time painting in large areas, as well as increase the perceived complexity of your bump map. Experiment with the different blending modes on each new layer to see what works best.

NOTES ON DISPLACEMENT MAPPING

In Animation:Master, displacement mapping works just the same as this bump-mapping method. Neutral gray (128,128,128) means the surface will not displace in either direction. Darker colors push the geometry into the surface; lighter colors pull the geometry out. The amount of detail on a model's mesh can be greatly increased with displacement maps and bump maps applied at the same time (see Figure 12.54). As long as you paint back to neutral gray near the edges of your decaled patches, you will have no problems with displacements.

You can use these same techniques to paint bump maps for any part of your character that will need them. The hands, especially the knuckles, will need some bump mapping. Stitching on your boots or belt can also benefit from a good bump. Seams on cloth like under the arms or running up the sides of the legs can only be feasibly created with bump maps. The list is fairly endless, and you could obsess over every minute detail of a character. You can find all the maps for the various parts of Captain on the CD-ROM in the Chapter 12 directory.

ON THE CD

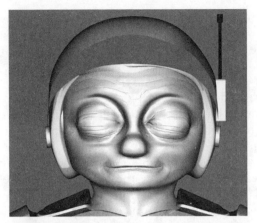

FIGURE 12.54   Displacement and bump maps working together can produce fantastic results.

Continue with the face now. You have defined the bumps and wrinkles for Captain's features, but there are other aspects that you will want to work on. If you look at the skin of most people you will notice that some areas are more shiny or specular than others. This is due to the way oil builds up on the skin. Right now, the captain has an even sheen all over his features. It would be nice to change the intensity of the specularity on the captain to be more realistic. The specular intensity map will allow you to do just that.

You can work in the exact same Photoshop document that you used for the bump, and in fact, doing so is ideal. By using this same document, you can save out a decal that lines up precisely with the bump map that you have already applied. Start by saving your doucument as a new Targa file (be sure to select the as Copy check box on the File Save dialog so that your Photoshop document will remain open) and name this one FaceSpecIntensity.tga.

Back in A:M, load your new decal into the Images folder of the project. You want this decal to be stamped on the mesh exactly the same place that the bump map is. And while you could go to the trouble of aligning and stamping the image into place and hope that it aligns properly, it is far easier to simply use the stamp that is already in place. In the model, expand the PWS tree until you come to the image folder for the decal you have already added to Captain. Bring up the contextual menu for the image folder and choose Add Image, and then simply select the specular intensity map from the list.

If the image is not already in the project, choosing "Other…" from the bottom of the image list will present an Import dialog that will allow you to simultaneaously add a new image to the project and the decal.

This places the image on the face of your character using the exact same stamp as the first decal. If the images were not the same size, then the new image you added would be scaled to fit in place based on the size of the first image in the decal. If the images are the same relative size (say, perfectly square) then this is not a problem, if, however, the images are of different relative sizes there would be some stretching or compression of the new image.

Now that the image is applied, change its Type property to Specular Intensity, and get to work on painting the map.

First, hide all layers except the background. Start from the same 50% gray background. Once all the old layers are hidden, add two new layers exactly as you did for the bump map—one to lighten and one to darken—and reveal the wireframe guide.

Start by painting on the dark layer with a fairly dark color the areas that you don't want to be as shiny: the lower parts of the cheeks, the area between the upper lip and the nose (not the tip or bridge of the nose, which are very shiny), and the area along the temples (see Figure 12.55).

Once you have painted out the areas that you don't want to be shiny, it is time to pull up the oilier areas of the face. On the Lighten layer, paint white at the tip of the nose and then up the bridge, almost solid at the tip and with a lighter preasure on the bridge. Then lay in a large area of white at the forehead. The lips should also be very specular, so paint them in to almost white. The result should look like an inverted raccoon mask of sorts (see Figure 12.56).

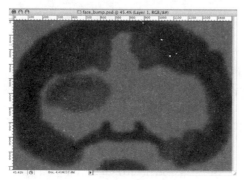 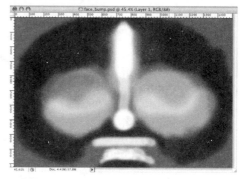

FIGURE 12.55   Reduce specularity with dark areas on the map.

FIGURE 12.56   The higher specular areas get painted with a light color.

Save this out over the top of the FaceSpecIntense.tga you saved earler, and do a test render in A:M. You should see some distinct areas of higher and lower specularity.

If you look at the wrinkles you added to the skin earlier, you can see that, while they do show depth, they are also fairly flat looking. This is pretty normal, but can make for flat-looking bumps. You can increase the perceived depth of a crack or height of a bump by adding a diffuse map that darkens the surface as it falls into a crack and lightens it as it rises. If you think this sounds very similar to the way you painted the bump map, you are correct. In fact, you can start your diffuse map for the face by duplicating the dark and equalize layers you made for the bumps and working with them.

Once you have duplicated the bump layers, set up a new layer for your whites. Diffuse maps assign no change to a white pixel and lower the diffuse falloff as the color of the image approaches black; so in order for your bump map to work as a diffuse, set the background color to white. If you don't, the resulting map will have a visible line where the effect ends. Create a new layer, set it under the other diffuse layers, and fill it with white (see Figure 12.57).

Save this image as a Targa copy named FaceDiffuse.tga, and add it to the decal container. Set the Type property of the new image to Difffuse and do a test render. The lines in the face may now look darker, but they also look a little too harsh. In Photoshop, apply a Gaussian blur to the Darken layer to soften the wrinkles you painted. Save again, and do a second test render. If the lines look less harsh (not considering the darkness of them, just the edge value) you can work on the darkness. The easiest way to asjust darkness is to simply lower the value of the image in the decal. Adjust the value down to 50% to get a nice result similar to Figure 12.58.

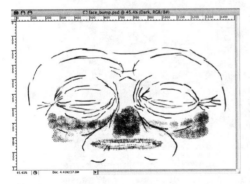

FIGURE 12.57   Your diffuse map needs a white layer for the background.

FIGURE 12.58   The wrinkles are better defined and a little softer with the addition of a diffuse map.

This gives us a good foundation for the Captain's face. The color from the underlying procedural is broken up and given some depth thanks to the bump, specular, and diffuse maps. You could add some more detail with color maps with very specific details and alpha channels that would allow us to, say, add a little color to the cheeks or the lips. If the captain were in the habit of wearing makeup, you could apply it in the same manner.

The process of decaling the hands is the same, with the wrinkles on the knuckles painted in the same fashion as those for the lips. So, move on to something slightly different. The armor in the character's costume is a good place to add some detail. It is very likely that the captain will have had a bump or two in his long career, and even though he works very hard to polish his armor and keeps it looking its best, scratches are just going to be part of the trade. You will want to add scratches and deeper wear at key points to give the armor a lived-in look.

Start just as you did for the face. Hide all but the parts you are looking to decal, which in this instance is easy, as it is simply the armor group you applied the plastic material to earlier. Select it and hide the rest of the model. Next, create a new pose in the model that allows you to prepare the mesh for decaling. You could set up each part of the armor and make decals one at a time, but it will be easier to paint and apply if you only have to deal with it once. To that end, you will be adjusting the position of the various armor plates to show in a single view for easy stamping and painting later. The best view to work in is probably the top view. From here, select and manipulate the points for each armor plate so that they lie flat from the top view, as shown in Figure 12.59.

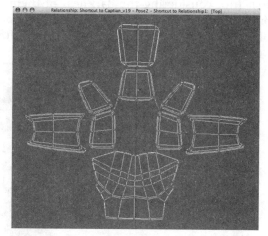

FIGURE 12.59   You move the control points in the armor to allow you to paint the maps more easily.

Take a screen capture of this window, and as with the face, save out a decal image named ArmorBmpSpecRef in Targa format. Stamp it so that the wireframe aligns with the geometry in the Pose window. Once this is stamped on the mesh, change its type from color to bump, and it's back into your paint program to work up the decals.

Start with a layer of scratches that lower the specular intensity and reflectivity of the armor where it has been scratched. This will be one image that will be applied to the armor three times: once as a bump map, once as a specular map, and once as a reflectivity map. Set up the decal for the bump map first, exactly as you did for the face: a dark-color layer and a light-color layer set to overlay with a neutral gray background. On the Dark layer, set down random crossed lines of varying darkness. These will be the large area of scratches on the surface of the armor (see Figure 12.60).

Once the overall scratching has been painted, go back and add in a little depth on the high wear areas. Since you apply this same map as bump, reflectivity and specularity will dull those areas more as well. The corners and edges of the armor will have received more wear than the rest of the surface, so adding a little darker area along the edges will add a nice bit of wear (see Figure 12.61).

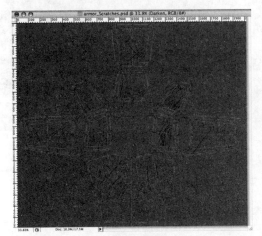 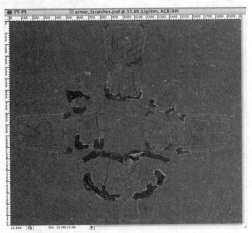

FIGURE 12.60   The start of the scratches for the armor.

FIGURE 12.61   Adding a little depth with darker colors along high wear areas.

If you do a quick render, you should be able to see a fair amount of wear on the armor just from bumps. But go ahead and add the image two more times: once as a specular intensity map and once as a reflectivity map. This makes the illusion of scratches and wear complete, as the areas that are scuffed and worn become dull and nonreflective. This is a great way to break up the surface color on your model. If you wanted, you could add more specific details into these maps, such as mould lines for the armor or perhaps blaster marks from major battles. You can also use color maps with alpha channels to give the armor some identifying logo or other markings. All of the images can and should be painted in the same Photoshop document to ensure that they line up with the underlying mesh and other decals perfectly. When you are done with the captain's armor, it might look like Figure 12.62.

Proceed with the exact same process for the remainder of the character.

Boots: Need bump maps to add stitching and wear, as well as the subtle cracking of the surface. Those same maps can be used for specularity. They will also need color maps with alpha channels to indicate areas where the polish is worn and the leather is lighter in color (see Figure 12.63).

Eyes: A color map for the iris and a subtle bump to give the iris muscle some definition. Veins can be painted in as well to make the eyes look more realistic (see Figure 12.64).

FIGURE 12.62 The armor can be detailed as much as you like.

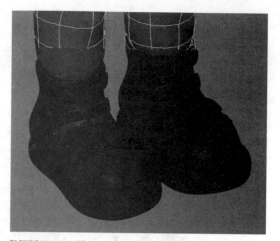

FIGURE 12.63 The surfaced boots.

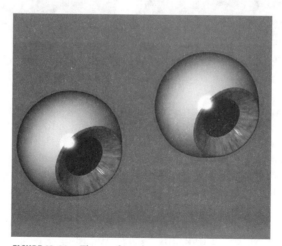

FIGURE 12.64 The surfaced eyes.

Helmet: Gets the same treatment as the armor. Separate the parts and flatten the shapes, then paint in scratches and areas of higher wear along with any insignia or other details you might like (see Figure 12.65). Each portion of the character can be given as much or as little detail as you like. The real key to this process is to break it down section by section and to keep the level of detail relevant to the character as a whole. When you are finished you might have something like Figure 12.66.

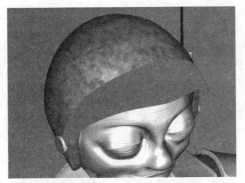

FIGURE 12.65   The surfaced helmet.

FIGURE 12.66   The finished, textured character.

ANIMATED DECALS

A single image gives you a lot of power for texturing, but there are times when you will want a series of images to play in sequence on a model—for a television screen, for instance. You apply animated images the same way you do static images. The only real difference is how you import them into A:M. Rather than double-clicking the Images folder, bring up its contextual menu and choose Image Sequence from the Import heading. This allows you to browse your hard drive for a sequentially numbered series of images. If the series of images are contained in a QuickTime or AVI file, then it is imported in the same way as a standard decal.

The animation of decals is done with the frame property on the image. Simply setting keys for the frame will progress the animation through each image in the sequence.

STAMP EDITING

Suppose after applying a decal you notice that it is slightly out of position. If you want to, you can delete the stamp and reapply the image, but it might be easier to simply edit the position in the stamp. If you bring up the contextual menu for a decal stamp, you will see Edit as an option. Selecting this opens a new window with the decal image in it and a flattened version of the area of the model where the stamp was applied. By adjusting the control points in the stamp-editing window, you can make slight adjustments to how the decal appears on the model. This is great for minor changes, but unsuitable to major shifts. If you need to make a larger change in a decal's position, you are better off deleting the stamp and reapplying it.

PATCH IMAGES

Sometimes you want each patch in a group to have a particular image applied to it, such as for leaves on a tree. Rather than positioning a cookie-cut map over each patch and making a stamp, add an image to a group and A:M places a copy of the image on each patch when rendering.

This can also be used to place a bump map for pores on the arms and hands of a character, or scales on a snake. Almost any surface that might use a tiling image map can use a patch image. The image will scale down to fit completely onto the patch, which can be used to your benefit for pores and surface bumps, making them smaller as the area that they are covering gets smaller.

POSITIONING MATERIALS

The only materials discussed so far are ones that do not need to be placed precisely, but rather cover a global area. However, for some materials the position they have in 3D space is critical to how they appear on the model. Take Figure 12.67 as an example.

FIGURE 12.67   This eye was textured procedurally and required the material to be aligned precisely with the mesh.

The texture on the eye was created with a set of nested spherical attributes, which require them to be placed on the center of a spherical mesh and scaled to fit before they will work properly. If the eye is on the origin of the Model window, then no adjustment would be needed, but the chances that a mesh exists exactly on the center of the window are not very good. For this, you will need to move the center point off the material to match the center point of the mesh.

To find the center point of the mesh, simply select all the points and look at the properties for the group. Under the pivot disclosure triangle, the 3D coordinates for the pivot at the center of the group are listed. You can align any material to this group's center quickly and easily.

When a material is applied to a model or a group, the shortcut to that material has a set of properties that can alter the way the model treats that material. Scaling it or moving the center point is done by changing the coordinates in the transform group of the material's properties. By typing the position of the eye mesh's pivot into the translate position of the material you can align the center of your material with the center of the group. Then you can adjust the scale until the material fits on the model as you intended when creating it.

Because materials transport easily from one model to another, this gives you a way to ensure that you can adjust a complex material to fit models with drastically different proportions.

MATERIALS AS BUMPS

We need to talk about one more attribute before we wind this discussion down: using procedural textures for bumps and displacements. Any material can be applied to a model to do the same work as a displacement or bump map. This allows you to create a procedural texture and then create a second to use as a bump. For example, if you create a cellturb texture for a scaly hide, as shown in Figure 12.68, the surface will not be truly convincing until there are bumps to match the stones in the surface.

FIGURE 12.68   Without bumps, this surface looks unconvincing.

At the same time, painting a bump map to match the procedural is difficult, and aligning the two on the surface is next to impossible. Instead, you can create a second material with the same combiner trees as the first, but set the final attributes to shades of black and white. Then after you apply it to the model, simply give it a bump percent value to make it act on the surface bump rather than the color channels. Together, the color and bump materials line up and make the surface of the model more realistic (see Figure 12.69).

FIGURE 12.69   After a second material has been applied as a bump map, the surface looks much more realistic.

TOON SHADING

A:M has a built-in toon-style renderer that can generate high-quality cel-style renderings. There are three aspects of toon shading: lines, color, and falloff. Each can be set on a group, model, or scene-wide basis. The settings for each level are the same; the only difference being the level of control they have. The base level is set at the model. Changing the settings on the camera or group level will override the model's settings. However, before you can see any effects of the toon render at all, you must first enable it on the camera's properties, either in the Choreography or on the Rendering tab of the Preferences panel.

Lines are created based on the same principle as edge threshold gradients. If a surface is falling away from the camera, then that surface will create a line. The thickness of this line is set on the surface properties. The decision for how far a surface must fall away from the camera before it creates a line is determined by the bias setting on the camera or the Rendering tab of the Preferences panel. The lines are either a specified color, or a percentage of the object's color, whichever you prefer.

Color is determined by the surface attributes of the object, but take care when creating the surface to make sure that it looks good when toon shaded. For the classic cel-shaded look, a flat-shaded render creates a good look. When you are shading a model that you intend to be toon rendered, be careful to make the surface as simple as possible. This goes for details in the modeling as well. The less detail the better. Bump maps and other irregularities that are critical to realistic surfacing are detrimental to toon shading.

Falloff comes in four flavors: standard, flat, toon, and toon with falloff. Standard uses the same 3D falloff shading as normal rendering, controlled by the diffuse falloff attribute. Flat ignores all falloff and renders every surface as a solid area of color. This simulates the classic Warner Brothers style of cartoon shading. Toon uses a gradient to shade the surface, and selecting it as the method adds the gradient box to the properties. The shading is based on the light position where those areas on the left of the gradient are shaded as the surface falls away from the light, with the areas directly facing the light shaded as the right of the gradient.

There are two methods that the surface can be shaded in the gradient: either the gradient indicates a percentage of the surface color with black being 0% and white being 100%, or a specific color can be used. Try the Thermo preset to see the latter option. This method of shading shades the surface the same, regardless of the proximity of the light. Toon shading with falloff is the same as toon shading, but it also takes the proximity of the light source into account for its calculations. The farther away from an object the light source is the more the left-hand side of the gradient will weigh in the shading; the closer to the surface, the more the right-hand side will apply. Figure 12.70 shows an example of toon rendering.

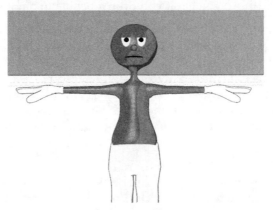

FIGURE 12.70   A traditional cel animation style can be achieved with A:M's toon rendering system.

PLUG-INS

A:M also ships with a number of plug-in procedural texture types that perform specialized tasks, and users with the SDK can develop their own plug-in materials. Following is a brief look at them.

The plug-ins are organized by the developers that created them: Hash, Inc., Alibi, ToonNation, Darkling Simulations, and Wata.

Hash, Inc.'s included plug-ins are Basket Ball, Environment Map, Projection Map, Sim Cloth, and Wave.

Basket Ball creates a black-and-orange pattern like the one found on basketballs. It has no parameters to change.

Environment Map is used to add a reflection map to an object to simulate reflections without the need for ray tracing. It takes an image map and applies it to the object spherically. You can vary the opacity to blend with the underlying surface, and make the colors of the map additive, meaning that they will brighten the underlying color of the model. An environment map does not stick to a surface; like reflections, it remains stationary and slides across the surface of the object as it moves.

Projection Map is included, but all the functions of this plug-in are duplicated with standard decals in with more control. Prior to version 9.0, this plug-in allowed you to use spherical and cylindrical map surfaces.

Sim Cloth is a special dynamic surface that is investigated in depth in Chapter 13, "F/X." It is where you set the properties for cloth simulation. Having this as a material allows you to bank up libraries of material types, so that you can find the cloth settings that work for heavy cotton, for instance, or silk, and not have to reinvent the wheel every time you need a cloth simulation.

Wave affects the bump of a surface only, simulating concentric waves like those you get if you drop a pebble in a pond.

Andy Whittock of ToonNation has contributed a staggering number of useful plug-ins for A:M—so many that we are not able to go into the specifics of them here. Included with A:M2002 you will find: Brick, Cellular, Dusty, Eyeball, Gooch, Ink Pen, Ink Stroke, Joyce, Lake, Landscaper, Macro Photo, Metallic, MultiSky, Ocean, Sketch, Rim Lit, Spots, Villa, Water Color, Weave 2, and X-ray. The best way to get an understanding of these plug-ins is to visit Andy's Web page at *http://www.toonnation.co.uk*, and, of course, to experiment with them on your own. There are four plug-ins from Alibi: Crumple, Dented, Planet, and Scales.

Crumple and **Dented** are bump-only materials. Crumple is intended to resemble crumpled paper, while Dented is intended to look like damaged or abused metal or rock. They can both be used to great effect when texturing rocky terrain. The controls for each are very similar. The size attributes can stretch the material in a given direction. Bump size is a very touchy control and can completely disable the effect or make it so intense as to make it unusable. It is recommended that you only adjust it +/– 5 from its default. Frequency and amplitude control the noise pattern that generates the texture. Octaves increase or decrease the level of complexity. Weight changes the way the texture treats the valleys and peaks; a lower value will create a sharper drop-off from the peak to the valley, a higher value can balloon the valley up. Seed allows you to change the random pattern generated by the material so that various textures can look different.

Planet creates random land masses, oceans, and polar caps on the surface of a sphere to simulate planets. The attributes of this plug-in determine the size of the oceans, polar caps, land, and features of the planet. Experimentation can produce anything from a desert world to a rich ocean-covered planet.

Scales is intended to simulate the scales on snakes or the hide of a rhino, but can also be used to create parched, cracked desert floors. It is a bump-only material that creates plates with gaps between them, based on turbulence patterns. Size behaves the same as for all the other materials discussed. Bump Size, as the attribute of the same name for Crumple and Dented. is a touchy control best left +/– 5 from the default value of 60. Edge determines how much of each plate will fall off into the valley. Valley determines how wide the space between each plate will be. Rounding determines how much the plates protrude from the surface. The default value is recommended. Slope 1 and Slope 2 change the way that the edges fall into and out of the valley. Seed changes the pattern to make the texture appear more random. Some experimentation with the settings will go a long way here.

Darkling Simulations has created a plug-in called **Simbiont AM**. This is not in itself a texture type, but rather a host for "shader" files that are created with Darkling Simulation's Dark Tree texture creation application. The Simbiont allows you to load in any of Dark Tree's complex shaders and apply them to your models. PC users can find a demo version of Dark Tree on the CD-ROM.

ON THE CD

Darktree is a visual procedural creation environment that uses numerous types of combiners and effects to create procedural textures that would be difficult, if not impossible, to duplicate with A:M's built-in texture creation tools. These textures are then brought into A:M through the Darktree Simbiont plug-in. Alternatively, they can be exported from Darktree and used as tiling image maps.

Wata has provided one plug-in for us: Grid

Grid is similar to the gridturb turbulence looked at earlier. It produces a number of different grid patterns based on the input values. Unlike gridturb, however, this plug-in only produces the lines of the grid.

SUMMARY

Texturing is at least one-third of what makes good CG work. We have covered the tools and concepts here that will let you apply as realistic or stylized surfaces as you may need to your models.

Part of what makes A:M such a powerful application is the choices that it gives you without making the process too complicated, and this holds true in its surfacing tools. Whether you use decals or procedural textures, or a combination, A:M will let you create any surface you might need.

The basics of surfacing are the same for a character as they are for a streetlamp. Both are merely objects with discernable properties. Break them down to their base elements and accurately surfacing them is a snap.

ADVANCED TOPICS

13

F/X

In This Chapter

- Particles
- Sprites
- Dynamics
- Flocks
- Volumetrics

In this chapter, we discuss A:M's F/X tools, including particle systems, flocking, and dynamics. We explore how these tools are used in real-world situations and explore alternatives where needed.

By the end of this chapter, you should have an understanding of the available F/X tools, how they are used, and have a basis for further exploration.

PARTICLES

A particle system is a collection of 3D masses that are acted upon by physics in a 3D scene. A:M has four types of particle systems built in: hair, streaks, blobbies, and sprites. We look at all four types, but the focus here will be on sprites, the most powerful. Unless there is a specific need for one of the other three types, sprites will give you the best results. Particle systems are used to simulate things that would be difficult or impossible to model, such as fire, smoke, rainfall, fields of grass, explosions, rivers, and sparks. Sprites can go beyond these, limited only by the images you use in the system.

In A:M, all types of particle systems are materials. You create them in the same fashion you do a combiner: bring up the contextual menu for the base attribute in a new material and choose the type of system you need from the Particles heading. The main difference between particles and other types of materials is that they cannot be nested, meaning that a particle cannot emit particles itself.

Before you can work with particles, you need to be certain that you have them enabled in A:M. If you turn off Particles for any reason, they will not draw and will not render. Particles are enabled on the Global tab of the Options panel. Of all the particle systems we discuss, only sprites can be seen in full effect without rendering. Sprites can be drawn real time in Shaded or Shaded Wireframe mode, making them the easiest to tweak.

Hair

The simulation of realistic hair and fur is one of the most sought-after aspects of any 3D software. A:M comes with a very robust set of hair controls built in that provides tools for creating hair for characters, fur for animals, or fields of grass (see Figure 13.1.)

Hair in A:M is provided by dynamic particle simulation, which can add to render times.

FIGURE 13.1   The fur on this character was produced with A:M's hair system.

It can take a number of frames for a particle system to be fully populated and under the control of the gravity of a scene. This is less of an issue with hair than with the other types of particles, but can still have bearing. Increasing the preroll attribute calculates the system over a number of frames before the animation begins, ensuring that the system is ready when you start rendering.

Cast Shadows tells A:M to either use the hair to determine shadows or to ignore it. If you can get away with turning this property off, your render times will reduce, as A:M will not have to spend as much time calculating shadows for each strand of hair.

Control Points determines the number of points that will be given to the guide hairs for the system (more on guide hairs later) directly determining how the system can be styled.

Dynamic Options toggles the dynamics on the hair and the properties that control those dynamics

Density controls how much hair will be emitted by the system. The higher the density, the more complete coverage a hair system will have.

Length specifies the absolute length of the hair. If you set it to 10, it will be that length even if you scale the model that you apply it to in the choreography. You will need to adjust the length for every model.

Thickness indicates how thick each hair strand should be. The thinner the hair, the better it will catch light, and the higher the density will need to be to ensure coverage. The higher the density, the longer it will take to render.

Kinkiness adds a wave to the strand of hair

Kink scale determines the overall scale of the wave you add with the kinkiness property.

The Real-Time Group contains the properties that determine how (if at all) the hair will render in real time. This allows you to optimize the drawing of hair for your system's performance, without affecting the render-time appearance of the hair.

Instead of an attribute, such as combiners and other material types have, hair systems have an emitter that contains more information about the hair system. A single hair system can have any number of emitters that will all contribute to the overall appearance of the system.

Image. This allows you to use any image in the project as the basis for the hair. You can load an image of a tree, for instance, and have a hill emit a forest. You can use an image of a feather and coat a bird. The image uses any alpha channel to shape the hair as it emits.

Cap Ends. When this is on, each hair will have its strands capped; when this is off, each hair is a hollow tube. Turning this off can reduce some of the geometry the system is creating and can save on render time. It can, however, create odd-looking hair, if the hair is less than a full tube.

Density. This indicates how much hair the system will emit. More density will put more hair on each patch. The higher the density, the more resources will be needed to draw and render the hair. This will equate to longer render times.

Length. This determines the percentage of the full system's length that this emitter will achieve. This allows different emitters to have differing lengths.

Variation. Many emitter properties have a variance subproperty and they all do basically the same thing, they make the property in question less regular across all the hair from that emitter. Length Variation for instance gives each hair a slightly different length within the range of variance you specify.

Position Variation. Hair can be emitted in regular grid like rows, or it can be more random across the surface that is emitting it. The lower this property, the greater the regularity the system will show.

Direction Variation. Similar to position, each hair comes out of the patch following the guide hairs by default. The direction variation property allows you to let each hair have a slight change in that direction.

Surface Attribute properties. This property group is identical to a material property. It allows you to set the surface color of each hair in a system using the same properties that you use for all materials and combiners. A:M also allows you to change the properties along the length of the hair. If you open the Timeline and set it to channels, you will notice that the Timeline portion is now showing percentages. These percentages represent the value of a given property as you edit it along the length of the hair. This is applicable to a number of properties for hair. If you leave any property in the surface group unset, the hair system will pull its properties from the underlying patches of the model, meaning that you can stamp a pattern such as a zebra or tiger and the stripes in the fur will be driven by the color of the decal. Likewise, other materials on a group will drive attributes for hair.

Brightness. This allows you to change the brightness of a hair system. This looks similar to raising the diffuse falloff of a surface.

Variation. This property is similar to the subproperties of the same name, except that it sets the variation on the surface color and brightness of each hair.

Thickness. This sets the physical thickness of each strand of hair. The overall look of a system is greatly affected by the thickness. Both the coverage and density of a system will have a greatly different look. If your hair is very thin you will need a higher density to ensure coverage. Variation: gives each hair a slightly different thickness.

Bow. Hair can be emitted as tubes or it can be unrolled into flat shapes. The bow amount determines how "rolled" a hair tube will be. Variation: Like all variation properties, this one lets each hair have a slightly different bow.

Kinkiness. This sets the amount of wave each strand of hair in the emitter will have. This can be altered by the global property of the same name. Variation: allows each hair from the emitter to have a slightly different kink value.

Kink Scale. This sets the "tightness" of the wave in the hair, a smaller value will produce more frizzy hair, a larger value will make the hair more wavy. Variation: allows each hair on the emitter to have a different kink scale.

Face Camera. When a hair is not in a tube shape, it can appear two-dimensional unless it is asked to face the camera. This will keep the flat side of the hair toward the camera. The percentage here indicates how many of the hairs in the system should face the camera, which keeps a system from looking too regular. Variation: again allows the hairs for this emitter to have different camera-facing attributes.

Brighten Facing Hair. This lightens the surface for hairs that are facing the camera. It can make a system look more convincing.

When a hair material is applied to a surface, it emits hair in the direction of the normal from the patches in the group that has the hair on it. Grooming mode also becomes available. In Grooming mode, A:M presents the user with "guide splines." These splines work just like regular splines. They don't render and you cannot add more of them, and they simply emit from the CPs in the group that has the hair on it. In Grooming mode, you have access to a new set of tools explicitly designed to help you determine how the hair will grow from the patches that it is applied to. Grooming tools are similar to Modeling tools, except they function explicitly on guide splines (see Figure 13.2).

FIGURE 13.2   The hair grooming tools.

Edit (standard) allows you to select any point on a guide spline, and move the entire spline.

FK mode allows you to select and move any point on a guide spline, but will not alter the remainder of the spline. This is identical to how FK manipulation of bones works.

Brush mode allows you to move the circle of influence over the guide splines to "brush them." The circle will appear around the cursor and is fixed in size. If you want to affect more of the surface at once, zoom the view out so that the object appears smaller in relation to the brush. Likewise, for finer control, zoom in on the surface to make the area larger. Simply click and drag the brush around the window to push the hairs around.

Lengthen allows you to make a portion of the hair system longer or shorter. Simply click the end point of the guide spline for the area you want to change, and drag the guide. As you move the point in and out along the spline, you should see the hair in the system lengthen or shorten.

Density allows you to increase or decrease the hair density for the system at a given guide hair. This tool works exactly the same as the Lengthen tool does. Click and drag the end point of the guide spline, and as you move it away from the surface, the system will grow denser. As you drag it closer, it will become less dense. This allows you to sculpt bald spots into your character's hair.

Once you understand the various elements of a hair system, you should be ready to apply this to a character. Take the captain, for instance, and add some eyebrows as well as a bit of hair coming out from under his helmet.

The first step in adding hair to a model is determining where to apply the hair material. In some cases, you can apply this directly to the model, but in other cases you will need to change the spline layout or, often more preferably, add additional geometry to specifically emit hair. For instance, you can sculpt a set of patches to look similar to an eyebrow and place them just under the captain's face where you want the hair to emit from, as well as a few patches inside the helmet (see Figure 13.3).

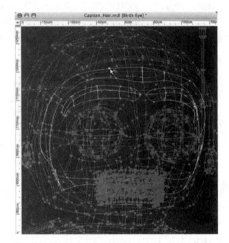

FIGURE 13.3   Set up emitting geometry.

Select all the points in the geometry that is to emit hair and create a group for it. Once you have your group set, it is a simple matter of creating a hair emitter material. You can leave most of the settings at their default values. The only settings you need to worry about are the thickness and diffuse color of the hair. You can choose any color you like for the hair. For thickness, there are a few things to consider. The first thing is the scale of the character. Hair thickness and length are global settings and do not take the size of the character into account. It is therefore difficult to give simple values for your model. The best way to decide on the thickness is to simply apply the material to the group and adjust it until it feels right to you.

If working with the hair is slow, turn down the real-time density on the hair system.

With the hair emitter in place, enter Grooming mode. In Grooming mode, start with the brush to move the guide splines to lay down along the face of the character. Once the rough brushing is done, go back over the brow and adjust any individual guide splines until you like the style of the hair (see Figure 13.4).

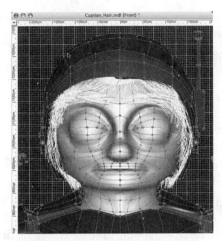

FIGURE 13.4   After the hair is combed.

Once you have combed the hair, adjust the length and the density. Switch to Length mode and start pushing and pulling the guide splines to set the length of each set of hair. You will notice as you change the length of a guide spline that the hair in the patch contained by the guide will average the hair in that patch by all the guides that border it.

Once the length is set, do a test render to determine if the hair is providing enough coverage. If it isn't, you have two options: increase the thickness of the hair in the system or increase the density. Many times the solution is a mix of the two. You can change the thickness and increase the density incrementally until the coverage is acceptable (see Figure 13.5).

FIGURE 13.5   The final hair system adds a great deal to the appearance of the character.

Streaks and Blobbies

Blobby particles are small spheres that are emitted from a surface in the same direction as the surface's normal. As it moves, it checks to see if it is near other blobby particles;

if it is, the two particles glom onto one another to form a new, larger blobby. These particles act similarly to water, exhibiting surface tension characteristics.

A streak emitter emits particles along the direction of the normal of the surface to which it is applied. As it moves, it leaves a tail or streak behind it, similar to how rain is perceived. You can also use this for creating fire or smoke effects, as you can see in the *Art of Animation:Master* manual that comes with your software. To truly understand how particles function and how to create effects on your own, however, you need to understand what the properties are and how they work. The primary properties for streaks and blobby particle systems are the same. We discuss the common properties first and then cover the properties that make each type distinct.

Force is used to override the gravity in the choreography. If, for example, you want your particles to rise up as if there is no gravity you need to set the force of the emitter to 100% in the *y*-axis. If you look in the properties for a choreography you will see that it has a force setting there as well. Further inspection reveals that the force in the *y*-axis is –100%, which simulates earth's normal gravity for all dynamics in the choreography. Changing this setting affects every physics simulation in the choreography, so to localize the adjustments, change the force on the emitter.

Preroll advances the calculations for the emitter by a number of frames. For example, at Frame 0 the emitter will have no particles coming from it, and for each frame a number of particles will be emitted. If you want the particle system to be in full swing on the first frame, like a fountain or fire, adjusting the preroll gives the system a history before the first frame from which to start its calculations. So, a fire can appear to be roaring at the start of the animation.

Life Expectancy measures the length of time in seconds that a particle will last after it leaves the emitter. The longer a particle lives, the more time it will be visible in the frame. This can make particles appear fleeting for fire or long lasting as in smoke.

Rate of Emission specifies the number of particles that are released by the system in a single second. The larger this number, the more particles that are on screen at any given time and the longer the system takes to calculate. Because particles are 3D objects, this means that shadow calculations will require more time for each particle in the frame.

Initial Velocity determines how quickly the particles will move as they are emitted. The faster a particle moves, the longer it will take gravity to reduce the speed of the particle and pull it downward. For some systems, such as fire, you will want very fast particles, but to simulate bubbles in water or other such systems, a slower velocity will likely produce better results. Velocity is expressed in distance per second, with the distance being measured in the current unit of measurement for the project

Bounce indicates how much energy is left in the particle after a collision. The energy left in the particle moves it away from the surface that it collided with at an angle opposite to the initial collision. The amount of bounce depends to a degree on the type of material the particle is intended to represent.

Viscosity describes the amount of drag that the surrounding atmosphere exhibits on the particles. The higher this value, the sooner the energy of the particle is spent.

Die on Impact makes the particle disappear upon coming in contact with any surface or particle, as long as the collision properties are on. This works for things such as particle rain, where it is not effective to continue to calculate a particle after it has hit a surface (such as the ground).

Object Collisions indicates whether the system should check particles to determine if they have hit geometry in the scene. If this property is off, Bounce and Die on Impact have no effect, and particles will not interact with the geometry in a scene.

Particle Collisions indicates whether the system should check for collisions between the particles in the system. This will not calculate between particles in other systems that may exist in the choreography. If this is on, Bounce and Die on Impact settings affect not only collisions against objects, but also the particles themselves.

There are other properties that are used only for streak or blobby systems specifically.

Streaks have three additional properties.

Tail duration indicates how long after the streak has passed that the tail will be visible. This tail is always a straight line and never follows the path of the particle as it arcs and curves. The tail is a line calculated by the current position, direction, and velocity of the particle, as if it had traveled along this line for the full length of the tail duration. For effects such as steady rainfall, long tail durations can give a great effect, but shorter durations work better for particles that have more motion.

Thickness describes the width of the particle and its tail. Wider streaks work well for fire and smoke effects. Rain needs a thinner streak.

Additive color adds the color of overlapping streaks together, making the cumulative effect brighter. This is useful for fire and other self-illuminating effects.

Blobbies have two additional properties:

Size indicates the diameter of the blobby sphere at various points in its lifecycle as indicated by the values in this group. At birth is the size at which the blobby is emitted. Percent at death is how much the particle will have shrunk or grown at the end of its life expectancy. Tolerance indicates how much larger or smaller each particle can be when emitted. The lower the value, the more consistent the sizes between particles will be.

Blobbiness is the tendency of particles that collide to stick to one another. A high value on this setting will create large masses of blobbies, while a lower setting will maintain a larger number of separate particles.

The other major difference between blobby and streak particles is that blobbies can use any type of combiner or plug-in as the attribute, while streaks are limited to plain attributes. Note, however, that materials do not stick to the surface of a blobby. Rather, each particle changes its surface attributes as it moves through the material field in the choreography.

Blobbies and streaks both have uses, but they are processor and render intensive, and in most cases, a sprite emitter will produce better, and more flexible, results.

SPRITES

Sprite emitters emit 2D images, which are called sprites, in a volumetric fashion to make smoke, fire, rain, grass, sparks, fairy dust, explosions, snow, marching armies, waterfalls, exhaust fumes, and practically any particle-based effect you can imagine. The secret to how to create a good sprite emitter is in the images that you use in the sprites. Figure 13.6 shows a few sprite systems and the images that were used to create them.

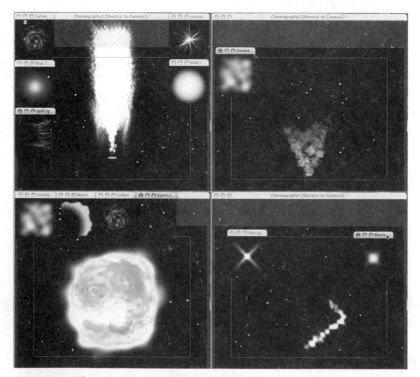

FIGURE 13.6   These sprites created the effects you see here.

Sprite systems consist of two parts: the emitter and the individual sprites. The system's properties affect the properties of the individual sprites in the system, allowing you to adjust the overall appearance of an already established particle system and to more easily animate the properties of all the sprites at once. First, look at a sprite and its properties, then at a system as a whole. Finally, look at what makes a good sprite image.

Each sprite is an image, a series of images, or a QuickTime file. These can be loaded into the sprite with the image property. This is very similar to how images are imported into a decal. Clicking the None value brings up a pop-up menu listing all images currently in the project. The properties of the image group are also similar to those in decals, the exception being there is no type value. If the image is a sequence or a movie file, there will also be a frame property that allows you to choose a particular frame in the sequence. The frame property for an image sequence is animateable, as is the actual image used. This means you can change every instance of a particular sprite to a completely different image or sequence of images.

The single particle allows you to specify that only one of the images at a time is used as a sprite. This single sprite is replaced by a new sprite at the end of the life span of the first one. This could be used to create a visible emitter object that other sprites can appear to come from, or it can be used to dynamically control a single object. Some properties such as rate of emission are not available to single sprites.

Life indicates how long each sprite emitted will exist in the choreography.

Rate of emission determines how many sprites will be released from the emitter in 1 second.

Initial velocity indicates the speed and the distance the sprite will travel in 1 second.

Drag is analogous to the viscosity setting for blobby and streak emitters, indicating the amount of drag that the atmosphere exerts upon the particle.

Color method allows you to specify a single color, or a range of colors based on a gradient, that will be used on the sprite.

Over life is a single animateable color attribute. You specify how the color will change over the life of the sprite by changing the color attribute, then advance the frames either by clicking on the frame ruler in the Timeline or typing in a frame number on the frame Toolbar. This allows a sprite to change its color over the length of its life.

Random from gradient allows you to specify a range of colors from which the sprites will take their colors. This is the same gradient system that toon shaders use, but you are more likely to want to create your own custom gradient. To create a custom gradient, simply click under the gradient bar to add a new marker. Each marker is termed a key and indicates the position in the gradient where it is a particular color. To change the color of the key that you have added bring up the contextual menu for the key and choose Key Settings. In the Key Settings dialog, choose a specific color or a percentage of object setting and click OK. Your new color marker should affect the gradient bar. Add as many keys to your gradient as you need to give the full range of colors you want. If you will be using the gradient for other elements in your scene, bring up the contextual menu for the gradient and choose Create from the Presets heading. Once named, the gradient will be available to all sprites and toon-rendered objects.

Additive Color toggles the additive state of each sprite. If a sprite adds its color, it will get brighter with each object it overlays. This is great for fire or other self-illuminating types of particles.

Opacity is an animateable property that allows you to vary the transparency of each sprite. The opacity is the setting at birth for the sprite. Variation allows the sprites to vary in their opacity from sprite to sprite, helping add interest to a sprite system.

Over life indicates the opacity of the sprite at the end of its life span.

Size indicates the physical size of the sprite. Like the Opacity property, this is the size at birth, with the Over life indicating the change at the end of the sprite's life span and the variation giving each sprite a range of values to determine its size.

Gravitational affect is similar to the force on other types of particles, except all it does is increase or reduce the effect that gravity has on each sprite. This can vary for each sprite in the emitter, so that a low-hanging fog can roll across the ground while mysterious sparks shoot up and away from it, all in one emitter. The variation and Over life settings are the same here as for the other properties.

Angle method determines how the sprite will be angled when released. Since sprites are 2D images that always point at the camera, the rotation of each sprite is what gives a system its character. There are three ways that a sprite can determine its initial angle: Align to Motion, Random, and Specify. Align to Motion forces the sprite to be aligned to the vector it is emitted along, which is the same as the direction of the surface normal for the patch that emits it. Random emits the sprite at a random rotation. Specify allows you to require each sprite to be emitted at a specific angle. Both Align to Motion and Specify allow you to call out an angle. For Specify, this angle is the absolute angle at which the sprite is emitted, while Align to Motion uses it as an offset. Variation can also be specified for these two methods to give a range to the angle of each sprite. Spin is available for all three angle methods. The spin on a sprite indicates how far it will rotate from its initial angle in degrees over the course of its life. Variation allows sprites to spin more or less, which will alter the rate at which they spin, again giving added interest to the emitter. Over life allows you to spin the sprite faster or slower as it ages.

Given these properties, you can control a large number of aspects in a sprite, but since an emitter can have more than one sprite, changing properties for a number of sprites and keeping the same relative values is difficult. To handle this, A:M has a set of percentage properties on the base emitter that correspond to and influence how the sprite's properties are calculated. Life, rate of emission, initial velocity, drag, opacity, size, gravitational affect, and spin are all directly related to the properties of the same names on the individual sprites in an emitter, acting as an enforcement percentage similar to those found in relationships and constraints. Preroll precalculates the entire system to a number of frames to allow it to fully populate before the first frame of animation. Tint is used to alter the coloration of the entire system by blending it with the tint shade at a specified percentage. If your tint is blue and has a strength of 50%, for example, and your system emits a sprite that is specified to be red, the final color of the sprite will be purple. This allows you to change a previously constructed sprite's color. If the color method is random from gradient and the gradient specifies a percentage of the object color, then the color that it is based on is the tint, and the strength property has no effect.

The key to making good effects with a sprite system is in using the right images in the system. The image itself will have the greatest amount of control over what the effect looks like.

The best images for most effects are created by a small white image with the desired shape created in the alpha channel. Images such as these brought into A:M as 32-bit Targa files can make convincing fire, smoke, spark, or grass. The coloration will be assigned in the particle system, and using simple white sprites makes them usable for a variety of sprite systems. The pivot point of each image is in the exact center of the image and is crucial to getting the emitter to do what you intend.

The center of the image is the point of the sprite that is touching the surface of the emitter object at birth. This means that if you try to use an image like Figure 13.7 to produce lightning, the results will likely be unexpected. Figure 13.8 shows a lightning-bolt image that performs more predictably. Notice that the beginning of the bolt is in the dead center of the image.

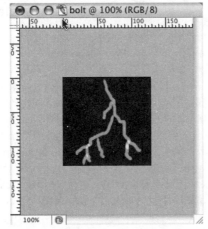

FIGURE 13.7   Placing the start of this bolt on the edge creates unexpected results.

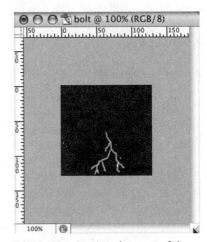

FIGURE 13.8   Putting the start of the bolt at the center of the image makes it work as you would expect.

The pixel size of the image matters very little when the particles are created, so making the images as small as possible is a good idea as it will require less RAM and render faster. Images down to 32 × 32 pixels can be used effectively. On the CD-ROM is a folder of sprite images you can use to get started. To save space, they have been saved as 8-bit Targa files. To create good 32-bit images, paste them into the alpha channel of a new image.

ON THE CD

With a little experimentation, you can make almost any effect that you can think of with sprites.

DYNAMICS

Dynamics in 3D are a way to get models to exhibit properties such as mass, and to detect the surfaces and collide with other objects in a realistic fashion. This is not used to keep a character from reaching through a glass or anything so subtle, but rather to allow a ball to bounce on a ground plane or some other more broad application.

A:M has four types of dynamic systems: cloth, constraints, spring systems, and rigid bodies. Cloth systems are based upon dynamic simulation of the splines and points off the mesh. You apply it to where the points are assumed to have mass and the splines have tension and elasticity. Constraint-based dynamics are applied to bones and give easy control over dynamic reactions in single bones or chains of bones, allowing you to drive secondary motion in characters or build hang and swing into ropes and chains. Spring dynamics are based on the concept of masses that are connected with springs. These masses and springs can be attached to bones allowing you to drive simple motion on meshes. Ridgid-body dynamics in A:M are provided trough the Newton game physics engine and can be used to simulate complex physical interactions—everything from bouncing balls to rows of dominoes. Dynamics allow you to let the computer calculate accurate physical interactions that save you a lot of time later.

Cloth

Immediately after fur on the buzzword list comes cloth. The typical expectation for cloth is that you simply apply the cloth material to a character's shirt and it magically behaves like a real-world shirt. However, unless the model is constructed to the optimal shapes and density for the task the results can be less than desirable. If you keep in mind that it is a *cloth* material, not a *clothes* material, you will be happier with the results. That being said, A:M's cloth systems are second to none and provide a very robust set of tools to arrive at a desired result.

The first thing to know about cloth is that it requires slightly denser geometry than you would otherwise build. This is especially true if you want the cloth to interact with a surface. You create a new cloth material just as you would any other material, and change the attribute node to Plug-in > Hash inc > SimCloth. Before you can make the best use of it, you need to understand its properties.

Object Type determines what function the material plays in the simulation. There are two types of objects: cloth and deflector. A cloth object is dynamically simulated to be a soft, flexible surface, whereas a deflector remains rigid and interacts with cloth. Cloth will only collide with a deflector. Any geometry that is not defined as a deflector is ignored in collision detections.

Particle Mass determines the rough weight of each CP for the simulation. The heavier the cloth, the higher the mass should be.

Collisions is a group of properties that determine the behaviors of the cloth surface when colliding with other objects. The two subproperties are Self Collide and Friction. When Self Collide is on, the cloth looks to its own surface to determine if there are intersections. This can make a cloth surface look more realistic, but requires more computations when running the simulation. Friction simulates the amount of drag a cloth surface will have against any colliding surface (be that self-collision or a deflector). A rougher cloth will have more friction than something smooth like silk.

Forces are a group of properties that determine the structure of the cloth being simulated. The properties determine how the cloth will stretch between control points and how likely the splines are to expand and contract.

Stretch type can be set to either Stretch/Shear or Spring. The difference is subtle but important. In a Stretch/Shear system, the cloth is presumed to have a structure as shown in Figure 13.9 with stretch along each spline and shear across the center of the patch. In this way, the patch can be distorted beyond its default shape, but only so far as the shear will allow.

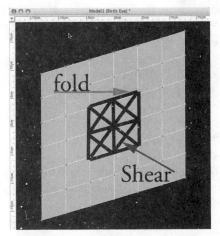

FIGURE 13.9   The structure of stretch/ shear cloth.

Spring type cloth removes the shear portion of the equation. It only uses the Stretch, allowing much greater distortion of the shape.

For each of these types there are stiffness and damning properties, which each in their turn reduce the dynamic range of the forces on the cloth. Stiffness indicates how rigid each given portion of the system is. If a cloth system has less give, it will not stretch or sag as much. Dampening reduces the "bounce" in an aspect of the system. If you have a high amount of dampening, then the Stretch/Shear or Spring will want to return to its resting length as much as possible, but will absorb most of the energy the system might accumulate by stretching.

Bend type allows you to determine how you want A:M to calculate the folds in the cloth system. There are two choices: Bend Angle and Bend Springs. The difference is extremely subtle, and it is not likely you will ever need to change the default, but the Bend Springs type produces slightly more flexible cloth at the same stiffness and dampening settings.

Air drag determines how much the atmosphere affects the cloth. A lower number results in less drag, as you might get from a mesh surface; while a higher number represents more, as you might get with thick cloth.

In addition to these properties, models and groups also have a set of plug-in properties available to them. This group contains a set of properties for all plug-ins that access group properties (currently Newton Physics and SimCloth). For SimCloth, you have the following group-level properties:

Attached makes a group that is part of a cloth group respect and follow the motion of the bone that controls the point. This is often used to "pin" cloth in place.

Collisions turns the calculations for collision detection for the group on or off. This excludes this group when the simulation is run, which can make it run faster.

Self Collide overrides the self-collide attribute on the cloth material if this group is in a cloth type.

Check Intersections tells A:M to consider this group for intersections. If this is on, A:M tests to see if the surface is intersecting a dynamic body. If it is. it recalculates to find the point where the surfaces intersected. This can prevent points in the cloth from getting "trapped" inside another surface.

Scale scales the group down when the simulation starts. This is used to bring cloth groups into contact with the surface of the model. A waistband on pants, for instance, can be modeled large to avoid the initial collision with the deflector surface of the waist, but can be brought in to rest on the hips with the scale property.

If you recall when you modeled the captain, you made groups for cloth. One was to be a deflector group, specifically for the body under the cloth. Then you created a group called Cloth Attach and a group called Cloth. In order to make this simulation work, you need to create two materials. One will have its type set to Deflector, and the second will have a type of Cloth. The Cloth type is applied to the Cloth group on the model, which makes this group capable of dynamic simulation.

The deflector cloth material is, as you might surmise, applied to the Deflector group. The attached group doesn't need a material, but you need to set the attached property (in its plug-ins group) to on. This holds the cloth in place and keeps it from falling to the ground.

In order for the cloth simulation to react properly to the deflector and to not move from the attached group, you need to make it aware of those groups. This is done by bringing up the contextual menu on the SimCloth node of the shortcut for the material on the model and choosing New Group. This adds a "custom group" to the properties. From this group, simply choose the attached group from the pull-down menu, and then do the same for the Deflector group.

Now, simulate the cloth in an animation and start to tweak its settings to achieve the desired results. You already have some animation with this character from Chapter 10, "Animation," so you can just work with that. First, simulate what you have, to see what kinds of tweaks you need to make. Simulations are made by bringing up the contextual menu for the choreography and choosing Plug-Ins > SimCloth Simulate. A:M steps through the animation and simulate the interaction of the cloth as it hits the surfaces of the character.

After the simulation, step through the animation to determine what tweaking, if any, needs to be done. Adjust the Stiffness/Dampening and other attributes of the cloth material until they look like the type of cloth you want when simulating.

You will need to resimulate your cloth every time you change a portion of your system.

When you have the cloth looking right for most of the character, you might still have a few points that are not behaving as you would like. In these cases you can simply adjust the motion of those points directly. Cloth simulations return simple muscle motion, so all points can be animated and changed later. In this way, you can get the cloth "close enough" and fix any minor imperfections with muscle motion.

All cloth simulations need several frames to come to a rested state, to let the springs find their length, and to detect and stop at any surfaces. This is similar to the concept of preroll for particle systems, except that you need to allow actual frames of animation time to pass. Any surface already colliding with a mass in the cloth can cause problems, which are typically countered by scaling the portions of the model that will contact the cloth down, then over the first 10 to 15 frames of the animation scale, then up into the cloth. This gives the system time to calculate the initial state of the masses and prepare for collision detection. Since Captain is off-camera the first few frames of your animation, this is not so much a problem but is something you should keep in mind.

Spring Systems

As with most things in A:M, the key to understanding is starting simple. The simplest spring system that can be created is two masses connected by a single spring. You start with this to learn how the settings of a system affect the various components in

the system. Until you understand the settings and what they do, it will be very difficult to know how to create and adjust systems that are more complex.

Start by opening the Springs_basics.prj project from the CD-ROM and creating a new action for the simple tube model. Before you can add springs to this
model, create a new spring system to hold them. Do this by bringing up the action's contextual menu and choosing Spring System from the New heading. This
creates a new action object, which is indicated by the bone that holds your
springs and masses under it. Notice that the Dynamics Mode button is now available. Clicking it enables Dynamics mode and changes the tools to those used to
create springs and masses.

Clicking the Add button enters you into Add Lock mode, much like modeling, except instead of laying down control points and splines you are setting up
masses and springs. Clicking sets a mass in place, and between each mass that you
create a spring is drawn. This is the basic way that all soft-body dynamic systems
are created. By changing the properties of the masses and the springs, you control
the way that they react to gravity. Go ahead and draw two masses with a single
spring between them. you will use this as your test unit.

A mass reacts to gravity by being pulled down by it. The greater the mass, the
more pull it has to reach a surface. The direction it is pulled is defined by the gravity settings in the action or choreography that the system is in. By default, a mass
is pulled down. The properties for each mass are simple and are augmented by
mass properties on the main system as well. Look at the properties for a single
mass and then those for a system. Figure 13.10 shows the properties for a mass.

Properties		
⬇ ▽ Mass3		
Translate	X:-39.98 Y:-54.12	Z:0
Fixed		OFF
Override System		OFF

FIGURE 13.10   Properties for an individual mass
indicate how it will react to gravity and other
surfaces.

Mass determines how heavy each point is. The larger the mass, the faster and
harder it will be pulled down.

Collision Radius indicates how far away from itself the mass will test to see
if it is intersecting a surface.

Fixed toggles the masses mobility on and off; a mass that is fixed is not affected by gravity or by springs that it may be attached to. This is how you
anchor systems in place.

Override System tells A:M that you want to set the properties of this particular mass here, rather than use the mass settings on the system's properties.

If you look at the properties for the entire spring system (see Figure 13.11), you
will see a portion of the properties there are similar to the ones on an individual

mass. If the masses don't have their Override System properties on, then these settings will be used instead. Specifically Mass, Mass Drag, and Collision Radius are used to control all the masses in the system that are not specified to override.

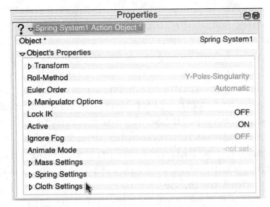

FIGURE 13.11   These properties on the spring system control all masses that are not overriding the system.

Of these properties, the one you need to look at specifically is Mass Drag. Drag is the same property that you looked at when examining particle systems, and the masses in a spring system can be thought of as individual particles. Drag indicates the amount of resistance that the atmosphere has against the masses.

The other components in a spring system are the springs. The springs tie masses to each other and use the gravity of each mass to push and pull other masses in the system. Like masses, springs can be controlled by the system settings or individually (see Figure 13.12). The settings for each are the same. Understanding one helps you understand them in conjunction.

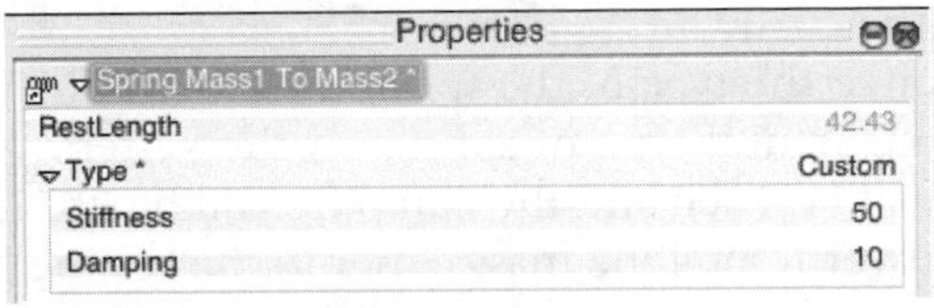

FIGURE 13.12   The properties for a spring control how the system moves between masses.

Stiffness indicates how strongly the spring resists pulling by a mass. Very stiff springs, with perhaps 1,000 or more for stiffness, will not be pulled much, if at all, unless the mass that is attached to it is very heavy. Damping indicates how much the spring pulls on the two masses that it is between. Damping will pull at the masses until the spring is at its resting length. Rest length is the length that the spring was initially drawn at and represents the length that the spring would like to be if no force is being applied to it.

Changing the position of masses after they have been drawn will not change the resting length of the spring. Rather, it will either pull or compact the spring, giving energy to the system. If you move a mass and want the new length to be the resting length for the spring, bring up the spring's contextual menu and choose Reset Rest Length.

Type indicates how you want to apply settings to the spring, either using one of the four types listed on the main properties for the spring system or using the properties on the spring itself. The four types of springs that can be set on the system level are System, which uses the base settings; Structural, Fold, and Shear. The last three you can use in your systems to give different springs different jobs. As a system grows more complex, this becomes a timesaving way to make minor adjustments. The fifth type of spring, Custom, uses the settings on the spring's properties rather than the ones on the system, much like the Override System property does for masses.

So how do these properties work together to make dynamic simulations? Look at the most basic simulation first. In the two-mass-and-one-spring system you created, select one of the masses—because masses are drawn incredibly small in the interface, this is easier done by selecting it in the PWS—and set it to be fixed. This keeps our masses from simply falling and gives us a chance to examine the spring and how it works.

Advance 1 second into the action, and change to Bones mode. Select the bone that controls the spring system, and move it slightly to one side. You do this because the spring simulation only lasts as long as the action it is in, requiring at least one keyframe to give length to the action.

Change the mode back to Dynamics, and bring up the contextual menu for the action and choose Simulate Spring Systems. Animation:Master will progress through the action one frame at a time and use physics to determine how the spring and mass will behave. Once the simulation is complete, you can step through the action and watch how the mass pulls down on the spring. You can find a render of this on the CD-ROM.

ON THE CD

Change the type of the spring to structural, and examine the default settings for the structural type of spring on the system's properties: The stiffness of the spring will be 1000 and the damping will be 20. These numbers give the spring a lot of power to pull the mass closer to the resting length of the spring. If you simulate this system, the spring will hardly show any stretching at all. Now try a spring at the default fold settings: stiffness of 5 and damping of 0.25. This is the same stiffness that was used on the first default spring, but the damping is only one-quarter the strength. If you simulate this, you will see that while the mass pulls the spring down, the spring doesn't pull the mass back toward its resting length much, if at all.

The settings for Shear are the same as those you have for fold, so will produce the same results. Experiment with each of these settings until you have a general idea of what they are doing. Apply a higher drag and see how it affects the mass.

You can put this single spring to work as a simple way of controlling a pony-tail or the ends of a bolo tie for a cowboy. With more complex spring systems, you can control cheeks, ears on a dog, or a strip of hair, or even clothes.

FLOCKS

You have already looked at flocks as a tool to populate scenes with grass or to put leaves on a tree, but their traditional use is for simulating animated models in groups.

There are three basic types of flocks built in to A:M: birds, crowd, and swarm. Each is named after the type of behavior that it is expected to simulate. Birds simulates the patterns that a flock of birds uses when flying; crowd simulates the way groups of people act as they move in large groups; and swarm simulates the behavior of flying insects.

Creation of a new flock is done from the choreography's contextual menu, as discussed in Chapter 6, "Inorganic Modeling."

The majority of the properties for each type of flock are the same, with the only differences being with the last several properties of the crowd flock (see Figure 13.13).

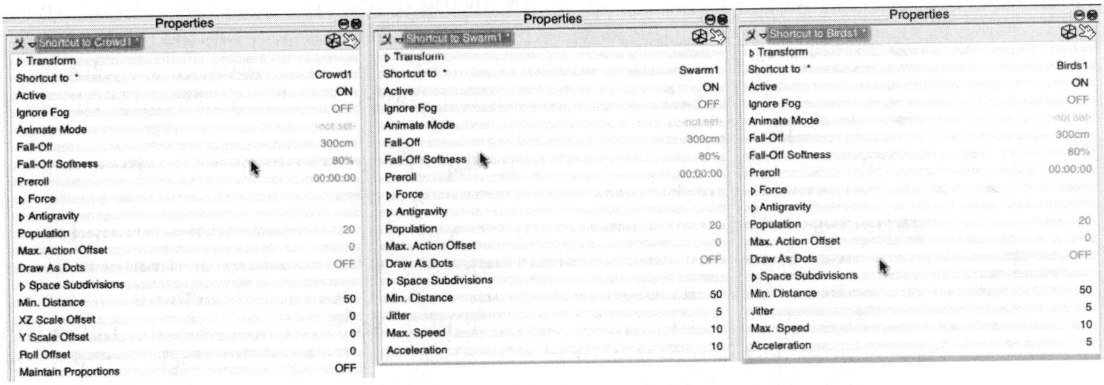

FIGURE 13.13   The properties of the various flocks vary only slightly.

Type indicates the shape of the area that the flock will occupy. The default spherical shape works well for most applications, but you may also choose box, cone, or cylinder. These are similar to the types of lights and identical to the types of volumetric effects discussed briefly in the next section.

Falloff indicates the furthest extent to which a member of the flock will go from the center.

Falloff softness is similar to how lights behave, with the greatest concentration of models in the flock existing at the center of the influence shape and falling off toward its edges. This is used to control the density of the population.

Preroll is identical to the same property on particle systems. This allows a flock to be fully populated and in motion starting at the first frame of animation.

Force is used to indicate the portion off the area of influence that the flock will prefer. This is unlike particles in that it is not used to counter gravity. You have a different property to accomplish that.

Antigravity counteracts the force of the choreography but in subtle increments rather than on a one-to-one fashion, for in their own way the area of influence will hold the population of the flock in place. For most things, the default setting of the antigravity will do as needed, keeping both birds and swarms in the air and crowds along the ground (or stuck to an irregular surface with the flock to surface constraint). But by changing the antigravity, you can force the flock to move out of the area of influence. Lowering the default y antigravity forces the flock's population to fall down just as for particles. However, giving it a value in the x- or z-axis can move the entire flock along those axes, which can give additional motion and realism to crowds.

Population indicates the number of objects that will exist in the flock.

Max action offset changes the starting frame of a looped action applied to a flock member to be slightly different from the other instances of that model in the flock. This keeps all the members of the flock from moving in lockstep. For the leaves on your tree from Chapter 6, for example, you could create a simple action that rotates the leaf to various angles, then with Action Offset the individual leaves on the tree would all have slightly different positions.

Draw as dots speeds up real-time display in the choreography by replacing the models in the flock with simple dots.

Space subdivisions indicates how the area of influence that surrounds each flock is to be divided for detecting the proximity of other members of the flock. The behavior of each member of the population depends on knowing when another member is within its area. A higher setting here gives more accurate detection of the other members of the flock but requires more resources for the computations.

For the birds and swarm types, there are three more properties not available to crowds. Crowds have four properties that are unique to themselves.

Jitter is a measure of the chaos of the flock. The higher the setting, the more often the members adjust their direction and position.

Max speed simply indicates the fastest that any member of the flock may travel. The lower this number, the slower the movements of the flock. If it is reduced to 0, the members remain still.

Acceleration is reminiscent of the cornering capacity of a car. The higher the acceleration, the more capable of turning and more agile the movements of the flock will be.

Crowds are intended to be characters and used as extras, but since a street full of characters with the exact same proportions would look odd, there are properties to vary them.

XZ scale offset indicates the amount of variance a model can have in these two axes.

Y scale offset does the same for the *y*-axis

Roll offset changes the facing direction of each member of the flock slightly. If you want a military parade, be certain to turn this value down.

Maintain proportions forces the Y scale offset to remain proportional to the XZ scale offset. This keeps a model from becoming excessively stretched along one axis.

Once the flock is in place, you add members to it and position it exactly as you did in Chapter 6 to place the grass in your scene. However, there is one other thing to take into account for crowd type flocks, and that is the behavior of the members of the flock on uneven ground.

It would be difficult to position 15,000 pebbles on a beach even if it didn't bring your project to a grinding halt with its complexity. A flock would make this task exceptionally easy, performance issues aside, if only you could keep the members of the flock along the irregular surface. This is exactly what the flock to surface constraint is designed to do.

It behaves exactly like the surface constraint, but only with a single target. The target being the surface that the members of the flock should remain attached to. It is only available to a crowd type flock in the choreography and can be found under the other subheading of the flock's New Constraints contextual menu.

Note that if the default flock types do not create the behaviors you want, they are plug-in-based functions, and if you are familiar with programming you can use the Hash SDK to create any behavior you may require.

VOLUMETRICS

The air that makes up your environments isn't perfectly clean. It has dust and water vapor suspended in it. When these particles are thick enough, they are easily visible. This phenomenon is called volumetrics. Animation:Master ships with three types of volumetric effects: dust, steam, and mist.

All three of these have the same set of properties, the only difference being in the appearance of the rendered volumetric effect. Dust works best as small puffs, for example, when someone is walking on a dusty floor. Steam works well for sewer grates and hot water, but looks best in small columns. Mist is a ground-covering volumetric that works well for low-to-the-ground fog that covers a larger area.

You can create volumetrics as stand-alone objects in the PWS or as part of a model. You may also create them directly from the action or choreography window's contextual menu. However it is created, you can only see the effects of the volumetric effect through a final quality render or rendering to file. The progressive render will not display them.

The first property of the volumetric is the type, which changes the shape of the area of effect that the volumetric will use. It also slightly changes the properties available to the volumetric object. An effect can be a cone, box, cylinder, or sphere. These shapes are similar to lights, with the additional cylinder shape being a blend of the cone and box area types. Like lights and flocks, the greatest concentration of the volumetric will be in the center of the area of influence and will fall off toward the edges.

> **Width** is only available to cylinder, box, and cone types, and specifies how wide the area of effect is at its base.
>
> **Width softness** is related to width and indicates how soon the falloff will occur from the width to the edge of the area of effect.
>
> **Falloff** indicates how far the area of effect will reach. For spherical types this is described as a radius; for the other types it is the length of the shape.
>
> **Falloff softness** tells the shape when to start falling off. A lower value pushes the falloff closer to the end of the falloff distance of the area.
>
> **Cone angle** is only available for the cone type, and it indicates how many degrees the angle between the sides of the cone is.
>
> **Quality** is the setting for a volumetric that determines how the area renders. A very low quality can make the effect not visible at all or cause visible banding in the effect. A higher value generally produces better results but takes longer to render. You should experiment to find a value that produces a good result in a time that you can live with.
>
> **Brightness** increases the visibility of the effect.
>
> **Contrast** increases the difference between those areas that have volumetric particles and those that don't. A high value for this produces discernable areas of volumetric and nonvolumetric, while a lower value makes the entire area more homogenous.

Volumetric effects have inherent animation, so that the area appears to be under the effect of a moving atmosphere. The speed property makes the movement of the effect more or less pronounced.

> **Swirl** increases or decreases the frequency with which the volumetrics change direction when moving.
>
> **Scale** increases or decreases the turbulence of a volumetric, making the areas in it larger.

All volumetric effects have a default fractal sum turbulence applied to them. This turbulence indicates the areas that will be more or less volumetric similarly to a turbulence material. You can add other turbulences or remove the default turbulence from the volumetric effect, and changing or adding new turbulences is the easiest way to change the character of the effect (see Figure 13.14).

FIGURE 13.14   Each image is rendered with a different type of turbulence applied to the mist volumetric.

Summary

The F/X tools in A:M are by no means the focus of the program, but with sprites, layers, and the physical simulation tools in A:M you aren't limited to just character animation. The tools are not simple, however, and take a lot of experimentation and patience to master, but if the result is a better piece of animation, then it is time well spent.

RENDERING AND COMPOSITING

In This Chapter

- Render Options
- Output Options
- NetRender
- A:M Composite
- Post Effects
- Layers

In this chapter, we discuss the settings, options, formats, and qualities of render that you can get from Animation:Master. You explore the render options in depth and learn how to set up and render your animation. Also looked at is Hash, Inc.'s NetRender package and how it can help with your projects.

You also look at A:M Composite, A:M's built-in compositing tools, and learn how to tweak and sweeten a render without the lengthy process of rerendering.

RENDER OPTIONS

When you click the Render to File button, A:M uses the current viewport to render the scene to disk. This means that if you are looking at a side or top view of any workspace, that view is rendered to file. If you are in a choreography and are ready to render your animation out to final quality, it means that you need to be viewing the scene from the camera view before you click the Render button.

Of all the views in A:M, only the camera gives us complete control of all aspects of a render, from framing to effects like DOF. Most of these settings can be accessed either on the camera's properties or on the Render panel.

The settings for the camera allow you to change the quality of a render or to disable portions of the render, such as shadows. To get the most out of Hash, Inc.'s renderer, you need to understand the settings and how they impact both render quality and render time. You will look at these settings in the context of the camera's properties, but they are the same settings that you find on the Render panel.

Open your animation project from Chapter 9, "Expressions," and select the shortcut to the camera under the choreography in the PWS. The properties should look like Figure 14.1.

FIGURE 14.1   The camera properties.

You should be familiar with the first set of properties from dealing with bones and models. The properties focused on are the 12 render options for the camera:

- Quality
- Multi-Pass
- Motion Blur

- Depth of Field
- Shadows
- Ambience Occlusion
- Reflections
- Draw Particles/Hair
- Fog
- Toon render
- Field render
- Stereo
- Plug-in shaders

Quality changes the type of rendering that A:M produces.

Final quality is a full a-buffer/ray-traced render of the scene from the camera view. This is the highest level of quality and takes the longest to render. Final quality shows all the surface attributes and effects in the shot.

Default uses the Draw mode of each item in the choreography to determine how to render it.

Wireframe shades everything in the choreography as if using the Wireframe Draw mode; it renders quickly and is useful for animation tests.

Shaded uses the real-time Shaded Drawing mode for all items in the choreography. It takes slightly longer to render than Wireframe, and is used to get quick previews of animation and a basic feel for lights and shading.

Shaded Wireframe mode combines the shading of wireframe on top off the Shaded mode rendering. It is used to preview animation, showing things more clearly than Wireframe and can help you point out problem spots in your mesh that Shaded mode might hide.

Multi-Pass is a special rendering technique by which a frame is rendered multiple times; each time is referred to as a "pass."

Passes indicates how many times A:M should render each frame, or the number of subframes it should average. The more passes you render, the higher the quality of the final image will be. Each pass is a full quality rendering of the image without the antialiasing step, A:M renders as many passes as you ask it to and then averages them together to arrive at the final image. The benefits are in the flexibility of the rendering (you can render with just one pass and get a much faster final quality render than with no multi-pass) and the options it opens up to you. The downside of Passes is that A:M must render the entire scene more than once per frame and can cause very high render times.

Soften causes A:M to use a filtering on the render pass that averages each pixel slightly based on its neighbors, which gives each pixel a softer look. This can increase the perceived quality of an image with fewer passes.

Motion Blur tells A:M to blur objects as they move. This is a rendering trick that simulates the property of film to blur objects in motion. When you render animation, Motion Blur can greatly enhance the perception of motion. There are two types of Motion Blur, which both function the same but depend upon the Multi-Pass setting. The technical difference is not so important for you to understand; the visual difference is what is more important. Look at Figure 14.2, which shows a frame rendered once with Multi-Pass motion blur and once without. Note the differences in the blur of the sphere, and most notably on the shadow. A:M only blurs objects with standard final quality render, whereas multi-pass motion blur averages the actual pixels of the frames to get the blur. This is an important difference to understand: with Multi-Pass on, A:M averages the actual subframes. You can use the nature of Multi-Pass motion blur to achieve numerous effects—some of which are discussed shortly—that would not be possible otherwise.

Blur Percent tells A:M how much to blur moving objects. Technically you are telling A:M what percentage of time *between* frames should be considered when determining the blur of an object. If this were a real-world camera, this would indicate the amount of time that the aperture remains open between frames. The higher the percent, the more an object is blurred as the camera tracks more of its motion between frames.

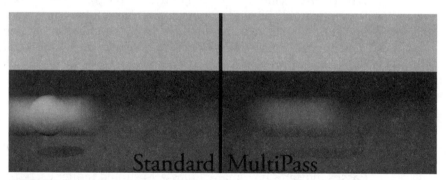

FIGURE 14.2   These two frames are identical except one is rendered with Multi-Pass and the other is not.

Depth of Field toggles A:M's rendering of camera focus effects. When you take photographs or use a film camera, not everything in the image is in perfect focus. There is a specific point that the camera lens is focused on, and anything closer to or farther away from the camera is more or less in focus. In 3D graphics, your camera inherently has an infinite depth of focus. This can make your images look less realistic or convincing to an audience.

Focal Distance is the exact point that the camera is focused on. Anything that is this far from the camera is in crisp focus.

Near Focus indicates the point where objects start to lose focus as they get closer to the camera; measured as distance away from the Focal Distance property toward the camera. For example, if the Focal Distance is 100 and the Near focus is 20, any object closer than 80cm to the camera is rendered out of focus.

Far Focus indicates how far past the Focal Distance the camera retains its focus. This is measured similarly to the Near Focus as a distance away from the Focal Distance property.

Depth of Field, like motion blur, has two styles of rendering that depends on the Multi-Pass render setting. Look at Figure 14.3 and again notice the differences in the renders. The most obvious difference is that the background sky color is not blended into the ground with the non-multi-pass blur. This is because, like Motion Blur, when Multi-Pass is on, you are sampling the actual pixels of the image at various depths to create the blurred image, while only the actual objects are considered when Multi-Pass is not active.

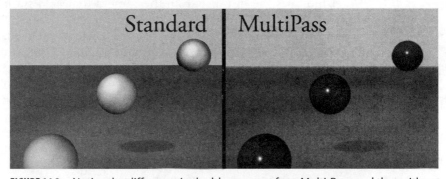

FIGURE 14.3   Notice the difference in the blur you get from Multi-Pass and that without.

Shadows toggles shadows on or off for the whole scene. In some shots, Cast Shadows might not be necessary for a convincing rendering, and the scene calculates much faster if they are not active.

Ambience Occlusion toggles the calculations for Ambient Occulsion.This gives objects a rough shadowing based on the proximity of one surface to another and is typically used in conjunction with Image Based Lighting Techniques. This property lets you toggle the effect for a particular camera in a chor and alter the amount of influence you allow it to have on the scene.

Reflections enables ray-traced reflections in the scene. If this property is turned off, the image is created without using reflectivity.

Levels determines how many times a ray will bounce to calculate reflectivity. Turn this down as low as possible because each level increases the time it takes to render a scene. You may need to increase this value if you need multiple reflective surfaces to accurately show the scene.

Soft invokes A:M's soft reflections rendering. This, as you may suspect, softens the reflections rendered on an object. The subproperty of Quality indicates the sampling each ray uses to determine the reflection. It is necessary to raise the quality for softer reflections. Soft uses the specular size of the surface to determine how soft it should be. A surface with a specular size of 10 will have much sharper reflections than a surface with a specular size of 100. Note that this setting can, and will, drastically increase your render times and should be used sparingly.

Draw Particles/Hair toggles on or off A:M's particle systems. Turn this on when you have images or animations that rely on any of A:M's particle systems, including hair for characters or sprites. If you are simply testing your animation, you might turn this off to increase render speeds.

Fog applies a fog effect to the camera cone. Fog, by default, is the same color as the background property of the camera. It starts at 0% opacity at the start distance and increases to 100% at a distance away from the camera determined by the end property. Note that this property will not affect any object that has its Ignore Fog property turned to on.

Start indicates the distance from the camera that A:M starts adding fog into the image. Anything closer to the camera than the start distance will have no fog affecting it, while those beyond it will be affected.

End indicates the point at which the fog becomes 100% opaque. Anything beyond this point will be completely obscured by the fog.

Image lets you specify any image you want to be used in place of the camera's background color. Fog is typically used to create the appearance of haze or atmosphere in renderings, but can be used to more drastic effect.

Toon Render turns on the toon-rendering engine. Enabling it allows you to change the toon-shading parameters of the entire scene. These parameters are the same as found on toon-rendered materials. See Chapter 12, "Surfacing," for a more complete discussion.

Field Render helps in matching imagery to a video image. Television signals are made up of a series of interlaced images, called fields, where alternating rows of the same image are displayed one after the other, giving the impression of a single, larger image. By default, Animation:Master renders noninterlaced images, which is generally what you want; but if you are trying to match 3D imagery to video from an analog source, you will want to render the image in fields. If you render in fields, you need to know which field you start with in your video source, either odd or even (sometimes referred to as upper and lower). If you are unsure, try a render. If you have it incorrect, you will know right away.

Stereo is a way of rendering to give a 2D image the feeling of depth. The most commonly known type of this effect, called an anaglyph, is seen through blue and red 3D glasses. A:M has very robust support for creating stereo images. Turning on these settings opens a broad range of options that you can use to create free viewing, anaglyph, and interlaced stereo renderings.

Plug-in Shaders enables A:M's render shaders. A render shader is a way to bypass A:M's default rendering methods. This can be turned on and off at the shortcut, but the type of shader used can only be set up on the original camera object or as a surface property. A:M ships with 19 plug-in shaders: Ambience, Anisotropic, BlinnPhong, Brushed, CookTorrance, Glossy, Gradient, Gradient Light, Lambert, Lewist, NullShader, Oren

Nayer, Phong, Planet Glow, Schlick, Skin, Velvet, Ward, and Wastin. The Diffuse shaders are Skin, Planet Glow, Oren Nayer, Null Shader, Lambert, Gradient Light and Gradient. Space doesn't allow discussion about all the aspects of all these shaders here, but if you look to the online technical reference you should be able to get a fair start. Figure 14.4 shows the same image rendered with each of the diffuse shaders applied. Exploring these shaders can help you find a rendering style all your own.

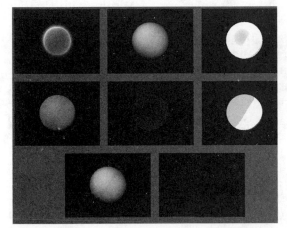

FIGURE 14.4   The Diffuse shaders can drastically alter the aesthetic of a render.

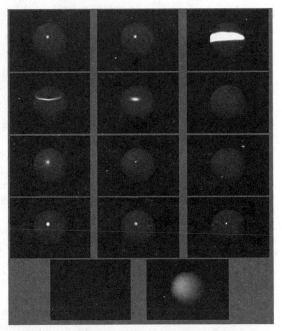

FIGURE 14.5   The Specular Render shader can alter the defalut specular highlights.

The Specular Render shaders are Westin, Ward, Schlick, Phone, Null Shader, Gradient Light, Glossy, Cook Torrance, Brushed, Blinn Phong, and Anisotropic. Figure 14.5 shows the same object rendered with each specular shader.

The Ambient shader simply allows you to specify a color for the ambience of a scene, so that instead of being simply less shadowed, the ambience can lend a subtle tint to the shadowed side of objects. This is similar to the Ambience color property on materials, with the exception that it applies globally to all objects in the scene and overrides the shadowed shading giving an entire shot a tint.

OUTPUT OPTIONS

The Output options grouping lets you set up the format, resolution, and render buffers for your images:

- Format
- Filename
- Range
- Resolution
- Gamma
- Buffers

Format is the type of file you want to render the image to. This can be any of the formats that A:M supports on your platform. A:M ships with plug-ins to read and write the following image formats: BMP, OpenEXR, JPEG, QuickTime Movie, PCX, PNG, Targa, and AVI (on PC only). Which format you render to is up to you and depends a great deal on how you intend to deliver your final image. If, for instance, you plan on putting your renders onto a Web site as a still image, PNG or JPEG might be perfect choices. If you are rendering a test animation or are publishing an animation to the Internet, QuickTime is a perfect choice. If you want or need to *composite* your image and use A:M's light buffer technologies then the High Dynamic Range OpenEXR format would be your choice. If you render an animation in any format other than QuickTime or AVI, A:M saves the frames as a numbered sequence of images based on the frame number being rendered. Regardless of the format, you render to the subproperty: Save Options gives you access to the compression and color depth settings for the given format, if available.

Filename allows you to specify what the file is named and where you want to save it on your hard drive. If you are creating a sequence of still images, you will want to name the file with a number of zeros at the end. A:M names still images in sequence starting at 0 and progressing normally. If you are rendering more than nine frames, however, this can lead to problems when compiling them into other formats since many applications and operating systems consider "frame10" to be lower than "frame2" in the naming sequence. Naming your file Untitled000, for instance, will provide enough padding for 999 frames without problems with the sequence.

Range is where you specify the frame range in the choreography to be rendered. This can start from frame 0 or any frame you like.

Resolution allows you to choose the size of the final render, either using one of the presets or by specifying a pixel dimension.

Gamma is the same as the post option of the same name, except that rather than applying the gamma to the pixels of the image, it is stored in a buffer that a paint program or other viewing application can use to correct the gamma on the fly.

Buffers holds a variety of optional buffers that can be created with the image. Which buffers are available depends on the image format you select for rendering. Some of the buffers are created inside the same file as the image information, while others store the buffer data in a separate file.

Alpha renders the image with a mask in the *alpha channel*. Any portions of the image that are not occupied with geometry are masked out of the image.

Light while listed for all image types is only truly useful when using the OpenEXR format. In an OpenEXR file, you can store more information than a traditional image. You can set this property to render the image as if it was lit by each light from the choreography, and then store each of those images in file on a separate "channel." You can then use A:M composite to change those channels to adjust the lights in a scene without having to rerender a scene. We go into this more when we discuss A:M Composite later in this chapter.

Shadows also creates an alpha channel in an image, but instead of rendering the other channels normally, it renders solid black and stores the shadows from the choreography in the alpha channel. This allows you to separate out the shadows for mixing your 3D with live-action footage. This is not needed if you are using OpenEXR for compositing in A:M, as shadows are broken out automatically.

Depth Buffers are only available when rendering to the OpenEXR format. It renders out a 32 bits-per-channel representation of the distance from the camera each point in the scene is. Currently, they are not completely useful. They store the information, but getting to it and using it elsewhere in A:M is not feasible at this time. Other ways to get Depth information out of the render are explored, as compositing is discussed later in this chapter.

Normals Buffers store the information of the surface normal for every pixel in the render. They can tell you what direction every pixel in your image is facing from the reference of the surface that was rendered to get the value of that pixel. Its use is very limited, and it is looked at only briefly later.

Apply Camera's Post Effects takes any Post Effects that may have been applied to the camera in the choreography and applies their effects to the rendered image. Under normal circumstances, most post effects are not rendered into the final image because this allows no adjustment of the effect later. So if you render with the effect in place, you have to rerender the entire image sequence to make any changes. Rather than spend the time rerendering, save the image and apply post effects in A:M composite. If you render to a final QuickTime, or if you just want the frame number listed on a quick render frame, then it could be benifical to render the post effect directly into the image. We go into much greater depth on these effects later.

NetRender

Other than the options that the base A:M package offers, Hash, Inc. also offers a network-rendering package that has additional features.

The primary feature in NetRender is the ability to distribute frames of animation to multiple machines across a network. This speeds up the rendering process, not by making the actual render times per frame shorter, but by allowing more than one frame per shot to be rendered simultaneously. It also has tools in it to manage renders for more than one project or choreography at a time. As your work becomes more complex you might find that you have a need for these tools. If nothing else, you might consider the time you could save by building an inexpensive render farm of a few machines. Each machine will mean more time to work on animation rather than waiting on rendering. Before you decide to run out and get a copy of NetRender, you should be capable of setting up a network of computers that can all share files among themselves. This is not complex networking but does require a little know-how. If you have questions, check the online Hash forums at *http://www.hash.com/forums/index.php?showforum=41* where other users can give you help and advice.

A:M COMPOSITE

A:M Composite is a feature of A:M that allows you to alter aspects of a render, such as light intensity and color, without the need to rerender the frames. In the long run, this makes it easier to experiment with lighting until you find something you like. You can separate out the various aspects of a light in a scene and effectively change most aspects of its illumination. The benefit is that you will not have to spend as much time rendering to make lighting changes. In order to use the Composite features, you need to have the data to work with in the first place. This data comes from buffers you set up at render time. The next few tutorials will go over how to get this data out of A:M and how to bring it back to composite it.

Starting Simple

When you start with a new feature, it makes sense to start with simple data and figure out what things do before you start to apply that knowledge to more complicated projects. To that end, you have a basic sphere over plane scene (see Figure 14.6).

FIGURE 14.6   A simple scene to get you started.

Not a fantastic image, but it does have what you need: data. Look at the image as if it had taken a long time to render and something you don't want to have to spend a lot of time rerendering. Presume that a client has you on a really tight deadline. You've been working late nights and somehow accidentally pushed your fill light from 20% to 200%. You set it up to render and went to sleep. When you woke up, the white spot on the sphere was completely blown out and your shadow was not dark enough. Did you really *mean* to make the key light that color? But you may not have the time to fix those things and rerender this for your client! Luckily you set up your project to render out to OpenEXR files with light buffers in them so you can make some adjustments.

Render Setup

Getting buffers out of a render is as easy as one, two, three:

1. Set the render type to OpenEXR Sequence.
2. Set the Buffer for Light Buffers to On and change it to each light in its own buffer (save the other options for another day).
3. Turn Multi-Pass rendering on.

With these settings, A:M breaks out the diffuse, specular, and shadow elements of each light into separate buffers (think of them like layers in Photoshop®) as well as breaking out the ambience and reflectivity of objects in the scene. Each of these elements is stored in what is called a buffer, which you can put to work in A:M Composite.

Starting a New Composite

A:M Composite is a special *image* type that lets you layer images and buffers together in ways other than the standard RGBA. We can use Post Effects (more on post effects later) to change aspects of any image you put into a composite, allowing you to make the adjustments that make your client happy without the time it takes to rerender the whole scene.

It is recommended that you composite in a new project file so after you finish rendering you can start a new project. In order to use composite, load in the sequence of EXR files you rendered out. This works just like any sequence of images in A:M. Right-click (control-click on the Mac) on the Images folder, and choose Import > Image Sequence. When you have the sequence in the project, take a look at what you have as far as data goes. In Figure 14.7, you see all the buffers that A:M split out for you:

- Color Alpha
- Diffuse
- Ambience
- LightDiffuse1
- LightDiffuse2
- LightDiffuse3

- LightSpecular3
- LightShadow3

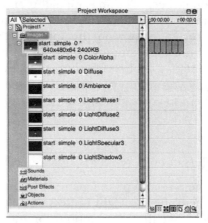

FIGURE 14.7   The render contains a number of buffers.

Color Alpha, the first buffer, is actually the image as A:M would output for a standard render in any format. It has the data from all the lights built right in. You don't use this much in compositing, though it does come in handy as a reference to what you started from.

Diffuse contains all the color data from the scene without any shading factored in (this is pretty much the same as a flat shade render out of A:M).

Ambience contains all the ambient light data from the scene. Any objects that have ambience set as a surface property will have that show up in this buffer.

Each light in a scene (as you rendered it) gets a buffer for the options on it that were enabled. In this scene, Light 1 and Light 2 have diffuse properties only, while Light 3 has diffuse, specular, and shadow properties.

You could go in and laboriously build up a composite for these elements to allow you to start tweaking elements by choosing New > Composite from the image folder's contextual menu, and then mixing and layering the elements together. Or you can just do it the easy way: Bring up the contextual menu for the EXR sequence in the PWS, and choose Build Composite and A:M automatically puts together a composite for you based on the data in the sequence. What you get is a series of "Mix" post effects, each of which has two children that are "mixed" together to produce a final image. You can adjust how much a particular buffer contributes to the final image by simply changing the value of its Mix percentage.

Identifying Your Needs

Before you get too far along with any composite, analyze your image and determine what you feel needs tweaking. While you can just load things and go at it through trial and error to see where you wind up with interesting results, if you want you or your client to be happy you need to identify the issues he has with your render and fix those.

You know that the white spot on that sphere is blown out, and it was mentioned that the shadow could be darker. Now that you think of it, the client really dislikes yellow lights, and you will need to fix that. These three things are probably enough to start with.

Once your needs are laid out, jump into the composite and find out what you have to work with.

A:M built a tree in the PWS for you when you asked it to build a composite. It contains all the data needed to produce the image as it was originally rendered. Your first step in your composite is finding the things you want to change in the image and the corresponding data in the composite tree.

Double-click the Composite object in the PWS. The new image window that opens shows the result of your current composite. If, however, you look at the PWS, you will see that after each element in the composite is a small circular icon that shows three possible states for each element. Green is the currently viewed element including any children of the tree that goes into making that element (so for now you have the root composite item selected to view, and all its children are in place). Dark gray/blue indicates that a particular element contributes to the currently viewed element (that is, it is a child of that element). Empty indicates that the element is neither being viewed nor does it contribute to the current view.

You can navigate through the layers that produce the composite by clicking on the circle to the right of its name. The first time you click a circle, it brings that element to focus making any of its children dark gray and all other aspects empty. If you click it again, the view is toggled to the full composite. This allows you to easily go back and forth to examine what a given branch is contributing to the composite tree. For instance, when you click the circle next to the first mix it will make that circle green and all the following circles dark gray, indicating that the first mix is the final compositing step. Given that information, you can rename the mix "Final Composite Mix." This is done just as you would rename any element in the PWS: Press F2 and type in a new name. Your next step is to look at each element in the composite and rename them all so that you know what each branch is doing (see Figure 14.8).

In the example, "start simple 0Composite RGBA" does not contribute to the final comp. Think of it as the "before" snapshot, which allows you to easily see what your changes have done to the image by showing you the original. It is this original that the post effects are acting upon to create the new composite. If you like, you can rename this image "original."

Adjusting Mix Levels

There are a few different ways in which you can handle changing the intensity of the light for the scene, but it is good practice to work with what you have in place before making gross changes. First, look at the values of your mix post effects.

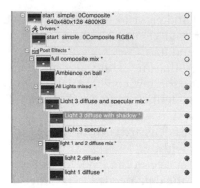

FIGURE 14.8 Rename all the items in the composite to indicate their function.

Starting at the "all lights mixed" post effect, which is where our Fill and Key lights come together, its data into your composting window so that you can see what is going on. Click the circle next to it in the PWS. This mix contains all the light data fed into two channels. The first is the key light in the scene, and the second is the fill light in the scene. You can look and be fairly certain that the fill light is the source of most of your intensity problems, so it makes sense to start by bumping the mix percentage down for input 2. Drop it to 50%, and you should see a change similar to Figure 14.9

If, however, you go back to the root of your composite tree, you see something like Figure 14.10.

FIGURE 14.9 Lowering the mix input adjusts the intensity of the fill light.

FIGURE 14.10 The change is not propagating back to the root of the tree.

Your change has not made its way back to the root of your composite tree, leading you to wonder what's going on. There must be something between the lights and the base of the composite that is causing trouble, which (in this case) leaves just one thing: the ambience on the ball is pushing the light on the ball to be too bright. You can adjust it at the first Mix branch of your composite. On Full

Composite Mix, change input 1 (the ambience level) down to 10%, and you should see something like Figure 14.11. Problem 1 solved.

FIGURE 14.11   The reduction of the ambience makes the render levels correct.

Breaking Out Shadows

Once the levels of the light look good, the shadow becomes your next concern. So, like the light data, look at your composite tree to see where the shadow might live.

The element renamed LightDiffuse3 with shadow looks to be the most likely suspect. Isolate it in the composite by clicking the circle next to it in the PWS (see Figure 14.12).

FIGURE 14.12   The shadow is revealed by isolating the layer for light 3.

Looking at the composite here, it's all bundled in with the diffuse elements of this buffer, and you just want to darken the shadow not the diffuse elements. There is a way you can separate out the shadow though, which given your goal will be necessary.

If you look at the original OpenEXR image you imported (see Figure 14.13), there is a buffer split out for shadows on light 3. It's just not anywhere to be found in your composite. Why? Well, it's not needed to build the image because the shadow is also right there in the diffuse element of light 3.

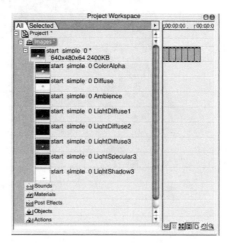

FIGURE 14.13   There is an unused shadow buffer in the Open EXR file.

In order to adjust only the shadow, first remove the shadow from the diffuse layer and then put it back in with your desired adjustments to the darkness. There is, thankfully, a simple way to do exactly that.

First, remove the shadows. This is done by simply bringing up the contextual menu on the light 3 diffuse with shadows element and choose Insert Post Effect > Hash Inc. > Divide. This adds a branch directly above the item. You brought up the menu for making the original buffer the first input in this new branch. Go ahead and rename it "Light 3 diffuse no Shadow". Now you need a second element to this branch before it will function correctly.

What it does is divide the pixels of one element from another, effectively lightening them inverse to the brightness of the pixels in the second image. If you know that shadow layers are multiplied in to adjust a level, this makes perfect sense, but it might seem weird if you don't. This is all computer graphics talk for how the image from one layer is combined with an image from another. If you are familiar with Photoshop, you are likely already familiar with this concept, which is called Blend mode there. All you need to know for this (right now anyway) is that those shadows you see are multiplied into the diffuse image, and divide (being the opposite of multiply) will remove them. So for your second element, simply drag and drop the LightShadow3 buffer onto the Divide you just created, and you should have something similar to Figure 14.14.

Now is a good time to rename the Divide layer so that you know what it does later. Name it "light3 shadow removed divide" or something similar. It is a good idea to keep the name of the post effect in the PWS element just to make it clear what you are adjusting. Before you can adjust the shadows, put them back into your composite. Multiply the shadow back into the now shadowless diffuse element for this light. And it needs to come after you have divided it out. So you want yet another branch in your composite. This time, right-click on the divide branch and choose Insert Post Effect > Hash Inc. > Multiply. Now drag and drop the shadow element onto this new branch to complete its input, and you are right back where you started with one difference: Now we can adjust the darkness (and other aspects) of the shadow without effecting the diffuse elements of this layer. You should have a composite tree similar to Figure 14.15.

FIGURE 14.14   Dividing can quickly remove the shadows from a layer.

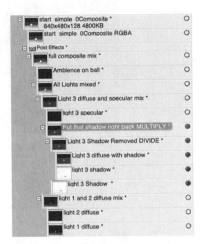

FIGURE 14.15   This is your current composite tree. Note the renamed Multiply branch.

Adjusting Shadow Darkness

Now you want to go into the shadow buffer and change the darkness of that shadow, so that it is more pronounced on the ground. This is actually very easy: Add a new branch to the composite by bringing up the contextual menu for the shadow buffer and choosing Insert Post Effect > Hash Inc. > Exposure. A lot of learning how to make Composite sing is in figuring out each post effect and what it does. We explore each post effect in depth shortly.

Look at what Exposure does. It has the following Properties: Active, Exposure, Brightness, and Contrast.

Active, of course, just shuts the effect off and lets the elements past the branch just filter through. Exposure has to do with the HDR aspects of your image. It allows you to push highlights past white and shadows under black. If you have an underlit scene, an exposure adjustment allows you to bring the render back into the range where you can see what is going on. In your case, start with Brightness and Contrast. You want the shadow to be darker, so drop the brightness from 50% (normal/default) to 30% to get something similar to Figure 14.16.

The readily apparent issue is that this casts a pall on your entire scene rather than just darkening the shadow area (which it has done). What you need to do is to push the light gray to white and allow the shadows to stay black. This is what contrast does. Push the contrast up to 90% and you get something similar to Figure 14.17.

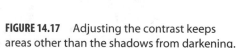

FIGURE 14.16 Lowering the brightness of the shadow buffer.

FIGURE 14.17 Adjusting the contrast keeps areas other than the shadows from darkening.

With the shadows darkened and the highlights from the fill brought under control, you have just one task left on your list: changing the color of the key light to a color other than yellow.

Light Color and Adjustment

In order to truly adjust the color of a light in a scene you need to adjust the actual *light* and leave the underlying surface properties of the geometry alone . . . Which, if you know anything about how light works in the real world, can be pretty confusing. In the real world, the color of a surface is actually determined by light. The surface bounces back certain wavelengths of light and absorbs others (speaking in a very simplified way). The light leaving that surface is then picked up by your eyes and bounced around your rods and cones to determine how bright that light is and what color you see the surface as being. In 3D, you cheat this quite a bit. Each surface has its own color regardless of what's going on in the scene; then you shoot light rays at that surface, and the color of the light alters the color of the surface by Multiplying the light into the surface. So when you want to change the color of a light, you need to be able to pull just the information that the light is contributing to a surface regardless of the color that surface might have. So how do you separate out the light data? The same way you separated out the shadow data. First, look at your available buffers (see Figure 14.18) for what you need.

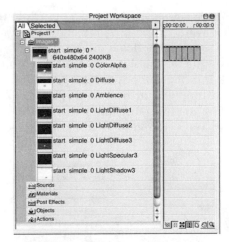

FIGURE 14.18   Look at the buffers. You are looking for either a buffer that just holds light data or one that just holds surface color data.

The buffer that you are looking for here is the Diffuse buffer, not the diffuse buffer for any of our three lights, mind you. Those contain the diffuse color of a surface and the effect of lighting. No, you need the Diffuse buffer that contains *only* the diffuse surface colors for the objects in the scene, which is the one right there at the top: start simple 0 Diffuse.

This is what is called a flat, shaded version of the scene (see Figure 14.19): what the scene looks like without any lights added in at all. It's not much to look at but it does give us something to divide your diffuse light elements with to get to just the light data.

FIGURE 14.19   The Diffuse buffer shows a flat, shaded version of your scene.

Go to your composite and add a branch to the Light 3 diffuse with shadow element. You want to add a Divide branch just as you did to remove the shadow, but this time drag the global diffuse buffer to the branch to complete it. Again, just like you did for the shadow, you need to multiply the diffuse elements of the scene back into the composite after you do the Divide. It is a good idea to simply insert the Multiply right now while you're thinking of it, if for no other reason than it keeps you from forgetting about it later. Rename your new branches, and you might have a composite tree that looks like Figure 14.20

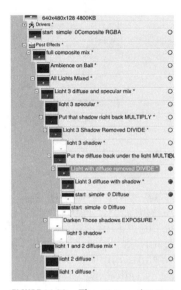

FIGURE 14.20 The composite tree after dividing out and multiplying back in the diffuse buffer.

If you toggle between the multiply and divide branches, you probably won't detect a huge difference, but that's because our surface colors aren't really set. They are all default white. If you had any variation off that default white in the scene, you'd see pretty vast differences. Now that you have the light separated, you can see that it is indeed yellow in hue, and you want to make this light a cool color. There are a couple ways that you can go about this. You can either use the tint post effect, or you can use the HSE post effect. Do tint here and explore HSE on another layer.

Tint takes the range of color in an image and reduces it to just brightness of each pixel, which you can then map to two colors. One will supplant the dark tones in the image, and the other will alter the light tones. In the print world (and in Photoshop), this is called a duotone. It is used to give images that old-timey sepia tone look to them or to simply take a color image and make it black and white.

The Tint branch is added to your composite tree in the same manner that you have done for all other post effects. Right-click on the Divide branch you just added, and add a new Tint post effect. The new branch defaults to making your image black and white. There are a number of other presets available to you: Colbalt makes the darks of the image black and the lights a rich deep blue; Sepia turns the image into a sepia tone, where the darks are a dark rich burnt umber color and the lights are a light brown; X-Ray makes the dark tones white and the light tones black. Or we can use a custom set of colors, as shown in Figure 14.21.

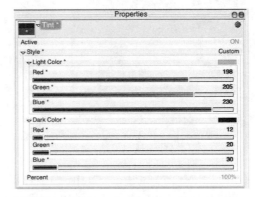

FIGURE 14.21   The colors for your tint are a very dark blue-gray and a brighter version of the same color.

The last little bugbear is the yellow/orange fill light: light 1 diffuse. Tackle this just like you did light 3: First, divide out and multiply back in the Diffuse for the entire scene, then add a branch in to change the color of the separated-out light data. This time, use the HSE effect to do it.

HSE stands for Hue Saturation Exposure. The simple way to think of this is: Hue determines the color, Saturation determines how vivid or washed out the colors are, and Exposure determines how bright or dark the colors are. In the way of computers, seemingly simple concepts are actually pretty complex if you keep digging, but this base understanding is enough for now. So, at the point where you have the light data broken out of your composite (that is, on the divide branch), right-click to add a new HSE effect. This effect will allow you to shift the hue from the yellow range that it is in to a cooler color range. To understand what the hue shift will do, think of a color wheel and think of your color as being a fixed point in space—not really a color, but a coordinate that points to a color on the wheel. When you adjust the hue, you rotate the wheel without changing the location of the point of your color so that now it points to a different color entirely. The upshot is that you can change an entire color range without affecting the variations across a surface (as with tint). Hue takes a value from −180 (rotate the wheel counterclockwise 180 degrees) to 180 (rotate the wheel clockwise 180 degrees). With a little experimentation, you can find a color that you like. For this example, give the wheel a value of 50 (shifting the color wheel 50 degrees clockwise moves the green range of color under your point). At this point, you have a full composite that looks like Figure 14.22, which is a whole world of difference from where you started (see Figure 14.23).

FIGURE 14.22   The final composite.

FIGURE 14.23   The original render.

The actual time to build and adjust this composite will likely be under 20 minutes, which if you are talking about an animation with hundreds of frames that you want to adjust is a huge timesavings on rerendering. If this is what you want, it's a simple matter to commit to this: Right-click the composite in the PWS, choose Save As Animation..., and your composited image is saved to disk in the format of your choice. If we send this to your client and they decide they want the fill to be purple instead of green, no problem: just change the hue (–150 would probably do the trick) and save as animation. Total rerendering time: 0 seconds. Let that sink in. You just changed something that affects the look of every frame of your animation and the total time to render that change to file is 0 seconds. Suddenly the render is a reusable asset that can be used again and again, changed slightly, and output with no real hit to your time.

The thing to remember here is that composites aren't just for fixing problems; that's really the least of their use. Mostly, they are about giving you the freedom to try different things all at full resolution all over the full length of an animation all without having to render a scene dozens of times.

POST EFFECTS

Before you can truly understand Composite, you need to understand the tools you have at hand. Most of these tools are in the form of post effects.

A little experimentation with them can go a long way in determining if they are needed for your images. Some of these are best suited (or explicitly intended) for use as render-time post effects (applied to a camera in the chor), but all of them can be used in a composite.

Alias Edges is intended for use on a camera at render time. It removes any antialiasing from the edges of an object in a render. This allows A:M to antialias the internal aspects of an object (such as textures and decals) without smoothing the edges. This is primarily used to create "sprites" for games.

Auto Levels compresses the color range of an image so that the lightest color is white and the darkest color is black. This is done so that images that have a high range of data do not exhibit "clipping" when exported to a format with a lower range of color (going from open EXR to JPG, for instance).

Bloom simulates another common artifact of film that digital images don't have. Bloom comes from the brightest areas of an image bleeding into and slightly overexposing other portions of an image. This is most noticeable around heavy specular hits.

Blur applies a simple blur to any buffer. It can be used for basic shadow softening or other simple effects.

Clamp is similar to auto levels in that it limits the range of the colors in a composite (from 0 to 255), but does it by locking all values at this level, whereas auto level attempts to maintain the overall distribution of values.

Dither blends colors by altering pixels in the transition among the available colors. When an image is rendered, it is limited to a finite number of colors, and large shifts in color can cause a visible banding if there are not enough colors to transition smoothly between them. To alleviate this problem, you can tell A:M to dither. This simulates a greater range of color than is available.

Divide has been used a number of times and its properties already discussed. Basically it divides the value of the pixels in the first input by the same pixel in the second input, in effect lightening the image based on the luminosity of the second input.

Exposure is looked at earlier. It sets up a basic way to adjust the brightness and contrast of an image, but goes a step further and offers exposure controls. Exposure allows you to adjust the range of values by compressing or expanding the overall range of the image without clamping the max or min value.

Film grain can be used to add grain like noise to your images. In live action, the chemical process used to create images on film creates a visible artifact called film grain. This artifact is more or less noticeable, depending on the type of film used and the length of time it is exposed. This is especially visible on dark images. Because most movies are shot on film, audiences have come to expect this artifact, so much so that a perfect digital image without it is perceived to be of lesser quality.

Frame Burn is intended to be a render-time camera effect. It simply puts the number of the frame into the image of the frame as it is being rendered. This allows you to pinpoint frames of animation that need to be tweaked.

Gamma is a scale that changes the perceived brightness of an image. Every type of viewing device, from computer monitors to television sets, has a property that indicates its basic color range. Even different computer platforms have different standards. These values are represented by what is known as gamma. If you are targeting a particular medium such as NTSC television, you can adjust the gamma of your render here.

Hue Saturation Exposure is looked at earlier. This effect allows you to shift the color of an image by altering its reference to the color spectrum or by desaturating it. The same exposure controls that are in the Exposure effect are here to allow brightness adjustments without clamping.

Min Med Max samples a radius of pixels and adjusts the value of each pixel based on this sample range. It either makes the pixel equal to the Minimum value, the Maximum value, or some value in between (Medium). The result in general is that Min darkens an image while Max lightens it. It is possible to get very artistic effects with this post effect.

Mix allows you to specify the amount each of its two inputs contributes to the final image.

Multiply is the opposite of divide and takes the value of each pixel in the first input and multiplies it by the value of the pixel in the second input. The overall result is a darkening of the image in relation to the luminosity of the second input.

Over layers one image (with an alpha channel presumably) over a second. The order is reversed from what you might think, but follows the hierarchy of the rest of A:M's PWS, where the lower image is placed on top of the first input image.

Tint changes the overall color of the render by changing the color to grayscale and applying two colors based on luminance values to the image. With it you can create subtle black-and-white film effects or make an image look old and worn with a sepia tint.

Video Safe adjusts the color on any out-of-gamut colors (not viewable on television screens) to fit within the range that an NTSC monitor can safely display. This prevents oversaturated or "clipped" colors. This is most noticeable in the red color range and can produce less than desirable effects. You may need to use other post effects to move the range before making it video safe to prevent unsightly color banding.

Each of these effects is in itself useful, but as you have learned it is in the layering and compositing of these effects that they reveal their power.

LAYERS

A:M allows you to use 2D images in a number of ways: rotoscopes, decals, and sprites. Another powerful use of 2D images comes in the form of layers. A layer is a 2D image that can be used without any geometry in a choreography. This allows basic compositing and traditional multiplane camera-style features. The most common use for layers in A:M is to place previously rendered background elements, and other set pieces, into a shot without requiring the associated geometry. This can do a good deal for speeding up rendering and lends a certain amount of flexibility in shot creation.

There are other more innovative uses for layers that can speed other aspects of a production or achieve effects that would otherwise be difficult to produce or expensive to render. Most of the more innovative uses for layers simply come from knowing what can be done to a layer beyond positioning it in the choreography.

At the most basic level, a layer can be thought of as a single patch with a cookie-cut map applied to it, primarily intended to create backdrops or multiplane effects. Multiplane is a reference to a type of camera developed at the Walt Disney Studios to shoot layers of animation with depth applied. It operated by means of a series of glass plates on various levels under a camera (see Figure 14.24). The layers could be moved individually to give a great sense of depth to otherwise flat 2D animation.

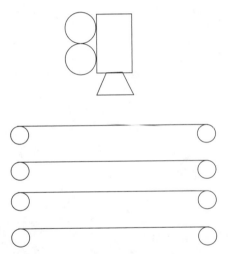

FIGURE 14.24 The original multiplane camera operated by using layers of glass.

Layers in A:M can also be used to give depth to otherwise 2D aspects. For example, a background can be rendered out, or taken from a photograph, and applied to various layers in a project. Since layers are simply 2D images, they render incredibly fast. The layers can then be positioned in front of the camera and at various depths to create a true depth without the need for all the extra geometry.

Beyond that, you can use a little creative tweaking to make layers do varied and interesting things, like simulated cutout animation. Cutout animation is created by moving cutout pieces of paper one frame at a time, in a similar fashion to stop-motion Claymation. To do this, add nulls to the layer and change the position of the default bone in the object. Once this has been done, it is a simple matter to create kinematic chains of layers that can be animated easily.

SUMMARY

Finding the correct settings for any render is largely a matter of trial and error. We don't have much need for much of the control that A:M gives us, but for those times when it is required you will be glad to have it built in.

The largest effect on perceived quality comes from the antialiasing of the image. The smoother the colors and transitions are, the better the image appears. Using multi-pass techniques is probably the best way to get this quality into your images.

GROUP PROJECTS

In This Chapter

- Getting the Ball Rolling
- Online Collaboration and Project Management
- Asset Management

I n this chapter, we look at the tools that A:M has that allow you to start and manage a collaborative animation project over the Internet. The focus is on sharing and managing files, but also touches on setting up and maintaining project management.

You need no files for this chapter.

GETTING THE BALL ROLLING

The most difficult part of any project, whether it is a feature film with hundreds of artists or a short film done by one person, is just getting the process started and keeping the momentum going. Finding people to work on any project, especially when you consider that most will be spare-time projects, can be very difficult. The best way to start is to develop relationships in the A:M community. The online forums at *http://www.hash.com/ forums* are a good place to start. Or you might investigate the Community panel inside A:M where you can chat with other A:M users in real time. However you go about it, the relationships you develop may evolve into collaborative partnerships. Or you might find a larger project underway and offer your help. A perfect example of such a project is the Tin Woodsman of Oz film that Hash, Inc. has used as the development focus for the 2006 subscription cycle. This project has driven the features that are discussed in this chapter as well as several of the improvements and tools that you have already looked at.

Getting a group together is only half the battle though. Time constraints and life can and will get in the way. Finding the perseverance to push a project along despite all the setbacks can be more daunting than the work of animation itself. Setting realistic goals for a film and meeting them can go a long way in keeping people involved; shooting for too much often leads to frustration.

ONLINE COLLABORATION AND PROJECT MANAGEMENT

Once you have a crew together working on a project, the next hurdle, especially when talking about Internet-based projects where individuals might live thousands of miles apart, is getting everyone on the same page. This process can be sped up by using a common forum where people can look at each other's work and offer comments, critiques, and most importantly encouragement.

At the vary base level, make a list of what is needed as early in the process as possible. Take the script and break it down into scenes, and then list the milestones and other aspects of the scene that need to be met before it is finished, from storyboard to voice recording all the way through compositing final renders. Break the tasks down into small bite-sized pieces so that members of the crew can always find something relatively simple that they can work on. If you have access to a Web server of your own and are either comfortable setting up server software or have a competent system administrator at your disposal, you can set the entire list up in a project management environment, such as dotProject. At the very least, you can simply use a forum and a set of threads to keep track of everything where the crew can post comments or progress for review.

Once everyone is talking and the tasks have started to be assigned, the problem comes in keeping track of all the data in the project and maintaining revisions from multiple artists. From the first spline in the first model to the last pixel of the last rendered frame, every file must be tracked and kept in place. This is actually a very important and complicated set of problems. Keeping all the members of a project current on all the potentially hundreds of files in a project would be daunting if A:M didn't have integrated tools for just this need.

The foundation of management is the file-naming structure that you will develop (as discussed in Chapter 1, "Interface"). As long as everyone understands where to save and how to name the files in a project, the remainder can be handled by A:M.

ASSET MANAGEMENT

SVN is a tool used by programmers to allow effective collaboration on pieces of code, where more than one person can work on a file at the same time. The files are stored both on the local computer of the individuals working and in a central repository. When you start working on a project, you check out the files that currently exist and save them to you hard drive. Then as you work, you send up changes to the server and receive the changes that other people might have made. In this way, two programmers can work on the same piece of software code simultaneously. Hash has leveraged this same technology into A:M to allow groups of far-flung individuals to work collaboratively over the Internet.

As of this writing, SVN is integrated into the Community panel of A:M, but this may change, especially for private projects. The focus of the asset management on the Community panel is TWO, but it can work with any project that has an SVN repository set up for it. The first step then is to get a running SVN repository. If you have a Web server and are very familiar with setting up programs for it, you can set up your own or simply use one of the free or low-cost hosts available. We will not go into how to set up an SVN server, as that is far beyond the scope of this book.

Once you have a server, it is a simple matter of setting it up for use in A:M. This may change from the time of this writing as it is a very new feature and still being finalized by Hash, Inc. As of now on the Community panel in A:M, click the TWO Movie tab. Click the button on this tab that says Receive to start the setup process for the Repository. Give a local location for the files on your computer, and then provide A:M your log-in information for your repository, including the address of the server. By default, the SVN points to the TWO movie repository, but you can direct it to any server you choose. Once you are set up, A:M connects and downloads all the files in the repository to the local folder you indicated. This initial download can take a fair amount of time if there are a lot of files on the server. Once that is accomplished, any changes you make to the files for the project can be sent to the server by simply clicking the Send button. This uploads all changes to the server. Likewise, the next time you click the Receive button, you get the most up-to-date versions of the files in the project. The URL for the current project repository in A:M can be changed from the SVN tab on the Options panel (see Figure 15.1).

From this panel, you can change the current SVN URL by simply clicking the Repository URL button. A:M works with only one repository at a time, however, so if you want to work on multiple projects you need to change the URL you use here each time you need to change your access. You can also change the local folder (which, if you work on multiple projects, changes with each project).

The important thing to note is that the repository system allows two people to work on a given file at the same time. For instance, if you and a partner both work on a character, perhaps you add decals to it and your partner adds the bones for rigging, you would both have a different version of the file—your partner's without decals and yours without bones. You would both send the file up to the

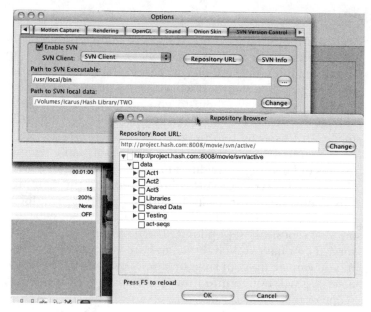

FIGURE 15.1 The SVN options let you set up other servers.

repository, at which point the SVN system would merge the files. You would then each receive a new version of the file. This version would have both the decals and the bones in it. If, on the other hand, you both change the same part of a file, say your partner animates a character on frame 10 and you do the same, the change would be in conflict with one another. If there is a conflict, someone must clear it before the new file is merged into the repository. That person is typically the director. The director looks at each animation and determines which one to keep. In this manner, everyone working on a project can keep up to date with very little effort.

SUMMARY

Animation is hard, and while it can be a solitary endeavor, there is nothing that says it *must* be. If you choose to work with other artists, A:M and the Internet can provide critical tools to drive you and your projects toward completion.

16

MISCELLANY

In This Chapter

- Preferences and Settings
- PWS Filters
- Creating an Animatic and Other Basic Editing Tricks
- Getting More Help

In this chapter, we look into things that don't fit other places, and topics that don't need quite the depth of coverage of some of the others. We discuss the organization of a workspace and some of A:M's preferences. And finally, we include a list of resources for finding help both online and off. You'll need no files for this chapter.

This chapter wraps up the discussion of A:M. You should be prepared now to move forward with the tools that A:M provides. We look forward to seeing your work.

PREFERENCES AND SETTINGS

All the tutorials and examples in this book have gone under the assumption that the preferences and settings for A:M are at their default values. But most users will want to customize the settings to complement the way they work. A few of the settings have already been discussed, such as the lathe settings, advanced properties, and show particles/fur. But you can find a number of new features and customize the way A:M behaves by changing the preferences. You can find the preferences under the Tool menu.

The options, as A:M refers to them, are broken down by groups on tabbed panels. Finding a set of options that complements your working style takes time, but for the most part you shouldn't need to change much. There are settings here to improve performance and to change the way the tools work. You will use the Modeling tab most often. To change the lathe settings, you can always come to this tab by simply holding the Shift key when clicking the Lathe button. Most of the other settings can be toggled with keyboard shortcuts (see Appendix A for a complete list of shortcut keys) or are set once and left alone.

If there is one setting that can make A:M more stable and enjoyable on your machine it is the Undo setting. A:M is capable of unlimited undos, but each level requires more RAM and resources to track. It is recommended that you turn the number of undos available as low as you are comfortable with; a setting of 3 for an experienced user is generally good enough. As a rule of thumb, if you aren't sure about something you are about to do, save a new version, and you should save for anything that will take you more than 5 minutes to do again.

The other settings are found on the Customize panel. These change the way A:M looks and behaves, allowing you to turn off or customize the toolbars or even create new ones. You can also change the keyboard shortcuts or create shortcuts for tools you use often. This is not recommended until you have more familiarity with A:M though, and remember that most tutorials assume that you are using the default key bindings.

If you need to change all the settings back to their defaults, simply select Reset Settings from the help menu and restart A:M. All settings will be restored to their factory defaults.

PWS FILTERS

The PWS holds a lot of information designed to give you easy access to any given set of properties at any time. The upside is that you have access to a wide array of data that you can use to create complex relationships. The downside is that it can be difficult to locate the information that you need when you need it. To solve this problem, A:M uses filters.

Two filters are always available in the PWS: All and Selected. All shows every item in a project; Selected shows only the currently selected object. You can create new filters to show exactly what you need when you need it. For example, say you want to work on a particular character; you could create a filter for only that character's name (see Figure 16.1).

You make new filters by clicking the PWS filter button—the square button with the triangle on it at the top right-hand side of the PWS window. Clicking this button and selecting New Filter brings up the Edit Filter dialog (see Figure 16.2).

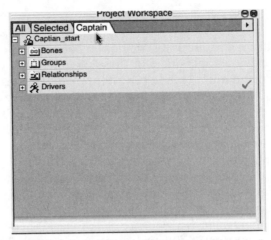

FIGURE 16.1   Using a PWS filter to isolate individual characters.

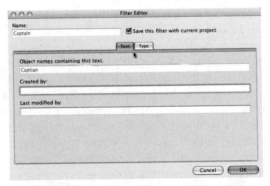

FIGURE 16.2   The Edit Filter dialog allows you to set up tabs and define what they display.

From here, you can name the tab that will be created and specify the types and names of objects that will be shown.

To create a tab for a single character, type that character's name into the object names containing this text field. When you close the editor, a new tab is placed at the top of the PWS that shows only your model, including every instance of it in a choreography. This is handy for animating a single character in a cluttered choreography, as it excludes lights, cameras, and other models.

Using this, you can create a set of tabs in a project for any grouping you may need. Saving these settings with the project allows you to create a set of filters for a group, allowing each individual to work on his area of a project without the need to dig through the clutter of everyone else's work.

CREATING AN ANIMATIC AND OTHER BASIC EDITING TRICKS

We talk a lot about using compositing or editing applications for assembling work or creating an animatic, but these programs can cost hundreds or thousands of dollars, and not everyone can afford them. For the starving artist or student, A:M has come to the rescue. It has a basic set of editing and compositing tools built in.

Often, animation is rendered as a numbered series of Targa images, making the quality of the images lossless and lets you interrupt a render and resume it later. However, Targa sequences are not easily played back or shared, For that, most people want a QuickTime movie of the sequence. You can use a camera rotoscope to place the series of Targas into the camera view and then quickly render the sequence to a file, scaling the output and applying compression.

You can create an animatic in the same way, taking your storyboard drawings and naming them as a sequence of Targa files. Then by animating the frame property for the rotoscope on the camera, you can control how long each image is shown.

You can also create simple editing with decaled image sequences. Decal one patch with an image sequence, then add the other sequences you want to edit together to the decal. Make each sequence a color image, turn the ambience of the patch to 100%, and place it in a choreography. In the camera's properties, change the type to orthogonal. This removes all perspective from the camera. Place the patch in front of the camera so that the decal fills the camera view. Now you can animate the frame and value properties of the individual layers of sequences. If you make the color of the patch that you have decaled black, you can even create a simple fade to black by lowering the value of the images to 0. If you have sounds that you want to apply, you can create a new action for the patch and add in all the sounds you might want. Adjusting their starting and ending points in the Timeline allows you to align them with the action, while animating the volume or mute properties on the sound itself allows you to fade in or cut out particular sounds. Dropping this action on the patch model in the choreography tells A:M to render the sounds into the QuickTime file.

Need to superimpose a watermark on your renders? Try using a layer or a camera rotoscope that is always on top. The same technique can be used to overlay a binocular mask or a gun scope. It's not as full featured as Apple's Final Cut Pro, perhaps, but Final Cut Pro costs $999.00. With a little creative thinking you can find a way to accomplish almost anything you need to do with editing right in A:M.

GETTING MORE HELP

This book has tried to cover a lot of ground for the new user and to expand that information rapidly. Due to the limitations of space and time, not all topics could be covered in the depth that they deserve. The programmers at Hash are also working hard to add new features and to improve the ones that already exist. This makes information a moving target, and makes any attempt to cover it all in one volume next to impossible.

When approaching topics like animation or lighting, which are very deep by nature, we have only touched on the basics. There is a great deal of information available on all the various topics of animation and 3D that is not specific to any one software package, as well as a number of tutorials and other resources for A:M.

Online

Hash, Inc. Forums: *http://www.hash.com/forums/*. The official online forum for Hash, Inc. remains the go-to source for tips, tricks, and camaraderie among A:M users. This is maintained and frequented by the programmers and other folks at Hash, Inc.

The A.R.M. (A:M Resource Matrix) *http://www.lowrestv.com/arm/*. Your one stop for tutorials and other A:M-related resources.

Hash.com *http://www.hash.com*. The home page for Hash, Inc., where you can find links to user sites, image contests, galleries of user work, and more. Stop by and check for the latest information and software updates.

Eggprops.com *http://www.eggprops.com*. Purveyor of fine models and textures as well as video tutorials on various aspects of A:M. The quality of the models offered here is amazing. Prices are better than models of lesser quality available from other sources. If you need a prop or animal or a full canyon set, consider this site a good source. Even if you don't, the skill exhibited in the construction of the models is worth its weight in gold as a learning tool.

Anzovin.com *http://www.anzovin.com*. Anzovin studios offers training videos on some of the more technical aspects of using A:M, as well as the SetUp machine, a tool for automatically rigging characters.

The Katakata Atelier: *http://home9.highway.ne.jp/katakata/*. If your interest is in creating anime-style characters and animation then consider the Katakata Atelier a must see. The site is in Japanese, so if you do not read that language, you will need the assistance of a Web site translator. The effort is worth it for the wonderful imagery alone. The tutorials and DOS utilities that are provided as free downloads are a bonus.

Books

The Animator's Survival Kit™ **by Richard Williams (ISBN 0-571-20228-4).** Richard Williams encapsulates all the fundamentals and many of the secrets to great animation into this book, and it is a must read for any serious student of animation. The level of detail in this book makes it the most thorough book on the techniques for animation on the market. If you own only one book on animation, this is the one to have.

Cartoon Animation **by Preston Blair (ISBN 1-56010-084-2).** This is the seminal work on how to animate; it has long been the one book that you will find on the desk of almost every animator in the business. Preston

Blair offers insight into the basics and moves through the process of animation in a simple fashion, illustrating the principles clearly and providing an indispensable reference for the creation of various cycles.

[digital] Lighting and Rendering **by Jeremy Birn (ISBN 1-56205-954-8).** Jeremy Birn not only covers aspects of lighting in a software agnostic fashion, but also discusses color theory, surfacing techniques, and composition techniques. This volume offers the most comprehensive look at making your renders more attractive than any other book on the market.

Other

Community. This is actually part of A:M. A community window can be opened allowing you to talk with other Hash users while you work; sometimes you can find the programmers or support staff online. It is similar to other instant-messaging software, but is accessed directly from the A:M interface. A great way to keep in contact with collaborators.

#hash3d. Users also gather online on a dedicated IRC server and have been trading tips and tricks for a number of years. You can join with any IRC client by pointing it at the server *obnomauk.dnsalias.org* port 6667 and joining the channel #hash3d. The server runs 24 hours a day, seven days a week, but Wednesday evenings are designated gathering nights.

SUMMARY

ON THE CD

That's it. This is the end of the book! Be sure to look on the CD-ROM, if you haven't already. We hope that you found this book helpful in your explorations of Animation:Master. This is a very deep program, and learning all of its ins and outs can take years, but it is simple and elegant enough that you can be creating animation in as little as a month. The tools are just the beginning of the journey; the techniques and art that make animation great is a lifetime of learning and growing.

ANIMATION:MASTER KEYBOARD SHORTCUTS

Mac

COMMAND	DESCRIPTION	SHORTCUT
File:Open	Open an existing document.	Command+O
Project:Save	Save the active project.	Command+S
View:Project Workspace	Show or hide the Project Workspace panel.	Command+0
View:Libraries	Show or hide the libraries window.	Command+1
View:Properties	Show or hide the property panel.	Command+2
View:Pose Sliders	Show or hide the pose sliders panel.	Command+3
View:Community	Show or hide the Community window.	Command+5
Tools:Options	Change options.	Command+P
Help:Help Topics	List Help topics.	F1
Add Lock Mode	Enter Add Lock mode.	A
Add Mode	Enter Add mode.	Shift+A
File:Exit	Quit the application.	Command+Q
Move Down	Move the selected object down one pixel.	Down Arrow
Move Left	Move the selected object left one pixel.	Left Arrow
Move Right	Move the selected object right one pixel.	Right Arrow
Move Up	Move the selected object up one pixel.	Up Arrow
Attach Control Point	Attach control point.	`
Back View	Set the selected window to Back View.	Num 8
Bird's Eye View	Set the selected window to Bird's Eye View.	Num 7
Bones Mode	Enter Bones Editing mode.	F6
Bone Visible	Make the selected bone visible.	J
Bones Visible Branch	Make the bones visible for the branch.	Shift+J
Bottom View	Set the selected window to Bottom View.	Num 0
Bound Branch	Set the draw mode for the branch to Bound.	Shift+B
Break	Break the selected spline.	K
Camera View	Set the selected window to Camera View.	Num 1
Edit:Invert Selection	Toggle the state of all control points.	.
Curved Branch	Set the draw mode for the branch to Curved.	Shift+C
Decrease Subdivisions	Decrease the subdivisions in Shaded mode.	Page Down

COMMAND	DESCRIPTION	SHORTCUT
Default Draw mode	Use model's Draw mode.	7
Delete	Deletes the current selection.	Del
Edit:Deselect All	Deselect all selected control points.	Return
Detach Point	Detach the selected control point.	Shift+K
Choreography Mode	Enter Choreography mode.	F9
Bound	Bound.	B
Curved	Curved.	C
Vector	Vector.	V
Edit:Copy Keyframe	Copy the selection to the Clipboard.	Command+C
Edit:Cut Keyframe	Cut the selection and put it on the Clipboard.	Command+X
Edit:Paste Keyframe	Insert Clipboard contents.	Command+V
Edit:Redo	Redo the previously undone action.	Command+Y
Edit:Undo	Undo the last action.	Command+Z
Edit Mode	Enter Edit mode.	Escape
Extrude Mode	Enter Extrude mode.	E
File:Close	Close the active document.	Command+W
New	Create a new document.	Command+N
Flip Normals	Flip the normals of all selected patches.	F
Jump To Frame	Enter the frame number to jump to.	Command+F
Front View	Set the selected window to Front View.	Num 2
Show Grid	Toggle the grid on and off.	3
Edit:Group Connected	Select all control points connected by splines.	/
Group Mode	Enter Group mode.	G
Edit:Select Spline	Select all control points on the spline.	,
Hide CPs	Hide all unselected control points.	H
Hide More	Hide all unselected control points.	Shift+H
Increase Subdivisions	Increase the subdivisions in Shaded mode.	Page Up
Insert	Insert a Point along the selected spline.	Y
Toggle Interrupt	Toggle interrupted drawing on/off.	2
Invisible Mode	Set the draw mode for the object to Invisible.	I
Invisible Branch	Set the Draw mode for the branch to Invisible.	Shift+I
Lasso Draw Mode	Enter Lasso Draw mode.	Shift+G
Lathe	Lathe the selected spline.	L
Left View	Set the selected window to Left View.	Num 4
Light View	Set the selected window to Light View.	Num 3
Modeling Mode	Enter Modeling mode.	F5
Move	Enter Move mode.	M
Muscle Mode	Enter Muscle Motion mode.	F7
Select Deeper	Jump to next object behind current object.	]
Next Frame	Advance to the next frame.	+
Next Keyframe	Advance to the next keyframe.	Shift - +
Next Object	Select the next object.	Tab
Next CP	Select the next control point.	}
Show Normals	Toggle normals on and off.	1

COMMAND	DESCRIPTION	SHORTCUT
Patch Group Mode	Enter Patch Group mode.	Command+P
Peak	Peak the selected control points.	P
Perspective	Toggles perspective mode in this view.	\
Previous Frame	Jump to the previous frame.	-
Previous Keyframe	Jump to previous keyframe.	Shift + -
Previous Object	Select the previous object.	Tab
Previous CP	Select the previous control point.	{
View:Refresh	Redraw the current view.	Space
Render Lock Mode	Enter Render Lock mode.	Shift+Q
Render Mode	Enter Render mode.	Q
Right View	Set the selected window to Right View.	Num 6
Rotate Group Images	Rotate group images.	Shift+R
Rotate Mode	Set manipulator to Rotate mode.	R
Scale Mode	Set manipulator to Scale mode.	S
Edit:Select All	Select all control points.	Command+A
Toggle Shading	Toggle shading on and off for the object.	X
Shaded Branch	Toggle Shaded on and off for the branch.	Shift+X
Shaded	Set the Draw mode to shaded.	9
Shaded/Wireframe	Set the draw mode to Shaded with Wireframe.	0
Skeletal Mode	Enter Skeletal Motion mode.	F8
Smooth	Smooth the selected control points	O
Edit:Snap Group To Grid	Snap the selected control points to the grid.	'
Toggle Back Face Culling	Toggle back face culling.	Shift+6
Show Decals	Turn Decal drawing On/Off	D
Show Particle/Fur	Toggle particle/fur drawing on and off.	Shift+8
Top View	Set the selected window to Top View.	Num 5
Translate Mode	Set manipulator to Translate mode.	N
Turn	Enter Turn mode.	T
Vector Branch	Set draw mode for the branch to Vector.	Shift+V
Toggle Full Screen Mode	Toggle Full Screen Mode on or off.	F11
View Settings	Open View Settings dialog.	Shift+4
Toggle Wireframe	Toggle the wireframe for the object.	W
Wireframe Branch	Toggle wireframes for the branch.	Shift+W
Wireframe	Set the draw mode to wireframe.	8
Zoom	Enter Zoom mode.	Z
Zoom Fit	Zoom to fit in window.	Shift+Z
Edit:Paste Mirrored	Paste the copied keyframe while mirroring.	Command+ Shift+V
Edit:Make Keyframe	Force a keyframe on the current frame.	Insert
Loop	Toggles looping mode on and off.	Home
Play Range	Play the selected range of frames.	End
First Frame	Jump to the frame 1.	Shift+Home
Last Frame	Advance to the last frame.	Shift+End

PC

COMMAND	DESCRIPTION	SHORTCUT
File:Open	Open an existing document.	Ctrl+O
Project:Save	Save the active project.	Ctrl+S
View:Project Workspace	Show or hide the Project Workspace panel.	Alt+1
View:Timeline	Show or hide the Timeline panel.	Alt+2
View:Libraries	Show or hide the libraries window.	Alt+5
View:Properties	Show or hide the Property panel.	Alt+3
View:Pose Sliders	Show or hide the Pose Sliders panel.	Alt+4
View:Community	Show or hide the Community window.	Alt+6
Tools:Options	Change options.	Ctrl+P
Edit:Snap Group To Grid	Snap the selected control points to the grid.	'
Next Keyframe	Advance to the next keyframe.	+
Edit:Select Spline	Select all control points on the selected spline.	,
Previous Frame	Jump to the previous frame.	-
Edit:Invert Selection	Toggle the state of all control points.	.
Edit:Group Connected	Select all control points on the selected spline.	/
Shaded/Wireframe	Set the draw mode to Shaded with Wireframe.	0
Show Normals	Toggle normals on and off.	Shift+1
Toggle Interrupt	Toggle interrupted drawing on/off.	Shift+2
Show Grid	Toggle the grid on and off.	Shift+3
View Settings	Open View Settings dialog.	Shift+4
Onion Skin	Toggels Onion Skin mode.	Shift+5
Toggle Back Face Culling	Toggle back face culling.	Shift+6
Default	Use model's draw mode.	7
Wireframe	Set the draw mode for this view to Wireframe.	8
Show Particle/Fur	Toggle particle/fur drawing on and off.	Shift+8
Shaded	Set the draw mode for this view to Shaded.	9
Next Frame	Advance to the next frame.	Num +
Add Mode	Enter Add mode.	A
Edit:Select All	Select all control points.	Ctrl+A
Add Lock Mode	Enter Add Lock mode.	Shift+A
Bound	Bound.	B
Bound Branch	Set the draw mode for the branch to Bound.	Shift+B
Curved	Curved.	C
Edit:Copy Keyframe	Copy the selection and put it on the Clipboard.	Ctrl+C
Curved Branch	Set the draw mode for the branch to Curved.	Shift+C
Show Decals	Turn Decal drawing On/Off.	Ctrl+D
Extrude Mode	Enter Extrude mode.	E
Flip Normals	Flip the normals of selected patches.	F
Jump To Frame	Enter the frame number to jump to.	Ctrl+F
Group Mode	Enter Group mode.	G
Lasso Draw Mode	Enter Lasso Draw mode.	Shift+G
Hide CPs	Hide all unselected control points	H

COMMAND	DESCRIPTION	SHORTCUT
Window:Tile Horizontally	Arrange windows as nonoverlapping tiles.	Alt+H
Hide More	Hide all unselected control points	Shift+H
Invisible Mode	Set the draw mode to Invisible.	I
Invisible Branch	Set the draw mode for the branch to Invisible.	Shift+I
Bone Visible	Make the selected bone visible.	J
Bones Visible Branch	Make the bones visible for the branch.	Shift+J
Break	Break the selected spline.	K
Detach Point	Detach the selected control point.	Shift+K
Lathe	Lathe the selected spline.	L
Move	Enter Move mode.	M
Translate Mode	Set manipulator to Translate mode.	N
New	Create a new document.	Ctrl+N
Smooth	Smooth the selected control points.	O
Peak	Peak the selected control points.	P
Patch Group Mode	Enter Patch Group mode.	Shift+P
Render Mode	Enter Render mode.	Q
Render Lock Mode	Enter Render Lock mode.	Shift+Q
Rotate Mode	Set manipulator to Rotate mode.	R
Rotate Group Images	Rotate Group Images.	Ctrl+R
Scale Mode	Set manipulator to Scale mode.	S
Turn	Enter Turn mode.	T
Vector	Vector.	V
Edit:Paste Keyframe	Insert Clipboard contents.	Ctrl+V
Window:Tile Vertically	Arrange windows as nonoverlapping tiles.	Alt+V
Vector Branch	Set the draw mode for the branch to Vector.	Shift+V
Delete	Deletes the current selection.	Delete
Move Down	Move the selected object down one pixel.	Down
Play Range	Play back the selected range of frames.	End
Edit Mode	Enter Edit mode.	Esc
Help	Display help for current task or command.	F1
Help	Display help	Shift+F1
Toggle Full Screen Mode	Toggle Full Screen Mode on or off.	F11
Modeling Mode	Enter Modeling mode.	F5
Bones Mode	Enter Bones Editing mode.	F6
Muscle Mode	Enter Muscle Motion mode.	F7
Skeletal Mode	Enter Skeletal Motion mode.	F8
Choreography Mode	Enter Choreography mode.	F9
Loop	Toggles looping mode on and off.	Home
Move Left	Move the selected object left one pixel.	Left
		Shift+Left
Decrease Subdivisions	Decrease the subdivisions in Shaded mode.	Page Down
Bottom View	Set the selected window to Bottom View.	Num 0
Camera View	Set the selected window to Camera View.	Num 1

COMMAND	DESCRIPTION	SHORTCUT
Front View	Set the selected window to Front View.	Num 2
Light View	Set the selected window to Light View.	Num 3
Left View	Set the selected window to Left View.	Num 4
Top View	Set the selected window to Top View.	Num 5
Right View	Set the selected window to Right View.	Num 6
Bird's Eye View	Set the selected window to Bird's Eye View.	Num 7
Back View	Set the selected window to Back View.	Num 8
Increase Subdivisions	Increase the subdivisions in Shaded mode.	Page Up
Edit:Deselect All	Deselect all selected control points.	Enter
Move Right	Move the selected object right one pixel.	Right
View:Refresh	Redraw the current view.	Space
Previous Keyframe	Jump to previous keyframe.	Shift+Num -
Next Object	Select the next object.	Tab
Previous Object	Select the previous object.	Shift+Tab
Move Up	Move the selected object up one pixel.	Up
Wireframe	Wireframe.	W
Window:New Window	Open another window for the active document.	Alt+W
Wireframe Branch	Toggle wireframes on and off for the branch.	Shift+W
Shaded	Shaded Mode for the Selected Model.	X
Edit:Cut Keyframe	Cut the selection and put it on the Clipboard.	Ctrl+X
Shaded Branch	Toggle Shaded on and off for the branch.	Shift+X
Insert	Insert a control point along the spline.	Y
Edit:Redo	Redo the previously undone action.	Ctrl+Y
Zoom	Enter Zoom mode.	Z
Edit:Undo	Undo the last action.	Ctrl+Z
Zoom Fit	Zoom to fit in window.	Shift+Z
Perspective	Toggles perspective mode in this view.	\
Select Deeper	Jump to next object behind current object.	]
Attach Control Point	Attach control point.	`
Previous CP	Select the previous control point.	{
Next CP	Select the next control point.	}

B

GLOSSARY OF TERMS

A

Action The specialized workspace mode for creating motion on characters and objects.

Action Overloading Using one action to replace the motion or a portion of the motion of a previously existing action.

Alpha The bias control that changes the direction a spline enters and exits a control point perpendicular to the gamma.

Alpha Channel The fourth channel of a 32-bit image that is typically used to indicate which portions of the RGB channels show and which are hidden.

Animatic A rough indication of the timing in an animation, created by stringing storyboard images together.

Animation The processes of creating motion by a series of images that change slightly. Shown one after the other.

Anisotropic Any surface attribute that is different, depending on the angle at which it is viewed.

Antialias The process of averaging the pixels of an edge with the pixels around it to reduce the jagged edge that aliased pixels exhibit.

Anticipation Indicating a motion before it happens by adding a slight motion in the opposite direction.

Average Normals An advanced property that smoothes creases and lumps in a mesh by averaging the normals at render time. (This property is replaced by the porcelain material in v10.0 and up.)

Axis One of the three planes used to plot coordinates in 3D space in the Cartesian coordinate system.

B

Bias The controls for how a spline enters and exits a control point, specifically magnitude, gamma, and alpha.

Bloom A lens artifact exhibited in film production where the brightest areas of an image are blown out making them appear softened. Most prominent in bright specular highlights.

Bone A control used to manipulate numbers of control points at the same time during animation. Also used to create animation control rigs via constraints.

Boolean In modeling, a shape that is used to cut away the surface of another shape. A property of a bone. (See also Hierarchical Boolean.)

C

Channel A graphical indication of the interpolation of motion between keyframes displayed in the Timeline; also called function curves or channel graphs.

Character Animation Animation specifically geared toward the movement and performance of characters.

Choreography The virtual set in which components are assembled to produce final rendered animation.

Constraint A way to control various aspects of a bone by targeting it to similar aspects on other bones.

Control Point The points along a spline or patch surface that allow for direct manipulation. The smallest unit of a model.

Creasing An artifact found in modeling from a variety of causes including incorrect patch techniques and bad spline continuity.

D

Decal A bitmap image applied to the surface of a model used to alter various surface aspects.

Dope Sheet Tool used to automate the process of lip synch.

E

Ease Term used to indicate the slow acceleration and deceleration of an object. In path constraints or actions applied in a choreography, it is an animateable property used to indicate a percentage along the path or through the action.

Expression A formula used to drive the value of a given property, which can include mathematical components and other model properties.

F

Five-Point Patch Specialized modeling tool used to close holes of five control points; common in shoulder and hip joints.

FK Forward kinematics. An indication of how bones in a chain are manipulated, specifically indicating that the position of a bone at the end of the chain has no effect on its parents and that any manipulation of the parent bones will be carried down the entire chain. A preferable way to animate hands and arms.

Flocking A system where models are placed into a group governed by behavior, specifically: crowd, swarm, and birds.

Four-Pont Patch The most optimum layout for single patch, where there are four points describing its perimeter comprised of two or more splines.

Function Curve See Channel.

G

Gamma The bias control that changes the direction a spline enters and exits a control point based on a reference to the points further along the spline.

H

Hierarchical Boolean A function of the hierarchy of bones where any control points that are assigned to a bone that is a hierarchical child of a bone that is designated as a Boolean cutter will remain unaffected by the Boolean operation.

Hook A tool used to ease areas of higher density into areas of lower density in a model. Rather than connecting a spline to a control point, it is hooked along a spline.

I

IK Inverse kinematics. An indication of how bones in a chain are manipulated, specifically indicating that the position of the chain is determined by a target at the end of the chain. Moving the target causes all bones up the length of the chain to move to accommodate reaching the target. A preferable system of control for legs or hands that must contact a surface.

Interpolation How the value of a property moves from one keyframe to another.

K

Key Drift A motion artifact caused by too few keyframes and spline interpolation.

Keyframe A specific point in time, where the value of a property, or properties, are recorded. Animation is based on moving from one keyframe to the next.

L

Lecia Reel See Animatic.

M

Magnitude The bias control that changes the shape of a spline as it enters and exits a control point, specifically indicating how sharply the spline passes through the point.

Manipulator One of the tools used to control points or bones in a specific manner, either translation, scale, or rotation.

Map See Decal.

Mass A point that is given weight; used in soft body dynamic simulations with spring systems.

Material A way to describe the surface attributes of a model with procedural algorithms.

Mode One of the specific ways an object may be manipulated, specifically model, muscle, bones, skeletal, distort, dynamics, or choreography.

Model A collection of splines and control points used to describe a 3D object in A:M.

N

Normal When light hits a surface the "normal" of that surface indicates what direction the light will bounce. It is used to indicate how a surface is shaded. Also used for particle.

emissions, dynamic collisions, and radiosity calculations.

Nonlinear Animation (NLA) The process of animating motion in small chunks and layering them via action overloading to produce the final performance of a character.

O

Origin The point in a workspace where all three axes cross. The zero point of all the axes.

Overlapping Motion Traditional animation term used to indicate that all portions of an object should not start and stop moving at the same time.

P

Particle System A group of 3D points emitted from a surface and under the effects of physics in a choreography. Used to simulate fire, water, and other special effects that would be difficult with normal models.

Patch A rendering surface composed of at least three control points (but no more than five) and two splines.

Path A spline drawn in the choreography. Typically used to move an object along using a path constraint.

Phoneme The basic blocks of sounds that make up individual words; not to be confused with single letters.

Pivot The center point of any manipulator. Defaults to the center of a selected group of control points or the base of a bone. For control point manipulation the pivot can be defined by the user.

Porcelain A special material that when applied to a model gives control over surface smoothing. This material is normals aware and can cause artifacting if the normals on the model's surface are not aligned properly.

Pose The basic components of action strung together over time to create animation.

Pose Slider A relationship tied to a slider control used to change properties or drive other relationships in a model.

Project The container for all aspects of an animation: models, materials, actions, lights, choreographies, and so on.

Proxy A low-resolution version of a model substituted to speed drawing in the interface while animating.

PWS Project Workspace. The window that displays the project and all the components related to it.

R

Radiosity A rendering algorithm where light energy is transferred from surface to surface.

Ray Trace A rendering algorithm used to create realistic reflections and refractions in a scene.

Relationship A way to tie the value of one animateable property to another, creating a link between them.

Render The calculations performed by the computer to create the final image.

Render Farm A network of computers used to distribute frames of animation, allowing more than one frame to be rendered simultaneously.

RGB Red, Green, Blue. The three colors that are blended to create all colors on a computer monitor; also the color channels in a typical bitmap image. The Additive color palette.

Rigid Body Dynamics The physical simulation of mass and weight on an object as it interacts with other objects.

Rotation The method of manipulation where the object is moved in arcs around the pivot point and measured in degrees.

S

Scale The method of manipulation where the object is enlarged or shrunk from the pivot point and measured in percents.

Secondary Motion Term used to describe small motions that follow the larger motions of animation, such as hair, clothes, or the ears on a dog

Shortcut An instance of an object that refers to, but makes no permanent changes to, the original object; used in choreographies and actions for animation; also used with materials on models.

SmartSkin A relationship driven from the rotation of a bone.

Soft Body Dynamics A system of springs and masses used to simulate objects that are not rigid and their reaction to physics.

Spline A mathematical curve between points used to indicate the surface of a model and to create patches.

Spring A spline used to connect masses. When simulated, it stretches and shrinks in reaction to the masses and gravity according to physics.

Staging How elements of a scene are positioned in relation to one another and the image frame. Used to compose compelling shots.

Story Reel See Animatic.

Storyboard A series of drawings used to visualize a story before production begins.

Surface Normal See Normal.

T

Three-Point Patch A patch composed of three control points and at least two splines.

Timeline The window that displays the keyframes generated over the course of an animation.

Toolbar An interface element that presents commonly used tools or functions.

Translation The method of manipulation where the object is moved in straight lines along one or more of the three axes.

V

Viewport The window that displays the current working mode such as modeling or action.

Volumetric Effect A 3D simulation of airborne particles such as smoke or dust.

Volumetric Light A light that exhibits volumetric properties.

W

Wizard Tool designed to automate complex or commonly performed tasks.

Workspace See Viewport.

World Space The axes used in the Choreography window.

X

X-Axis One of three cardinal axes. When a viewport is viewed from the front view, the *x*-axis runs from left to right.

Y

Y-Axis One of three cardinal axes. When a viewport is viewed from the front view, the *y*-axis runs from top to bottom.

Z

Z-Axis One of three cardinal axes. When a viewport is viewed from the left or right side view, the *z*-axis runs left to right.

C

ABOUT THE CD-ROM

This book is meant to aid you in learning A:M and the CD-ROM that accompanies it is integeral to that process. Since many of the aspects of the software are very visual and difficult to explain without showing you what we mean, we have decided to use the CD-ROM to provide more information in the form of project files.

In the Chapter folders, you will find Project files for the projects discussed in the book. These should work with any version of A:M 2006 and higher, but most will not work with any version prior to 13. Due to the rapid development schedule, some features in A:M may have changed from the time that the projects were committed to this CD-ROM. If you have any difficulties with any of the projects, please check *http://www. am-guide.com/* for updates or information regarding the book.

You will need QuickTime 7.0 or better installed on your computer to view the video on the CD-ROM.

In the DarkTree Folder you will find a demo version of DarkTree, a Windows-only program for creating dark tree textures for A:M.

In the Figures folder you will find each of the figures from the book in color. This makes understanding some of the figures easier.

SYSTEM REQUIREMENTS

PC

- Windows 2000 or better
- CD-ROM drive
- QuickTime 7.0
- Animation:Master 2006 (v13)

Mac

- OS X 10.4 or better
- CD-ROM drive
- QuickTime 7.0
- Animation:Master 2006 (v13)

If your system can run A:M, it should more than meet any requirements for the CD-ROM.

INDEX